Keystone Nations

Publication of this book and the SAR seminar from which it resulted were made possible with the generous support of Eric and Barbara Dobkin through their commitment to scholarly enterprises that foster positive social change in our world.

**School for Advanced Research
Advanced Seminar Series**

James F. Brooks
General Editor

Keystone Nations

Contributors

James F. Brooks
School for Advanced Research on the Human Experience

Courtney Carothers
School of Fisheries and Ocean Sciences, University of Alaska, Fairbanks

Benedict J. Colombi
American Indian Studies Program, School of Anthropology, School of Natural Resources and Environment, University of Arizona

Sibyl Diver
Department of Environmental Science, Policy and Management, University of California, Berkeley

Erich Kasten
Foundation for Siberian Cultures

David Koester
Department of Anthropology, University of Alaska, Fairbanks

Marianne Elisabeth Lien
Department of Social Anthropology, University of Oslo

Charles R. Menzies
Department of Anthropology, University of British Columbia

Katherine Reedy-Maschner
Department of Anthropology, Idaho State University

Victoria N. Sharakhmatova
Russian Association of Indigenous Peoples of the North (Kamchatsky), United Nations Development Programme

Courtland L. Smith
Water Policy and Management, School of Language, Culture, and Society, Oregon State University

Emma Wilson
International Institute for Environment and Development

Keystone Nations

Indigenous Peoples and Salmon across the North Pacific

Edited by Benedict J. Colombi and James F. Brooks

SAR
PRESS

School for Advanced Research Press
Santa Fe

School for Advanced Research Press
Post Office Box 2188
Santa Fe, New Mexico 87504-2188
sarpress.sarweb.org

Managing Editor: Lisa Pacheco
Editorial Assistant: Ellen Goldberg
Designer and Production Manager: Cynthia Dyer
Manuscript Editor: Sarah Soliz
Proofreader: Paul Grindrod
Indexer: Margaret Moore Booker
Printer: Sheridan Books, Inc.

Library of Congress Cataloging-in-Publication Data

Keystone nations : indigenous peoples and salmon across the north Pacific / edited by
Benedict J. Colombi and James F. Brooks.
    p. cm. — (School for advanced research advanced seminar series)
  Includes bibliographical references and index.
  ISBN 978-1-934691-90-8 (alk. paper)
 1. Indians of North America—Pacific, Northwest—Fishing. 2. Indians of North America—
Alaska—Fishing. 3. Indigenous peoples—Pacific Area—Fishing. 4. Salmon fishing—Pacific,
Northwest. 5. Salmon fishing—Alaska. 6. Salmon fishing—Pacific Area. 7. Traditional fishing—
Pacific, Northwest. 8. Traditional fishing—Alaska. 9. Traditional fishing—Pacific Area.
 I. Colombi, Benedict J. II. Brooks, James, 1955-
  E78.N77K49 2012
  979.004'97—dc23
                              2012015736

This book was printed on paper containing 30% PCW.

Cover illustrations: Alaska, British Columbia, Washington, Oregon, and California have many
small communities where the presence of salmon and fishing activities are key to the culture and
economy. *Top left:* Aleut Dancers of King Cove, courtesy of King Cove Corporation, King Cove,
Alaska; *top right:* photo of Gibsons, British Columbia by Courtland L. Smith; *bottom:* Apayo Moore,
Native Alaskan artist, *Spawning Grounds*, 2008, acrylic on canvas.

Contents

Illustrations

Figures

Tables

Color plates

follow page 64

Preface

The histories and futures of Indigenous peoples and salmon are inextricably bound across the vast ocean expanse and rugged coastlines of the North Pacific. We title this volume *Keystone Nations* to signal this enmeshment—and to signal the marriage of the biological and social sciences that characterizes its chapters. Salmon stocks and Indigenous peoples across the region, we argue, are significant beyond their size in maintaining the viability and legitimacy of ecological and political systems. As such, both our species' futures are simultaneously bound to the conservation concerns of natural scientists and the political agendas of Indigenous sovereignty movements that arc across the northern hemisphere. If wild salmon vanish from the North Pacific, as they largely have from the North Atlantic, their absence will herald the cascading failure of a complex marine system. If Indigenous peoples vanish from the North Pacific, as they largely have in the North Atlantic, their absence will point to the failure of the world's dominant political powers to recognize the human right to cultural expression and survival. Both groups now serve, to use the jurist Felix Cohen's (1953:390) simile, as the "miner's canary…marking the shifts from fresh air to poison gas in our political atmosphere."

We begin with the world's most important fish: salmon (*Oncorhynchus* sp.). Long a subsistence staple of Indigenous diets, today salmon are at once a subsistence and commercial species, wild and domesticated, gifted and sold, a staple and a delicacy, found in cat food and in the finest restaurants, hunted for food and for sport. Mostly hidden from the public consciousness are the myriad cultural histories that Indigenous peoples share with these salmon, stories that illustrate how salmon have variously been conserved, exploited, cherished, and renounced in Indigenous life. The ecological matrix that unites the wide-ranging salmon's life cycle, northern Pacific Indigenous peoples, and their combined significance to the region's ecosystem lies at the center of this project.

Like Franz Boas's Jesup North Pacific Expedition (1897 to 1902), a partnership between philanthropist Morris Jesup and the American

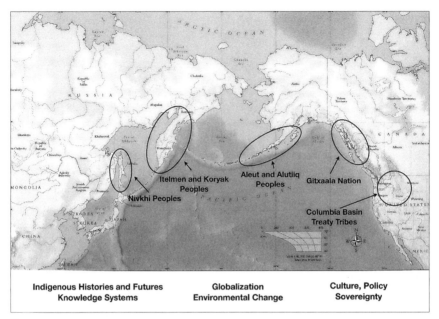

FIGURE 0.1

Map of northern Pacific region showing the case studies of Indigenous peoples and salmon in this volume. Source: adapted from Augerot 2005.

Museum of Natural History, this book also found its origins in a philanthropic vision, that of Eric and Barbara Dobkin, whose strategic projects in social change initiative at the School for Advanced Research (SAR) is designed to bring scholarly insight to issues of urgent social concern. Yet if the Jesup Expedition, wherein a dozen ethnographers sought to explore the biological and cultural connections between the peoples of Asia and North America, limited itself to human relationships as linked by salmon cultures, our seminar at SAR, crafted in partnership with the Wild Salmon Center and Pacific Environment and two years in the making, explored how peoples *and* salmon across the North Pacific—from Sakhalin Island through Alaska and south to the Columbia River—built their distinctive relationships and engaged with historical forces of change across the last two centuries (Fitzhugh and Crowell 1988; figure 0.1).

In May 2010 ten specialists from Germany, Alaska, Norway, Idaho, New Mexico, Canada, Arizona, and Russia convened in Santa Fe to discuss the social and historical transformations that link the Russian Far East and northwestern North America. Even this breadth cannot, of course, capture the full extent of human–salmon relationships in the region, but we sought a rich assemblage of cases that would provide both tangible depth and conceptual breadth to our inquiries. We further sought to combine empirical richness and theoretical insight by including both specific cultural and geographic case studies—the Nivkhi of Sakhalin Island, Itelmens and Koryaks of the Kamchatka Penninsula, Aleuts of the Aleutian Islands, Sugpiats of the Kodiak Archipelago, Gitxaała of northern British Columbia, Nimiipuus of the Snake River, and Umatilla, Warm Springs, Yakima, and Nez Perce nations of the Columbia River tributaries —with two far-reaching chapters that "bookend" the volume. The latter illustrate differing interpretive stances: one that seeks generalization around issues of management practices (Smith, chapter 1, this volume) and one that highlights the challenges ahead in defining the political and ecological valences of nature, culture, and indigeneity (Lien, chapter 11, this volume). These two essays also arc across the Pole to provide a comparison of the North Pacific and the North Atlantic.

Our diverse study team explored historical and cultural processes to investigate how salmon serve as pillars of culture, history, and economy in the North Pacific, and we focused specifically on themes of Indigenous knowledge about salmon, fishing policies, water and fishing rights, the tradition of treaties, co-management experiments, and commercial "cultivation" versus the preservation of "wild" salmon. Each topic alerted us to major threats to the future of both Indigenous peoples and salmon in intermeshed biological and political spheres. The essays speak to tensions swirling around the proposed Pebble Creek mine in the salmon-rich Bristol Bay region of Alaska, where Indigenous Yupik have relied on salmon for thousands of years in an area that also possesses one of world's largest deposits of copper, as well as gold. We also look to emerging contemporary issues, such as fish carrying high-level radioactive materials following the 2011 tsunami and crises at Japan's Fukushima nuclear power plant. Threatened inland fresh waters, non–point source pollutants, increasingly fragile ocean ecosystems, and the political strength of Indigenous peoples within their "host" nations are among the threads that bind our story.

Central to our understanding is salmon's unusual life cycle as an *anadromous* fish that connects ocean, estuarine, and freshwater ecosystems. Salmon spend two-thirds of their life gaining most of their biomass in the ocean. The salmon that spawn within the Bering Sea region, for example, may have traveled as far as 1,980 mi down the Yukon River and ranged over 3.5 million sq mi of ocean before returning to their spawning grounds. Salmon do not respect national or cultural borders, migrate across many jurisdictions and scales, and swim through many cultures and environments, creating complex social, political, and economic relationships.

Salmon serve as a *keystone species*, transport vectors that bring nutrients from the ocean to the freshwater environment, which means that hundreds of species—including Indigenous peoples—cultures, and indeed entire ecosystems rely on salmon (Augerot 2005; Cederholm et al. 2001; Power et al. 1996). In the North Pacific salmon populations have experienced local extinctions related to natural disturbances, including glaciation, volcanism, and other catastrophic events, but they survived by having diverse, independent reproductive regimes and have shown the potential to colonize new or recolonize old rivers, including entire watersheds. The studies herein illustrate how salmon have responded to periods of great change and how they reorganize themselves to cope with that change.

Yet parallel to their biological significance, salmon serve as a *cultural* keystone species as well (Garibaldi and Turner 2004) and indicate the cultural vitality and resiliency of the people who depend upon them for their livelihood. The Nez Perce tribe—(the Nimiipuus)—found Celilo Falls on the Columbia River—the first falls encountered by returning salmon—to be a place where they could harvest fish but also a meeting place where people could trade, marry, and hunt. They continue to visit the falls despite the fact that they are today beneath a reservoir, called Lake Celilo, created by the construction of the Dalles Dam for hydroelectric power and irrigation cultivators in the late 1950s. The Nez Perce now cultivate salmon on the main stem and tributaries of the Snake River, which flows through their reservation in Idaho, while stewarding the memory of Celilo Falls as timeless in cultural significance. Thus the hydraulic history of the American West (and the Russian Far East, as we shall see) is inseparable from contemporary concerns about tribal sovereignty and cultural sustainability: if the Nimiipuus are simply farmers of non-anadromous salmon, how do they differ from those non-Indigenous commercial salmon operations whose culture is largely that of the twenty-first-century marketplace?

Salmon husbandry runs deeper than twentieth-century dam-building and the agricultural metaphor, however. According to the innovative ethnoarchaeology of Charles Menzies, Gitxaała peoples successfully combine traditional and contemporary methods in managing the coastal watersheds of northwestern British Columbia, melding practices a millennia old with the latest knowledge of fisheries biology. We learn from Courtney Carothers and Katherine Reedy-Maschner, for instance, that in the Kodiak region around the Aleutian Islands, Indigenous peoples known as "people of the sea" have been sustained by salmon for more than seventy-five hundred years. Some 80 to 90 percent of their food came from this relationship, yet their rapid (and successful) entry into commercial fishing in

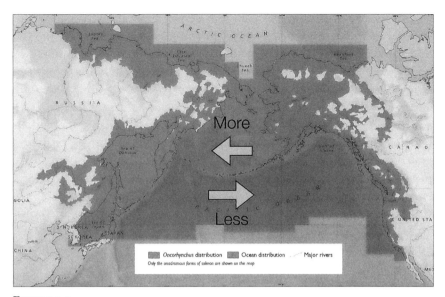

FIGURE 0.2

Current state of salmon biodiversity across the northern Pacific. Source: adapted from Augerot 2005.

the twentieth century embedded Aleuts and Sugpiaks in commodity chains that supply (when credit is available) boats, fuel, and tackle and increase their susceptibility to market cycles. Thus the Aleuts and Sugpiaks' recent receptiveness to oil exploration in the islands, which might yield a "second salmon" for their benefit. The Itelmens and Koryaks of the Kamchatka Peninsula, as discussed by Erich Kasten, David Koester, and Victoria Sharakhmatova, and the Nivkhi of Sakhalin Island, as treated by Emma Wilson, today face similar challenges as oil and gas exploration threatens to destroy spawning beds where some 80 percent of the world's wild salmon are now born, yet also entices with promises of reliable wage-yielding jobs and access to global seafood markets.

Clearly, Indigenous peoples are increasingly enmeshed in relationships with the larger global economy. And salmon, like people, are also caught in webs of larger influences. For example, salmon have become the world's first genetically engineered food animal, with AquaBounty, a Boston-based company and designer of genetically modified salmon, planning to raise the Atlantic salmon in inland tanks in Ohio. Known as transgenic salmon, this fish will reach maturity in eighteen months instead of three years through the incorporation of DNA from the ocean pout (an eel-like fish found in the North Atlantic) and the Chinook salmon, which will allow it to grow twice as fast (Goldenberg 2011).

Along with the many parallels and concordances across the reaches of the Pacific, we identified a significant "double movement" during the seminar, which provoked debate about how best to deploy the finding for policy purposes. This finding involves an inverse relationship between salmon biodiversity and Indigenous peoples' political standing directionally across the Pacific Rim (figure 0.2 and plate 3). In the richly biodiverse areas of the Kamchatka Peninsula and Sakhalin Island, Indigenous peoples find themselves to be virtually powerless spectators to local- and global-scale extractive industries: commercial fishing, roe poaching, copper mining, and oil and natural gas development. Yet in these biodiverse areas salmon represent a significant portion of the Indigenous diet, provide ecosystem services as an important keystone species, and have drawn global attention as a "stronghold" for ecological preservation (Quammen 2009). Indigenous nations in Canada and the United States, though they have a limited ability to exercise full sovereignty over their natural and cultural resources, have a stronger legal standing within their host nations from which to undertake that effort, even as they may be the only witnesses to the decline of salmon biodiversity in their own territories. In neither the Pacific West nor East do enmeshment in twenty-first-century economic exchange systems, Indigenous rights movements, or global environmentalism provide simple solutions. The challenge, as Marianne Elisabeth Lien (chapter 11, this volume) defines it, is to acknowledge that "the current state of both Indigenous people and salmon along the Pacific rim is in many cases deeply problematic," and yet "how can we draw on the rich variety of human–salmon relations to imagine alternative futures?"

We have been honored to work over these past years with the contributors to this project and the communities they represent. Our special gratitude goes to our discussants, Courtland Smith and Marianne Lien, whose deep experience, wisdom, and breadth of knowledge proved crucial to extending the project's significance. This book is just the first in an extended engagement with these issues; with the second we intend to address management practices and policies on the same hemispheric scale. We would also like to thank Eric and Barbara Dobkin for inspiring and supporting this series, our acutely insightful anonymous reviewers, and the always generous staff at SAR for making this book a reality.

Benedict J. Colombi and James F. Brooks
Tucson, Arizona, and Santa Fe, New Mexico
October 15, 2011

Keystone Nations

1

Introduction: Cultivating Capture Fisheries

Lessons from Salmon Culturing and Cultures

Courtland L. Smith

One of the central themes of anthropology has been the role of agriculture in changing not only relationships within societies but the structure of cultures. The "neolithic revolution" refers to the transition from foraging to farming in which subsistence increasingly came from domesticated plants and animals (Childe 1936), and the urban revolution followed as agricultural surplus supported the expanding state. Building on the theme that technological change in food production, metallurgy, and transportation structure society, a "science of culture" further elaborated the role of agriculture in the "evolution of society" (White 1949, 1959). In the twenty-first century, this materialist perspective (Harris 1979, 1980) receives less attention. More common is a critique of power, symbolism, discourse, and structural elements that is used to analyze the impacts and implications of industrial agricultural practices, address the disadvantaging of Indigenous and minority peoples, identify factors affecting the agency of actors, and review the neoliberal pressure for market-based solutions (Bourdieu 1991; Clifford 1986; Foucault and Gordon 1980; Geertz 1963; Nadasdy 2003).

The demands of urban and industrial growth have been widely identified as the main cause for the decline of salmon and other resources and for the loss of fishing and foraging cultures (Lackey, Lach, and Duncan 2006; White 1995; Wolf and Zuckerman 1999). Agriculture supporting urbanization and industrial growth leads to the extensive modification of landscapes for growing crops, trees, and animals. Industrial agriculture requires extensive transportation systems; the application of chemicals, fertilizers, and water; and the general reorganization of landscapes. Salmon and natural resource decline results from the physical presence of industrialized agriculture and systems for its support (Botkin et al. 1995; NRC 1996).

An industrial agricultural philosophy reinforces the idea that humans can modify ecological systems to make them more productive. Simplification, selection, and modification increase, for a time, productivity and the abundance of food and fiber. This productivity often comes at the cost of diversity both ecological and cultural. The authors in this book explore the experiences of North Pacific peoples who are at the forefront of the tension between growth and diversity.

"Cultivating capture fisheries" is a play on words that doubly reflects how agricultural metaphors affect salmon production and thinking. *Culturing* can refer to the aquaculture of stocks like salmon, steelhead, trout, and increasing numbers of other commercially important species. The first culturing technique for salmon mainly involved hatcheries. Culturing selects specific stocks for hatchery production based on their cultural value, productivity, and behaviors. Hatchery stocks only spend the early part of their life cycle in production facilities before being released into rivers and estuaries to travel to and mature in the ocean and then return to capture fisheries. *Culturing* also refers to salmon farming, which is artificial propagation that controls the growth of the fish stock throughout its life cycle. Another use of *culture* encompasses ways of thinking with respect to the environment and its management.

The cases in this book follow an arc across the North Pacific from Sakhalin and Kamchatka in Russia to Alaska, British Columbia, and the Columbia Basin. They serve to highlight some common patterns and processes across the North Pacific. Going from south to north by latitude, human populations decrease in concentration and size, and salmon habitats are less degraded, although mining and forest harvest still pose a threat. Moving clockwise from Russia to the Columbia Basin by longitude, salmon are in increasingly worse shape (Augerot 2000, 2005; Augerot and Smith 2011). Yet despite differing patterns, agricultural actions and metaphors affect salmon fisheries and fishing peoples in all areas. Forest practices, energy exploration, and food production activities restructure landscapes that are home to both salmon and the peoples who depend upon them.

In general, industrialized agriculture supported growth in human populations, provided nutrition to extend the average life span, enabled improved material well-being, and supported state societies. Much of the focus of political ecology is on those left out of these processes (Peña 1998; Sturgeon 2009; Wolf 1997). Nevertheless, the overwhelming majority of people gain their sustenance using culturing techniques, and the reliance on agricultural approaches structures values toward resources and nature. Industrializing nations came to regions of the North Pacific in the nineteenth century to explore and then to exploit salmon production for international trade.

EXPORTING SURPLUSES

Indigenous peoples of the North Pacific used large quantities of naturally spawning salmon. The exact amount is unknown, but estimates based on per capita use times population provide insights about the quantity (Boyd 1999b; Chapman 1986; Hewes 1947; NPPC 1986). Contact with explorers, missionaries, entrepreneurs, and settlers led to major changes in use of the salmon resource. Typically, this change included entrepreneurs who saw the possibilities for profit in salting, canning, and smoking salmon or taking eggs for export to distant places. The cannery is a measure of this early international trade. Salmon canners took the salmon heading to die, what they saw as the waste of natural production, and exported it to industrializing areas of the world. These canners acted as the agents for colonizing nations that were absorbing resources to fuel their industrializing economies.

Canneries spread up the Northwest Coast from the Sacramento River in 1864 to the Columbia River in 1866, the Fraser River in 1870, and Klawock, Alaska, in 1878 (table 1.1). In Asia, the first Hokkaido salmon cannery went into operation in 1913 (Augerot 2000:43). Russian salmon were not exported, but intercepting home-bound fish was more of an issue. The treaties between Russia and Japan allowed or disallowed each entry into the other's waters for the purpose of capture fishing.

Canning food was an early nineteenth-century French invention (Appert 1814), and it enabled the transport of salmon to emerging industrial areas. Courtney Carothers (chapter 7) details how the cannery affected Alaska's Alutiiq peoples and documents a seventy-five-hundred-year history of Alutiiq cultural dependence on marine resources. Built in 1882, the Karluk River cannery was followed by many others. Canners shipped salmon to the United Kingdom and British colonies throughout the world. The cannery was also a source of jobs both in the cannery and in fishing, a place to get loans and purchase goods, and a force that consolidated communities.

One detrimental effect of international trade in salmon stocks is the

TABLE 1.1

Timing of international events in development of salmon fisheries of the North Pacific

Date	Event
1604	Japanese grant Ainu exclusive fishing rights
1639	Russian explorers find huge quantities of salmon in the Armur River
1784	Russian settlement of Three Saints Bay southeast of Kodiak Island
1805	Lewis and Clark reach the Clearwater in Idaho
1864	First salmon cannery on the Sacramento River
1866	First salmon cannery on the Columbia River
1870	First British Columbia salmon cannery on the Fraser River
1875	Russo-Japanese Treaty of Saint Petersburg gives Japan fishing rights in Russian waters
1878	Klawock, first Alaskan salmon cannery built
1882	Karluk River salmon cannery built
1884	Russian Primore Law limits Japanese salmon fishing
1907	Russo-Japanese Fisheries Convention delineates Russian only fishing areas, Japanese get Sakhalin Island
1917	P. E. Harris salmon cannery begins the settlement of False Pass, Alaska
1920	Japanese take over Armur and Sakhalin fisheries
1937	Japanese intercepting increasing amounts of Soviet salmon
1937	Fraser River Salmon Convention mandates 50/50 US/Canada split
1977	Law of the Sea extends territorial limits to 200 mi, Soviets limit Japanese interceptions
1985	Pacific Salmon Treaty signed by United States and Canada
2008	UNDP Conference "Problems of Traditional Fishing by Indigenous People of the North and Prospects of Local Communities Based on Their Inclusion into Management of Fish Resources" brings international biodiversity concerns to Kamchatka

fishing for caviar described by David Koester (chapter 3). Caviar is produced from the eggs of female salmon, as well as other fish, returning to spawn. Fishing techniques that do not provide for live capture and the difficulty in distinguishing a female from a male fish means that as much as half the catch is not used for harvesting caviar. Some of the carcasses, critical to many ecological processes, are not returned to streams, and the eggs do not produce the next generation.

A second measure of international trade is treaties between nations that affect entry into fisheries. Japanese distant-water fishers have historically taken salmon returning to Russian waters, and in 1875 the Russo-Japanese Treaty of Saint Petersburg gave Japan the right to fish Russian waters. Russia regained the rights to its native salmon with the 1977 Law of the Sea Treaty.

The effects of international trade continue with the introduction of exotic species, principally Atlantic salmon, to the farms along the west coasts of Washington and British Columbia, mining and mineral exploration (Reedy-Maschner, chapter 6; Wilson, chapter 2), the influence of global nongovernmental organizations (NGOs; Colombi, chapter 9; Diver, chapter 10; Sharakhmatova, chapter 5; Wilson, chapter 2), competition from nonlocal fishers (Kasten, chapter 4; Koester, chapter 3; Menzies, chapter 8; Reedy-Maschner, chapter 6; Sharakhmatova, chapter 5; Wilson, chapter 2), and world market exchanges and labor requirements (Carothers, chapter 7; Koester, chapter 3; Reedy-Maschner, chapter 6).

The cumulative effect of international trade in salmon has been the reduction of wild stocks (Augerot 2005; FAO 2011; Netboy 1974). Initially, this loss came from fishing pressure and habitat loss. The combination of high catch expectations and the production of hatcheries led to declines in wild stocks mixed with heavily fished hatchery stocks. In addition, river modifications—including dams for energy to mill grains and produce electricity, water diversions for irrigation, and channelizing to protect land for farming, make rivers more easily navigable, and prevent floods—led to more losses (Lichatowich 1999; NRC 1996; Williams 2006).

AGRICULTURAL METAPHORS FOR CULTIVATING FISH

The agricultural metaphor has been applied with both important benefits and negative effects. Increasingly, industrial agriculture has been a powerful cultural process for feeding and clothing people. The technology for culturing plants and animals creates the primary subsistence base for industrializing nations, but it also brings significant changes to ecosystems well beyond the boundaries of the nation and threatens ecosystem services. This is not to say that small-scale horticulture does not continue to exist in many parts of the world, but the nineteenth-century efforts to harvest salmon and include this harvest in international trade provided high-quality protein and the "fast food" of nineteenth-century industrial workers (Smith 1979).

Harvesting, however, is also a metaphor that when applied to fish and wildlife management reflects a way of thinking that differs from the views of many Indigenous peoples (Nadasdy 2011). Metaphors structure thinking (Lakoff and Johnson 1980; Ortony 1993). Introducing industrial-agricultural thinking results in system simplification, resource specialization, system stabilization, density-dependent management, surplus production for exchange, sedentary living, hatcheries for production, environmental manipulation, damming and channelizing of rivers, rearing of farmed salmon, property rights, closed-system perspectives, genetic analysis and modification, and linear perspectives on evolution. Prior to the arrival of international trading entrepreneurs, North Pacific Indigenous communities co-evolved with their ecosystems, developing patterns that enabled many communities to survive the growth and decline of salmon populations, major floods, significant earthquakes, tsunamis, extensive drought, and major fires. The "maintenance of social relations" in relation to the components of the natural system that characterizes Indigenous perspectives is very different from the "wildlife management is agriculture" view of industrial agriculture (Nadasdy 2011:136). The concept of co-evolution recognizes that people who depend on a resource can develop a symbiotic relationship wherein the actions of each affect characteristics of the other (Durham 1991; Ehrlich 1968; Ehrlich and Raven 1964). Harvesting does not reflect a symbiotic relationship; it is a process of control over natural systems in which sowing and gathering a crop is the goal.

The application of culturing technology to maximize abundance and productivity changes this symbiotic link into more of a command and control approach to fisheries. The US Commission of Fish and Fisheries, established in 1871, designed artificial propagation facilities to increase fish production with the objective of sustaining commercial fisheries. In 1872 Congress gave the commission the task of fish culturing because studies showed resource decline along the New England shore and in lakes. With the help of the American Fish Culturalists' Association, the commission established a marine hatchery at its Woods Hole headquarters (NOAA 2006).

The culturing of fish improves productivity by reducing mortality in early fish life history and increasing growth, selecting for desirable traits and characteristics, increasing efficiency, and meeting societal goals for predictable and stable production. Greater productivity from the culturing of plants and animals is one reason that societies could expand in population and material goods. The cost has been lost abundance, decline in reproductive capacity, environmental modification, and reduced natural diversity for many fish and wildlife populations important to North Pacific peoples.

The evidence that fish culturing through artificial propagation in hatcheries improves production is contested (Bottom 1997; Hilborn 1999; Lichatowich 1999; Naish et al. 2007; Sharma, Cooper, and Hilborn 2005). Intuitions based on experience with artificial propagation have resulted in continued pursuit of fish culturing to increase the abundance of salmon and other species for capture fishing. In parallel with *agriculture*, fish culturing is called aquaculture or mariculture. An even more productive industrial-agricultural technique to increase abundance is salmon farming, pioneered in Norway in the 1960s (Lien, chapter 11). Salmon farming has come to create greater market abundance than capture fisheries do.

Agricultural metaphors are also found in fishery management, as in discussion of "harvest." Like "livestock," hatchery workers manage "fish stocks." They "plant" fish in streams. A major fishery management concept is "maximum sustainable yield," and Daniel Bottom (1997:586) writes that "maximum sustainable yield...was based on a logistic growth curve developed from animal populations held under constant food supply and environmental conditions (Barber 1988; Botkin 1990)." Maximum sustainable yield allowed for calculating the optimum point of fishing intensity that would continue to yield the maximum crop of fish indefinitely. Much as in forest management, the perspective developed that when a fish died from natural causes and was not used by humans, it was wasted.

Fishery management "increased total production of food...and increased net economic return to the fishermen" (Schaefer 1957:679). In the 1940s, fishery biologists and economists noted the limits of land-based production (Gordon 1953; Le Gall 1951; Schaefer 1957) and pointed to the potential for fisheries to produce additional protein needed by a growing human population. H. Scott Gordon (1953:442) emphasized, "The purpose of a fishery is the human use of a source of food. Fishing is carried on by human beings for human purposes."

Culturing metaphors are deeply rooted in how agricultural peoples address problems. John Perkins (1997:267) in a review of the green revolution observed, "Our relentless obliteration of nonhuman ecosystems in favor of agricultural ecosystems is a major force determining the balance between humankind and other species with whom we share the earth." C. G. Johannes Petersen (1903) emphasized the need to thin young fish, like one thins crop or tree plantings, so the remaining stock would grow bigger and more rapidly. This practice is an early formulation of the density-dependent perspective in fisheries, an agricultural concept in which the spacing of seeds and thinning of crops leads to greater productivity.

Density-dependent recruitment and growth were two concepts that structured fishery managers' arguments for increasing abundance and productivity after World War II (Beverton and Holt 1957; Ricker 1975). Before maximum sustainable yield in the 1940s (Finley 2009), a similar concept was discussed by E. S. Russell (1931, 1942:94), who wrote, "The rate of fishing which gives the maximum steady yield is of course not necessarily the most economical rate of fishing." Carmel Finley (2009) adds that this concept "also reflects an agricultural model of conservation, and a belief that fish populations are malleable and can be controlled for human benefit (McEvoy 1988) and that the oceans can be reordered to produce high-value species." In the North Pacific, salmon have been transplanted between streams and hatcheries that have promised to augment depleted stocks. Development of the Oregon Moist Pellet in the 1960s to feed hatchery salmon provided disease control and improved hatchery survival (Hublou et al. 1959), while also promoting belief in vastly increased production possibilities. The belief was that rearing of salmon could produce a "surplus" to support a vastly enlarged fishing effort. Salmon became a crop to be harvested (Bottom 1997; Bottom et al. 2009).

Charles Menzies (chapter 8) describes how Gitxaała people managed the environment related to their fisheries. Menzies argues that it is logical to conclude that these actions affected the rest of the Gitxaała ecosystem. Gitxaała people saw themselves as working with the other parts of the ecosystem to maintain their joint survival—an example of co-evolution.

Indigenous leaders have noted that non-Indigenous people who settled in the Northwest in the nineteenth century lacked an ecological perspective appropriate to the resources of the region, and tribal leaders have described the loss of cultural and ecological diversity. Late twentieth-century Native American leader Ted Strong (NPR, *Science Friday*, February 14, 1997) stated, "We are going to be vilified as those people who destroyed the innocents of this Earth, and that is something that Native Americans absolutely will not stand for."

Indigenous peoples have articulated and demonstrated that they are interested in fish for the purpose of meeting their cultural needs, and Indigenous North Pacific salmon cultures had beliefs that emphasized fish as partners of human beings. They had stories and beliefs that described their responsibilities to the ecosystem as a whole, for example, the Itelmen view of a river as a living being. Koester (chapter 3) relates how they worried that an axe could cut through a river and kill the resources.

Some biologists suggest "looking at things from the viewpoint of the salmon" (Larkin 1979:105). Peter Larkin (1979:105) goes on to say, "Protection, regulation, and enhancement should thus be bent to serve the interests of salmon as a resource rather than to those who use the resource."

Thinking "from the viewpoint of the salmon" is central to the perspectives of the four tribes who created the Columbia River Inter-Tribal Fish Commission (CRITFC) and a plan for Columbia Basin salmon restoration (Diver, chapter 10). Their philosophy is that "stewardship extends respect for life beyond the dignity of the human person to the whole of creation.… As long as nature is taken care of, nature will take care of the people" (CRITFC 1996). Diver details how CRITFC gained influence by participating in decisions about managing Columbia River fisheries and the allocation of resources for correcting the system of dams that severely damaged

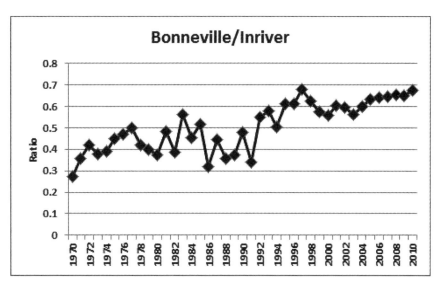

FIGURE 1.1

Ratio of number of fish reaching Bonneville Dam versus the total in-river run. Tribal fisheries on the Columbia River take place above Bonneville Dam. Source: Dave Ward, Columbia Basin Fish and Wildlife Authority.

the fisheries. In thirty-five years of working with Columbia River fishery managers, the co-management described by Diver increased the tribal catch from 5 to 40 percent of the total salmon caught (ODFW 2011). Between 1978 and 2008 CRITFC received the largest share (19 percent) of two billion dollars paid to contractors by the Northwest Power and Conservation Council (NPCC 2009:table 5). Evidence for CRITFC influence is the ratio of in-river salmon reaching tribal fishing areas above the Bonneville Dam. Figure 1.1 shows a pattern of increase in this ratio from 1970 to 2010. In many years prior to 1991, fewer than 40 percent of the total number of fish reached the dam. After 1992, the ratio reaching tribal fisheries was greater than 50 percent and many years exceeded 60 percent. The tribes fish the river above Bonneville, so when more salmon reach their fishing grounds, they have the opportunity to catch a larger share of the total run entering the river.

Ben Colombi and Sibyl Diver (chapters 9 and 10, respectively) note that in the mid-1990s CRITFC and individual tribes launched habitat restoration and conservation programs, both to help steward the salmon and broader ecosystem, as well as to raise salmon population levels to allow for increased catch. The tribal philosophy is, "Gravel-to-gravel management acknowledges the relationship between the biology of the fish, the degree of human pressures on them, and the condition of their physical environment throughout all life history stages" (CRITFC 1996).

Colombi and Diver document how tribal philosophy led to both the keeping and refocusing of hatchery programs in the Columbia Basin. Many biologists have been critical of the impact of hatchery fish on wild runs of salmon and have recommended ending or significantly modifying hatchery programs, but the tribes favored the perpetuation of hatcheries as mechanisms for supplementing lost salmon stocks. The tribes are concerned about the detachment of nontribal society, saying, "Contemporary society is removed from what traditional native thinkers of the Columbia Basin called the 'connectedness' or 'connection of all life'" (CRITFC 2011).

Menzies (chapter 8) discusses how Gitxaała values influence decisions regarding Canadian fisheries. The Columbia Basin and British Columbia experiences suggest the hypothesis that US and British Columbia tribes are exercising sovereignty to affect decisions on the future of salmon and other species important to tribal people. The Indigenous peoples in Russia are trying a similar path. Erich Kasten and Victoria Sharakhmatova (chapters 4 and 5, respectively) write about the constitutional rights of Indigenous peoples; however, rights relate very differently to agency when enforcement is lacking.

CONTROLLING THE COMMONS

To protect resources from the effects of industrial harvest practices, gear, area, and time limits were imposed, and limits to entry that created restrictions on those who fished followed gear, area, and time limits (table 1.2). The application of gear, area, and time rules was not significantly different in concept from rules that Indigenous people used to restrict catch. Menzies (chapter 8) shows how Gitxaała rules determined "who could fish, when they could fish, and how much fish would be taken." Further, fishing techniques allowed the release of nontargeted species and juvenile fish. Kasten (chapter 4) discusses how Indigenous communities operated fish weirs to allow salmon to escape to their spawning grounds, which is a practice common to Indigenous fishery management.

About the same time that gear, area, and time restrictions were imposed, limitations to entry were also prescribed. Similar rules restricting who can fish local stocks can be found among Indigenous peoples where a village leader or village territory may restrict who can catch salmon and other species (Harkin and Lewis 2007; Hunn and Williams 1982; Lake 2007; Thornton 2008; Williams 1980).

TABLE 1.2

Dates of activities related to managing fisheries in Japan, Russia, Alaska, British Colombia, and northwestern United States. Representative dates selected from a larger and more complete list.

Date	Activity	A[1]	H[1]	E[1]	F[1]	Q[1]
1855	Treaties with Columbia River tribes			E		
1859	Washington prevents nonresidents from taking fish	A				
1863	Miomote River artificial propagation, Japan		H			
1870	British Columbia promulgates fishing rules	A				
1870	US Fish Commission goal to augment salmon using hatcheries		H			
1872	McCloud fish hatchery established					
1872	First Oregon game laws, fish ways required over dams					
1875	Russo-Japanese Treaty of Saint Petersburg gives Japan fishing rights in Russian waters			E		
1877	Washington establishes closed periods	A				
1878	Oregon established minimum mesh sizes and closed periods	A				
1884	First British Columbia salmon hatchery on the Fraser River		H			
1888	Hokkaido salmon hatcheries constructed		H			
1907	Russo-Japanese Fisheries Convention—Sakhalin Island given to Japan			E		
1920	Japanese take over Armur and Sakhalin fisheries			E		
1924	Soviet quotas, closures, spawning protrection	A				
1924	White Act—Alaska fisheries oppose exclusive access rights			E		
1928	Soviet Union builds two hatcheries on Armur River		H			
1930	First Alaskan salmon hatchery built		H			
1937	Fraser River Salmon Convention establishes 50/50 US/Canada split			E		
1944	Japan operating twenty-two hatcheries on souther Sakhalin Island		H			
1952	Japanese Fisheries Conservation Law establishes marine ranching		H			
1960	Salmon farming experiments at University of Washington				F	
1968	British Columbia limited access initiated			E		
1971	First salmon farm with British Columbia license				F	
1972	Atlantic salmon farming begins in Puget Sound				F	
1973	Alaska Limited Entry Act			E		
1977	Law of the Sea extends territorial limits to 200 mmi			E		
1990	Russia builds Sakhalin Island hatcheries		H			
1995	Sablefish and halibut longline IFQs introduced in Alaska					Q
1997	Farmed salmon and trout surpass wild production				F	
2002	CQE authorized by North Pacific Fishery Management Council					Q
2006	Alaska king crab quota system introduced					Q
2008	British Columbia largest fish farmer in the North Pacific				F	

1. For the right five columns, A=area, gear, and time rules; H=hatcheries; E=entry limits; F=salmon farming; and Q=quota management that gives a property right.

Source: Augerot (2000) and personal communications; Langdon 2008; papers by Colombi, Carothers, Diver, Kasten, Koester, Lien, Menzies, Reedy-Maschner, Sharakhmatova, and Wilson; and administrative records of Alaska, British Columbia, Oregon, and Washington.

Gear, area, and time controls; limits to entry; and hatcheries tend to appear in close succession. Entry limits are seen as conservation measures. Koester (chapter 3) says that in Russia, "the most troublesome aspect is that licenses ('limits') for fishing are given by government authorities based on political influence." Further, catch allocations for Indigenous peoples are too limited to meet their basic needs, even though Indigenous peoples have a constitutional right to a catch share (Kasten, chapter 4; Koester, chapter 3; Sharakhmatova, chapter 5).

Katherine Reedy-Maschner (chapter 6) explains the problems faced by Aleut communities when traditional cultural patterns come up against pressing economic needs caused by continued production for international markets. The Aleut people are "becoming increasingly aware of their vulnerability and mortality," she writes. Sixteen Aleut communities have been abandoned, and population is declining in the consolidated communities. Reedy-Maschner writes, "But, salmon in the north are for the most part renewable, predictable, and harvested in mass quantities for subsistence and commercial ends with a global market in all five species." The state of Alaska's efforts to protect the biological resource have paid less attention to Indigenous needs. Salmon that Aleuts would normally take are instead intercepted by a large nonresident fleet coming from Seattle that takes the allowable catch in a very short time.

Since capture fisheries attract too much effort and the resource gets overfished, economists suggest establishing a property right to enable fishers to fish more safely, match catches to resource availability more effectively, and develop a stewardship interest among harvesters. These rights take the form of quotas. Quotas include IFQs (individual fishing quotas), ITQs (individual transferable quotas), CDQs (community development quotas), CFQs (community fishing quotas), and CQEs (community quota entities) (Langdon 2007; Carothers, chapter 7; Reedy-Maschner, chapter 6; Sharakhmatova, chapter 5). Quotas derive from microeconomic approaches to agriculture. A quota is equivalent to a land-based limit for a crop or like barbed wire that corals livestock for an owner. A fishing quota is a mechanism for establishing individual property rights. This mechanism is different from the allocation of a portion of the available catch to tribal fisheries. Community quotas allow a group to access a particular fishing area or stock, and part of the point of granting a property right is to reduce the number fishing. Quotas divide the whole among many different individuals or communities, but one impact of quotas documented by Carothers and Reedy-Maschner is the inequality they produce, especially the marginalization of Indigenous fishers in gaining their fair share of the resource.

Quota fisheries reduce the number of fishers and total catch to match the estimated "biologically acceptable catch." But fewer boats and less catch deplete community revenues and economic life. While the Aleuts have a CDQ program, investments have not brought economic well-being, village population continues to drop, and a debate goes on about whether petroleum exploration and drilling might offer better returns in their overall portfolio of economic activities (Reedy-Maschner, chapter 6). Reviewing CQE programs, Langdon (2008:38) finds these, too, have not been as effective as hoped and without modification "will exist only as an illusion."

CAPTURE TO CULTURE

The building of hatcheries increases survival of young salmon on the theory that if more survive the alevin, fry, parr, and smolt stages of the life cycle, salmon will be more abundant. Hatchery technology spread quickly around the Pacific in the late nineteenth century as fishery managers increasingly cultured salmon for greater production to meet the demands of capture fishers (see table 1.2, also Dodds 1959; Lichatowich 1999; Taylor 1999). Salmon are held in hatcheries to reduce early life cycle mortality. They are then released to complete the rest of their life cycle in estuaries, the ocean, and rivers, where they spawn.

Agricultural metaphors around the management and production processes in fisheries continued to increase, and about a century later, full-fledged farming brought about significant impacts. Farming salmon controls the whole life cycle in a pen or closed facility. Salmon farming increases productivity by reducing mortality throughout the life cycle and using feeds, antibiotics, and genetic modifications that increase rates of growth. The farming of salmon was an innovation that began on a commercial scale in the 1960s along the coasts of Norway and Scotland using Atlantic salmon (Lien, chapter 11). Experiments were going on at the same time at the University of Washington, and British Columbia opened its first salmon farm in 1971 (see table 1.2).

Farmed fish are most like industrialized agricultural products in that production is controlled throughout the salmon life cycle. As the volume of farmed fish increases, prices received by fishers drop, and worries increase about farmed fish escaping because they could interbreed with or outcompete native salmon. Concern grows about waste products and the use of antibiotics and other chemicals to increase productivity. The biggest concern, however, is loss of diversity as any kind of agricultural process involves selection for certain varieties, traits, behaviors, and life history characteristics. Perhaps it is ironic that Atlantic salmon are among the main species cultured on the Pacific Coast.

The growth of industrialized agriculture in providing food and fiber, producing animals, and supplying timber to meet human needs has also reduced spawning and rearing habitats for salmon, created obstacles in salmon migration corridors, introduced exotic species (many of which are harmful to salmon), and limited the area that salmon can inhabit. Salmon adapt to a diversity of landscapes in networks of rivers, streams, and tributaries. As a result of occupying different habitats, salmon develop different life history characteristics that tie them to a variety of highly variable natural conditions. Studies show that over a quarter of the fourteen hundred populations of US Pacific Northwest salmon have been lost since settlement (Gustafson et al. 2007; Nehlsen, Williams, and Lichatowich 1991). A focus on culturing removes much of this diversity, just as the sale to international markets creates competitive forces that reduce the diversity of salmon cultures (Augerot 2005) and small communities (Martin 2008).

Concern for abundance and productivity leads to the enumeration of fish produced and caught (Koester, chapter 3). The amount of hatchery salmon in capture harvest becomes of interest. Figure 1.2 compares the percentage of total capture harvest among five areas for the first decade of the twenty-first century (top line) with the percentage of that harvest in each area produced from hatcheries. The top line shows the percent contribution by region that comes from hatchery production (Augerot 2005; Knapp, Roheim, and Anderson 2007; Ruggerone et al. 2010; The Research Group 2009). Washington, Oregon, California, and Idaho (WOCI) have the least—less than 1 percent of the total for the five regions with 80 percent hatchery produced. British Columbia has approximately 2 percent with 70 percent hatchery produced. Japan produces nearly all salmon in hatcheries. Russia has the lowest percentage of hatchery production, 14 percent, and 39 percent of the total North Pacific catch. The capture harvest of chum is the largest, and twice as many chum are harvested as all other salmon species. Estimates vary from year to year due to environmental conditions, according to species mix, and with international market conditions. Alaska and Russia have better habitats and produce the most nonhatchery salmon (Augerot 2005). Japan uses mostly chum salmon from hatcheries for its capture harvest (The Research Group 2009:7). Alaska is successful with chum and pink salmon hatcheries. In Russia, the overwhelming majority of effort regarding artificial propagation has been devoted to sockeye and chum salmon (Augerot 2005). These data omit the production of farmed salmon.

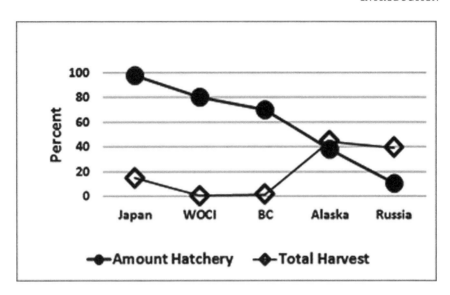

FIGURE 1.2

Diamonds show the percentage of the total North Pacific catch by fishing area for the first decade of the twenty-first century. Solid circles show the percentage that comes from hatchery production for each area. Thus, Japan has 97 percent hatchery-produced salmon and 15 percent of the capture harvest among the five areas. Russia has 39 percent of the capture harvest among the five areas, of which 10 percent comes from hatcheries. Source: adapted from Augerot 2005:33; Knapp, Roheim, and Anderson. 2007; Ruggerone et al. 2010; The Research Group 2009.

These comparisons show several north–south patterns. First, Russia and Alaska in the north have very low numbers of people and density relative to Japan and WOCI. A higher percentage of the north's population includes Indigenous peoples. In the Columbia Basin and British Columbia, a greater portion of the resource is allocated to Indigenous communities than in Russian and Japan.

When looking at the north, we see that it is richer in numbers of salmon and salmon diversity. In Kamchatka and Alaska, both numbers and biodiversity are greater because the habitat has been in better condition during the first decade of the twenty-first century. The best habitat remaining for salmon is in northeast Russia and Alaska, although Kamchatka and Sakhalin Island habitats are currently under threat from mineral extraction, oil and gas development, and illegal poaching for salmon (Kasten, chapter 4; Koester, chapter 3; Sharakhmatova, chapter 5; Wilson, chapter 2). However, Emma Wilson provides an example of how mineral exploration and extraction can provide help for Indigenous peoples to adapt to new conditions while maintaining cultural practices. The Nivkhi of Sakhalin's northeast coast retained the centrality of salmon to their culture. They developed leadership and were able to collaborate in the design of the Sakhalin Indigenous Minorities Development Plan, which gained financial and program support from oil and gas companies.

One of the significant habitat changes meant to support agriculture is the building of dams on the Columbia River. For agriculture, the dams provide three benefits. First is irrigation water; second is electricity to pump water; and third is "a river highway" to move agricultural products downstream. Energy and fertilizer supplies return upstream. Colombi (chapter 9) describes how the Nimiipuus are leaders in an effort to remove dams on the Snake River, a major tributary to the Columbia, that inhibit salmon from leaving and returning to their home rivers—Clearwater River in Idaho and Grande Ronde in Oregon.[1] Colombi also notes that the Nimiipuus are leaders in restoring watersheds and in efforts to increase Snake River salmon stocks through supplementation practices designed to mimic natural processes. He writes that the Nimiipuus also use their reserved water rights to help the downstream migration of salmon. While Colombi refers to the Nimiipuu case as "sovereignty through salmon," he also documents how the Nimiipuus are building salmon through use of their sovereignty.

The quantity of farmed salmon has grown dramatically. From 1950 to 2009, farmed salmon have increased from next to nothing to over 60 percent of the total quantity of salmon produced worldwide (FAO 2011:top graph). The total salmon production shown in figure 1.3 is the amount captured from naturally spawning and hatchery stocks, plus the amount farmed, and these aggregated global data come from a diversity of sources and protocols. Further, these data reflect quantities, not value: chinook, coho, and sockeye salmon and steelhead trout command higher prices than the more abundant chums and pinks. Figure 1.3 shows the general pattern of change toward greater reliance on farmed salmon. In 1996 the amount of farmed salmon exceeded wild and hatchery-born salmon for the first time. As table 1.2 shows, farming of salmon is a relatively late addition to the North Pacific salmon story.

DISCUSSION

The exporting of perceived surpluses by entrepreneurs from dominating nation-states, application of agricultural metaphors, efforts to control the commons, and increasing use of culturing techniques highlight four ways that agricultural metaphors and the actions that follow from them are detrimental to salmon and salmon fishers: First is the impact of

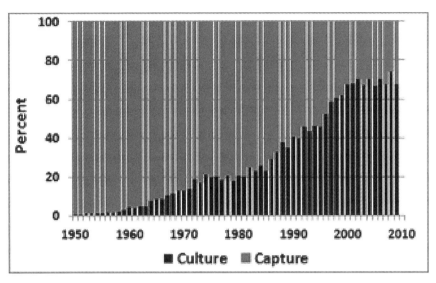

FIGURE 1.3
Wild and hatchery capture production versus farmed salmon production for 1950–2009. The graph shows the increasing percentage of production by aquaculture that has overtaken the percentage from capture fishing. Source: FAO 2011.

agricultural metaphors that have become part of fishery management. The goal of maximum sustainable yield implies the continuation of a maximum surplus production, but salmon stocks are highly variable due to a variety of natural processes, and command and control management of salmon fisheries has not matched fish abundance to the efforts of fishers. Second is the direct effect of fish culturing to increase abundance, which was the original use of salmon hatcheries and continues to be the case. The simplification and selection practices at hatcheries greatly reduce salmon biodiversity. Third is the growth of fish farming, whose effects are less direct. Fish farming competes with capture fisheries in world markets, putting pressure on fish prices and thus the incomes of capture fishers, and many fear that fish farming will damage natural runs of salmon. Fourth is the impact of industrial-agricultural production on the habitats of salmon, whether they will retain their historic diversity in a network of streams that enables them to adapt to natural and human disturbances. An examination of culturing thus reveals a dire list of threats to salmon populations and fishing peoples.

These case studies of North Pacific salmon fishing peoples show the impacts of culturing, but also the adaptability of culture. The cases suggest that portfolio building, resource quota allocations, sovereignty and leadership, and values are ways of creating alternatives to the impacts of industrial agriculture, and all show a diversity of subsistence resource portfolios that come from adaptation over thousands of years. Each Indigenous group had a portfolio of activities from which they derived their well-being. Historically, as reflected in Kasten's (chapter 4) description of the paired economies of marine Koryaks and reindeer Koryaks, salmon peoples relied on a diversity of subsistence activities. Kasten notes the diversity of Koryak subsistence resources: fishing; hunting sea mammals, snow sheep, and fur-bearing animals; collecting sprouts, wild onions, berries, and roots; and trading with reindeer herders. In Koester's chapter, Tatiana Petrovna reflects on Itelmen foods including salmon and many other fish, a variety of plants and roots, birds' eggs, and seals, bears, ravens, foxes, gulls, mice, and many other hunted animals, all of which are threatened by industrial agricultural perspectives and practices of productivity maximization, stabilization, and simplification.

The Nimiipuus, too, are portfolio builders. Colombi (chapter 9) points to Nimiipuu "narratives built on harvesting several different runs of chinook, coho, chum, and sockeye salmon; cutthroat, lake, Dolly Varden, and steelhead trout; and different varieties of whitefish, sturgeon, suckers, lampreys, and pikeminnows." Colombi goes on to say that in addition to fish, the Nimiipuus used plant resources for food and "medicinal and industrial purposes." With the coming of Protestant missionaries, the Nimiipuus added farming to their portfolio. They became successful small-scale farmers and outstanding animal breeders.

Catch quotas are a second approach to creating options for capture fishers. Victoria Sharakhmatova (chapter 5) reports on how Russia allocated salmon to outside businesses and prevented Indigenous people from catching salmon from the runs that could have provided for an Indigenous catch. In other words, Indigenous Kamchatkans do not receive the benefit of salmon runs because Russian economic development plans allocated catches to non-Indigenous commercial fishers. Sharakhmatova describes a United Nations Development Programme (UNDP) to help Kamchatka Indigenous peoples obtain fishing rights using the CDQ concept. Here is a potentially complementary impact of caring for salmon ecosystems: the UNDP is concerned about biodiversity, and Kamchatka Indigenous peoples are concerned about getting their Indigenous rights; the UNDP/GEF (Global Environment Facility) Kamchatka Salmon Biodiversity Project has a global interest in biodiversity that is complementary to a local interest in gaining catch shares to pursue in traditional ways.

Catch is increased by the application of Indigenous sovereignty. Diver (chapter 10) discusses the 1855 treaties that recognized tribal sovereignty signed with the Nimiipuu, Umatilla, Warm Springs, and Yakama nations. As Diver points out, the Columbia River Inter-Tribal Fish Commission (CRITFC) worked to secure the allocation of catch in which legal decisions were interpreted "in common" to mean equal shares (Cohen 1986). The treaties, which are agreements between sovereigns, are a critical factor in Columbia Basin tribes being able to retain their rights and have the ability to affect fishery management decisions (Cone 1995).

A hopeful sign for Indigenous participation in fishery management is Diver's review of CRITFC's role in co-management. Diver tells the story of the emergence of co-management between CRITFC and other groups interested in the management of Columbia River salmon fisheries. She points to how CRITFC grew out of the 1935 Celilo Fisheries Committee, which enforced regulations to uphold sharing of traditional fishery resources, limited access to tribal fishing places by outsiders, and determined the timing and location of Indian dip-net fishing.

Leaders who bring vision and the ability to implement new practices make sovereignty more effective. Wilson (chapter 2) explains how the Nivkhi were able to develop the leadership to think strategically about the future. Reedy-Maschner (chapter 6) points to how leadership allows the Aleuts to undertake new development ventures. Gitxaała leaders guided fishing practices and relations with the Canadian government. CRITFC leaders showed how to use tribal perspectives to restore Columbia Basin salmon fisheries. Colombi (chapter 9) documents Nimiipuu leadership in bringing attention to the problems of hydroelectric dams in the Columbia Basin and the potential benefits of their removal.

A diversity of values brings a diversity of options to resource use planning. One of the values that salmon fishing peoples bring is the idea of giving something back for the gifts received from nature (CRITFC 1994). Tribal people are thought to have a more reciprocal relation with salmon and ecosystems, and the First Salmon ceremonies common to the Northwest Coast honor salmon and an abundant, animate earth (Gunther 1926; Swezey and Heizer 1977). Another characteristic of Indigenous cultures is that they tend to limit what they take from ecosystems and do not seek to maximize productivity (Butler and Campbell 2004; Lake 2007; Langdon 2008; Thornton 2008; Thornton and Manasfi 2010). Certainly, there are exceptions (Krech 2005, 2007), but common to many salmon peoples discussed in this volume is an ethic to protect and preserve salmon and the habitats they require.

Kasten (chapter 4) describes the cultural ethic of not taking more than is needed, practices of knowing the environment and not polluting the river, and ceremonies to honor the fish. While the marine Koryaks had paired economies with the reindeer Koryaks and needed salmon to feed their sled dogs as well as people, they were careful not to take more than they needed. These actions show a concern for the resource. Kasten tells of Koryak people giving back by returning some fish to the river "'so that there would be many fishes in the future'" and of their concerns that too many fish are being taken to provide caviar. He summarizes, "In contrast to Soviet or Western ideology, Indigenous people were aware that they would never be able to 'conquer'...or to control nature." As the fisheries of Kamchatka became commercialized, Indigenous peoples were forced to resort to poaching, "a grassroots social response to the inequitable distribution of natural resource rent." In other words, poaching occurs when fishery management is not seen as fair and reasonable.

Menzies (chapter 8) says that the actions toward and modifications of their environment by the Gitxaała "are framed in terms of relations with nonhuman social beings and humans." He continues, "This implies and requires a structure of obligation and reciprocity." Menzies argues that Gitxaała care for the environment is one of the factors that keeps fish stocks from declining—that declines correlate with the outlawing of Gitxaała conservation practices by government managers. While it might not be *the* answer, the hopeful message is that values diversity creates an array of options to consider.

CONCLUSIONS

Each region is affected differently by agricultural metaphors and their applications. The future may be fish farming, but Russia, Alaska, and the Columbia Basin still do not have fish farms. Salmon farming is very extensive in British Columbia, where fish farmers and capture fishers are actively hostile toward each other. Even without a physical presence, fish farms in Europe and Chile have an impact on all North Pacific salmon peoples. Fish farms affect the international trade in salmon by lowering the price received by capture fishers, while also making salmon more available and cheaper for consumers. A market in wild-caught salmon exists, but it is small relative to the overall salmon market. Further, many of the "wild-caught" salmon are hatchery produced. Thus, the hatchery component of fish production plays very directly into the opportunities for salmon peoples in all areas. In the first decade of the twenty-first century, the Columbia Basin and British Columbia relied most on hatcheries, Russia the least.

Alaska, the biggest producer of salmon, relies on hatcheries for 40 percent of the wild-caught harvest.

Threats to salmon habitat from the urban-industrial footprint affect all the groups discussed. Whether mining and oil extraction in Russia; the timber harvest in Russia, Alaska, and the Pacific Northwest; or extensive agricultural development in the Columbia Basin, the demands of urban and industrial growth threaten capture fisheries. Japan is an example of a place where capture fisheries exist only because of hatchery production. Agricultural metaphors and the practices they engender cause loss of natural and cultural diversity and raise concerns about the future.

With the loss of salmon biological and cultural diversity has come new forms of diversity—in production practices, such as using hatcheries to augment salmon abundance, in the complexity of ecosystems for conserving and restoring salmon, and in fish farming systems. Salmon are important to many diverse groups of people. They are living metaphors of wildness and tenacity, while also important for catch and release, commercial, recreational, and trophy fishing. Some salmon live natural life cycles, others are hatched and ocean ranched, while still others have their life cycle controlled by farming. Fishers include people using Indigenous, tribal, recreational, commercial, trolling, set-net, dip-net, purse seine, gillnet, and hook and line methods. Salmon are distributed as first foods for Indigenous peoples, local ceremonial and subsistence purposes, and commercial sale in local, national, and international markets. Fisheries are managed according to values that range from neoliberal to deep ecology. Despite the abundance of salmon for some purposes, there are not enough for all purposes, and many of the purposes conflict. Resolving this human diversity dilemma is a critical problem that is being addressed in each of the case studies in this volume. While many patterns may be similar, solutions will likely vary from location to location.

The North Pacific salmon history and these nine case studies show a pattern of change that most often has worked to the disadvantage of salmon-dependent peoples, who use capture techniques. The result has been marginalization and the loss of opportunities to practice traditional culture, secure traditional rights, and pursue traditional resources. Industrial-agricultural metaphor and practice point to a difficult future for capture fisheries. Yet principles from each of these case studies suggest options for the future: what new portfolios, use rights, sovereignty, leaders, values, cultural understandings, restoration activities, and partnerships can abate the devastation that culturing exerts on capture fisheries?

Note

1. *Nimiipuu* is the Indigenous name for people who make up the Nez Perce Tribe.

2

The Oil Company, the Fish, and the Nivkhi

The Cultural Value of Sakhalin Salmon

Emma Wilson

INTRODUCTION

Sakhalin Island in the Russian Far East is home to about 20 percent of global Pacific salmon stocks.[1] Salmon is a mainstay of the traditional diet of Sakhalin's Nivkh people, many of whom live in Noglikskii District in northeastern Sakhalin, which is also the location of major offshore oil and gas projects. Since the earliest documentation of Nivkh practices, fishing and preparation of salmon and other fish species have been central to their livelihood activities (Shternberg 1999). While the lifestyles and prospects of many Nivkhi have changed over the past century, fishing and fish preparation have retained their central place. Since the commercial exploitation of large-scale offshore oil and gas fields began in the late 1900s, Sakhalin's economy has shifted from one based largely on fishing and fish processing to one where oil and gas production dominates—at least in terms of revenues, if not in terms of employment or significance for livelihoods. The Pacific salmon remains important for today's Nivkhi, not only economically, but also from a social and cultural perspective.

Damage to the Sakhalin salmon fisheries has historically come from heavy logging, overfishing, and the onshore oil and gas industry (from the early twentieth century). New threats have been posed by the offshore oil and gas industry that is rapidly transforming Sakhalin into an oil and gas export economy. At the same time the multinational companies engaged in the offshore developments are offering support to salmon conservation and the Indigenous communities that depend on the salmon fisheries— support that is much needed and largely unavailable from other sources. This support inevitably raises questions about the implications of close engagement between traditional resource users and powerful industrial interests and the nature of any mutual dialogue.

By focusing on one company—Sakhalin Energy Investment Company Ltd. (Sakhalin Energy)[2]—and one particularly vocal Indigenous group—the Nivkhi—I seek to highlight some of the tensions around use and protection of Sakhalin's salmon fisheries in the context of major offshore oil and gas development. I consider some of the reasons for a multinational company to promote Indigenous traditional activities and conserve salmon and for the Indigenous people themselves to engage. While we are aware of the risks of large-scale multinational interests "co-opting" local organizations and interest groups through "participation" (Cooke and Kothari 2001), the case study of the Nivkhi and Sakhalin Energy offers some useful insights into the kinds of choices that people face in such situations. In it I view the Nivkhi not as passive players, but as people who have made clear choices about how to engage (albeit within a limited range of options) and have made efforts to remain true to their traditional values. Pacific salmon is central to the choices that have been made, from both a practical and symbolic perspective.

Salmon fishing and the location of fishing activities are seen as intimately bound up with Nivkh identity and the ability to leverage other livelihood benefits. Salmon was the foundation for early trading relationships, and it was the main resource for collective fishing bases to which the Nivkhi were forced to move in the 1930s. In the post-Soviet era, the Nivkh relationship with salmon has provided justification for Indigenous identity, underpinning claims for priority fish quotas, enterprise support, and access to land. Traditional forms of salmon preparation are seen as a differentiator between Nivkh and Russian identities. Today fish and fish products are still traded on the open market and exchanged within networks of family and friends. And as this chapter demonstrates, salmon also acts as a symbolic tool of protest and leverage in negotiations with international oil and gas companies.

The status of "Indigenous" (in Russia as in other countries) is partly determined by resource use activities. According to the Russian law On Guaranteeing the Rights of Russia's Indigenous Northern Minorities, the Indigenous peoples should live on the lands of their ancestors and preserve their traditional ways of life, occupations, and trades. In the case of the Sakhalin Nivkhi, this means fishing (and making traditional dried fish or *iukola*) on the rivers and coastal bays where their ancestors used to fish. Of course, other residents of Noglikskii District depend on salmon and other fish resources for their livelihoods. For the Evenki and Uil'ta (or Oroki), for example, who live in the same region, fishing is a traditional subsistence activity to supplement reindeer herding. Non-Indigenous fishers include local residents who fish for recreation (using a rod) on weekends, small-scale fishing enterprises that operate in the near offshore waters, and larger enterprises that fish further offshore. Poaching is also relatively common, with people coming (often from outside the region) to poach fish on the rivers, frequently taking the caviar and leaving the fish to rot by the riverbank.

Sakhalin's recoverable oil reserves are estimated to be around 5 billion barrels, while its natural gas reserves total approximately 34 trillion cu ft.[3] Sakhalin has six offshore oil and gas projects in various stages of development,[4] and its onshore oil and gas industry (which began in the early 1920s) is still producing small volumes. In this chapter I focus in particular on the Sakhalin-2 project, led by Sakhalin Energy, a consortium involving Shell and Gazprom. This focus is partly because of the high levels of transparency practiced by this consortium and the considerable amounts of international attention it has attracted over the years, which have resulted in significant volumes of published materials relating to the project. It is also due to the relationship that Sakhalin Energy has forged with the local Indigenous peoples (largely represented by the Nivkhi) through the Sakhalin Indigenous Minorities' Development Plan. Other companies are also operating in the same area, but either their projects are less well advanced, or (in the case of ExxonMobil's Sakhalin-1 project) much less information is published about their activities.

This chapter first of all offers a brief history of fishing and the oil industry in northeastern Sakhalin. It then focuses on several Nivkhi who were fishing on Nyiskii Bay, one of Sakhalin's northeastern coastal lagoons not far from the Sakhalin-2 project offshore oil and gas fields, in the early stages of the Sakhalin-2 project. The chapter then reflects on the way that the Nivkhi of Sakhalin have engaged with Sakhalin Energy since the late 1990s and the role that the Pacific salmon has played in these engagements. In the chapter I draw on my experience of environmental activism while based in the Russian Far East between 1994 and 1997; field research undertaken for my PhD in 1999 (Wilson 2002b), including some previously published case-study material (Wilson 2002a); subsequent visits to Sakhalin Energy as a consultant between 2002 and 2006; and more recent anthropological research collaboration and engagement with people working in the region, alongside analysis of relevant literature to the present day.

A BRIEF HISTORY OF FISHING AND THE OIL
INDUSTRY IN NORTHEASTERN SAKHALIN

With a length of 1,000 km and an area of over 76,000 sq km, Sakhalin is Russia's largest island and is shaped somewhat like an elongated fish. It lies in the Russian Far East, over 10,000 km and seven time zones to the east of Moscow and just 40 km north of Japan. Noglikskii District lies in the northeast; its coastline faces out into the cold Sea of Okhotsk, which is rich in fish as well as oil and gas. The Sea of Okhotsk is where most of Sakhalin's offshore oil and gas projects are located; the Sakhalin-2 project's famous Molikpaq platform lies 16 km from the coast of Noglikskii District (figure 2.1).

Sakhalin is home to eleven salmonid species and is the third richest salmon region in the world after Alaska and Kamchatka. Millions of pink, chum, cherry, and coho salmon, Dolly Varden and white spotted char, and endangered Sakhalin *taimen* return to Sakhalin's rivers each year (Wild Salmon Center 2008:12). Sakhalin's northeastern coastline is laced with a string of shallow lagoons used by local people for recreational and subsistence hunting, fishing, and gathering. These are wetlands of international conservation interest as bird habitat, while the coastal waters beyond the lagoons are the summer mating grounds for the endangered western Pacific gray whale (Newell and Wilson 1996).

According to the last Russian census in 2002,[5] Sakhalin's population was just under 550,000, a decline of nearly 20 percent from 1999. The population includes Russians (84.0 percent), Koreans (5.4 percent), Ukrainians (4.0 percent), and others. The Nivkhi (Sakhalin's largest Indigenous group) number 5,287 or 0.5 percent of the total population, and their population has remained stable. Many Nivkhi now live in the district center Nogliki (population 10,729) or in other districts to the north and east. Some Nivkhi and most of the Uil'ta and Evenki (who number just a few hundred) live in rural settlements to the north of Nogliki.

Up until the late nineteenth century, the Nivkhi held fishing, hunting, and gathering grounds in clan ownership. The nomadic Evenki and Uil'ta started to arrive on Sakhalin from the mainland (unchallenged by the Nivkhi) in the sixteenth and seventeenth centuries (Shternberg 1999). The Indigenous groups traded their natural resources with each other, the Ainu in southern Sakhalin, and the Manchurians and Japanese (Vysokov 1995). In the mid-nineteenth century, Russians began exploring Sakhalin's mineral resources. In the 1860s, Japan and Russia came into conflict over fishing grounds in northern Sakhalin, forcing the Nivkhi to define their own rights to the contested resources (Grant 1999). From 1875 to the early 1900s czarist planners used convict labor to exploit Sakhalin's resources.

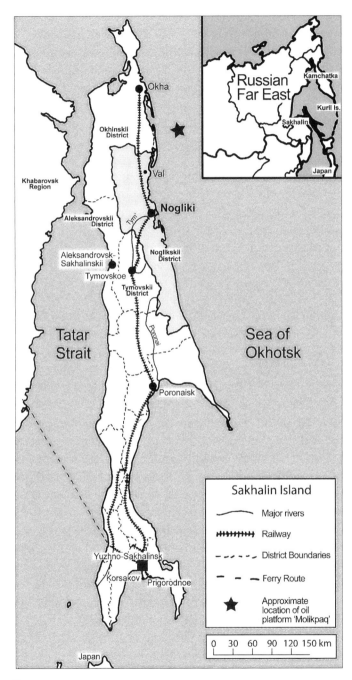

FIGURE 2.1

Map of Sakhalin. Source: Gavin Wood.

In the 1890s commercial fishing associations were set up by Russian business magnates, notably Grigory Zotov, who also discovered Sakhalin's first oil reserves in 1904 (Stephan 1971). After the Russo-Japanese war of 1904–1905, Japan gained the southern half of Sakhalin, and in 1920 Japan invaded northern Sakhalin, exploiting the oil reserves of the northeast until Sakhalin was returned to Russia in 1925 under the Soviet government. From 1925, workers throughout the USSR were encouraged to migrate to Sakhalin. The oil reserves became vital to the Soviet government as the only known reserves in eastern Siberia at the time (Stephan 1971).

The Soviet government attempted to settle the Nivkhi into collective fishing enterprises through policies of collectivization in the 1930s and village amalgamation and sedentarization in the 1950s–1960s. The Nivkhi were progressively marginalized from their traditional fishing grounds, their children were forced to attend the *internat* (boarding school), and their systems of customary law were broken (Roon 1999). Hundreds of Indigenous villages were closed; the northern Sakhalin coastline is scattered with these deserted villages, as is the Russian north as a whole. The state also guaranteed markets and subsidized transportation such that traditional economic activities became entirely dependent on state support. This practice made the shock even greater when, in the postsocialist era, state support was withdrawn from traditional enterprise. The Indigenous populations were gradually assimilated into the incomer populations. In fact, as the following snapshots of Nivkh life illustrate, older Indigenous residents of Noglikskii District express their nostalgia for the early days of collective fishing enterprises, prior to the period of amalgamation in the 1950s, when they were forced to move to Nogliki. It is these old fishing villages that the Nivkhi now return to in summer. The collective fishing enterprises offered security and a guaranteed income, good housing, land for growing potatoes and keeping animals, as well as access to rich fishing grounds close to the homes. The trauma of being moved from those villages is understandably still with the elders.

The demographic upheavals were characterized by nonconsultative meetings to inform people about decisions that had already been made. People did not expect to be consulted, nor did they try to protest. One of Bruce Grant's (1999:188) informants commented in 1990: "The tragedy is that nothing happened. The empty houses in Nogliki were all ready.... Most people just got up and moved. That's the tragedy—that there was no tragedy." The initial expectations of elderly Nivkhi about the multinational oil companies operating on Sakhalin were based on their experience of Soviet resettlement programs and other planning processes. While public meetings were common under the Soviets, they never led to meaningful involvement: "Whether one consciously believed in the officially proclaimed goals was less important than the act of participating in routine official practices, perceived as inevitable" (Yurchak 1997:168). This pattern led to a deep cynicism about power, a public disengagement from the state, and a "personal non-involvement in the official sphere" (Yurchak 1997:163). The deep cynicism has been difficult for older generations to shake off, and even younger people do not always believe that they can influence externally led industrial interventions. The situation is not helped by today's top-down style of government and the typical nature of public consultation led by oil companies. Nonetheless, by contrast to the official sphere, people display a surprising degree of agency in the realm of subsistence activity and social interaction (Wilson 2002b). To some extent this agency can explain the evolution of Nivkh engagement with Sakhalin Energy, as this chapter attempts to demonstrate.

Until the late 1990s, fishing and fish processing were the main sources of income for the Sakhalin region. The Kuril Basin and Sea of Okhotsk are some of the richest fisheries in the world, providing more than 60 percent of Russia's total fish harvest and exports to the United States, Japan, and Korea. Salmon fishing remains a major job provider. According to the Wild Salmon Center (2007:12), the salmon fisheries provide around 50 percent of rural jobs, with about thirty-two thousand jobs being linked to the salmon fisheries. Sakhalin's fisheries have been heavily exploited for more than a hundred years, and overfishing—including by large foreign fishing vessels—continues to be a major cause of fisheries degradation. Throughout the twentieth century, heavy logging also contributed to the fisheries' decline, along with the onshore oil and gas industry. The more recent offshore oil and gas industry has posed further threats (including pipeline construction across spawning rivers)—though there is no evidence of major negative impacts to date.

In response to general fisheries decline, fish quotas for Noglikskii District have been reduced, a situation local fishers feel is unfair as it has been brought about by outsiders. The reduction of fish quotas has also exacerbated tensions between the Indigenous people (who benefit from priority fish quotas due to their Indigenous status) and the non-Indigenous people who believe they have an equal right to this local resource. This chapter attempts to elucidate local perceptions of fishing rights and regulation. While the greatest damage to fish stocks results from illegal fishing far out to sea, it is difficult to police, and very little information is available on this issue locally. Regulators find it difficult to catch those poachers who come from outside the area to local rivers, and some may deliberately turn a blind eye to such activities. Yet minor cases of Indigenous people fishing more than their legally allocated fish quotas are frequently policed in quite an aggressive manner, despite the relatively small impact on overall fish stocks that these practices must have. As I illustrate, while local Nivkhi view the law as frequently arbitrary, sometimes aggressive, and generally unfair, local social norms at the same time encompass quite a clear moral code around what is acceptable and what is unacceptable fishing practice.

Today, the oil industry is taking over from the fishing industry as number one in the region. Since the 1990s, the budgets of Noglikskii and Okhinskii districts have been almost entirely dependent on revenues from the local oil company Rosneft'-Sakhalinmorneftegas (SMNG), particularly in view of the collapse of other former state industries (especially the timber industry). The first oil from the offshore reserves was produced in 1999 at the Sakhalin-2 project's Molikpaq platform. In that year and subsequent years, Sakhalin has been second only to Moscow for foreign investment. Phase 2 of the Sakhalin-2 project included erection of two more offshore platforms, construction of 300 km of offshore pipelines and more than 800 km of onshore oil and gas pipelines, an onshore processing facility in Noglikskii District, and, in the south of the island, an oil export terminal and Russia's first—and the world's largest—liquefied natural gas (LNG) plant. According to Sakhalin Energy, oil and gas from the Sakhalin-2 project alone represented 50 percent of exports from the region in the first half of 2010.[6] There is some evidence that overall standards of living have improved on Sakhalin since the start of the offshore oil and gas developments, while unemployment has dropped to below-average levels for Russia (AEA Technology 2007).

From the earliest stages of project development, international environmental nongovernmental organizations (NGOs) raised concerns about threats to the island's fisheries, largely due to onshore pipeline construction (Newell and Wilson 1996). The Sakhalin-2 project crosses 1,084 rivers and streams, many of which are home to salmon (Sakhalin Energy 2005). While engagement between Sakhalin Energy and potentially affected Indigenous peoples of Sakhalin was ongoing from the mid- to late 1990s, Indigenous peoples' issues rose to international attention following the "Green Wave" protest by Indigenous groups in January 2005 (Roon 2006). Sakhalin Energy responded by setting up the Sakhalin Indigenous Minorities Development Plan, which initially attempted to address environmental issues through dialogue and now primarily allocates funds to Indigenous enterprises and social projects (Sakhalin Energy 2006).

The following section views the early stages of the Sakhalin-2 project through the eyes of local Nivkhi who fish on one of Sakhalin's northeastern coastal lagoons—Nyiskii Bay. I attempt to illustrate the priorities and perceptions of those living and fishing on the northeastern coastal bays against the backdrop of the oil and gas developments taking place in the coastal waters. The oil and gas developments were seen initially as mysterious, sinister, and distant, in comparison to the very real conflict people were facing with fisheries regulators and the real problems of catching enough fish to meet their families' needs and those of the more vulnerable members of local society. The subsequent section of the chapter discusses the later evolution of relations between Sakhalin Energy and the Nivkhi, a period characterized by a much greater degree of agency and control on the part of the Nivkhi, albeit within a very limited sphere of influence (i.e., the allocation of funds to enterprises and social projects).

NYISKII BAY

Nyiskii Bay is one of a string of shallow lagoons that international observers fear to be most at risk from Sakhalin's offshore oil and gas projects. With their narrow mouths and shallow waters, they would suffer hugely if an oil slick hit. The value of these bays as nesting and migrating sites for rare birds was internationally recognized in the mid-1990s (Newell and Wilson 1996). Less was known internationally at the time about the importance of these bays for local subsistence and leisure activities.

I first met Tetya Nadya outside her hut in the "closed" village of Nyivo, on a narrow spit of land between Nyiskii Bay and the Sea of Okhotsk.[7] Tetya Nadya would spend every summer on the shores of the bay practicing traditional subsistence activities—catching and preparing fish and gathering berries. She would spend the harsh winter months living closer to relatives in her wooden home in the poorer part of Nogliki (known as the *kolkhoz* part of town). At that time, in September 1999, a big scandal had arisen involving the special police force (OMON). The Fishing Inspectorate had asked OMON to help out with fishing regulation, and—we were told—the special police had behaved aggressively and violently, even firing several shots through the fishing boat of another summer resident as it was propped up outside her hut.

Tetya Nadya explained to me: "We used to live here freely, caught as much fish as we wanted, and dried it, salted it. Before, we didn't have the problems we have now.... Why don't they let us catch this fish?... It's our food!" (personal communication 1999). To local people such as Tetya Nadya, this incident was an act of invasion and unnecessary force by "outsiders" and an arbitrary enforcement of the law. "Why don't they go after those poachers who catch the fish, take the caviar and throw the rest away? We make iukola [dried fish] and salt it and everything" (personal communication, August 1999). Tetya Nadya emphasized her own moral entitlement to the fish resource by comparing the wastage of commercial poachers to her own traditional (and complete) use of the resource. Iukola is an important cultural symbol for the Nivkhi. Significantly, the Russians do not make it.

Tetya Nadya had considerable nostalgia for the old days in Nyivo, where she was born in the early 1940s. People had "good houses" and gardens, they grew potatoes, and some even kept cows and pigs; the town had a shop, a club and a *banya*. Children traveled on dogsleds to the internat in Nogliki. Tetya Nadya's father was a brigade leader in the fishing kolkhoz New Life (Novaia Zhizn'). The workers used to receive money for the fish they handed in to the kolkhoz and were allowed to claim some of the catch for themselves. In the late 1950s the villagers of Nyivo were told by the authorities to move to Venskoe, another Native village, as Nyivo was apparently in danger of flooding. Tetya Nadya remembered: "Our people didn't want to move away...but we had to and that was that" (personal communication, August 1999). Later, in 1964, they were all moved to Nogliki when three villages were amalgamated. Despite the move, the Nivkhi retained strong emotional ties to their former settlements and their fishing grounds. In the 1990s they began to return to their old villages to fish, to rediscover their roots and cultural practices, and to find tranquillity away from the stress of the town. Tetya Nadya would return to Nyiskii Bay every summer. She fished to make soup and iukola and collects berries and leaves to make tea: "As soon as it is summer we can't wait to come here" (personal communication, August 1999).

Natalya Grigorievna, another Nivkh resident of Nogliki, was born in 1934 in a small Native settlement, Tymyt', which was renamed Gafuvich ("There's an oil tower there now" [personal communication 1999]). In 1939 the population of Tymyt' was moved to Dagi and the kolkhoz New Way of Life (Novyi Byt). In 1950 Natalya and her fellow villagers were forced to move to Chaivo. They were given one week's notice: "They came and held a meeting" (personal communication, September 1999). In 1964, for reasons of "nonprofitability," the three collectives were joined together to form Kolkhoz Vostok, based in Nogliki: "Nobody asked the people. It was all decided by party officials" (personal communication, September 1999). By 1968 Kolkhoz Vostok was in debt, and plans were not being fulfilled, so its members started expeditions back to deserted villages to access the fish resources of those places. Since then, the kolkhoz has been fishing in most of the bays, including Nyiskii. Before the collapse of the Soviet system, Kolkhoz Vostok used to have the status of "indigenous enterprise" (*natsional'noe predpriyatie*), which meant that the collective enjoyed privileges such as extra fish quotas. As in other Indigenous enterprises in the Soviet Union, the workforce of Kolkhoz Vostok became progressively less Indigenous. Today Kolkhoz Vostok uses a "scientific quota" of salmon for Nyiskii Bay, arranged with the Yuzhno-Sakhalinsk-based Institute of Fisheries and Oceanography.

The conflict over the fish of Nyiskii Bay is one of access to the limited resources of a particular place. The Indigenous summer residents have both a traditional entitlement and a legal entitlement defined in federal legislation. However, in practice, access is officially determined through allocation of fish quotas. At the local level, quotas are fixed by a commission in the district administration. Recommendations on who is to receive fish must be approved by officials in Sakhalin's regional capital, Yuzhno-Sakhalinsk. District quotas are worked out in Yuzhno-Sakhalinsk; regional quotas are determined by Moscow. Local residents mistrust the scientific research that determines the allocation of fish quotas for their local area.

Indigenous communities (*obshchiny*), families, and clan enterprises are allocated fishing grounds and accompanying plots of land on Nyiskii Bay and other bays in the district. In 1999 clan enterprises had to reregister as ordinary commercial enterprises but retained the right of access to the bays. Indigenous residents are allowed personal quotas of 100 kg of salmon per person every year, while their enterprises are allowed a certain priority in the distribution of commercial quotas and are allowed to fish in the bays. Other local (non-Indigenous) fishing enterprises and some registered elsewhere on Sakhalin can get quotas for coastal fishing according to a strict distribution procedure but do not fish in the coastal bays. Deep-sea fishing is carried out by international vessels, with quotas allocated by Moscow. Illegal fishing in the Okhotsk Sea is probably the greatest threat to overall fish resources and the most difficult to police.

In the late 1990s, non-Indigenous locals were complaining that they could not buy fish in the shops or on the market, while the clan enterprises could sell their fish elsewhere for a profit: "People are not very different. All are unemployed; all are looking to the rivers to get something to eat" (local fish inspector, personal communication 1999). Some local bureaucrats no longer accepted the Nivkh entitlement to fish quotas and were making efforts to withdraw that privilege. Tetya Nadya perceived their discourse as one of exclusion, not equality: "They say to us: go and build yourselves dachas, plant cucumbers and tomatoes. Why would I want cucumbers when I want to dry this fish?" (personal communication, August 1999). Here again she emphasized the Russian–Nivkh difference through use of cultural food symbols.

Vasya is a Nivkh who works as a pipeline engineer for the Sakhalin oil company SMNG. He lives with Zina, who is half Nivkh and half Russian and has three children from a previous marriage to a Russian man. During Vasya's vacation the family travels to Nyiskii Bay and stays in his parents' hut. The children collect mushrooms, pine nuts, and berries and help Vasya with fishing and Zina with preparing fish and caviar. In the late 1990s, Vasya was fishing the combined quotas of his large family. Zina's three children still received their full fish quotas despite being three-quarters Russian. Zina joked: "Nivkhi are proud of being Nivkhi, especially when it comes to fish" (personal communication 1999). The family's 100 kg quotas combined amounted to two barrels full of fish. However, Vasya and Zina fished to fill six barrels, with the aim of selling four of them: "We don't eat that much fish," said Zina. "I want a car" (personal communication, September 1999).

Vasya would sell their surplus fish to Russians who sold it on. If they are not registered as an enterprise, Nivkhi are not entitled to sell the fish themselves since, legally, their personal fish quotas are for subsistence only. Legislation paradoxically serves to criminalize certain traditional economic activities such as informal trade. Selling fish on the black market, moreover, is a business not without its dangers. One Nivkh entrepreneur was allegedly blown up in his car by the fish mafia. Nivkhi do not consider fishing over their quotas to be a crime. Most local people believe that the large-scale poachers (who come from outside) are a more serious cause of declines in fish populations. Regulators do not reveal information on large-scale poaching. As one official commented: "We don't have facts about big poaching...we don't see the poachers" (personal communication 1999).

The practice of fishing over the allocated fish quota also serves social purposes within the community. Zina fulfilled a key social role in the local community in the poorer kolkhoz quarter of town. She and her family shared their supplies of fish and caviar with other family and friends. Even when there was no fish, family, friends, and neighbors (Indigenous and non-Indigenous alike) often visited the house and were fed soup, bread, or *pel'meni*. Zina also helped her neighbors address problems with alcoholism and finding housing. According to Zina, the former head of the Fishing Inspectorate used to understand the Nivkhi, and he would turn a blind eye if they fished a little over their quotas. The new head, a long-term Russian resident of Sakhalin, had a different outlook: "Everyone should be the same. Why should Nivkhi get special treatment? Especially if they work for an oil company" (personal communication 1999). At the same time he recognized the moral debt owed by the incomer populations to the original Indigenous resource users: "Moving people from their own settlements and own lands—that is another issue" (personal communication, October 1999).

Indigenous people who are unable to catch their full quota of fish themselves are put onto a list by an Indigenous fishing enterprise that fishes for them. The enterprise catches fish on behalf of the listed people, while the quotas are also used to catch additional fish to cover the costs of fuel and equipment and to provide a source of personal profit. But the system is open to abuse. For example, one Indigenous entrepreneur asked Zina to coordinate the list of people whose quotas he would use. However, he did not provide everyone with the fish he owed them, though he still managed to send some fish to southern Sakhalin to sell. Zina was distraught at this betrayal of trust and at having been forced to betray the trust of her neighbors. From Zina's point of view, her family had a moral right to fish more than their personal quotas and trade the extra fish on the black market, as these quotas have been set by outsiders (using dubious scientific calculations) and are regulated by outsiders (who sometimes act violently toward her people). The entrepreneur, on the other hand, was unable to justify fishing more than the official allocation as he was unable to provide fish for the people whose quotas he had used. His deception was compounded by the fact that he managed to get fish to market to make a personal profit.

In the late 1990s, complex moral codes and legal obligations appeared to be well understood in relation to subsistence fishing. In comparison, the responses of local residents to the multinational offshore oil and gas developments were much less confident. At that time local people were beginning to relate changes in the local environment, particularly the increased numbers of sick, wounded, and poisoned fish found locally, to the Molikpaq platform that had just appeared on their horizon. Over tea at the local museum one day in September 1999, my conversation with several local women turned to the problem of increasing numbers of fish smelling of oil or phenols. With some humor, the women related stories of mutant fish ("with three eyes, or was it one eye?"), fish with distended bellies, and an unnaturally long flat fish ("I only saw it when it was cooked"). The women laughed as they said that there was nothing they could do as the evidence had been swallowed, but deep down they acknowledged the serious state of affairs of people eating deformed fish out of hunger and not knowing what is happening to their environment. Their impotence was translated into humor.

Although Tetya Nadya did not like the idea of big oil companies drilling for oil off the coast where she lived, she felt unable to influence events. When asked if she had been at meetings with the oil companies, she replied: "No they didn't ask our people, they made deals with someone there, then came here and that was that" (personal communication, August 1999). Tetya Nadya's response echoed earlier responses to Soviet resettlement. Outsiders make decisions and strike deals with no prior consultation before coming to inform local people about what is going to happen. Local fatalism can be exploited by oil companies during their consultations, where the message "it's too late to change anything" tends to be implicit. Outsider organizations—such as international environmental NGOs and human rights groups—are often the ones to stand up to multinational oil and gas companies. In the late 1990s, organizations such as Sakhalin Environment Watch, Pacific Environment, and Friends of the Earth–Japan were engaged in battles with the oil and gas companies, drawing attention to threats facing gray whales and salmon fisheries. However, such battles were taking place almost entirely outside the sphere of experience of local people and—at that time—did not serve to reduce local fatalism or encourage political mobilization.

SAKHALIN ENERGY: COMMUNITY ENGAGEMENT AND SALMON PROTECTION

Despite the controversies surrounding the Sakhalin-2 project (including global concern about potential threats to endangered gray whales, damaging construction work on salmon river crossings, and high-profile Indigenous peoples' protests), the project is frequently highlighted as pioneering in many aspects of social policy in the oil and gas sector for several reasons. In the early days of Sakhalin Energy's social engagement, a key driver was the head of the company's social team, who had had previous experience on ExxonMobil's Chad–Cameroon pipeline. Her personal commitment and the support of her line manager resulted in some innovative early engagements with Indigenous land users, which drew on the experience of local anthropologists. Moreover, the operator of the Sakhalin-2 project and lead shareholder in the Sakhalin Energy consortium was Shell. Shell's previous experiences—with conflict in the Niger Delta, and in particular the execution of local Nigerian activist Ken Saro Wiwa in November 1995, and efforts to overcome this devastating legacy in its approach to the Camisea project in the Peruvian jungle—had led to the development of progressive environmental and social policies. While the Sakhalin-2 project still offered much to criticize, Shell's commitments

did at least translate into a high degree of responsiveness to external stake-
holder concerns.

Another key factor in the progressiveness of the Sakhalin-2 project
was its being financed by the European Bank for Reconstruction and
Development (EBRD) and other international financial institutions.
EBRD had strict project finance conditionalities relating to management of environmental and social risks (based on those developed by the
International Finance Corporation—the private-sector arm of the World
Bank). Representatives of the EBRD undertook a prolonged period of
due diligence prior to making a decision on a second loan to the project. This due diligence culminated in a decision not to go ahead with the
loan (because of concerns about impacts on salmon rivers). However, it
did result in Sakhalin Energy committing itself to a suite of environmental
and social policies and action plans. Furthermore, the presence of international financial institutions and the openness of the company itself led to a
high degree of scrutiny and challenge from international and national civil
society organizations (such as Pacific Environment, the International
Union for the Conservation of Nature, and the World Wildlife Fund–
Russia). These organizations also supported local groups such as Sakhalin
Environment Watch in their efforts to monitor and hold the company to
account. By contrast, ExxonMobil, which has been operating in the same
region from the same period, using its own finances, and keeping a much
lower profile, has received much less international attention.

In the mid-1990s Sakhalin Energy was funding a range of initiatives
typical of oil company social investment programs, including cultural
and sporting events, environmental projects, scholarships, internships,
and junior achievement awards. In the early stages of the Sakhalin-2
project, Sakhalin Energy identified that the Evenk and Uil'ta reindeer
herders would be directly affected by pipeline construction across the
coastal pastures that had already been significantly degraded by the onshore
oil and gas industry. Meetings were held on the reindeer pastures between
the herders, Sakhalin Energy staff, and representatives of Noglikskii
District administration. This engagement—a pioneering approach to public consultation at the time—fed into the development of the Sakhalin-2
project Social Impact Assessment, and a suite of compensation and assistance measures was devised for the reindeer herders (Roon 1996).

Sakhalin Energy developed a Resettlement Action Plan, which identified all land users directly affected by the project through land-take and
calculated compensation for each affected land user (household or enterprise). The Social Impact Assessment also highlighted threats from incomer

workers who might engage in hunting, fishing, or gathering in local areas, thus damaging the resource base. As a result, Sakhalin Energy developed a policy of "No Hunting, Fishing and Gathering" by any company workers, unless they were from the local area. In addition, the company established a network of community liaison officers, including two for Noglikskii District (one of these being an Indigenous woman), and a Grievance Procedure for communicating and resolving issues reported by local residents about construction work or other issues relating to the project. In response to pressure from project lenders and environmental NGOs, following reports of poor pipeline construction work across rivers, Sakhalin Energy set up a river crossings monitoring program and published reports on their website from third party monitoring of all their pipeline construction activities.[8] At the same time, Sakhalin Environment Watch, an NGO based in Yuzhno-Sakhalinsk, carried out independent expeditions to the pipeline construction sites and took photographs and made reports of any cases of environmentally damaging construction work—these were also published online.[9]

Initially, the Nivkhi were considered by Sakhalin Energy to be only *indirectly* affected by the project as they had no official use rights to land or resources that would be directly affected by construction activities. The company assumed that any issues would be addressed by their Grievance Procedure. However, not only did the Nivkhi find the form-filling nature of the Grievance Procedure inappropriate for their predominantly oral culture, they also felt that the company had been ignoring them. They believed that they were in a vulnerable position, given that they practiced fishing in lagoons that would be highly sensitive to any oil spills. Furthermore, the community had a great deal of anxiety about existing water pollution and damage to fish stocks, including the incidence of mutant fish referred to previously. A mysterious mass die-off of Pacific herring off Sakhalin's northeastern coast in June 1999 only added to local anxieties. While these incidents were unlikely to have been caused by the Molikpaq platform—and were more likely due to other factors, including the legacies of the onshore oil and forest industries—Sakhalin Energy made little effort at the time to allay community fears or to explore the reasons for the reported pollution of the fish stock. Dissatisfaction grew. On January 19, 2005, Sakhalin's Association of Indigenous Peoples, together with local environmental organizations, including Sakhalin Environment Watch, organized the first Green Wave protest in Nogliki, blocking the road to an oil facility. A press release stated: "The indigenous peoples of Sakhalin, who practice a traditional self-subsistence economy based on fishing, hunting, reindeer herding and wild plant gathering, are bearing the brunt of the negative ecological impacts of the Sakhalin extraction projects."[10] The protesters called for an ethnological expert review to be carried out for the Sakhalin-1 and Sakhalin-2 projects—to identify potential impacts of the projects on Indigenous livelihoods, which were not captured in existing impact assessments—and they called for the establishment of an Indigenous people's development fund and an advisory council to take part in decision-making related to protection of their local natural environment.

By the time the second Green Wave protest had been organized—a two-day roadblock of another oil facility in June 2005—Sakhalin Energy had started work on the Sakhalin Indigenous Minorities Development Plan, guided by a globally recognized anthropologist with experience in working for international development banks on similar projects. Sakhalin Energy's initiative (which committed US$1.5 million over five years for the first phase) involved addressing specific aspects of the project that were of particular concern to Indigenous communities and allocating targeted funds to support traditional enterprise development and social programs (health, education, culture, and capacity-building, including a "School for Young Leaders"). The first five-year plan came to a close in 2010, and the second five-year plan (2011–2015) was officially launched in December 2010 (notably with full participation of the previously sceptical Sakhalin government).

As part of the plan the company developed a process of dialogue to address Indigenous people's concerns relating to negative project impacts on their environment and livelihoods. This process included arranging face-to-face meetings between Indigenous representatives and company scientists and engineers. As of July 2010, twenty-eight of the original thirty issues (including concern about impacts on fisheries from offshore platforms and pipeline construction) had been resolved, while the outstanding two were still being monitored: the sufficiency of emergency oil spill response capacities and the appropriateness of the company Grievance Procedure for Indigenous communities. Three additional studies were commissioned to analyze project impacts on the Indigenous peoples and identify gaps in the existing project impact assessments and other documentation.

These dialogues were a unique opportunity for Indigenous peoples' representatives to discuss environmental threats directly with the company's scientific experts. However, the dialogue itself did not endure, despite the determined efforts of the leader of the Indigenous peoples' association (a Nivkh) to attend the meetings. Admittedly, the construction phase of the Sakhalin-2 project was over, but there had been no final resolution of many of the local community's anxieties about long-term impacts on their fish resources. No new issues were raised, and some issues that remained contentious were simply "closed." Other Indigenous representatives tended to prefer the discussions and planning around the allocation of funds to the enterprises and social programs. This outcome can be viewed in different ways. On the face of it, one might conclude that the Indigenous representatives were more interested in securing financial support from the development fund than keeping track of the environmental issues that were causing such anxiety to their communities. On the other hand, the breakdown of the dialogue on environmental and scientific issues can be seen as a classic example of the language of a dialogue being inadequate to engage both sides. "Participation" tends to require local people to adopt the language of "expertise" (Cruikshank 1998), which limits the ways in which they can articulate their concerns and undermines their ability to question "experts" with any authority. Philip Goodwin (1998:494) notes that local people's legitimacy and authority derive from their relationship to place and their intimate involvement in local social practices. These elements did not form the basis of the dialogue on science and environmental impacts, but they did form the basis of the discussions around support to Indigenous enterprises and social programs.

Between 2006 and 2010, Sakhalin Energy's Indigenous peoples' development plan provided around US$650,000 to finance eighty-nine projects as part of the traditional enterprise support program. The program supported business plans to enhance the capacities of Indigenous enterprises, which are frequently not so competitive in the open market due to the social function they tend to provide and due to lack of experience with business planning. The program also offered self-sufficiency grants to help Indigenous families maintain a traditional lifestyle. Fourteen business plans were financed, of which three supported wild plant processing, four supported fish processing, and one supported reindeer herding. Self-sufficiency grants were provided to purchase snowmobiles, boats and boat engines, freezers, power generators, and other food-processing and storage equipment. An Indigenous beneficiary was cited in a review of the first five-year plan: "Much of our culture has been lost due to the *Internat* system and so now we are trying to revive our culture.... We were separated from our culture and now we are trying to re-learn how to fish and gather wild plants" (Guldin, Kapkaun, and Konkov 2010:29). An important aspect of the program was that Sakhalin Energy encouraged Indigenous representatives to take an active role in the governance of the development plan, including a supervisory board and several committees overseeing disbursal of funds. However, conflicts inevitably arose over the distribution of the funds. Family rivalries were deepened; accusations were made that the Nivkhi, as the dominant Indigenous group represented in the governance structure, had too much influence over the grant allocations. Sakhalin Energy's Grievance Procedure was adapted for usage by the Indigenous peoples, but it has since been used purely to resolve issues over the allocation of funds by the traditional enterprise support program.

At the same time, Sakhalin Energy has also been supporting efforts to revive the salmon fisheries themselves. In 2004 the Oregon-based Wild Salmon Center (WSC) brought together multiple stakeholders, including energy companies, Indigenous groups, commercial fishermen, and local government officials to develop a conservation strategy called the Sakhalin Salmon Initiative (SSI). In early 2008, WSC and Sakhalin Energy signed an agreement to fund a wild salmon conservation program for Sakhalin. The program (US$8.8 million over three years) includes establishment of a watershed council network, an island-wide salmonid conservation plan and monitoring program, support for sustainable fisheries initiatives, and educational programs. In 2008 efforts began to certify salmon fishing enterprises to international sustainable fisheries standards. If the certification is successful, it will open up international trade opportunities for Sakhalin's fishing enterprises (Wild Salmon Center 2008). If Sakhalin Indigenous enterprises were to be involved in this process, they could increase their revenue from fishing activities in the future. Yet, there is some concern about how Indigenous enterprises might be able to benefit from such a scheme. Certification is a complex, long-term process, and many Indigenous enterprises may not have the capacities to complete it or to expand their current activities for international market trade (Sakhalin Energy 2010). Furthermore, certification may indicate sustainably harvested fish, according to established criteria, but it does not guarantee the sustainability of the human community engaged in the fishing, which has cultural and social dimensions that are not captured by certification (Reedy-Maschner, chapter 6, this volume).

Twelve years after the first oil was pumped from under the sea to the Molikpaq platform, it is difficult to find complete information on the actual impacts of the offshore oil and gas projects on the salmon stocks. Over the years many articles by the media and NGOs have speculated on or warned of *potential* threats, while photographic evidence of damaging construction work across salmon rivers has been produced by Sakhalin Environment Watch. However, little information on or analysis of the state of the fish stocks has been available since construction work on pipelines was completed for the Sakhalin-2 project. According to Vladimir Radchenko, Olga Temnykh, and Viktor Lapko (2007:19): "In 2005, the coastal pink salmon catch in the Sakhalin–Kuril Islands region reached 137,747 t exceeding the previous record of 1991 (128,333 t)." Reports produced by the Sakhalin-2 project lenders' consultant, AEA Technology (2009:5), note that there was "another record salmon year in 2009," while monitoring has revealed no long-term impacts in most of the rivers crossed by pipeline construction, with just four out of eighty-four rivers of high sensitivity remaining under observation (AEA 2010:47).

REFLECTIONS: THE COMPANY, THE SALMON, AND THE NIVKHI

In this chapter I have attempted to explore the role of Pacific salmon in the lives of Sakhalin's Nivkh people in the context of considerable socioeconomic changes that have taken place over the past century, particularly in relation to the oil and gas industry. As the Nivkhi have adapted to these changes, the Pacific salmon has retained its central role in their lives and livelihoods as a food source, product of trade, and enduring cultural symbol. The arrival of major international oil and gas projects to disrupt the lands and waters of their ancestors appears to have yielded more opportunities than threats—to date. The symbolic significance of Pacific salmon has only increased in this context. A small but significant number of Nivkhi still fish in the waters fished by their ancestors and still prepare fish in the traditional manner. The enduring cultural value of these practices has enabled them to justify a special place in the discussion around distribution of benefits from the offshore projects.

The Sakhalin Nivkhi are not alone in seeing the offshore oil and gas developments not so much as a threat to their traditional way of life but as a way of maintaining it (Reedy-Maschner, chapter 6, this volume). While their success at engaging in meaningful dialogue with Sakhalin Energy has been limited to the development of a fund to support traditional enterprises and social programs, this achievement should not be undervalued. The engagement has provided the Nivkhi with an arena where they can engage in their own language of expertise (that of local place and social practice) and where they have been able to direct support to livelihood activities that are in decline.

Nonetheless, the Nivkhi do experience a sense of disillusionment. Following their protests in 2005, the Nivkhi have opted for a relationship of compromise and collaboration with Sakhalin Energy, stepping back from their confrontational stance and somewhat disappointing the environmental lobby. (Organizations such as Sakhalin Environment Watch refuse to take money from oil companies as a matter of principle.) Priority access to oil company funds has been seen as unfair by the local non-Indigenous communities; even within the company itself there were some who strongly objected to the process of implementing the Indigenous peoples' development plan. And within the local Indigenous community, factionalism and conflict have been exacerbated by the involvement of Indigenous representatives in funds disbursal. The paradox is that a major oil company that poses a very real threat to the fish resources upon which local people depend for their livelihoods is at the same time among the few supporters of the social enterprises of local Indigenous peoples, while also taking a leading role in funding salmon protection. This situation creates a delicate and somewhat imperfect balance. It remains to be seen whether these efforts will ultimately result in enhanced socioeconomic well-being and self-sufficiency for the Nivkhi along with the conservation and sustainable use of Sakhalin's salmon fisheries.

Notes

1. See www.wildsalmoncenter.org/press/SakhalinPink_PR.php, accessed March 7, 2012.

2. From 1992 the Sakhalin Energy consortium was made up of Shell, Mitsui, Mitsubishi, McDermott, and Marathon, with Shell as the operator. Marathon and McDermott subsequently dropped out, and in 2007 Gazprom paid $7.45 billion for a 50 percent plus one share. Shell kept a 27.5 percent less one share, Mitsui 12.5 percent, and Mitsubishi 10 percent.

3. See www.eia.gov/emeu/cabs/Sakhalin/pdf.pdf, accessed March 7, 2012.

4. See www.eia.gov/emeu/cabs/Sakhalin/pdf.pdf, accessed March 7, 2012

5. Russia was due to hold another census in 2010, but this has been postponed until 2013 due to the financial crisis (www.regnum.ru/news/1206699.html, accessed March 7, 2012).

6. See www.sakhalinenergy.com/en/default.asp?p=channel&c=1&n=379, accessed March 7, 2012.

7. Real names have not been used in this chapter.

8. See www.sakhalinenergy.com/en/default.asp?p=channel_home&c=8, accessed March 7, 2012.

9. See http://bankwatch.org/files/Pipeline_Photo_Report_PE-FoEJ-SEW _5.30-6.1.08.pdf, accessed March 7, 2012.

10. See www.sakhalin.environment.ru/en/detail.php?slice=8b4cb37fba47da1c76cf 3e44aa940cd2&sitemid=22121, accessed March 7, 2012.

3

Shades of Deep Salmon

Fish, Fishing, and Itelmen Cultural History

David Koester

In 1944 at the age of twenty-five, Indigenous Itelmen educator Tatiana Slobodchikova (later Lukashkina) wrote her first "autobiography," a kind of résumé that was often needed when changing employment in the Soviet Union. She had just finished working for a small school at a reindeer herding camp in northern Kamchatka and had moved to a larger village. Her autobiography offers a good starting point for this chapter about salmon in the lives of Itelmen people because she identifies her family and herself, at least in part, with fishing: "I, Tatiana Petrovna Slobodchikova, was born on the 12th of February, 1918 in the village of Sopochnoe in Tigil District of the Koryak National Territory. Up until the revolution my parents engaged in fishing and hunting. After the October Revolution they engaged in fishing and hunting. In 1930 they joined the *kolkhoz* [collective farm or work unit] and since then work in the kolkhoz" (Lukashkina 1944).[1]

In later versions of her autobiography, Tatiana Petrovna deletes the obvious and odd repetition, but the line about her parents being engaged in hunting and fishing remains. The idea of identifying her parents as representatives of a particular cultural type based on their primary mode of subsistence paralleled Soviet Indigenous policy. It was an idea that permeated deeply into the education of Soviet Indigenous peoples. State-determined ethnosocial categorization had a long history in Russia, well before Soviet social engineering took hold. In the pre-Soviet period, the peoples of the North were defined by officials as "migratory, nomadic and sedentary," and ethnologists added the category of "semi-nomadic" (Jochelson 1928:187; Slezkine 1994). During the Soviet period, mode of production became a more salient criterion for distinguishing groups. As the *Great Soviet Encyclopedia* reported for the so-called Small Peoples (Malye Narody), "The basis for dividing these peoples into particular groups... was the general trend of their economic life (hunting, reindeer breeding, fishing and, in a few regions, sea mammal hunting)" (Gurvich 1974). State policy-making depended on identifying where peoples were located on the scale of cultural progress toward civilization and ultimately socialism. The *Encyclopedia* (authored by I. S. Gurvich [1974]) continued: "The economic activities of the Small Peoples of the North were founded on primitive technology—they used bows and arrows and stone points on harpoons and spears. Thanks to Leninist national policy the Small Peoples of the North shed themselves of their backwardness and went from their archaic form of economic activity to a socialist form."

Tatiana Petrovna understood that her community's economic activity had gone from an archaic form of fishing and hunting to a socialist form. Initially, the categorization "fishing and hunting" defined who the Itelmens were economically and politically. For Tatiana Petrovna, reflecting in 1944 (and in future autobiographies up until the end of her life), her parents were frozen in this past. They were killed in the repressions of the 1930s and 1940s and did not live on into the newly mixed, ambiguous, hybrid Soviet society. For her they represented the last monolingual, "uneducated" (*negramotnoe*) generation.

Fishing societies held a special place in the social evolutionary theories that informed Soviet Indigenous policy. Because of their catch and storage technologies and tendency to live in nonmigratory settlements, fishing societies were considered to be at a stage higher than simple gatherers.[2] In fact, Friedrich Engels (1902:29) in *The Origins of the Family, Private Property and the State* followed Lewis Henry Morgan in identifying fishing as a key indicator in the assessment of stages of social progress. According to the theory, fishing allowed primitive foragers to move out of their familiar foraging grounds to fish up and down rivers and streams, along the coast, and eventually around the globe. Fishing was a key to progress in the Morganian scheme because its greater flexibility corresponded to a second stage of human social development that included more complex social relations, the use of fire, and sedentary settlements. In world ethnographic literature where social progress comparisons were made, Kamchatka's Indigenous Kamchadals/Itelmens were represented as fishing peoples par excellence.[3]

Tatiana Petrovna's identification of her parents as fishers and hunters was not a simple assessment of her experience of life growing up. Many other activities filled her and her parents' days. If she were to have measured the time or effort put into the full spectrum of her subsistence experiences, including the gathering of firewood, berries, roots and grasses, those activities would be as much a part of her economic identity as fishing and hunting. Nevertheless, though the state's definition was contrastive rather than descriptive, and a fuller economic portrait would be more realistic, hunting and fishing were of primary importance in Itelmen life. Hunting, if not critical for food, was vital for producing goods to be exchanged. Before the advent of money in Kamchatka, furs operated as currency, sometimes capriciously valued but always useful for obtaining needed goods (Bergman 1923:120–121). At the same time, the hunting of sea mammals and particularly seals was important both for the sealskin and the meat (Starkova 1974). Both of these were exchanged with Koryak people for reindeer meat and hides, among other things.

Historically speaking, fish were unquestionably the fundamental basis of subsistence for Itelmens. Fishing stands out in the historical accounts because of the overwhelming bounty of the resource.[4] The classic description was written by the usually unimpressed German explorer Georg Wilhelm Steller (2003:103) in the mid-eighteenth century: "The most extraordinary aspect of life on Kamchatka is without a doubt the fishery, full of many rarities and almost unbelievable circumstances.… The inhabitants of Kamchatka live almost exclusively on fish, although the country's rivers and lakes do not have a single Indigenous fish as other places do that are not close to the ocean. Nonetheless, one may well ask whether any country on this earth has a greater abundance of the best and tastiest fish than Kamchatka."

It is a tribute to the significance of the Itelmen catch that the scientific Latin name for king salmon derives from the Itelmen word *chavicho*.[5] Steller went on to say that the fish diet was particularly healthy, citing the good health and longevity of native Kamchatkans. Similarly, Waldemar Jochelson (n.d.) wrote over 150 years later: "The Kamchadals [Itelmens] had been and still remain a genuine fishing tribe.… Fish, different species of salmon, ascend the Kamchatka rivers in such abundance that they amply satisfy the needs in food."

The identification of Itelmens with fishing by both others and Itelmens themselves has continued on to the present. Itelmen ethnographer Nadezhda Starkova (1976:35) wrote: "Itelmens' main activity was fishing and this, above all, determined the location of their settlements." Itelmen elder

Georgi Zaporotskii, from the village of Kovran, commented that the village of Kovran was always known as a fishing place and the kolkhoz was a fishing kolkhoz. Georgi moved to Kovran after his home village of Moroshechnoe was closed by the Soviet government: "I came here for the first time in 1964. There was a kolkhoz here.… Red October it was called. In those days it was a 'millionaire.'[6] It was a fishing kolkhoz. In the beginning the river was so full of fish. I saw it myself. When the fish were running at the mouth of the Kovran River, if you threw out a pole, you'd think it would go downstream, but instead, on the fins of the fish, they dragged it upstream. There were probably several layers of fish" (interview with author, February 18, 2008).

Starkova, speaking about pre-Soviet and early Soviet Itelmen life, and Zaporotskii, speaking about the middle Soviet period, situated Itelmen life in relation to the abundance of salmon at particular places. Zaporotskii went on to speak of changes, however, saying that the last time he saw comparable runs of fish was probably in the 1970s.

In this chapter I will explain the broad range of ways that salmon are discussed, reflected in institutions, and presented in Itelmen expressive culture. The statements I have quoted represent ideas, practices, and historical trajectories that are shadows and reflections of salmon in people's lives. From the earliest statements about Kamchatka's fish bounty to the recognition on the part of elders of the changing state of the resource over time, salmon have made their appearance in subtle and deep ways. My aim will be to elucidate people's connections to salmon, important moments of disconnect, and increasing alienation between the two.

ALIENATION IN SOVIET FISHING

The peculiar repetition in Tatiana Petrovna's statement about her parents—that after the revolution they engaged in hunting and fishing—indicates much about the matter-of-factness of the changes taking place in Indigenous lives at the time. Although the "hunting and fishing" activity to which she referred appeared to be the same as in the first iteration, the second instance pointed to a new phenomenon under the Soviet government. While hunting and fishing were primarily family- and secondarily community-organized activities in Itelmen settlements before the Soviet period, later they were organized collectively. Tatiana Petrovna made this connection in her next statement. Her parents joined their local kolkhoz in 1930, which meant that instead of family outings to fish or gather plants, or household preparation of fishing nets and hunting equipment, these tasks were communally organized as the coordinated effort of the village kolkhoz.

Indeed, her parents were hunters and fishers before the revolution; after the revolution they continued to hunt and fish (and gather) but under new rules and work relations.

New productive relations were a first step during the Soviet period along a road of increasing bureaucratization and rationalization. One of the many ironies of Soviet development was that the consequences of Soviet policy were and continue to be multiple levels of political, economic, social, and personal *alienation*. In the Marxist economic and social theory on which Soviet policy was based, alienation was a social defect that the socialist revolution was supposed to counteract. It was a crucial thread that linked the philosophical and social analyses of Karl Marx's early philosophical writings with his later political economic theories (Andersson 1997; Boettke 1990:44; Roberts 1971). Marx's analysis began with the principle, earlier expressed by John Locke (1969:133-137), that when a man mixes his labor with the commons of raw nature—for example, hunts a deer, chops down a tree, or fills a pitcher with water—the object or substance so worked— the deer, the tree, or the water—becomes his property. Marx (1970:54– 57) took the classic philosophical concept of alienation and applied it to reveal the position in which workers found themselves within the capitalist political economy (Wendling 2009). Alienation comes about when this link between the natural productivity of the earth and human need and effort is broken. In industrial labor, workers become alienated from the objects of their labor, the goods they make.

Amy Wendling has argued that the distinction that Marx drew between the objectification inherent in creating an object as a product and the alienation resulting from the object becoming a commodity was key. Whereas Georg W. F. Hegel recognized both objectification and alienation as levels or forms of alienation/estrangement (Wendling 2009:17–18), Marx distinguished them in order to identify the injustice in the bourgeois economy. Capitalism, Marx argued, was fundamentally unjust because the value of the produced goods came from a worker's labor, but labor-infused objects ended up alienated from the worker as commodities. In industrial relations of production, workers used the technical equipment and machines of a factory or plant owner and produced goods of value. The owner of the means of production, the capitalist, compensated the workers for their labor and could sell the goods produced on the market and keep the surplus value that had been created by the labor of the workers. Economist and Sovietologist Paul Roberts (1971) has argued that it was these alienating relations of production that early Soviet policy sought to overcome:

they were thought to be the root of social injustice in capitalist society. The irony of Soviet policy was that numerous new forms of alienation were introduced as leaders sought to avoid the capitalist forms.[7]

Roberts argues that Soviet central planning was at first not an attempt to catch up with the industrialization of the West, as historians and Sovietologists came to argue, but to break down the foundations of alienated productive relations. Goods would in theory go from producers to consumers on the basis of corresponding needs and productive capacities. But rather than operating truly centrally planned or socialist production and distribution systems, the Soviet economic regime as it actually functioned created a polycentrically organized, dysfunctional capitalist system. Production targets were set on the basis of production history rather than on needs and distribution capacity. Instead of avoiding alienation, the system rendered production inefficient by thwarting the market pricing signals that could have regulated the creation, manufacture, and distribution of goods (Roberts 1971:110 ff.). What this meant at the far reaches of the Soviet empire was that alienation from renewable raw resources like salmon came at first not from commoditization but from collectivization, industrialization, and forced resettlement. Itelmen people found themselves alienated from land, from resources, and from their cultural heritage in a process that crescendoed through the end of the Soviet system and into the post-Soviet period.

To understand Itelmen modes of fishing, we must first understand the nature of Itelmen households and the place of fish production in the annual household cycle of production and consumption. The typical Itelmen domestic unit in pre-Soviet and early Soviet periods consisted of a set of structures that could include a house or hut (or in earlier times a semisubterranean shelter), a grass-roofed *balagan* (a hut on four poles about 2 to 3 m above the ground—in Itelmen *mem*), a livestock shelter or windbreak, fish-drying racks, and a raised cache (*ambar* or *ambarchik*). Temporary dwellings or storage huts made of thatch on a tentlike wooden frame (*shalash*) were often set up out away from the household, at fishing or gathering sites. Fish-drying racks were typically built under a balagan, but fish could also be hung on the balagan's upper platform. All of these structures belonged to specific households, and they were storage places for the products of local family labor (see Starkova 1976:35–68, for a thorough description of both pre-Soviet and Soviet Itelmen domestic arrangements). Fish became the property of the household whose members caught and processed the fish. Families held their stores of fish on drying racks under their raised huts or otherwise out of reach of the dogs, in pits, and, when salting became a regular practice, in barrels. The most common form of stored salmon was *yukola*, split salmon, air and sun dried; it was known as Kamchatkan bread. The drying racks were called *yukolniki*. In traditional (early Soviet) Itelmen villages we can understand the degree to which yukola was understood as property from a story Tatiana Petrovna told of mischievously stealing it. She recounts a time when, in the late spring, virtually everyone was out of yukola. She and some other children were planning an outing, and one of the children suggested taking some yukola from her uncle Nikolai's balagan without permission. They sent her in and ended up fleeing when they noticed her elderly uncle approaching. She told this story as an example of mischief rather than crime, but it demonstrates the sense that yukola, on someone else's rack, was not common property. Salmon as a product of labor belonged to the individual household unit.

This system began to change with the advent of the new Soviet government's labor policies. In rural Kamchatka, the first step in the process of reorganizing labor was the creation of *artels*—work units consisting of individuals who contributed their labor to a collective activity. Before Tatiana Petrovna's parents even joined the kolkhoz, they had begun contributing labor to the local artel. This was the first alienating step in the changing nature of fishing production. Although individuals received fish for themselves, their labor contributed to the production of fish not necessarily for themselves but for redistribution to everyone. As more and more of the fish caught were either for the collective or to be sent for consumption elsewhere, household economies began to change. The salmon that you ate was less and less likely to be a salmon that you or a family member had caught.

New government-organized labor brought another new dimension to relations with salmon: the enumeration of the catch. My good friend Georgi recounted to me that as a twelve-year-old boy he was recruited to keep the books for the fish camp on the Moroshechnoe River. Although schools existed in some Itelmen communities before the revolution, the Soviet government introduced schooling to many small communities in Kamchatka for the first time. There was some education for adults, but primarily the children learned to read and do arithmetic. This education meant that the young were often the most capable and recruited to meet the needs of the Soviet state in reporting and accounting. Georgi would make written records of the salmon catch each day, summarize them in reports, and then send the reports to the regional capital, Tigil. When I spoke to him about record-keeping activities, he did not recall the actual amounts that were caught, but he thought that the records ought still to be accessible in Tigil. The local community had gained a new way of representing salmon—as public, written numbers. Quantity was in fact measured and discussed prior to the Soviet period, and government statistics for fish catches were recorded already in the nineteenth century. And Itelmen families were not, in the absence of state accounting, lacking in means of measurement. On a daily basis, any fishing family had racks of dried fish, and the quantity could be measured at a glance by looking at the hanging space covered on the available racks. What was different was that quantity was no longer measured against a physical space but expressed every day as a number—numbers of individual fish of each species. Later they would be measured in kilograms. This quantification of the catch came to have increasingly profound implications.

Despite the introduction of industrial forms of production, Itelmens in small villages did not lose their sense of connection to fish. We should recall that Tatiana Petrovna's statement quoted at the beginning of this chapter was written in 1944, well after the first working artels were formed and the kolkhozes had been organized. She saw her parents as hunting and fishing people both before and after the installation of the new government, despite the fact that they had become artel workers and were producing fish for the collective. Thus, despite a level of alienation introduced by the new work pattern, Tatiana Petrovna's sense that Itelmen life was closely tied to fish continued as her parents continued hunting and fishing after the October Revolution.

REFLECTIONS, REFRACTIONS, AND SHADOWS OF SALMON

These preliminary reflections on Soviet personal and familial identity suggest that salmon fishing was embedded in Itelmen lives at the personal, familial, communal, and state levels. From a variety of perspectives, many social theorists presume that economic centrality or economic importance will be associated with cultural centrality and importance. This presumption is present in materialist perspectives that see the overarching superstructure to be a reflection of some economic infrastructure. It is also present in idealist perspectives that see central symbols and root metaphors as providing meaningful bases for complex cultural wholes. One of the classic indicators along these lines is language: a language has so many words for snow, wind, yams, or cedar trees that the concept must be of fundamental importance. In the case of the Itelmen language, one could point to the existence of a specific verb, əŋch'ekaz, "to eat fish," as indicative of the daily importance of the activity. While salmon clearly were and are an overwhelming contributor to Itelmen subsistence and hence to many of the activities of daily life, this fact has not led to equally overwhelming elaborations of this centrality in expressive culture. My aim in what follows is to characterize the reflections—bright and shaded—of salmon in Itelmen narrative.

Tatiana Petrovna, in her 1991 memoir, sought to make the case that in Itelmen conception salmon were central culturally as well as economically. Her book *Skazki babushki Petrovny* (Tales of Grandmother Petrovna) opens with the description "My Homeland" about the village of Sopochnoe where she grew up. After a brief portrayal of the surrounding tundra and forest landscape followed by a short poem, she turns to the river. It is rich with fish, she says, "coho salmon, king salmon, dolly varden char, red salmon, and grayling" (Lukashkina 1991:6). After then briefly listing the plants of the tundra and forest and describing a river festival, she returns again to fish: "Many tales about fish have been composed among the peoples of the North." She narrates the tale of "How Kutkha Traveled by Humpback Salmon" (1991:7), a story of the classic trickster raven Kutkh. In the tale he convinces some humpback salmon to be hitched to his dugout canoe and to drag him around like dogs pulling a sled (1991:7–9). Including this tale, a substantial portion of the first four pages of Petrovna's book are associated with salmon and their importance. Along similar lines, Elizaveta Orlova, who worked as a young ethnographer in Kamchatka when Tatiana Petrovna was growing up, wrote that fishing was the overwhelming preoccupation for Itelmens. She said that fish were both a part of legend and tales and figured constantly in daily conversation (Orlova 1999:48). Curiously, though, fish are only mentioned as food, and even then mostly with the word *yukola* (dried fish), in all of the fifteen tales Orlova (1999:127–157) recorded.

In fact, while salmon and fish are generally thought to be commonly represented in Kamchatkan myth and folklore, this does not seem to be the case in the corpus of tales that has been recorded and published over the past three hundred years. Stepan Krasheninnikov and Georg Wilhelm Steller conducted extended ethnographic work in Kamchatka in the eighteenth century. Their research was not, of course, like modern anthropological ethnography, but nevertheless a component of both of their projects was dedicated to describing the lifeways and worldviews of the people of Kamchatka. Of the five stories recorded by Steller (2003:195–202), one mentions fish, and this only in the form of dried fish eggs. Krasheninnikov (1972:238) recounted only the Itelmen story of the origin of the universe, and neither that story nor any others to which he briefly referred mentioned fish. Of the forty-one tales collected by Waldemar Jochelson at the beginning of the twentieth century (Worth 1961), not one features salmon in the central way that Tatiana Petrovna's story did. Two of them are about "codfish," which played nothing like the role of salmon in the Itelmen diet. The large Soviet collection *Tales and Myths of the Peoples of Chukotka and Kamchatka* contains forty-eight Itelmen stories (Menovshchikov 1974), twenty-two of which are from the Jochelson collection. Of the remaining twenty-six, one tells a variant of the sled-team salmon tale. One tells the story of a bored woman who took a humpback salmon for a husband, and one mentions in passing that Kutkh's son Ememqut was welcomed by the char people after he was thrown into the water (Menovshchikov 1974:560–562, 526).

What can we learn of Itelmens' attitudes toward salmon from the few stories that have been recorded? While it is true that absurdity and fantasy were important tropes in Itelmen storytelling from the earliest period of recording the stories, we can cautiously examine the two narratives in which salmon have an active role for larger attitudes toward and understandings of salmon. What levels of consciousness or agency are attributed to salmon? How are they like or unlike people?

In the sled-team salmon stories, the fish express very little in speech. Tatiana Petrovna recounted that they conspired in *gorbusha* (humpback salmon) language to haul the boat out and tip it over to rid themselves of Kutkh. The story tells us nothing more of their conversation. In the other tale, told by Mikhail Zaev from the village of Utkholok in 1929, the fish are quoted as saying only "feed us" (Menovshchikov 1974:506; Orlova 1999:143). This was to be their reward for hauling Kutkh around on his joy ride. When he reneged on the food, the salmon became active characters. They displayed both will and collective decisiveness in deciding to abandon Kutkh to drown. The greatest level of salmonid anthropomorphizing comes in the story of the battle between Kutkh and Ememqut recounted also by Mikhail Zaev (recorded by Orlova [1999:151–154] in 1929 [Menovshchikov 1974:524–527]). In one of their contests, Kutkh threw Ememqut into a river. Ememqut ends up in the underwater world of the Dolly Varden char (*golets*). There, the story tells us, he is well received, and an elder of the char world gives a short speech (Menovshchikov 1974:526). The elder urges the others to receive Ememqut well and cook a big meal of char for him. These fish are thus presented as socially stratified and as recognizing status in age differences, and their social lives seem to operate in accord with local principles of hospitality and authority in public speaking. Although intriguing, this scene occupies only a tiny and not particularly important part of the story, 7 lines out of 123 in the Soviet edition with no further reference to this fishy world.

Salmon in the "dog-team" story are characterized by a will and sense of status. The story indicates that they do not want to be exploited and manipulated, and they purposefully and intentionally carry out Kutkh's punishment. Curiously, this level of activity and will was attributed to gorbusha, the humpback salmon. In none of the other stories are king, dog, chum, or red salmon even mentioned as characters, let alone given an active or willful role.

In contrast, in the story of Kutkh and the crab, Kutkh wakes a sleeping crab and convinces the crab to carry him around on an excursion (Worth 1961:93). The crab, like the humpback salmon, wearies of the journey and abandons the hapless Kutkh at sea. Unlike the humpbacks, however, the crab talks back to Kutkh, first telling Kutkh not to bother him and then telling him he is about to pay for annoying a sleeping crab. Crabs, at least in this example, have more human characteristics than salmon. In comparison to the representations of other species in the full collection of Itelmen tales, in which bears, ravens, foxes, gulls, mice, and many other animals are active characters, the representation of salmon is curiously subdued and, with the exception of the char elder, little anthropomorphized.

Many beliefs associated with salmon had to do as much with salmon habitat as with the fish themselves. The river was treated as a living being that would react to human transgressions (Orlova 1999:90). Orlova (1999:90) wrote that "it was forbidden to use a steel axe for pounding stakes for a weir into the river bed;…the stakes were pounded with wooden sledgehammers because it was believed that an iron axe could 'cut through' the river and if that happened there would be no fish in it." She noted that legends told of a similar attitude toward the use of steel axes in the forest in the early days because they had the power to be so destructive; Itelmens believed that their use would cause the forest to die (1999:90). If we were to draw the analogy with the forest somewhat further, cutting the river would harm the river, causing it to die, meaning that it would have no fish.

The river was also sensitive to human sexual difference and women's procreative powers. Pregnant women crossing a river could have the same effect as the steel axe: the act would cause the river to lack fish. We do not have enough information about these beliefs to understand or interpret them as part of an overall masculine-feminine psychology, but clearly gender differences were deeply associated with aleatory aspects of subsistence. A husband's bad luck in hunting was explained by his wife's bad behavior or would be predicted if she happened to be pregnant. Trouble with a rifle could be explained by a woman having stepped over it. Women in general were not allowed to cross the river at the places where weirs were set up.

They would have to cross farther upstream so as not to affect the inward run of fish (Orlova 1999:90). Women's capacity to affect the fish in the river went beyond their sexuality or fertility. Old women were not to bring root foods (*kemchiga* and *sarana*) taken from mouse caches across a river for fear that they could stop even an active run of fish. Orlova (1990:91) adds the comment: "In this case, in truth, it is difficult to understand: kemchiga and sarana or old women have power that could hold back a run of fish?"

This intersection of old women, mice, and subsistence "stealing" reflects a fascinating triadic shading in the overlap between subsistence logic and anthropomorphic ideas. The earliest recorded tales and some of the longest Itelmen tales recorded in the twentieth century have to do with the mischievous machinations of mice and their dealings with the hapless hero Kutkh. In the oldest recorded full-length Itelmen folktale, mice are central characters. The story tells how they bury a seal in the sand on the beach in order to hide it from the irrepressible Kutkh. Their trick is found out because of an immature and careless mouse, and Kutkh takes the seal home. The mice seek return of the seal, and Kutkh requests that they delouse his head. Two of the four mice say that they cannot because they are tired from digging roots. This point in the story expresses the affective and social values that could be present in the beliefs about carrying roots across the river. The story begins with the concept of "stealing" from the mice, exaggerating what would usually be a small cache of roots to a whole seal. At the same time, it also indicates the unfairness of stealing from mice by telling of the effort the mice put into caching root vegetables. After Kutkh steals the seal, the mice take revenge, which incurs Kutkh's wrath. They beg his forgiveness and promise to supply him with gathered root vegetables if he does not annihilate them (Steller 2003:197–198). Here the story becomes a kind of fable about how the mice came to supply roots for people. This tale also seems to reflect in mythical form relations that are very close to those between Itelmens and Russians/Cossacks. The Cossacks refrain from killing the Itelmens if the Itelmens continue to provide goods, especially furs. In this tale, then, the tensions of subsistence and political rule are reflected in the relations between Kutkh and the mice. The act of taking roots from mice had to be done respectfully and carefully and put elder women in a compromised or charged status that in turn posed a danger to another sensitive site of labor and productivity—the river.[8]

This last detour to understand the intersecting powers that were associated with ideas of salmon and their habitat again underscores several layers of reflections. Elder women bearing stolen roots, pregnant women, and women near weirs were forbidden from crossing the stream for fear that their charged status would harm the salmon runs. As with the axe that might cut through the river and inhibit the salmon, the cause and effect relation is not directly from humans to salmon. Instead, a human action affects the river, and the damaged river, in turn, affects the salmon. The images of salmon expressed in these beliefs parallel the subdued ideas about salmon in the folktales as well. Salmonids are rarely mentioned in the entire corpus of recorded Itelmen stories and, except for the case of the Dolly Varden who graciously hosted Ememqut, are not given roles as individual characters. Only humpback salmon appear to act and react united as a group, as do salmon in rivers affected by steel axes or women in charged states.

What are we to make of this relative lack of reflection on salmon in Itelmen expressive culture? Is it just a sampling coincidence or a result of the ethnographers' selections rather than a reflection of the stories told? Or are the salmon so important as to be part of the unconscious "doxa" of Itelmen life?

In fact, if the salmon were little mentioned because they were part of the unconscious, unsensed pattern of social and economic life, their place in the Itelmen conceptual world cannot simply be explained as invisible doxa. As used in sociological contexts, *doxa* refers to an unconscious level of theoretical and practical understanding shared in a social group, typically that part that precludes conscious reflection. It refers to "systems of classification which reproduce, in their own specific logic,...objective classes...by securing the misrecognition...of the arbitrariness on which they are based" (Bourdieu 1977:164). In other words, the doxic substrates of the conceptual world of any culture or discursive system are those that are pushed out of conscious reflection. Salmon, however, are anything but a suppressed, arbitrary classification. Their suppression, if we can call it that, seems to have more to do with their role as a matter-of-fact, unexceptional part of daily experience, closer to what Pierre Bourdieu, following Marcel Mauss, called habitus. The truly doxic beliefs related to salmon were the ones underlying the ideas of the powers of women and steel axes over rivers. Such beliefs and the prohibitions that arose from them contrasted with the equally deeply held unconscious understandings and corresponding daily discourse founded on the habitus of salmon production. At another level, Sten Bergman, Waldemar Jochelson, and other observers' discourse about salmon seems to express an overt *orthodoxy* about the centrality of salmon. In contrast to other peoples, salmon seemed central to the Itelmens. Thus, we must recognize the interrelationship of authorship, context, and levels of conscious reflection or expression. Salmon may have been key, but the degree to which they would show up in any particular genre of expressive culture could be inversely related to the habitual yet deep appreciation of these waterborne, seasonal arrivals. In the next section, I discuss the consequences of disrupting the nonarbitrary and deep ties to salmon in Itelmen life.

ALIENATION IN THE POST-SOVIET WORLD

The alienation that began with the creation of the artels and the enumeration of the catch continued throughout the Soviet period. As records were kept of numeric quantities, fish were given to individuals and families in shares. Large numbers were still needed to feed the dogs on whom everyone depended for winter transportation, and this function was well served by collective action. By the time that most of the Itelmen villages were closed in the early 1960s, a significant portion of Itelmen fishing had been transformed into an industrialized practice. People were removed from traditional areas of settlement and given work in dairies, fish factories, and government offices. V. A. Turaev's (1990:118) Soviet history of Itelmen economic development described the post-WWII developments as if they were an inevitable process: "Kolkhoz fishing developed intensively. A network of state-run fish industry corporations developed in the District. The Ptichi Island fish factory opened production sites at the mouths of the Khairiuzovo and Kovran rivers. The basic form of kolkhoz production by the end of the war was the *brigade*.... Animal husbandry, agriculture and fishing became independent branches of production."

The factories are particularly important for understanding the transformation that was happening within Itelmen fishing. Instead of catching fish to be hung on family drying racks or placed in one's own pits for winter storage, people caught fish that were to be given to the factory for processing. This kind of fishing became another level of alienation for Itelmen "workers," much like Marx's description of alienation, except that, in theory, the "profits" were owned collectively. The aim of the kolkhoz was first to collectivize the work but also to produce surpluses that could be directed into the stream of national Soviet production. The fish products of rural Kamchatka, once salted, dried, or smoked, could be shipped out as commodities not only to nearby Petropavlovsk or Magadan, but also to Moscow and elsewhere. The actual alienation that took place was exacerbated by the Soviet resettlement policy. In order to consolidate production and facilitate delivery of administrative services, the Soviet government closed small villages from the late 1950s to the early 1970s. Not only were people alienated from the product of their labor, families were alienated from their ancestral sources of production.

As indicated in the earlier statement by Georgi, Kamchatkan salmon runs have declined precipitously over the past few decades. In some ways, the story of the Kamchatkan salmon's decline echoes the histories described in David Montgomery's (2003) *King of Fish: The Thousand-Year Run of Salmon.* Montgomery follows the cases of Atlantic salmon in both the British Isles and North America and of Pacific salmon in the American Northwest. When he tells of Indigenous fishermen, who take only 2 percent of the catch, being blamed for salmon decline, it sounds very much like Kamchatkan officials who today claim Indigenous overfishing. The story of competing interests and multiple layers of blame that allow those most responsible to hide from their culpability also sounds familiar. In the cases Montgomery outlines, the first stresses on the salmon runs came from overfishing, including the use of weirs and nets that inhibited the salmon from spawning. The most significant problems, he found, had to do with the destruction of habitat: not just that the introduction of dams and other obstructions prevented the fish from getting to their spawning grounds but also that the productive biota of the watershed were being cut down and removed and replaced by polluting farms and factories. Rather than the forest producing logs that helped to create a good riverbed for salmon spawning, the treeless farms emptied field runoff, and the factories dumped industrial pollutants. At the same time, in all cases, the demand for salmon increased, as did the number of people trying to obtain them. Noncommercial fishermen also took part in preventing salmon from getting to their spawning grounds, in some cases spreading fishing nets and weirs across entire rivers to catch as many fish as possible. Legislative means were introduced, but the collective tragedy of the commons allowed each group to shun responsibility for declining salmon numbers. In recent history the attempts to revive Atlantic salmon stocks were thwarted by another threat: aggressive industrialized salmon fishing at sea (Montgomery 2003).

In Kamchatka as in Britain and the United States, powerful interests, particularly mining and oil development companies, have worked against legislation to protect Russian salmon resources from environmental damage. Kamchatka has been very different from the British and American cases, however. One of the primary differences is that there has been relatively little development of farms or industry along Kamchatka's rivers (except for the central Kamchatka River). On many Kamchatkan rivers of the west coast, one can travel for miles without so much as seeing signs of human activity, let alone farms or industry. If the stocks are declining in these rivers, it is not primarily because of habitat destruction.

The other difference from the North American and British cases is the peculiar value that is attached to one specific product, the roe. Whereas in all the cases Montgomery examined salmon were valued for their flesh, in Russia the lofty price of salmon caviar in the post-Soviet context of high unemployment has given salmon a new monetary meaning. Salmon can be caught by the hundreds, opened for their roe, and then discarded, with the flesh being thrown away because of a lack of means (or sufficient incentive) to process it. One morning I went to observe people installing a weir not far from a small village. When we arrived at the site along the riverbank, we found a boat filled with hundreds of salmon that had been cut open during the night and discarded. Only the females contain the roe, so half of the catch produced only roe while the other half was totally wasted. The intense, cash-incentivized focus on roe has created another form of alienation. For both those who produce caviar and waste the fish and those who are limited in fish production because of the caviar craze, the relation to salmon as a carefully respected source of livelihood has been severed. This separation constitutes a striking example of how the alienation caused by commodification can be total. Cash-driven labor focuses all effort on creating a substance of marketable value, breaking with traditional practice and causing economic harm at the same time.

The practice of counting the catch, first in numbers and then in kilograms, has also had alienating echoes in the post-Soviet period. The numbers, once generated as a *descriptive* result of salmon catches from the villages, are now being used to devise forecasts and *prescriptive* quotas for particular rivers. Quotas for salmon catch are determined by government agency specialists. Setting conservation quotas would not in itself be a bad practice if the quotas were distributed according to needs. But the most troublesome aspect is that licenses ("limits") for fishing are given by government authorities based on political influence. Fishing rights for the small Kovran River have been granted to fishermen from Moscow, the Kamchatkan capital of Petropavlovsk, and the nearby Russian village of Ust Khairiuzovo. In some years, native villagers have been given no authorization to fish commercially on their own river, and Indigenous villagers have been offered individual licenses limiting them to as little as 50 kg of fish. A resource that could once be satisfyingly known by the concrete presence of the fish on household drying racks is now prefigured and permitted in numbers that have no connection to local livelihoods.

These are probably the last stages in the alienation of salmon from Itelmen people. Fish are being taken at sea before they can even enter the rivers to be caught or spawn. In violation of the Russian Constitution, which guarantees Indigenous people a right to traditional subsistence, the very resource that determined where Itelmen people established their settlements is being sucked away before it even reaches those locations. Salmon that were once the foundation of the Itelmen diet and by their daily consumption inalienably incorporated into Itelmen bodies have become mere bearers of a valuable substance: roe. Salmon as food have been transformed into salmon for cash by the most alienating human institution, money. And finally, to the extent that salmon runs are still occurring, people have literally been alienated from their own local rivers, forbidden to fish for food or caviar, while others are being given the rights. In this ultimate form of alienation, it is not just that the salmon are alienated from individuals through the productive process. The river itself, the sensitive unit that the community sought to protect from inexplicable forces, has been lost.

RENEWAL

In Kamchatka there has been a reassertion of links between Itelmen identity and salmon that has spawned significant activities centered around the theme. Although I think a description of the contemporary movement for salmon rights should be left to Indigenous participants who know the issues and stakes in far greater detail than I (Sharakhmatova, chapter 5, this volume), it is nevertheless important to include here a brief account of what salmon mean today.

One does not have to look far in Kamchatka to see that the fate of Kamchatka's salmon is one of the primary topics of interest for both Indigenous and long-term Kamchatkans. Virtually every issue of the monthly Indigenous newspaper *Aborigen Kamchatki* has articles and notices about salmon festivals, salmon quotas, salmon rights, or the state of the salmon fishery. The September 2009 issue, for example, featured an article about the festival called Salmon Keepers (*Хранители лосося*), held on the twelfth of September. This festival was also advertised with a very short article in the August 2009 issue. The article was titled "Let's Protect the Chief Wealth of Kamchatka" ("Zashchitim glavnoe bogatstvo Kamchatki") and described the goal of the festival as "presentation of the results of work by schools and ecology groups in the study of salmon; combining of forces and the forming of an understanding of the necessity to preserve salmon and their habitat; recognizing the importance of salmon and of traditions in the life of the Indigenous population of Kamchatka and the necessity of the rational use of salmon."

The festival itself consisted of a series of activities that gave children the possibility to express their understanding of the importance of salmon in their lives. Salmon camps held near the Itelmen village of Kovran allow children to write stories, draw pictures, and sing songs as they learn about their heritage and the importance of salmon. And these camps and festivals have produced booklets and posters that maintain the spirit of the activity in children's lives beyond the actual event.

Now, as the process of increasing alienation started during the Soviet era and continuing in the post-Soviet period has reached what should be its ultimate limit, the unconscious, taken-for-granted side of salmon culture has been replaced by an active mode of discussion and rich new forms of expression.

Notes

1. All translations from Russian sources are the author's. In cases of translated works, the reference is given to the published English translation.

2. Marx (1972) and Engels (1902) took the question of the origin of society very seriously. They insisted on using examples of peoples whom they thought to be like Europe's ancestors to develop a full historical trajectory from nomadic, foraging prehistory to settled agrarian life to industrialization, capitalism, and then socialism/communism.

3. *Kamchadal* was the Russian word for Itelmen in the early literature.

4. Starkova (1978:75) noted that 69.7 percent of the population had fishing as their main occupation in the 1926–1927 census.

5. The name *Oncorhyncus tshawytscha* comes from the Itelmen *ch'uvai, chavicho* (eastern dialect/language; Steller 2003).

6. To say that a kolkhoz was a millionaire meant that it had a total value, in terms of annual production and assets, of more than a million rubles. They produced large enough quantities of fish to be able to export them.

7. Concern with alienation as a moral and social ill has more recently been rejected in postmodern critique as founded on essentialized notions of humanity bound to but separated from nature. Derrida and others found the assumption of an initial, natural, unalienated state from which alienation emerged to be metaphysical speculation (Skempton 2010). As a consequence, philosophical attempts to transcend the alienation of modern society were criticized as resting on the assumptions about the truth of original, natural conditions, the "state of nature," and accompanying inherent identities. Yet, as Skempton (2010) has more recently argued, postmodern deconstruction, rather than disabling the concept, can more usefully be used to develop a theory of de-alienation, a critique that can lead to overcoming the social and political conditions that lead to alienation.

8. Tatiana Petrovna spoke explicitly of the concern that when taking from mice caches one needed to be cautious not to take too much, leave enough for them to survive, and be grateful to the mice.

PLATE 1

Fish weir across the upper Kamchatka River near Mil'kovo. Source: Friedrich Heinrich von Kittlitz, watercolor, ca. 1848. Photograph courtesy of Andreas Lörcher.

PLATE 2

The modern village of Old Harbor looking northeast toward Kodiak. The boat harbor shows the community fleet of purse seine vessels and many smaller skiffs. Source: Courtney Carothers.

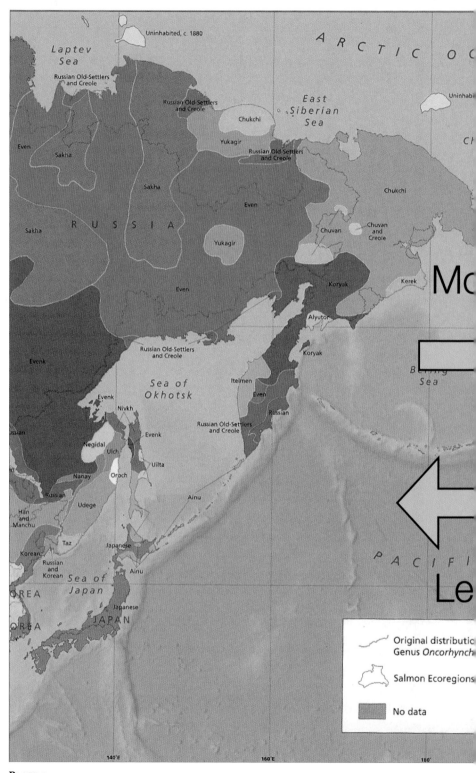

PLATE 3

Current state of Indigenous peoples' political standing across the northern Pacific. Source: adapted from

Augerot 2005.

PLATE 4

Raw fish heads, eaten immediately after the catch, are considered a delicacy even by the young, near Palana, 2006. Source: Erich Kasten.

PLATE 5

Drying salmon on stacks, near Tymlat, 2010. Source: Erich Kasten.

PLATE 6

Tkapp *(wooden fish weir), near Anavgai, 2001. Source: Erich Kasten.*

PLATE 7

Cutting salmon at the Iča River, 1998. Source: Erich Kasten.

PLATE 8

Family on the beach at K'moda. Source: Charles R. Menzies.

PLATE 9

Half-moon-shaped stone trap at K'moda. Source: Charles R. Menzies.

PLATE 10

Stone traps in Kxenk'aa'wen. Source: Charles R. Menzies.

PLATE 11

Stone alignments at Kxooyax. Source: Charles R. Menzies.

4

Koryak Salmon Fishery

Remembrances of the Past, Perspectives for the Future

Erich Kasten

INTRODUCTION

In this chapter I will reflect on and analyze views of Koryak elders, how they remembered changes in their salmon fishery over the past decades, and how these affected attitudes toward salmon and its role as the most prominent economic resource and as an important element of the socio-cultural fabric of these peoples. Besides the political dimension of securing environmental protection and a sufficient quota for local consumption, my particular focus will be on the behavioral dimension, on shifting ethics toward sustainable use, and how corresponding traditional values may be preserved or revitalized. The regional focus will be on coastal Koryaks (Nymylans) living in or near the village of Lesnaya on the west coast of northern Kamchatka, and I will also draw upon supplemental data from coastal Koryaks living in or near Ossora and Tymlat in the Karaginski District on the opposite side of the peninsula on the Pacific coast.

THE ROLE OF SALMON IN THE NATURAL SYSTEM OF NORTHERN KAMCHATKA

First, I will give some general characteristics of salmon and other fish species that are encountered in the rivers of western Kamchatka (Bazarkin 1996:71ff., 140ff.) and to which local informants will refer later. *Chinook salmon* (*Oncorhynchus tshawytscha*, Russian: чавыча) is the biggest of the various salmon species of Kamchatka, and its weight can reach 50 kg or more. It begins to enter the rivers in mid-May, but its main run is in June and the first half of July. *Pink salmon* (*Oncorhynchus gorbuscha*, Russian: *горбуша*) is the most numerous salmon species on the west coast of Kamchatka where this salmon species is of greatest importance for the human diet. It begins to enter the rivers in August, and its main run is in mid-August. *Chum salmon* (*Oncorhynchus keta*, Russian: *кета*) is almost as numerous as pink salmon and can in some years even exceed its numbers. It begins to enter the rivers at the end of June; the main run is in the second half of July and in the beginning of August. The migration of *sockeye* (*Oncorhynchus nerka*, Russian: *нерка/красная*) begins as soon the water is warmer than 4 degrees and continues over a longer period of time, from May to August. It spawns in rivers or lakes where juveniles spend one or two years in freshwater conditions. After migration to the sea, most sockeye live two to three years in the ocean. The first *coho salmon* (*Oncorhynchus kisutch*, Russian: *кижуч*) enter the rivers at the end of June. Their time of spawning might continue until November. *Cherry salmon* (*Oncorhynchus masou*, Russian: *сима*) are a species that prefers warm waters. It is not encountered in large quantities on the west coast of Kamchatka.

The spawning places of the *redspotted trout* (*Salvelinus malma*, Russian: *голец*) are located at the upper reaches of the rivers. After living two to three months in the sea, it comes back to the rivers to stay there over the winter. Similar to the redspotted trout, in its life cycle and form, is the *whitespotted char* (*Salvelinus leucomaenis*, Russian: *кунджа*). *Rainbow trout* (*Parasalmo mykiss*, Russian: *микижа*) is like the *Kamchatka steelhead* (*Parasalmo penshinensis*, Russian: *камчатская семга*). The latter lives in the Tigil' River and farther south and is on the Russian List of Endangered Species, whereas rainbow trout is allowed to be fished all year. *Pacific capelin* (*Mallotus villosus catervarious*, Russian: *уёк, мойва*) is a small fish with a length of about 12–15 cm, sometimes up to 19 cm. It is sporadically plentiful close to the coast in June, where it is fished with special nets from the shore. In most places it is seldom or no longer fished that way. This tradition has been preserved, however, among the Nymylans of Lesnaya. For them this fishing time is still important in their annual life cycle, apparently not only for economic but also for social and emotional reasons, as was often expressed by them in personal communications.

The aforementioned salmon and other fish species hold a central position in the ecosystem in Kamchatka. They are of great importance not only for human subsistence, but are also a most significant element of the food chain for other animal species, especially in coastal regions where they provide large amounts of food for seals, bears, birds, and other animals. Furthermore, changes in the salmon population or its quality related to human consumption would have tremendous effects on local, and particularly Indigenous, people, as for many of them salmon is still their traditional food.

Monitoring the quality of the water of the spawning rivers is therefore very important, especially as relates to possible pollution from nearby mining industries. In the Khailino area, in northern Kamchatka, Indigenous fishermen—who usually watch the outer appearance of fish very closely (see what follows)—have noticed some new strange features and expressed their concern that some fish look very different from how they did before (anonymous, personal communication 2002). More in-depth geochemical research on this issue has been conducted by Elena Dul'chenko (2007) in the Bystrinski area in central Kamchatka where mining also takes place and where she could trace unusually high amounts of various hazardous microelements in dried fish. I should add that according to Indigenous food traditions, fish is often consumed raw. Thus the quality of the water and the natural environment from which fish feed themselves can have even more immediate effects on the health of local people who prefer to consume these fish in their raw, dried, or salted—in contrast to fried or cooked—state. However, the substantial distance from population centers and the absence of industrial activities in most other salmon-spawning basins in Kamchatka minimize, at least for the time being, anthropogenic impacts (Bugaev and Kirichenko 2008:266).

Harvest statistics beginning in 1992 and continuing to the present day indicate that localized pressure on almost all commercial species in the Kamchatka River (the main river in Kamchatka) has increased significantly and, in certain instances, exceeds allowable limits. The exploitation of the more valuable fish species, the Pacific salmon, now comes in three forms: at-sea drift-net fisheries, coastal and in-river fisheries, and unsanctioned poaching within the watershed itself (Bugaev 2007:180).

However, the year 2009 brought such an abundance of fish, especially on the east coast of Kamchatka, as had not been witnessed for many years. Thus we are facing the paradoxical situation that even in times of abundance, fish becomes less available to local—and especially Indigenous—people as the fishing quotas imposed on them are probably too small. Consequently, the information that we receive from Indigenous people, though relevant, can sometimes be misleading when they complain about having less access to fish than before. Most likely we are dealing not with the problem of decreasing salmon resources alone, but of how their distribution is managed by state authorities. That issue is discussed more thoroughly in its proper political context by Victoria Sharakhmatova (chapter 5, this volume), whereas this chapter will concentrate on other themes.

THE PARTICULAR ROLE OF SALMON AS THE MOST PROMINENT ECONOMIC RESOURCE BASE FOR LOCAL COMMUNITIES AND FOR THE CULTURES AND IDENTITIES OF INDIGENOUS KORYAK PEOPLE

From early accounts of scientists who traveled to Kamchatka starting in the eighteenth century (Steller 2012[1774] and others)[1] and from later comprehensive ethnographies from the beginning of the twentieth century (Jochelson 1908), we know about the importance of salmon for coastal dwellers not only as the main staple for their own subsistence, but even as a significant trade good for obtaining materials and goods from others. Thus salmon became for them the central element in creating and maintaining necessary trade networks and cultural exchanges with reindeer-herding Koryaks and for weaving a corresponding sociocultural fabric between coastal and inland groups. Indigenous peoples at different places all over the northern Arctic had developed a model of "dual or paired economies" over the last several centuries, which turned out to be a most appropriate means for successful human adaptation to the particular natural environments of these regions (Krupnik 1993:213). As Vladimir Jochelson described:

> The food of Reindeer Koryak does not exist of reindeer-meat alone. To a considerable degree they resort to the fish and seafood of the Maritime Koryak.... As soon the snow is in good condition for driving, the Reindeer Koryak begin to appear on sledges in the villages of the Maritime Koryaks to obtain "seafood," and barter entire carcasses of frozen seal, oil, dog-salmon, and skin of the white wale. Each Reindeer Koryak has among the Maritime people a friend who supplies him with sea-food, and who, in his turn, later on visits the nomad camp of the Reindeer Koryak to get reindeer-meat. [Jochelson 1908:575–576]

Those trade networks were based either on intermarriages, as will be illustrated in the example of the Urkachan family from Lesnaya, or on the (aforementioned) *priyateli* institution of long-lasting transgenerational partnerships that continued even through Soviet times and sometimes up to the present. They are still well remembered by elder people today, as by reindeer herder Ivan Kavavovich Leginov: "In summer, my father went to the coast where the Kakhtanincy [Koryaks] lived. There he received his fish supply for the winter and other sea mammal products. When winter set in, his *priyatel* Poman came to us, and immediately a reindeer was slaughtered and everybody was in a good mood."[2] For the Itelmens, living farther south, Georgi Zaporotski remembers a similar encounter with reindeer herders from his childhood (Dürr, Kasten, and Khaloimova 2001).

The frequent mention in later interviews (see following) of previously existing and obviously well-functioning local exchange systems might make us rethink if or how these could be taken up again in resource management plans that have to take into account the viability and future persistence of Indigenous communities (see Sharakhmatova, chapter 5, this volume). To this end, information on how Indigenous people experienced their past should not be ignored, including information on periods when traditional exchange systems had become apparently well integrated with newly introduced farming and livestock breeding techniques (Kasten 2011:315). However, the memories of "golden" *kolkhoz* times described in recorded life histories can be somewhat biased as speakers contrast these times with the presently felt shortcomings of supplying more distant communities with necessary products and services.

Besides its significance within the translocal socioeconomic system, salmon played a prominent role in maintaining the Koryaks' local subsistence system that also relied strongly on sea mammal resources such as seals. Seal populations in turn depended on sufficient salmon stocks. As was reported to Jochelson (1908:586), a great famine occurred in the late 1870s along the coasts of Penzhina Bay, when both main food resources failed at the same time because they were closely related to each other. Unfortunately, almost no salmon entered the rivers in that particular region at that time, though the reasons why remain unclear. However this example shows the fragility of the entire ecosystem and of the human food chain that relied strongly on salmon.

For coastal Koryaks, sufficient stocks of salmon and Pacific capelin have been indispensable to feeding the dog teams that almost every family needed for winter transport between hunting sites and to trading or bartering for provisions from other settlements. In some villages, especially those with few opportunities for wage labor and where people cannot afford snowmobiles, such as in Lesnaya, dog teams are still the major means of winter transport between nearby hunting sites and the village, although they are now seldom used for long distance travel, as still recalled by elder people today.

INDIGENOUS SALMON HARVESTING AND PROCUREMENT STRATEGIES WITH REGARD TO SUSTAINABLE RESOURCE USE

To answer the main question of this chapter, we shall first look into relevant earlier accounts on western Kamchatka by scientists and travelers from the past three centuries and then listen to what elder people today remember about salmon harvesting and procurement strategies with regard to sustainable resource use.[3]

During his travels and observations among Itelmen people who live farther south from the coastal Koryaks on the western coast of Kamchatka, Georg Wilhelm Steller (2012[1774]:141–176) noted in the mid-eighteenth century their particular salmon-harvesting and procurement strategies and gave detailed descriptions of the various salmon and other fish species and their behaviors.

Although Itelmen fishermen would have been in a position to close a river entirely with their fish weirs (plate 1), they did not do so, as they were obviously concerned about letting a considerable number of fish pass upstream to where relatives and others had set up their settlements over time. From Steller's observations we can conclude that various families who lived in small settlements along a particular river system formed a local group that expressed its close ties during the feasting cycle in fall and early winter when members visited each other to conduct the reconciliation ceremonies toward nature, which are still held in Lesnaya today (see following). Presumably, the families were concerned about leaving sufficient fish resources for upstream settlements in order to keep them prosperous both because these settlements could provide additional resources from their territories and so that those families would not have to turn to downstream relatives in case of need. Such systemic—in contrast to now more prevalent individualistic—views are still reflected in accounts of elder people today. These views also correspond to a more "symbiotic" relationship with regard to ecological reciprocity (see Smith, chapter 1, this volume).

According to Semion Trifonov Urkachan, a Nymylan-Even hunter and fisherman from Lesnaya (now living in Palana), Indigenous people have well aligned their activities with the seasonal cycle of nature, which they monitored very closely. They followed its specific rhythm in their daily and seasonal tasks—which meant that they might have worked at times day and night, "as fish do not wait, but then relax for longer periods of time" (figure 4.1). Everybody knew what he or she had to do, so that they did not need orders from others; consequently, they were annoyed and frustrated by the strict time rules set up by newcomers in Soviet times.

FIGURE 4.1
Fishing during the peak season at the upper Lesnaya River, 2002. Source: Erich Kasten.

Indigenous people have learned from experience how to understand and to follow the signs of nature that provide them the most reliable schedule for planning their activities. Semion T. Urkachan remembers: "As soon the trees dropped their leaves in autumn which then began to float on the surface of the river, people knew that they had to get ready for setting up their particular devices, because soon rainbow trout would show up" to start its migration down to the mouth of the river. In a similar way Vladimir Sergeevich Yaganov from Lesnaya reports: "When we move to the coast in June to fish the Pacific capelin, we initially rest at the shore and set up nets. From the whitespotted char, that we usually get first, we open the stomach and look if we can find some capelins in there. If this is the case, we know that the capelin stocks are not far anymore, and everybody gets up and begins to prepare his fishing gear."

Aleksandra Trifonovna Urkachan, the sister of Semion Urkachan and the daughter of a Nymylan mother and a Even reindeer herder, told us: "When we hear the cuckoo singing in a particular way (tut-tut-tut) around mid-June, we know that soon the first fish will come to us." Sergei Antonovich Popov from Lesnaya agreed: "We will have many fish and capelins, when the cuckoo sings that way [*тупулг'атыӷ*], which sounds like beating a drum." And he continued: "When we earlier cut the fish, we watched very carefully

71

the condition of the scales and the entrails. For example, if the inner hide formed a kind of a pocket, we knew that there would many fish that year." Daria Upit and Khristofor Tanvilin from Tymlat on the northern east coast of Kamchatka remembered similar predictions, such as one could expect many fish when there was some reddish shine on the snow in spring.

S. T. Urkachan informs us about the seasonal fishing cycle of the people of Lesnaya: "After winter, in May, the first fish we take are redspotted trout that are on their way down to the coast. Those fishes are immediately consumed and not stored, and from some we make fermented fish to be used as bait in the specific weirs that we set up." In June, families are moving to the coast to fish the Pacific capelin there. After that, as soon the various salmon runs set in and bring waves of fish upstream (chinook, chum, and pink—see "The Role of Salmon in the Natural System of Northern Kamchatka"), they move up the river to their particular family fishing sites that their ancestors have used from time immemorial. During the following two months, in July and August, they prepare—especially by means of drying—the main fish supply for themselves and for the dogs for the rest of the year and until the next spring. Fishing slows down in September and October and ends with the run of rainbow trout, whereupon the main hunting season on sea mammals, snow sheep (until October), and fur-bearing animals (from November until February) begins. From June until September, women and children collect sprouts, wild onions, berries, and roots that are used as important ingredients for particular traditional dishes, often in combination with fish. S. A. Popov informs us about the important role that capelins once played (and still play), especially as dog food. He was told by elders "that in earlier times reindeer herders procured their fish supply around Тайӈыгытг'ын [Sacred Lake], far upstream at the Lesnaya River where the sockeye went up to spawn, while at that time of the year, in June, we were still occupied with getting our capelin stocks at the coast; consequently we did not pay much attention to sockeye."

Fish is prepared in various ways from which people make—often in combination with wild plant and animal products—nutritious dishes. From experience they have found out that these dishes are the most appropriate use for their main resource under the particular natural conditions of the north, as was acknowledged already by Steller (2012[1774]:302) with keen appreciation in the eighteenth century. Today such useful Indigenous food traditions are becoming less common, although they still exist in some places and mostly among the elder generation.

S. T. Urkachan became really enthusiastic about explaining to us in detail how earlier people were masters of preparing fermented fish in pits:

"The pit was accurately laid out with willow branches and fish, and fish heads were placed between the layers, whereupon the pit was closed" to let the fish ferment for a while. "When they later opened the pit, the smell had such an aroma that it would dissolve on the tongue," he expressed. "It was very different from the aroma of the fermented fish that we prepared in a more simple way for dog food." Another method was applied in fall, when whole chum salmon were hung up to first let them ferment for a while and then to freeze for later consumption in winter. "Then, after cooking, the fish was cut and served with seal oil, and especially the fish roe, eaten with spoons, was considered a real delicacy." Tatiana Kotovinina from Tymlat describes special storage pits in the permafrost "like small houses, even with doors and stairs," where they stored slightly fermented fish to keep its particular delicious taste.

The heads of the spring's first redspotted trout were eaten raw after these had been cut into small pieces. Salmon heads were also, and are still, eaten raw during summer, especially the front piece that is considered to be particularly delicious and which contains, they might have learned from experience, almost no hazardous parasites (Russian: *глисти, гилминти*; plate 4).

People also made fish meal from salmon as part of their diet for the winter. S. A. Popov reports: "We went up the river, about 15 to 20 km to the spawning creeks of the chum salmon. There we collected the female fish [*шиголг'о*], which had become already weak and were about to die after spawning; we roasted them over the fire and made fish meal from the meat. But the hides we ate, so we did not throw away anything." T. V. Kotovinina points out that after a similar process of producing fish meal the hide was kept for the winter when it was eaten together with fat. For K. P. Tanvilin fish meal was an important staple for the winter, and he compares it with some humor with instant soups from China (or Korea) that have become quite popular recently in Kamchatka: "Within five minutes you can prepare it, and you may add dried wild onion or seal fat to it."

The main food staple, however, was dried salmon, called *yukola*. The fish were cut into halves in an accurate and even way so that flies could not place their eggs into holes, as maggots might later destroy a whole supply. K. P. Tanvilin acknowledges that even this careful cutting might not help when flies are swarming, so that one then has to clean maggots from the inner side of the cut fish every day. Therefore, he prefers late August and September for making yukola, when the flies' peak season has come to an end. According to S. A. Popov, however, the best time for drying salmon in Kamchatka is July and August, when there is little moisture in the air so

Figure 4.2

Drying salmon on stacks, Lesnaya River, 2002. Source: Erich Kasten.

that the fish can dry quickly and maggots have no time to develop.

After the cut fish are dried on stacks they are hung up under the platform of a *balagan*, a kind of storage hut on poles, where the fish is well dried by the wind while being sheltered from rain and from birds by nets (figure 4.2, plates 5 and 7). Later, the dried fish is stored in the hut above. Yukola is broken up into pieces and preferably dipped into seal oil before it is eaten. Yukola also serves as dog food in winter, and it was occasionally traded for by reindeer herders as emergency food for reindeer in late winter. A. T. Urkachan reports that yukola was prepared by some family members in March as a nutritious supplement for reindeer in order to give them additional strength when they are about to give birth, around the beginning of April.

Fish oil rendering is not practiced today in Kamchatka and has never been widespread there among Indigenous people (in contrast to Kosaks and Russians), as it is among some First Nations in the Canadian Pacific Northwest (coastal Koryaks and Itelmens always get sufficient amounts of oil from the great abundance of seals and from other sea mammals as well). Steller (2012[1774]:175), however, noticed that fermented fish was still occasionally boiled in dugout canoes that were filled with water and into which heated stones had been thrown, whereupon the oil was eventually scooped off the surface—in a very similar way to how it is collected among the Dzawada'enuxw of the Kwakwaka'wakw or Kwakiutl First Nation (Kasten 1990:54–68).

Around the middle of the eighteenth century, Steller (2012[1774]:168) observed among Itelmens their dislike of salted fish, while for Kosaks and Russians salting had been their preferred method of preservation. In 1843 J. K. E. Kegel noticed that at Koryak villages in the Karaga region salt was not used for conservation (Gülden 2011:192). And T. V. Kotovinina from the nearby village of Tymlat remembers even today "that we didn't know of salted fish, and in general salt was unknown to us."

Even smoking salmon had never been a strong tradition among Itelmens and Koryaks, like it was among other Indigenous people along the North Pacific rim. Steller (2012[1774]:174) noted that the fish sometimes got a bitter taste that he attributed to the use of not sufficiently dried wood. Evdokiya Lukinishna Nesterova from Lesnaya, however, explained to us how salmon is smoked in a traditional way by using pits. Only in the 1920s, when salt became available in larger amounts, did Koryaks start to salt and smoke salmon (*balyk*). Salting was promoted in Soviet times as more "rational" (as less labor was required) and is mostly applied today. However, the consumption of dried salmon, conserved in the traditional way, turns out to be healthier than the consumption of large amounts of salted fish. Consequently, the elder people say that an unusually high number of Indigenous people from that region now suffer from circulatory disorders that were not as common in earlier times.

According to A. T. Urkachan, dried fish roe was a particular delicacy and was consumed in various ways: "After we had peeled off the skin it was eaten together with cedar nuts. It was especially tasty that way, almost like milk, and it did not stick so much in between the teeth. We ate it usually for breakfast, or women brought it with them when they went into the tundra to gather sprouts, and where we ate it together with the pulp of cow parsnip [*Heracleum lanatum*], during our rests, when we had tea." K. P. Tanvilin explains with great enthusiasm how dried fish roe was eaten with the inner layer of birch bark and mixed with seal fat, "in the real Koryak way." Steller (2012[1774]:171–172) also described how dried fish roe was prepared together with certain plants as provisions for traveling. E. L. Nesterova points out that drying the fish roe in the right way by placing it on a mat made from woven grasses is important so that it does not get bitter.

Dried salmon roe was also used as an ingredient for the traditional dish *tylktyl* (Koryak: тыԓӄтыԓ, Russian: *tolkusha*). It consists of various kinds of dried and smashed plants, roots, and fish roe and was served foremost during feasts and as a ritual dish during the Ololo festival. This dish was prepared in different ways. S. A. Popov remembers: "When we went to the festivals of reindeer herders, they served us 'white' tylktyl [эӈ'ы тыԓӄтыԓ] to which they added the inner fat of reindeer. Another kind of tylktyl that contains dried and smashed inner pulp of fireweed [*Chamerion angustifolium*] is called 'black' tylktyl [йг'йрг'а тыԓӄтыԓ]."

Another prominent dish made from fish is *kylykyl*. It consists of smashed pieces of cooked salmon from which the bones are separated carefully and to which crowberries—which are not really tasty but are especially rich in vitamins—and seal oil are added. Or one can add any other kind of berry that is in season, such as cloudberry (*Rubus chamaemorus* L.) and blueberry (*Vaccinium uligonosum* L.), as E. L. Nesterova demonstrated to us. This dish is not only considered healthy, but it is particularly appreciated because it is also filling.

Last but not least, fish soup (Russian: *ukha*) has to be mentioned as a popular dish. It is especially popular during the summer when its taste is best if it is made with fresh salmon, long-rooted onion (*Allium ochotense* Prokh.), and—as in former times—Siberian springbeauty (*Claytonia tuberosa* Pall. ex Schult).

In general, the loss of Indigenous food traditions is certainly one of the main causes of numerous health problems among Native people today. Unfortunately, relevant Indigenous knowledge is no longer transmitted to the youth as before, and some traditional food resources have become less available or are no longer available to many Indigenous people. This unavailability includes, above all, reindeer food, as apparently many people suffer now from a lack of hemoglobin and calcium; many Indigenous people are increasingly missing the particularly rich supply of vitamins that are found in fish oil, as they have to consume less fish than they did before.

Another problem is the loss of traditional knowledge about how to prepare and consume salmon properly. For example, certain fish, such as sockeye, need to sit for about forty days after having been salted and before they are consumed so that their parasites will have lost their pathogenic effects (Elena Dul'chenko, personal communication 2010).

Therefore, the preservation of fish resources in combination with traditional Indigenous knowledge about how to prepare these resources for consumption in a most appropriate and healthy way stand out as an important challenge for the future. Beyond preserving the knowledge of how to prepare appetizing Indigenous dishes, researchers and activists should work to make such nutritious traditional food popular again, which will not be an easy task as "Western" food, promoted in the media, is seen by many younger people as more "prestigious" today.

As I have mentioned, fish served not only as the most important human food supply. According to the Indigenous worldview, people were obligated to use all parts of an animal and leave nothing, or at least as few remains as possible. Thus, the inner parts of salmon were used for dog food and were put into pits where they fermented together with other fish. A. T. Urkachan informs us that "close to the pits a pole was put into the ground that these could be found in winter, when they were covered by snow, and when the food was needed for the dog teams." Also for dog food the fish backbone (*ниэлӄев'*) together with its head was dried and hung up with the yukola under the balagan.

A. T. Urkachan remembers that in former times even the skin of late-running chum salmon was used as material for certain clothes such as coats, caps, and gloves, especially for maritime hunters, as these were light and provided good protection against wind and rain. T. V. Kotovinina reports the same and describes how fish skin was used for making glue, for example, to attach reindeer hide to the frame of a drum. D. Upit mentions that "from fish skin we made baskets for our gathering trips into the tundra." Zakhar Stepanovich Yaganov from Lesnaya tells us that when he was young, windows were occasionally still made from the skin of chum salmon: "They took the skin from an old chum salmon who was about to die after spawning, as these had almost no fat anymore. After having taken away the scales and having well watered and dried it, it turned already into a light and beautiful skin that they then stretched over the window opening. In the middle, they made a little hole through which they could look. In winter, however, when dogs were starving, they sometimes tried to eat the skin."

Indigenous groups on the east and west coasts of northern Kamchatka most often used a particular wooden fish weir called a *tkapp* for salmon fishing in the rivers (figure 4.3, plate 6). T. V. Kotovinina remembers how she helped her parents when she was still a child "to collect round stones into piles in order to close openings so that fish could not escape through them. This way we closed well [parts of] the river [near the trap]" (see Menzies, chapter 8, this volume, for a description of similar Gitxaała stone structures). The structure and function of the tkapp is explained and shown in detail by Aleksei Pavlovich Appolon (2010:79 ff.): "With a special fish weir the river was closed, but in such a way that fish could pass through to their spawning grounds." Friedrich Heinrich von Kittlitz (2011[1858]: 272–273) noticed around the mid-nineteenth century that such weirs were

FIGURE 4.3

Tkapp (wooden fish weir), near Anavgai, 2001. Source: Erich Kasten.

intentionally "built so low that fish could jump over it,...because otherwise too many of them would have been caught.... The wooden sticks of the container keep only the bigger fishes, whereas the younger ones are not obstructed."

According to Appolon (2010:79), "The tkapp had been constructed like this so that one didn't take everything on one day, as people were aware of the need to think about the next day." He remembers that these weirs had been widely used on the west coast of northern Kamchatka until the mid-1960s, whereas more recently fishing with nets and fish traps had become the more common practice.

Varvara Kondrate'vna Belousova from Kinkil (a small settlement near Lesnaya) remembers: "When using the tkapp we could see in the wooden container the exact amount of fish that we needed or that we were able to prepare. Then we lifted up the container, emptied it, and carried the fish home, leaving the weir open then for other fish to pass through." According to her, every family had a clear estimate of the amount of fish that was needed for the year for its own food supply and for the dog team.

S. T. Urkachan confirmed the same: "People took only as many fish as needed, and they knew very well their ration for the year. From early childhood we were exhorted to never catch too many at one time, but to leave enough fish to swim upstream to the places of their origin, where they would give life to new ones, whereupon the old ones would die. So we could be sure that there would be enough fish next year." And K. P. Tanvilin emphasizes that "we fish only so many as we need, then we stop, it's enough, we leave [other fish] for the next year. So we lived our life, until the radical change occurred."

From her childhood in the 1950s, A. T. Urkachan remembers similar situations, when they were told by the elders to never take too many fish.

> When I was young, I occasionally came with my father, who was a reindeer herder, to a fishing site close to the sacred place Stony Man [В'ывкаляк] near Palana. There we fished for a while together with our relatives who lived there and eventually we took fish in our baskets [lepkhe] back to the reindeer camp. There, at the fishing site, I noticed and first wondered why they threw certain fish back into the river, and they told me that these [female] fish will give birth to even more, so that later you and your children will always have enough.

Similar comments from others give evidence and are particularly striking, compared to today's attitudes toward natural resource use, in relation to how Indigenous people once perceived long-term sustainable resource use and how they embodied and taught particular responsibility to future generations.

People knew that they had to leave a sufficient number of fish to pass upstream "so that there would be many fish in the future," and V. K. Belousova added that to this end, they singled out female fish and threw them back into the river. She complained that today just these fish are taken in great numbers because of their special value for caviar production. S. A. Popov witnessed the same—that too many female fish are taken now in order to fulfill the orders of traders or businessmen (komersianti) who are in charge of the lucrative, but disastrous from an ecological point of view, caviar trade. "Once I was hired myself to work for them. But when I noticed that they were about to dump the remains of the fish, those from which they had taken the roe, in the tundra to let them rot there, I quit. You must never fish more fish than you are later able to prepare. You must think about how these fish are given to us."

V. K. Belousova informed us that earlier, when she was young, Indigenous people did not take much salmon caviar. They dried and used it, among other things, in smashed form as an ingredient for the traditional tolkusha dish that was served during the annual Ololo festival in early winter. Only in kolkhoz times, when salt became available in larger quantities and was used for conservation, did fish roe or caviar began to be stored in greater amounts in barrels and shipped to towns. Later, during the subsequent *sovkhoz* period, salmon caviar became an increasingly desired trade good and was collected in even greater quantities from individual fishermen and fishing brigades. Eventually, especially during and after perestroika, the caviar trade got more or less out of control, with its well-known consequences for the salmon populations in some rivers of Kamchatka.

From the remembrances of V. S. Yaganov we learn how the people of Lesnaya became gradually drawn into the new—increasingly "globalized"—economic system that began to focus, even more than the earlier fur trade, on salmon and other food resources. This system was appreciated by Indigenous people in the beginning because of its immediately felt advantages for them:

> After most families had moved in June to the coast to fish and prepare the Pacific capelin stocks there for dog food for the winter, they dispersed to their individual family fishing sites along the Lesnaya River, where they fished all summer. When we had prepared our own supply of dried fish and other wild plants and berries for the winter, we gave to the sovkhoz what we did not need for ourselves. For that we received, in return, supplies so that we could build warm cabins at our winter hunting sites, where we earlier lived in tents.

Although the shift to a new economic system had already become apparent, traditional worldviews and value systems of Indigenous people were still in place to control the overuse and abuse of salmon resources. After perestroika, however, the supposed blessings of a free market economy and Western lifestyles became increasingly attractive to Indigenous youths, and conflicts arose even within families over the use of salmon roe. While elder people such as Nadezhda Grigor'evna Barkavtova (AKD 1998) still insisted on drying salmon roe in small quantities in the traditional way, young people complained that this was a "waste," since salmon caviar had become their "money," as they called it.

In a similar way, more individualistic orientations toward the new market economy are coming increasingly into conflict with other traditional values of sharing that can still be witnessed among fishermen and hunters in more remote villages such as Lesnaya. S. T. Urkachan remembers "a certain number of fish of a good catch were brought immediately by boat or on horses to those who had become too old or weak to fish by themselves. It was deeply rooted in our way of life to help each other out." V. K. Belousova tells us the same: "I was taught by my father that, after a successful hunt or when we got plenty of fish, we had to share them with others, first of all with those who are in need, such as orphans or families with many children and with handicapped people. It was a strict rule, although I myself in the beginning did not really understand it." Originally, occasional surplus had been used to balance out inequalities within the local group, whereas during kolkhoz times the production of (unlimited) surplus—with its consequent pressure upon relevant natural resources—was directed toward feeding "the stream of national Soviet production" (Koester, chapter 3, this volume).

SALMON IN INDIGENOUS RITUAL AND WORLDVIEW

Indigenous people in Kamchatka expressed their particular respect for salmon by means of their "ritual of the first salmon." Especially when the expected fish run did not arrive in time, people went to the shore of the river and conducted there a certain ritual. According to Ekaterina Grigorev'na Yaganova, they called the fish using the phrase "Chchnu, chchnu, chchnu [чучуу], fish come here and swim by." And as A. T. Urkachan adds: "From giant meadowsweet [*Filipendula camtschatica*] they wove a figure that looked like a fish head. First they waved it in the water, and sang: 'Oh, how many are coming, come quickly,' and then they let it go with the current. And usually, after two to three days, the first fish showed up." People believed that the fish would be attracted by the strong smell of the plant and be guided up the river that way, as they were thought to have lost their orientation.

Another way to call the fish is reported to us by E. L. Nesterova as she remembers her early childhood: "At that time, when we fished for the *gospromkhoz*, there once was little fish, and my sister told me: 'Now listen how I will call the fishes!' She said: 'Take a flower of the Arctic bramble [*Rubus arcticus* L.],' and we went to the sea. With the flower we called the fish so that they would gather at the mouth of the river. We stayed there for a few days, and then the chum salmon came" (figure 4.4).

Natalya Ionovna Grigor'eva, a woman of Even and Koryak descent from Esso, informs us:

> When the fish come, [the people] go to the river and start a
> fire near the shore. Then they throw small offerings into the fire
> and say that we have come here to honor you. We had earlier

FIGURE 4.4

The wooden hammer for pounding fish trap stakes into the river can take the shape of a salmon, as even preparing the fish weir often requires ritual precautions, near Kovran, 1993. Source: Erich Kasten.

conducted offerings to the souls of our dead ancestors here; therefore, we made this procession to the river. Near the river we set up three poles, and then we throw small pieces of food into the water. During the ceremony we say: 'River, give us fish. We gave you food, and you will give us fish.' That way we ask the soul of the river, when the fish run sets in, that there be many of them. [AEK 2003]

Accordingly, rivers had to be treated with respect and almost as sacred places (see Koester, chapter 3, this volume). People were forbidden to relieve themselves near them, as the smell might irritate the fish, V. K. Belousova told us, and A. T. Urkachan added: "At times of the fish run it was forbidden to use [red] alder bark for tanning, as this would close the eyes of the fish, which then would not be able to orientate themselves anymore."

Those accounts show that Indigenous people knew about the sensitivity of salmon in their fateful search for their spawning grounds and that people were aware that they had to keep undisturbed the ecosystem in which fishes lived and reproduced.

In addition to the first fish rituals I have mentioned, the ritual dialogue with the supernatural is still conducted today by coastal Koryaks in Lesnaya during their Ololo festival, which is held each year in October by individual families. Through singing and dancing the souls of the animals killed during the past season, symbolized by wooden and woven figures that are hung up in a sacred tree inside the house, are honored and eventually sent off through the fire after they have been fed with a particular ritual dish (tolkusha). In the world beyond they would report that they had been treated well by the hunters and by the entire community, so that many of them would return next year (Kasten 2009; Urkachan 2002). In earlier times, each animal species that was hunted was honored through a special ceremony of its own, whereas the Nymylans of Lesnaya (one of the few places where those festivals are still conducted in the traditional way) now celebrate the Ololo for snow sheep and seals together.

Although this festival does not relate directly to salmon, it demonstrates the persistence of particular worldviews and attitudes toward nature, especially among the elder generation, that also affect the use of fish resources. People felt that as part of nature, they had to maintain a ritual dialogue in order to find out what humans might have done wrong and to show respect, even in their daily lives. In contrast to Soviet or Western ideology, Indigenous people were aware that they would never be able to "conquer" (Russian: *pobed*) or to control nature, but that they could only please the "owners of the game" through appropriate behavior. Such understanding is based on the idea that animals *give* themselves to humans, in contrast to "modern" thought in which people *take* more or less freely from nature (cf. Tanner 1979).

However, what is interesting in this case and might remain so for further discussion is the surprisingly minor role that salmon played in the mythology and ritual of the Koryaks, as with the Itelmens. David Koester (chapter 3, this volume) has found out and emphasized that for the Itelmens, fish—in contrast to other animals—was less represented in expressive culture.

However, this underrepresentation stands in sharp contrast to what we know from the other side of the North Pacific rim, where salmon is often a central element in creation myths (see Colombi, chapter 9, and Diver, chapter 10, this volume) and a frequent motif in the arts, such as with the First Nations in British Columbia.[4]

Not only at festivals, but also in their daily activities Indigenous people enter into some kind of dialogue with nature. Each territory contains a number of sacred places. According to K. P. Tanvilin, someone passing by these places is supposed to leave some small item, such as *lauten* (a particular marsh grass), beads, or ammunition, as an offering. Whenever a fire is started during a tea break in the tundra, small pieces of food are thrown into it. The fire is considered to be the main passage or route to the worlds beyond, where the spirits of ancestors and animals reside, and the gift giving is meant to show respect and to please them. Throwing fish and seal bones into the fire was strictly forbidden, however, as ritual behaviors toward those remaining parts of an animal are connected to another process, that is, their resurrection. T. V. Kotovinina told us that "the fish bones had to the thrown to the shore of the sea so that fishes would enter the river and come to us again. Some people do not understand this: you must not throw the bones into the fire, but into the water."

At the coast near Lesnaya some food was given to the sea when the first Pacific capelins arrived in 2005, while A. T. Urkachan said quietly: "This is for you, sea, you feed the people, and we are grateful to you that the capelins came and that you help us, that the [sea] hunters and fishermen will have luck." Even healing powers are believed to reside in the sea, as she later explained to us: "At times, we wove a little boat and laid the flower of the Arctic bramble [*Rubus arcticus* L.] plant with some food on top of it, and we pushed it into the sea, as this should protect us from illness."[5]

People asked the powers of nature for assistance in times of need, and they were concerned about maintaining the indispensable "exchange" with animals and the keepers of the game by means of a ritual dialogue. They knew that this assistance and bounty would be denied to them if they did not behave properly toward nature even in their daily activities (cf. Feit 2004; Sirina 2011:312–329).

Elder people today still consider leaving the remains of killed game or fish unused to be extremely sacrilegious, as already mentioned in previous examples. Consequently, almost all the elders whom we consulted and who are still bearers of traditional knowledge and values are upset and expressed their deep concern about the way in which salmon resources are treated by many people today, like those who take only the roe for caviar production and leave the rest of the fish to rot on the shore. They care not so much that a practice is illegal or a violation of environmental codes, but, as they all said, that "nature will take revenge"—which is for them still the highest and most powerful authority.

Although many now think such beliefs and rituals are obsolete from a rational-scientific point of view, these beliefs and rituals nevertheless reflect distinct perceptions of and attitudes toward nature that gave Indigenous people the guidance they needed to use their natural resources in a sustainable way. In addition, the particular set of values that includes sharing and a deeply felt responsibility for future generations, as I have shown, ensured a specific use of natural—and especially salmon—resources that is obviously in sharp contrast to what we see today.

CONCLUSION

Many Indigenous people, such as S. T. Urkachan, complain about the increasing pressure on salmon stocks from the outside: "They come with their large high-tech fishing vessels and are able to fish huge amounts from the sea, so that not enough fish are able to get into the rivers and to their spawning grounds. Nobody does really control the amount that foreign people fish, but for Indigenous people they fix limits that are by far too little for them to be able to feed themselves in the traditional way."

One the other hand, Indigenous people are also getting involved in poaching and in less sustainable ways of using salmon resources, although often as the last link in the chain of the caviar business that is largely controlled by well-organized syndicates from outside Kamchatka and, as often reported, not seldom associated with state authorities in one or the other way. Sergei Sinyakov (2006:52) puts it, although correctly, in a more sympathetic way: "In no way can poaching be condoned, especially as a large-scale, organized form of activity. But it should be noted that poaching, by its very nature, is a grassroots social response to the inequitable distribution of natural resource rent."

The examples that I have given in this chapter illustrate the dilemma—which is more than just a generational conflict—that many Indigenous fishermen face these days and that they cannot easily resolve simply by falling back on their traditional value system (see section "Indigenous Salmon Harvesting and Procurement Strategies with Regard to Sustainable Resource Use"). Others, even though I saw them participating actively at the aforementioned traditional reconciliation ceremonies, could not resist the temptation to join a poacher's crew, at least temporarily. While expressing feelings of guilt about it, they tried to justify it to themselves in reference to unfair state regulations that impede their access to the resources they had used before.

Under such circumstances, environmental organizations and state fishing guards have to accomplish a desperate task, as S. A. Popov has noticed: "I remember when they once went up to the upper reaches of the Lesnaya River, where they caught some [poachers] and fined them. But as soon the fishing guards had left, the poachers returned and continued their illegal work, as the komersianti for whom they worked were just after caviar."

In fact, in the wide and sparsely populated wilderness of Kamchatka it is, of course, almost impossible to post a fishing guard at every curve of the numerous rivers in order to get salmon poaching under control. Therefore, although legal measures against salmon poaching are certainly needed, they are extremely difficult to enforce under the given conditions. Consequently, laws alone are hardly enough to stop the destructive trend. From comments of elder Indigenous people we might conclude, however, that beyond environmental laws and codes, a renewed emphasis on traditional values and worldviews in relation to nature, and their transmission to younger generations, could be a more effective tool to ensure Indigenous sustainable resource use, in the way that it had been practiced before.

Therefore, the important question and challenge will be how to integrate traditional knowledge and wisdom with conventional science in future community and Indigenous resource management plans. Strengthened emphasis on social and environmental values (Dietz, Fitzgerald, and Shwom 2005) could give guidance to Indigenous decision makers and harvesters in order to halt the dangerous trend of moral degradation that Victoria Sharakhmatova addresses in chapter 5 (this volume). Admittedly, the discussion about the need for knowledge integration and natural resource co-management is not new and has been ongoing in the decades since Garett Hardin (1968) wrote about it. But despite a number of success stories in the American Pacific Northwest (see Colombi, chapter 9, and Diver, chapter 10, this volume) and in other parts of the world, the debate is relatively new on the Russian side (see Wilson, chapter 2, this volume) and therefore commands our renewed attention.

Sometimes a certain reserve can still be detected on the part of both sides to accept each other's authority and useful contribution to this dialogue. As a coordinator of a multidisciplinary research team in the mid-1990s, I myself witnessed occasional clashes between Indigenous activists and natural scientists, especially when Indigenous knowledge became connected to ethnicity and political empowerment and was attributed more truth than conventional knowledge. This kind of clash only evokes opposition on the other side and impedes the process that should pursue, in the first place, solutions for successful sustainable resource co-management. On the other side, for some natural scientists ritual behavior might appear—quite understandably given their professional background and training—as "irrational" and the social values and environmental ethics of Indigenous people seem a relatively new field to explore, which is often done now in collaboration with cultural anthropologists. Therefore, and not only in the Russian Far East, natural resource co-management often reflects more of a political compromise than a sincere mutual understanding and full acknowledgment of the particular kind of knowledge of the other side (cf. Nadasdy 1999).

To contribute to the important goal of knowledge integration, we have, over the years, developed in the Kamchatka case strong collaborations between scientists and Indigenous experts. One of the latest results is a database that will bring together observations regarding natural resource use in historical accounts over the last 250 years, academic information from natural scientists of the Kamchatka Branch of Pacific Institute of Geography, Far-Eastern Department of Russian Academy of Sciences (KBPIG, FED RAS), as well as videos and commentaries on relevant activities and worldviews by Indigenous practitioners in their own languages that have been recorded during field projects and are edited with Indigenous experts. From such a pool of integrated historical, conventional, and Traditional Ecological Knowledge, we have produced relevant learning tools and designed specific community programs and are continuing to do so (see Kasten, ed. 2011).[6] In addition to necessary legislation to secure Indigenous people a reliable base to continue their traditional economic activities, a particular focus should be on preserving and revitalizing Indigenous value systems and environmental ethics as a foundation for continuous or renewed implementation of traditional knowledge as part of sustainable resource use—before this knowledge is lost forever as it very soon may be.

Notes

1. Georg Heinrich Freiherr von Langsdorff, Adelbert von Chamisso, Friedrich Heinrich von Kittlitz, Georg Adolf Erman, Johann Karl Ehrenfried Kegel, and Karl von Ditmar were early German explorers who carried out scientific projects in Kamchatka for the Russian government during the nineteenth century. Their extensive and keen observations, particularly on Indigenous traditional resource use, cannot be referred

to or quoted here in detail, although their accounts of salmon fishing can be found at www.kulturstiftung-sibirien.de, where electronic editions of their books, published as hardcover editions in 2011 at the Kulturstiftung Sibirien, can also be accessed.

2. If not otherwise indicated, these personal recordings are from Kasten, ed. 2011, where they may be found in their entirety. (Translations into English are my own and are based on the work of Aleksandra Urkachan, who transcribed the spoken Koryak text and translated it into Russian.)

3. My focus will be on the accounts of Georg Wilhelm Steller as these provide the earliest and most detailed information (see note 1).

4. Similar issues will be discussed comparatively across time and space (around the North Pacific rim) in planned future studies on the role of the raven figure in the mythology of these peoples. The Kutkiniaku story "Big Raven and Fish Woman" in a forthcoming issue of the periodical *Echgan*, for example, features an informative combination of raven and fish characters and behaviors that further illustrate Koester's argument in chapter 3 (this volume). See www.siberian-studies.org/publications/echgan_E.html.

5. Such perceptions among Indigenous people might be understood in the context of the assumption (and real experience) that most infectious diseases came to them with foreigners and, specifically, sailors "from the sea." See *Forschungsreise nach Kamtschatka. Reisen und Erlebnisse des Johann Karl Ehrenfried Kegel von 1841 bis 1847* in Gülden 2011:272.

6. The three-DVD series *Itelmen, Even and Koryak Language and Culture* was primarily made for the school curriculum and cultural programs in Kamchatka, although it can be used as well in international research and in university courses. The DVDs have English and Russian subtitles. Booklets contain both the transcribed original texts and translations (www.kulturstiftung-sibirien.de/materialien_E.html). *Echgan* is a quarterly periodical that serves as a teaching tool in schools and other institutions of culture in Kamchatka. It is aimed at assisting the teaching of Indigenous themes, such as Traditional Ecological Knowledge and arts and crafts, in conjunction with Koryak language (www.siberian-studies.org/publications/echgan_E.html). The database "Local Knowledge and Sustainable Natural Resource Use in Kamchatka" brings together historical accounts, recent ethnographic recordings, and information from natural science. Thus traditional local knowledge is further enhanced by science and presented in modern ways (www.siberian-studies.org/publications/tek_E.html).

5

Indigenous Peoples' Traditional Fishing in Kamchatka and Local Community Development Concept Based on Sustainable Use of Fish Resources

Problems and Solutions

Victoria N. Sharakhmatova

INTRODUCTION

The fundamental problems of modern Russia are economic, environmental, and national policies, including state policy on Indigenous peoples. The solutions to many problems (social, cultural, economic, moral, and otherwise) have been deferred for many years. Today, the lack of clear coordination among federal, regional, and local authorities and local populations in this area, the destruction of the moral and ethical foundations of the society, and the degradation of human values cause serious problems for Indigenous peoples as well as people living among them and leading a similar lifestyle. Political, economic, and other shocks occurring in Russia in recent decades have adversely affected populations in remote areas. In particular, the Indigenous communities on the west coast of Kamchatka find themselves in an extremely difficult situation. There appear to be very few jobs available for local people. They have begun to look for seasonal work as fishermen, firemen, coal furnace stokers, and maintenance staff in organizations funded by regional governments' budgets. Coastal communities in Kamchatka have severely limited options for earning money. In particular, they have minimal access to salmon-fishing resources.

The only way to make money is to receive and fulfill quotas for natural resources. On the west coast are tribal communities of Indigenous peoples

(Russian: *obshchiny*) who are already working in this field. However, competing with large fishing companies is very difficult.

Industrial fishing is the basis of the peninsula's economy, and salmon is the main fish in both industrial and subsistence catches. Most rural inhabitants survive mainly on salmon and the other resources that they must harvest directly from the rivers and sea. Salmon alone forms the livelihoods of the Indigenous peoples of Kamchatka—the Itelmens, Koryaks, and Evens.

At the end of 2007, the federal law On Fisheries and on Conservation of Aquatic Biological Resources was changed in ways that significantly weakened the special rights of Indigenous peoples. As a result, Indigenous obshchiny in Kamchatka lost the right to fish in the traditional territories where they had fished for ages. They could not compete successfully with commercial enterprises that offered more favorable conditions to the state. Therefore, having no other choice, people are turning to poaching. At the same time, many potential entrepreneurs lack necessary skills in business and face insurmountable obstacles, such as the absence of seed capital and prudent lending.

In this situation, the easiest and most obvious way to earn income (and to support a traditional way of life and perpetuate traditional economic activities) is to develop a business that acquires rights to aquatic bioresources (fishing quotas). Several obshchiny on the west coast of Kamchatka have already begun working in the "salmon business." However, without support from the outside, the salmon businesses of these obshchiny can neither survive nor become self-sufficient in a developing market with serious competition from large-scale fishing and fish-processing companies.

The current official system for the allocation of fishing quotas makes the majority of aquatic bioresources available to large companies. Local populations lose quotas, become marginal users of aquatic bioresources, and lose status as stakeholders in the rational use, conservation, and sustainability of bioresources. Meanwhile, according to the Russian Federation Constitution, the natural resources, whatever they are (land or fish), must be used as the basis of the livelihoods of Indigenous (local) populations inhabiting the territory of these natural resources.

But favorable conditions have not formed in the Kamchatka *krai* to allow the local coastal populations to be involved in commercial fisheries. Right now, regardless of whether or not the local population forms a community (*obshchina*), profit from the use of fish resources has been considered an end in itself, rather than a tool for community survival and development.

The situation is further complicated by the fact that the population suffers from legal illiteracy—the result of centuries-old traditions of the peoples of our country for whom the knowledge of moral laws was definitely more important than knowledge of social laws. A local population's lack of knowledge in the fields of Indigenous rights, community activities, and business activities having to do with fisheries makes it practically impossible for them to understand how to pursue their own traditional and other economic activities.

The United Nations Development Programme/Global Environment Facility (UNDP/GEF) project Conservation and Sustainable Use of Wild Salmonid Biological Diversity in Russia's Kamchatka Peninsula had made some attempts to figure out how to handle the challenge.[1] Within the framework of the project there was developed the "Community Development Concept for Indigenous Communities of Kamchatka on the Base of Using Fish Resources." It took into account Alaskan peoples' experiences of using fish resources to provide sustainable development for the local population (the Community Development Quota program). The concept provided suggestions for development of the local shore populations in Kamchatka in view of conserving and sustaining Pacific salmon biodiversity. Legal mechanisms for realization of the points of the concept had been suggested in "The Collection of Normative Documents and Relevant Legislation Regulating Local Communities' Access to the Water Bioresources" (Yakel 2009). Materials and data collected during the study have been used in the work of the Association of Indigenous Peoples of the North, Siberia, and Far East of the Russian Federation, primarily, and by the Association of Indigenous Peoples of Kamchatka Krai.

The quota scheme was first used in Alaska in the early 1990s to catalyze the economic development of fifty-seven coastal villages of the Bering Sea (about twenty-one thousand people). Fishing here is socially rooted; it is an organic part of the lifestyle of the local community. The federal government used its right of control of marine biological resources in order to give quotas for 7 percent of the allowable catch to local communities. The communities of the coastal villages could return quotas to the owners of fishing vessels under the condition that the owners provided employment for local people on their ships, built onshore fish-processing plants, or paid a share of the profits from the sale of the quota to the villages (Pilyasov 2007).

Based on their similarities, issues related to the cooperative management of natural resources and resolution of conflicts over fishery resources in Alaska are most applicable in Kamchatka. Conflicts over identity and the management of salmon resources on the Kamchatka Peninsula are very like those in Alaska and are not fully resolved to this day. Perhaps a more detailed review of the Community Development Quota (CDQ) program will lead the way toward a solution for Kamchatka.

In 2005–2009, within the framework of the UNDP/GEF Kamchatka salmon project, concepts were reviewed and discussed in order to begin a policy discussion about rural economic development and the sustainability of the salmon resources of western Kamchatka. This work drew from the experiences of Indigenous peoples in western Alaska with a CDQ and attempted to adapt these experiences to the current economic situation in western Kamchatka.

RELEVANT ASPECTS OF THE COMMUNITY DEVELOPMENT QUOTA PROGRAM IN WESTERN ALASKA.

The CDQ program allocates to western Alaskan communities a certain percentage of the total allowable catch of all of the valuable species harvested in the commercial fisheries of the Bering Sea.[2] The most valuable species included in the program are pollock, Pacific cod, halibut, king crab, and snow crab. The program does not include species managed by the State of Alaska, such as salmon and herring. The sixty-five communities that are eligible to participate in the program formed six not-for-profit, tax-exempt organizations that apply to the federal government for a share of the CDQ allocations. They then license the allocations to fishing companies that pay a royalty to the CDQ organization for the right to harvest the quotas. The CDQ organizations, in turn, use the money to become active participants in the fisheries and to support economic and human resources development in their communities.

In many ways, though, the situations in western Alaska and western Kamchatka are very different. Numerous families in western Alaska participate actively in the local commercial salmon fisheries as independent permit holders and therefore have a personal stake in the conservation goals of the fisheries. Fishermen may have a relationship with a salmon processor, but they do not work for the processors. In addition, the State of Alaska has a very active management program that includes many ways of ensuring compliance with the laws and regulations and imposes significant penalties for fishermen or processors who violate those laws. The personal use of salmon for food is the highest priority use under both state and federal law. Regulations governing personal use are very liberal as families are able to harvest what they need and are not subject to individual limits, except in times of extreme shortage. In such times, other uses of the salmon, including commercial and recreational uses, must cease in order to provide the most salmon possible for food. Additionally, the activities associated with harvesting and processing salmon are important not only to obtain food, but are central to the way of life in western Alaska. And finally, western Alaska is very remote from population centers and the road system around Anchorage and Fairbanks. As a result, shipping large amounts of illegally harvested seafood to markets outside western Alaska would be very costly and difficult. Since all local residents have virtually unlimited access to salmon for food and as the processors face severe penalties if they are caught with illegally harvested salmon, little incentive exists on the part of residents to violate the fishing laws and regulations (Cohen 2005).

However, while discussing the key questions that must be answered as part of an effort to apply a similar program in western Kamchatka, we must be guided by the sustainable fisheries priorities of the Russian government as spelled out in the fisheries law On Fisheries and on Conservation of Aquatic Biological Resources.

When we compare Russian and foreign law enforcement practices, we can see that the fisheries law is not worse than other countries' legislation and that matters relating to the rights of Indigenous peoples to use aquatic biological resources are well regulated by federal and regional legislation. However, as often happens, those rights are violated by the authorities, their officials, and major companies conducting their business in the same territories as Indigenous peoples. And Indigenous peoples do not usually appeal to higher authorities or take legal recourse for different reasons: legal illiteracy, inactivity, and the unwillingness to enter into conflict with the authorities and big business.

Nevertheless, such claims are still received and can be quite effective in addressing specific issues. One could compile and categorize typical violations of Indigenous peoples' rights with regard to salmon production and prepare a list of typical claims. But we need to understand that violations occur where there are inadequate legal provisions. Gaps in legislation and conflicting laws are fertile ground for denying the specific rights of Indigenous peoples to use natural resources. Without addressing these gaps and enhancing the responsibility of the authorities for implementing solutions, the rule of law will never be fully realized. Thus, this multilevel problem can be solved only through an integrated approach, that is, taking simultaneous action on several fronts:

- improving the legislation (eliminating the gaps and conflicts)
- training personnel working in public institutions

- educating Indigenous peoples
- strengthening the responsibility for decisions made

Creating a methodical textbook on the practical application of legislation for the protection of Indigenous rights to the traditional use of fisheries is still necessary. Furthermore, we also need to describe an algorithm of actions in case of violations of rights of access to water resources, which would include instructions for court protection and a detailed description of possible situations, samples of procedural documents (claims, complaints, petitions, etc.), as well as examples of real court cases.

Among the complex of legislative regulations on fishing and preservation of aquatic biological resources, we can observe a dramatic situation relating to access to the aquatic biological resources of Indigenous peoples and local populations for personal consumption and for their economic activities. Fishing to continue traditional ways of life, fishing for personal consumption, and fishing to maintain traditional practices of Indigenous peoples are all descriptions used by Indigenous peoples, and federal fishery officials understand the goal of traditional fishing as catching fish exclusively for personal consumption.

Links between poaching prevention, community development, and meaningful incentives for sustainable use can be made, first of all, by promoting the "Community Development Concept for Indigenous Communities [obshchiny] of Kamchatka on the Base of Using Fish Resources." This represents a promising way to strengthen control over the use of salmon resources by local and Indigenous populations.

The issues surrounding traditional fishing by Indigenous peoples and commercial fisheries as the bases of social and economic development for local communities were discussed at various meetings and conferences in Kamchatka. In November 2008, the main provisions of the concept were discussed during the working conference "Problems of Traditional Fishing by Indigenous People of the North and Prospects of Local Communities Based on Their Inclusion into Management of Fish Resources," conducted by the UNDP/GEF. Also involved were members of the Federal Agency for Fisheries of Russian Federation Project "Conservation and Sustainable Use of Wild Salmonid Biological Diversity in Russia's Kamchatka Peninsula" and nongovernmental organizations (NGOs) including the World Wildlife Fund and the Association of Indigenous Peoples of Kamchatka Krai.

The objective of the conference was to analyze the possibility of using commercial fisheries as a basis for socioeconomic development of communities of the coastal areas in Kamchatka. After analyses of all the reports and presentations were made by participants in the conference, some measures were recommended:

1. To use materials based on fish resources by the GEF/UNDP project "Conservation and Sustainable Use of Wild Salmonid Biological Diversity in Russia's Kamchatka Peninsula," including "The Community Development Concept for Indigenous Communities of Kamchatka," also, "The Analysis of the Normative-Legislation Documents, Regulating Participation of Local Shore Communities in Fishing Aquatic Bio-resources" for application in the practice of local population development

2. To introduce some standards into regional legislation to regulate participation of the Indigenous communities and the other unions in salmon fishery management

3. To work out a mechanism of taxation for caught and processed aquatic bioresources, which would result in a return of moneys for a nonrecognized right to fish

4. To work out a strategy of use of the Pacific salmon resources by Indigenous people in the Kamchatka krai

5. To work out a program of Indigenous participation in fisheries and conservation of salmonids in Kamchatka

6. To work out a legal mechanism for participation of local people in protection of spawning rivers against poaching

7. To create a regional fisheries council of the Kamchatka krai

8. To set up regional ethnic-ecological councils to provide transparency and publicity in sharing resources and control for using resources allocated

9. To provide for equal participation of local communities and representatives of Indigenous people around fisheries' management of fish resources in the following organizations:
   a. The Fisheries Council
   b. The Anadromous Fish Species Catch Regulation Commission
   c. The Basin Council
   d. The Commission on Consideration of the Fishery Plots Allocation Applications

10. To work out a mechanism of coordination and allocation of fish resource quotas jointly with a plenipotentiary representative of Indigenous people in the Kamchatka krai

Participants in the conference then asked the government of the Russian Federation, the state duma of the Russian Federation's federal assembly, and the legislative assembly of the Kamchatka krai for consideration of the points, as follows:

1. To use federal law N166-FL, On Fisheries and on Conservation of
   Aquatic Biological Resources, issued on December 20, 2004; law of
   the Kamchatka krai N29, About the Fishery and Conservation of
   Aquatic Biological Resources in Kamchatka Region, issued on April
   14, 2008; and other legislative documents of federal and regional-
   level bodies, which would allow a complex solution to the problems
   of economic development without exhausting the resources and
   social stability of fishermen, members of their families, and young
   people in fisheries-based settlements, and to keep intact the fishing
   rights of Indigenous people, which entail:
   a. First priority in choosing fishery plots
   b. The ability to make contracts for using fishery plots without com-
      petition for the right to have a user's contract
   c. The use of fishery plots free of charge
   d. Spatial and temporal privileges in fishing aquatic bioresources
      (based on sex ratio, age structure, and fluctuation of runs)
   e. The exceptional right for fishing certain aquatic bioresource objects
2. To differentiate the current design of aquatic bioresources catch
   quotas—in order to provide for traditional lifestyles and the propagation of traditional economic activities of Indigenous peoples of
   the North, Siberia, and the Far East of the Russian Federation—into
   two parts:
   a. The quotas to provide traditional lifestyle (personal
      consumption)
   b. The quotas to provide traditional economical activities (sustain-
      able socioeconomic development)
3. To build Pacific salmon–based economic activities in view of annual
   stock abundance assessment and quotation by categories of users

In April 2009, the Association of Indigenous Peoples of the North,
Siberia, and Far East of the Russian Federation (RAIPON) held a legal seminar for presidents and leaders of regional organizations.[3] The problems of
existing legislation and the ways of improving it were discussed at the seminar. Another topic of discussion was the proposal developed by the UNDP/
GEF Kamchatka Salmon Biodiversity Project. As a result, the VI Congress
of Indigenous Peoples of the North, Siberia and the Far East of the Russian
Federation included the proposals for the improvement of legislation on
fisheries developed by the project in its resolutions. These amendments
were proposed by the Association of Indigenous Peoples of the North,
Siberia, and the Far East of the Russian Federation to be included in the
Action Plan for the 2009–2011 implementation of the "Concepts for the
Sustainable Development of Indigenous Small-Numbered Peoples of the

North, Siberia and the Far East of the Russian Federation."

In 2009 the federal government approved the "Concept for the Sustainable Development of Indigenous Small-Numbered Peoples of the North, Siberia and Far East of the Russian Federation," which is to be continued until the year 2025, and a "Range of Initial Methods for Realizing This Concept by 2011." Among the concept's goals and initial methods are

- The establishment of pilot territories of traditional natural resources use
- Legislative improvements to simplify Indigenous small-numbered peoples' access to traditional natural resources for fishing and hunting
- Acceptance and approval of a methodology for assessing damage to traditional lands caused by commercial companies' activities

Also relating to the UNDP/GEF Kamchatka Salmon Biodiversity Project, the collection of basic laws governing local communities' access to the use of aquatic resources was compiled and released. This compendium of legal documents was prepared for the regional associations, communities, and other associations of Indigenous peoples, NGOs, and authorities to study and practice the law in carrying out economic activities and decision-making in the field of fisheries and conservation of aquatic biological resources (Yakel 2009).

Salmon business plays an important social and economic role for the Kamchatka krai, and fisheries management is difficult because of:

- recent changes in controlling salmon fisheries (moving management of the fisheries from the federal level to the regional level, exclusion of Pacific salmon from the list of commercial species governed by quotas, allocation ["rental"] of fishery plots for the period of twenty years, and so on). As the principal legislative limits on salmon catches (total allowable catch or TAC) for various types of coastal fisheries have been off, the procedure of management must be improved and better defined, ensuring that salmon is both the long-term, sustainable basis of the ecosystem and an object that plays an important social and economic role in the region;
- the absence of an efficient fish conservation system to prevent mass poaching, masking catches, and illegal catches;
- a poor level of in-shore processing and high transportation and power costs, resulting in the trading of raw materials;
- an imperfect legislative basis to provide for the real participation of Indigenous people in commercial fishing and conservation of Pacific salmon.

Nevertheless, obshchina leaders and executive and legislative authorities drew from the idea of community development quotas, to discuss the concept of socioeconomic development of Indigenous peoples on the basis of fishery resources.

DEVELOPMENT OF THE "CONCEPT OF SOCIOECONOMIC DEVELOPMENT OF COMMUNITIES OF LOCAL POPULATIONS OF THE COASTAL AREAS OF WESTERN KAMCHATKA"

Working out the "Concept of Socioeconomic Development" will determine the general and specific targets of internal development of the Kamchatka krai. Also to consider and reconcile are the interests and strategic plans of individual businesses, valuation and use of the resource, infrastructure, and geo-economic potential, which will have a synergistic effect on the development of the region for a sustained period of time.

The "Concept of Socioeconomic Development" will concentrate investment resources on priority areas to identify "points of growth" where development will have the greatest effect. In turn, the points of growth will create clusters—groups of related, geographically focused organizations (producers, suppliers, service providers, research institutions, and other organizations that are mutually supportive and reinforce each other's competitive advantage).

The development of key elements of the cluster can stimulate the development of related sectors of the economy, leading to the concentration of the limited resources of the regional budget and privatization of investment in key areas. The consequence of the existing dominant domestic production and territorial organization of the majority of regions in the Russian Federation is the lack of competitive territorial clustering: dynamic and internally competitive networks of localized plants producing the same or related products together and providing a good market position for the country, region, and industry (Zhuravleva, Sharakhmatova, and Yakel 2009).

Like many other regions of the Russian Federation, Kamchatka krai has a dominant mono-profile economy and lacks established territorial clusters. The low spatial mobility of the population of Kamchatka is superimposed on the low qualifying mobility. If a person cannot move in space, following the market offers in his or her professional niche, he or she is forced to change professions to try to meet the employment demands in the place of residence. This immobility leads to a multifaceted situation characterized by

- the mass deprofessionalization of the population;

- losses from earlier gains made by the education investment;
- a general decrease in the quality of vocational education, based on the needs of the previous stage of development of the regional economy or, at best, the current situation;
- temporary but massive losses of the labor force as most people spend time on re-skilling with little hope of finding work.

The "Concept of Socioeconomic Development" for the region will be guided by the desire to improve the administration of all levels (republics, territories, regions, municipalities) in order to improve the welfare of the inhabitants of a given territory by increasing employment in the most productive sectors of the economy. Performance indicators should include (1) the creation of conditions for accelerated socioeconomic development; (2) a decrease in the proportion of the population living below the poverty line; (3) a reduction in differences in per capita income; (4) an increase in the gross regional product per capita; and (5) the development of the social and engineering infrastructure.

If an area has not achieved the status of the reference region, government support should be aimed primarily at ensuring equal access of the population of this territory to the budgetary services, thus implementing the constitutional rights of citizens. Off-budget investments to support strategic projects for regional development should be developed, and selective budget (grant) support for regional initiatives should be provided within the agreed strategic priorities for regional development.

Traditional land use, under the federal law On Traditional Nature Management Territories of the Indigenous Peoples of the North, Siberia and Far East of the Russian Federation, dated May 11, 2001, states: "It is not debilitating to use Indigenous fauna and flora and other natural resources." Traditional livelihoods are defined as the use by Indigenous people of renewable natural resources for direct personal or family consumption as sources of food, clothing, shelters, tools, vehicles. Potential livelihood depends on the biological productivity of ecosystems of the area.

The development of the traditional economy is affected by the choice of organizational forms: a sole proprietorship, limited liability company, production cooperative, joint stock company, community, nonprofit partnership. According to the organizational-legal forms, most traditional farms are nonprofit organizations. In the present condition, it is the only viable form of conducting such activities.

Adverse economic and social conditions in the settlements of Indigenous peoples engender the opacity of economic activity. The roots of this are most often incompetence or lack of managerial skills because of territorial remoteness, and this territorial remoteness deprives tribal communities of the opportunity to obtain reliable and timely information on changes in legislation regulating economic activities, taxation, and so forth.

One of the preferred ways to organize activity, in order to obtain rights to natural resources and tax benefits, is through the community. Its main goal is the protection of the environment and preservation of traditional lifestyles, farming, and crafts. The community is a nonprofit organization and operates in accordance with the federal law On Nonprofit Organization.

THE CONCEPT OF TRIBAL COMMUNITIES WITHIN THE MEANING OF THE FEDERAL LAW

Indigenous peoples are self-organizing persons belonging to small nations and are united by consanguine (family, genus) and territorial-neighborly ties that are created in order to protect their original habitat and conserve and develop traditional lifestyles, farming, fisheries, and culture (see the federal law On General Principles of the Indigenous Communities of the North, Siberia and Far East of the Russian Federation, 2000). The main idea of federal law is to create conditions for the development of local communities of the coastal regions of Kamchatka along with the preservation and reproduction of biodiversity resources of Pacific salmon. Three main problems must be solved within the framework of the concept:

1. The minimization of overfishing of salmon
2. The fight against poaching
3. The promotion of economic development of the local population of coastal regions of Kamchatka

The problem of overfishing should be solved in three ways:

1. Prioritize salmon fishing for personal consumption
2. Reduce the number of companies engaged in production of salmon resources
3. Track volumes of caught and processed salmon

The problem of poaching should be solved simultaneously in the following two ways:

1. Improve the effectiveness of monitoring compliance with legal requirements in fishing areas and markets where fish products are sold

2. Develop a mechanism to control "production-delivery to a processing plant, production, sales of products" that would be overseen by conservation authorities in order to track the volume of salmon resources consumed

The goal of the program of community development for the local coastal populations of Kamchatka is to motivate local governments to monitor compliance with legal requirements. To achieve the greatest social and economic effects of the program's implementation, a rational tax policy that is based on a differentiated approach must also be implemented. In particular, the differentiation principle for the resource region can be applied depending on the relationship between the larger economic environment and the local economies of the region in order to create equal starting conditions for the activities of small businesses in the material sphere. The selected approach will create a favorable entrepreneurial and investment climate in the region and increase the welfare and level of socioeconomic development of municipalities.

In May 2009, based on a resolution of the Russian federal government, the Kamchatka krai was recognized as a traditional territory of Indigenous peoples of the North. Thus, aboriginal peoples of Kamchatka—including Kamchadal peoples living in the southern regions of the peninsula (the Elizovsky, Ust-Bolsheretsky, Milkovsky, Sobolevsky, and Ust-Kamchatsky regions) as well as all other Indigenous peoples of Kamchatka (Koryak, Chukchi, Even, and Itelmen peoples)—received the rights to fish for traditional economic use and subsistence purposes. In the same year, fishing applications were submitted to government officials for Indigenous sites. Of the 330 Indigenous fishing groups referred to as obshchiny who applied, only 19 received fishing permits for economic use.

Based on the fish catch for personal consumption in the territory of Kamchatka in 2009–2010, the Northeastern Territorial Department of the Federal Agency for Fisheries set the volume of output (catch) of Pacific salmon and char to ensure the traditional way of life and traditional economic activities without obtaining the fishing grounds and permission for prey (catch) of living aquatic resources (shown in table 5.1). However, the current situation related to Indigenous peoples fishing in Kamchatka is very complicated. There is a conflict of interest between the business communities and Indigenous people caused by the uncertainty in the boundaries between industrial quotas and quotas for the support of traditional activities of Indigenous peoples.

Table 5.1

Distribution of aquatic biological resources (Pacific salmon) based on personal consumption per person for Indigenous peoples, 2009–2010

Municipality	Population of Indigenous Peoples of the North (peoples)	Total per person 2009 (ton)	Total per person 2010 (ton)
Petropavlovsk-Komandorskaya subzone			
Aleutian area	344	0.16	0.15
Bystrinsky area	1000	0.051	0.048
Milkovsky area	3124	0.041	0.048
Ust-Kamchatsky area	1355	0.058	0.048
Elizovsky area	2211	0.044	0.035
City of Petpropavlovsk-Kamchatsky	3217	0.051	0.035
City of Vilyuchinsk	490	0.044	0.035
Kamchatsk Kurilskay subzone			
Ust-Bolsherazk area	143	0.15	0.13
West Kamchatka subzone			
Penzinsky area	1783	0.115	0.1
Tigilsk area	2461	0.107	0.17
village of Palana	1603	0.055	0.16
Sobolevsky area	526	0.117	0.17
Bustrinsky area	250	0.117	0.17
Karaginskay subzone			
Olutorsky area	2611	0.382	0.255
Karagisnky area	1766	0.345	0.235

Source: Northeastern Territorial Department of Federal Agency for Fisheries, www.terkamfish.ru.

National public policy objectives for the fields of industrial and traditional fishing are fundamentally different, although the socioeconomic development of territories creates the preconditions for preserving traditional ways of life and national culture. The conflict arises when Indigenous communities obtain quotas for free as the basis for normal fishing activities on their own or by contracting with the fishing enterprises. The first option leads to aggravation over limited resources, rising imbalances in resources and fishing opportunities, and the exacerbation of the structural crisis in salmon farming. The second option—in which Indigenous communities form, obtain quotas for salmon, and subsequently resell quotas to fishery enterprises—leads to the capitalization of some groups of Indigenous people. They will receive rent for the use of local natural resources, and the fishery business will serve a specific purpose that, ceteris paribus, leads to a decrease in its profitability and competitiveness (Ksenofontov and Goldenberg 2008).

We need to understand why any local population of Kamchatka krai is trying to get access to traditional fishing resources. One reason is limited access of the local population to aquatic biological resources for personal consumption. Next is the competition over sites for long-term access to commercial fishing. The policy of the Federal Fishery Agency (Rosrybolovstvo) is aimed at consolidation and capitalization of coastal fisheries.

In summary, the existing conflicts of interest between the Indigenous and non-Indigenous population are caused by the situation that the Indigenous population receives free quotas of salmon allocated for the preservation of traditional lifestyles and free fish in the framework of social support programs, but the non-Indigenous population has no such opportunities.

At the present time, the Indigenous peoples of Kamchatka krai are deeply concerned about a message sent from the legislative assembly of Kamchatka krai to B. F. Basargin, the minister of regional development of the Russian Federation, which recommends excluding five southern municipal regions of Kamchatka krai (Ust-Bolsheretsky, Elizovsky, Milkovsky, Sobolevsky, and Ust-Kamchatsky), as well as two urban districts, from the official list of traditional territories and traditional economic use areas of Indigenous peoples of the Russian Federation. These areas are considered traditional territories of Indigenous peoples based on the resolution approved by the Russian federal government on May, 2009 (No. 631-r).

At the open forum of the Association of Indigenous Peoples of the North, Siberia, and Far East of the Russian Federation for Kamchatka krai, held on May 20, 2010, a resolution was adopted to hold an emergency Congress of Indigenous Peoples of Kamchatka Krai on June 3, 2010: "On the implementation of the resolution of the Russian Federal Government on May 8, 2009, No. 631-r." The congress was also concerned with "confirmation of the official list of traditional territories and traditional use areas of Indigenous peoples of the Russian Federation, and the official list of traditional use activities in Kamchatka Krai."

The presidium of the Association of Indigenous Peoples of the North, Siberia, and Far East of the Russian Federation for Kamchatka krai has also responded strongly to a separate initiative by the deputies of the legislative assembly of Kamchatka krai that would introduce changes to the resolution approved by the Russian federal government on May 8, 2009 (No. 631-r). In part, the proposed changes would ban the sales of catches from traditional fisheries by Russian Indigenous peoples of the North and Far East of the Russian Federation.

In October of the same year, a joint meeting of the Working Group (WG) and Presidium Association of Indigenous Peoples of the North, Siberia, and Far East of the Russian Federation was held. Actually, eleven WG meetings and three joint meetings with representatives of the Kamchatka authorities had been held since June 3, 2010. The members of WG had launched their work with the Kamchatka government authorities and the legislative assembly of Kamchatka krai before approving a normative document to form a conciliation commission and to regulate the order of the work that is expected but has not been issued yet.

Participants in the joint meeting decided by common consent to continue the emergency Congress of Indigenous Peoples of Kamchatka Krai and suggested using the rule of legislative initiative for the federal law On the Guarantees of the Rights of Indigenous Numerically Small Peoples of the Russian Federation, which allows the (non-Indigenous) residential permanent population to fish for personal consumption.

The Association of Indigenous Peoples of Kamchatka krai also has launched an initiative to provide ethnological certification of the tribal community for the validation of their representatives' and their stakeholders' Indigenous status. A commission made up of representatives of the Association of Indigenous Peoples of Kamchatka Krai and the Union of Tribal Communities of Kamchatka krai should be formed to work out certifying procedures.

Within the large complex of legislative regulations on fishing and the preservation of aquatic biological resources, the most dramatic situation may be observed in the matters relating to Indigenous peoples' and the local population's access to aquatic biological resources for personal consumption and for their economic activities. Urgent resolution of these access issues is extremely important since we are talking about that part of the country's population for which fishing is not only important, but actually the only possible source of livelihood. Regarding the federal and regional authorities, numerous complaints and petitions have been published in the mass media by citizens, organizations, and Indigenous communities of the North, Siberia, and the Far East who are concerned by the violations of rights to access fishing grounds and water resources.

Problems with the organization of Indigenous fisheries are created by ill-considered legislative and administrative decisions or by the lack thereof. First, the amendments introduced to the existing legislation in late 2007 destroyed the existing system for organizing fishing, which was to ensure the traditional lifestyle and traditional economic activities of Indigenous peoples of the North, Siberia, and the Far East. Then ill-conceived subordinate acts were adopted, and their implementation at the local level often turned out to be disastrous. As a result, the habitual way of life for many people was tragically destroyed.

The fisheries law artificially divided the population into those who are entitled to receive free fishing quotas for their own use (Indigenous peoples) and those who have no such right (non-Indigenous local peoples who live in similar conditions). Thus, we have created an environment that fosters the emergence of not only social, but also ethnic, tensions in the areas inhabited by Indigenous peoples.

The competitive distribution of fishing grounds has created a sharp increase in the number of Indigenous communities, and salmon continues to play a huge role in the lives of Indigenous peoples in Kamchatka. Existing fishing quotas for personal consumption cannot solve the current problem; thus, we must develop mechanisms that will completely satisfy the needs of Indigenous peoples for their ancient staple. This task should be considered a priority. However, we also need to solve the problem of the rights of non-Indigenous Kamchatka-born locals who also rely on fish to some extent.

CONCLUSION

The main problem of the traditional fishery is the decrease of fish resources concurrent with the need to provide the government and business enterprises with the best fishery areas. The high price of transport and other economic difficulties leads to very low profits in the industrial fish sector for both small and large organizations. In the new socioeconomic conditions, the problem of unemployment of Indigenous peoples, young people in particular, remains acute, with most engaged in the gathering of wild plants, fishing, and the hunting of animals and birds.

From 2001 to 2009 the number of associations of Indigenous peoples increased fourfold, reflecting the increasing interest of Indigenous people in the implementation of self-regulation of traditional economic activities in the krai. The number of registered tribal communities exceeds the number of existing ones. But not all tribal communities have adapted to new conditions of management, and one reason for the cessation of activity is the small fishing quotas that did not allow people to recoup the cost of production of fishery resources. The main problem faced by the traditional economy is the lack of material and a technical base.

One of the key, and complex, features of traditional natural resource use by Indigenous peoples in Kamchatka is the fact that these resources are also subject to use by the economy and population of Kamchatka as a whole, where Indigenous minorities make up only 4.3 percent (according to the Russian population census [Yakel 2002]) or 7.0 percent (according to data provided by Kamchatka officials for the Northeastern Territorial Department of the Federal Agency for Fisheries [Yakel 2010]) of the total population.

Government policy can contribute to a revival of traditional lifeways among Indigenous people, especially tribal communities. However, the present situation in Kamchatka is very complex and contradictory, and the traditional way of life is not oriented toward the market economy. Much depends on a change in the mindset and psychology of locals. The decentralization and demonopolization of Kamchatka's economy can contribute to traditional nature management in the North, and against the background of everyday problems, the national-cultural issues retreat to secondary status. With the gradual erosion of national specificity, the problem of preservation of ethnic traditions and cultural heritage of Indigenous peoples is exacerbated.

The revival and further development of Indigenous peoples of the North is impossible without state support. The complexity and uniqueness of their problems require concerted action by all levels of government and their active cooperation with these Indigenous peoples.

The introduction of more complex processes to the current stage of economic development requires the study of the environmental management principles of the Indigenous peoples of the north of Kamchatka. A lack of statistical information on the socioeconomic status of the Indigenous peoples, namely the tribal communities as a form of economic activity, complicates the process.

Therefore, to create conditions for the sustainable economic development of Indigenous communities, projects and businesses should be implemented through the use of natural resources by tribal communities (obshchiny).

The importance and complexity of the problem of socioeconomic development of the Indigenous peoples of the North require a separate office (ministry) for the Development of Indigenous Peoples within the structure of the executive authority. The activities of that authority should be directed at ensuring the flexibility of development management, at complex analysis and formulation of problems, and at centralized development strategy and process implementation.

Notes

1. The UNDP/GEF project Conservation and Sustainable Use of Wild Salmonid Biological Diversity in Russia's Kamchatka Peninsula was developed by the specialist Federal Fisheries Agency (Sevvostrybvod), Moscow State University, with participation by regional environmental NGOs, in order to demonstrate the possibilities of salmon biodiversity conservation and with a view toward the sustainable economic development of the territories, including fisheries.

2. A community in Alaska consists of recognized geographical locations that are governed by a city government or Alaska Native tribe, or in some cases both.

3. RAIPON is a public organization that has as its goal the protection of human rights; defense of the legal interests of Indigenous peoples of the North, Siberia, and Far East; and assistance in solving environmental, social, and economic problems and the problems of cultural development and education. RAIPON works to guarantee the rights of native homelands and traditional ways of life as well as the right to self-governance according to the national and international legal standards. The organization unites forty-one Indigenous groups whose total population is around 250,000 people. These people are represented by thirty-four regional and ethnic organizations that have the authority to represent them in both Russia and the international community. RAIPON's highest body is the Congress of Indigenous Peoples of the North, Siberia, and the Far East of the Russian Federation, which meets every four years. The coordinating council and presidium (consisting of RAIPON's president, the first vice president, and other vice presidents) lead RAIPON's current activity. The president is elected at the RAIPON congress by secret vote and from a ballot that has at least two candidates. All the regional associations' leaders, elected by people in their regions, are members of the coordinating council. RAIPON is built on territorial and territorial-ethnical branches (associations), and these associations are organizationally and financially independent.

6

Deprivations amid Abundance

The Role of Salmon and "Other Natural Resources" in Sustaining Indigenous Aleut Communities

Katherine Reedy-Maschner

INTRODUCTION

"Alaska's Salmon Fishery Certified as Sustainable" announced a press release issued by Alaska's Department of Fish and Game in 2000 (Rue 2000). Their abundance-based, escapement-driven management had finally met the "Principles and Criteria for Sustainable Fishing" standards set by the independent London-based Marine Stewardship Council (MSC). Eco-labels on fish would independently confirm that they were harvested from a well-managed, sustainable fishery, and certification would help boost Alaska's global market share. Quoting Governor Knowles, "The MSC certification confirms our view that Alaska salmon management provides a model for sustainable salmon fisheries worldwide."

This conceptual trend toward sustainability is also deployed in human communities. As a result of the Sustainability of Arctic Communities project,[1] sustainability was defined by arctic peoples through a list of specific conditions and goals. These can be broadly summarized as access to abundant subsistence resources; wage employment that is compatible with human–animal–environmental relationships; self-determination and local control over lands, resources, and politics; education of youth in traditional and Western knowledge systems; cultural preservation and enhancement; and improving infrastructure around the villages (Kofinas and Braund 1996). Sustainability depends upon the conservation of local resources,

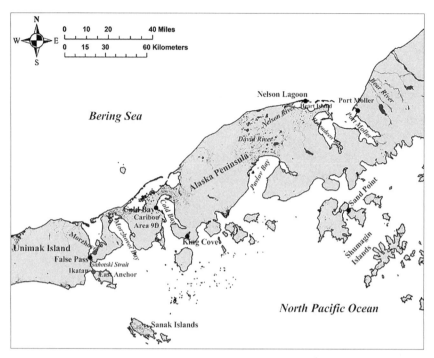

FIGURE 6.1

Map of False Pass and Nelson Lagoon regions. Source: Katherine Reedy-Maschner.

local communities' access to, respect for, and control of those resources, and people having both the money and the ability to maintain their homes in stable communities.

In March 2010, while sitting out another storm at the Bering Inn in the Aleut village of Nelson Lagoon, Alaska, I had time to think about the sustainability of this village, its salmon fishery, its history, and its future in light of the aforementioned conditions and goals, as well as through the lens of the salmon industry's "sustainable" global reputation of the past decade. Nelson Lagoon is a small village located on the shore of the Bering Sea in semi-vegetated black volcanic sand dunes (figure 6.1). The village is on a sand spit, making erosion a concern since an extreme high tide occasionally breaches sections between the lagoon and Bering Sea, and the inhabitants "are on an island sometimes," said elder Sherman Johnson of Nelson Lagoon (interview with author, August 19, 2009). Like its neighbors on the Alaska Peninsula, Nelson Lagoon is a commercial salmon fishing village, with a local fleet of about twenty-five boats. The primary salmon buyer is a cannery 25 mi across the lagoon that operates five months of the

FIGURE 6.2

F/V Julia Marie, *Nelson Lagoon, Alaska, August 2009. A boat out of water. Source: Katherine Reedy-Maschner.*

year processing mostly sockeye, king, and coho salmon. Most of the Nelson Lagoon fleet fishes by set gill net inside the lagoon, targeting sockeye in June and July and coho from August into September. They set their nets 1,800 ft apart by "gentleman's agreement" for fairness and space. A cannery tender vessel comes into the lagoon to collect fish from these boats and move the fish to its facility, paying the fishermen by the pound harvested, which is variable by species. Because of the protected lagoon, the fleet consists of both boat and skiff gill net fishermen, including women. There is no harbor, but locals anchor their boats in "the river," a channel that forms at low tide between the sand bars and the spit, or tie up to the dock during the fishing season, and they pull their boats up on land for storage in a dockside boatyard or next to their houses in the village off-season or when unable to fish (figure 6.2). Salmon is also a subsistence resource, and villagers take fish home from their commercial nets for smoking, salting, drying, freezing, and sharing. Other subsistence foods are harvested throughout the lagoon system.

This situation sounds good. All the concerns for community sustainability in the Arctic appear to be met. Nelson Lagoon is a small village with a seasonal, renewable economic base in salmon. Friends and relatives fish together on locally owned boats in local waters. The processor is close by, and fishermen can go home to their families at night after a day's catch has been delivered. Subsistence resources can be found throughout the area. The village has modern services: a school, a health clinic, and an airport. It is also part of a community development program that provides money for fisheries infrastructure, business opportunities, and educational and vocational scholarships for youth and that encourages socioeconomic self-sufficiency. Yet, the future of the village is in doubt.

False Pass is a nearby Aleut village with all the same attributes of Nelson Lagoon, but it also has access to commercial cod, pollock, herring, crab, and halibut fisheries. It has an active port—a crossroads for fishermen—with frequent barge service and a monthly summer ferry. A processor is located in the community and operates for the summer salmon season. A new harbor, dock, grocery store, liquor store, landfill, and an expanded airport have all been built. Whereas Nelson Lagoon meets the minimum requirements for sustainability, False Pass surpasses the requirements yet is failing, too.

How is it that the abundance, reliability, and "sustainability" of salmon are no longer supporting small Indigenous communities of coastal Alaska? Even with the best conditions that many other arctic villages dream about, the future of these villages is uncertain. What, then, are the implications for models of sustainability? How can sustainability be achieved? What or who should be sustained? Analogous languages of sustainability are applied to both humans and fisheries but for distinct purposes. The sustainability certification from the MSC has nothing to do with social conditions of Alaskan communities and is based on limited social data. The goals identified for human communities constitute unrealistic wish lists that, even if achieved, will likely sustain no one.

In this chapter I examine the development of the role of salmon in the eastern Aleutian region and explore its relationship to two small villages that are becoming increasingly aware of their vulnerability and mortality. This growing alienation from salmon can be linked to structural elements, including state fishing policies, the commoditized right to fish, a growing and self-traditionalizing transient fleet, cultural logics that devalue processing labor, and market efficiency goals. By focusing on the needs and perspectives of local villages, and their experiences with environmental management, capital improvements, subsistence and market resources, settlement history, and culture, we can expose the local–global constraints that make sustainability a difficult, and potentially meaningless, objective.

Constraints on salmon-fishing access and profitability have contributed to local interest in other resource developments (including the recently canceled offshore petroleum exploration) that could provide capital so that traditional fishing can remain intact. Even as people formulate strategies to improve their quality of life, new barriers and challenges appear.

SUSTAINABLE MANAGEMENT

Sustainability and sustainable development have been controversial as top-down approaches to ecosystem management (e.g., Escobar 1995; Sachs 1992) and as more successful localized applications supporting human and environmental systems (e.g., Crate 2006). Salmon-dependent communities are rarely of dominant concern in village sustainability models. Caribou- or reindeer-dependent villages, for example, rely on the health and strength of the herds and are vulnerable to climate change, petroleum development, land disputes, and political shifts, among other factors (e.g., Anderson 2000; Kruse et al. 2004; Vitebsky 2005). Whaling-dependent communities must contend with sea ice changes, whale population dynamics, international regulation, and environmentalists (Caulfield 1997). But salmon in the north are for the most part renewable, predictable, and harvested in mass quantities for subsistence and commercial ends, including a global market in all five species. The problem for coastal villages, however, is that the salmon are managed for biological health, not for how they support people economically, socially, or politically (Hilborn 2006; Robards and Greenburg 2007). As Charles Menzies (chapter 8, this volume) has described for British Columbia historically, Alaska's salmon are intentionally managed for greater productivity, creating harvestable surpluses (to follow the agricultural metaphor [Smith, chapter 1, this volume]) that *must* be collected for the health of the runs and streambeds and the people who are economically dependent on them. Yet local deprivations also exist amid this abundance.

Managers of aquatic systems often consider the role of resource-dependent communities, but the communities and their fishing cultures are not the focus for direct support. In many cases, Indigenous peoples' presence on the landscape, their knowledge, and their adaptive use of natural resources has contributed to long-term conservation (e.g., Stevens 1997; Western and Wright 1994), and in places where people are either removed from the land and resources or denied the flexibility to deal with changes to them, both the resources and the people suffer (e.g., Igoe 2004). In recent history, attempts to regulate Alaska's salmon fisheries to make them economically viable and keep access in local hands, such as the Limited Entry Permit plan of 1974, generated overcapitalization. Capacity and harvesting costs increased as the value of salmon and fishermen's earnings declined and the processing industry consolidated (Hilborn 2006). Further, Alaska's market share has been reduced by the farmed sector, and the values of both wild and farmed salmon have subsequently declined in tandem (Valderrama and Anderson 2010). New schemes to stay competitive favor quality control and efficiencies that are more easily achieved with privatization and total allowable catch (TAC) limits. The fisheries management goals of biologists require only that the fleet is efficient and easy to manage.

INSTITUTIONALIZED INFLEXIBILITY

A cursory history of eastern Aleutian villages and salmon fisheries offers a framework for this discussion.[2] Thin Point, Ikatan, Morzhovoi, Dora Harbor, Herendeen Bay, Port Moller, Sanak, Pauloff Harbor, Kasaska, Belkofski, Bear River, Ilnik, Unga, Squaw Harbor, Pirate Cove, and Wosnessenski are all Aleut villages in the Alaska Peninsula/eastern Aleutian region that were permanently abandoned at various times during the twentieth century for other villages in the region. The demise of each community was due to a change in fisheries or marine mammal economics. Thin Point, Unga, Sanak, and Pauloff Harbor had mixed cod- and salmon-salting operations that were no longer viable after the cod fisheries collapsed in the 1930s. Morzhovoi, Wosnessenski, Herendeen Bay, and Belkofski were sea otter–hunting stations, then trapping sites, and later participated in salmon fishing but were abandoned for larger communities springing up around salmon processors. Belkofski, Bear River, Ikatan, Pirate Cove, Unga, and Ilnik each had salmon fisheries but were not chosen as sites for supporting the salmon industry, and so people relocated to processor communities. The locations and economies of the modern communities of King Cove, Sand Point, False Pass, and Nelson Lagoon are directly related to the salmon industry; each formed in the twentieth century around canneries in prime locations for commercial fisheries. Many residents of these communities today were born or lived in a now defunct village in their younger days. The rise and relative stability of twentieth-century villages reflects the rise of salmon industry infrastructure.[3]

Villages in this region have thus emerged, closed down, relocated, dwindled, and expanded in the past century, but many of these same residents are still living in the region. Perhaps flexibility was a sensible strategy for life in the North Pacific–Bering Sea. The people who live here were sedentary but became mobile when it was practical to do so, when maintaining a living in their current location became too difficult and opportunities arose elsewhere. The abandonment of so many villages might appear to be a disturbing trend, what Chuck Martinson of False Pass observed as a sad tale of loss, since "tribes are now located in other villages" (interview with author, February 26, 2010).[4] Movement and economic shifts could be interpreted as testaments to Aleut resilience, which may have been true in the past, but today "whole cultures are under threat" according to Martinson (February 26, 2010), since there are fewer places left to go.

The Alaska Native Claims Settlement Act (ANCSA) of 1971 established permanent land boundaries, ending this flexibility of the early cannery period. Land selections were made by villages, cities, tribes, corporations, and the federal and state governments. ANCSA resulted in greater land and resource rights, local political authority, and investments in infrastructure, but it also had the effect of locking villages into specific locations, and "as global markets evolve and transform, producers associated with more sedentary village infrastructure are forced to adapt in place" (Robards and Greenburg 2007:25). Survival does not depend totally on land, and villages have not lost their cultures with each village desertion, but the flexibility of the past has been constrained as small villages cannot relocate in part or whole, and people instead migrate to larger communities or out to urban centers. Canneries can no longer easily set up shop in locations convenient to the harvests, as they did in False Pass and Nelson Lagoon in the early and mid-twentieth century. Aleut residents made village corporation land selections from available government lands surrounding village sites at the time of the legislation. The Isanotski Corporation in False Pass, for example, selected nearly the entire strip along both sides of Isanotski Strait between the Gulf of Alaska and the Bering Sea. Distantly owned selections are used for subsistence hunting, fishing, and trapping by shareholders and are sometimes preserved as habitat by the corporations. Land trades and sales have occurred since ANCSA; for example, in the 1980s the Nelson Lagoon Corporation traded with the US Fish & Wildlife Service sections of marsh for better hunting grounds, and in 2009 the Isanotski Corporation sold to a conservation group swan habitat lands that are managed by the US Fish & Wildlife Service. Acreage owned by the corporations has generally declined through sales and land trades.

ANCSA also had a less obvious effect on these communities by shaping harvest regulatory regimes with legal definitions of "customary and traditional" that limit the range of practices and species used that can be considered "Native" and ultimately closing off innovation and enterprise that could meet the needs of the present (Loring and Gerlach 2010). Alaska Natives may use these definitions as sources of power to maintain access to land and "country food." However, "it is the strategy of flexibility, and spatial and temporal patterns of land use, that is most traditional to these peoples, far more so than the specific harvest technologies and even the particular harvested animals" (Loring and Gerlach 2010:193). In the decades following ANCSA anthropologists have affirmed these narrow definitions of subsistence activities by not documenting the full scope of activities. This absence has subsequently been internalized by Alaska Natives in order to maintain rights to certain species and land and incorporated by regulatory entities into their management of access and rights.

If certain practices are not documented or embraced as part of the Alaska Native repertoire, how can we expect creation of regulations that provide for these practices? This current state of institutionalized inflexibility is implicated in the alienation of salmon access because "customary and traditional" does not include commercialization. Diversification into other fisheries (cod, herring, and crab, for example)—species that are abundant, valuable, and part of the Aleut fishing heritage—is still not part of the established record of the Aleut cultural matrix. Thus commercial fisheries in general are treated as new economic developments to which Alaska Natives do not have traditional claims. But False Pass and Nelson Lagoon are not just dependent on commercial fisheries, these fisheries are part of their culture. These Aleuts do not restrict themselves to those practices covered by ANCSA and instead have tried to change the ways government understands the necessity of a wide range of subsistence and commercial practices to their lives and communities.

These political conditions have only barely distressed the Aleut fishermen who continue to fish whether their practice satisfies traditional criteria or not, but their frustration with access is growing. For decades local and transient fishermen have fished alongside one another, even collaborating on the fishing grounds. In the smaller villages, however, the limited number of permits, the rates of transfer away from villages, the lack of "right of first refusal" to buy permits locally, and the general open market for permits has changed the ratios of local to transient. Inequalities of permit access, fishing territories, attention from processors, and influence on fisheries managers have driven emerging tensions.

ALEUT VILLAGES AND SALMON

The salmon fishery became a socioeconomic base in eastern Aleut villages, replacing the cod fishery after World War II. Since their founding, these villages have relied on salmon for sociocultural, political, and economic needs (Reedy-Maschner 2010). In every household, salmon dominate palates, tables, freezers and pantries, and labor efforts. Coolers of salmon are standard luggage and air freight as fish are sent out to relatives and friends living away from the villages. Children compete with one another for the best parts of salmon and choose these foods over mass-produced commodities, especially when they are first available in the season. Salmon are central to every celebration, birthday, anniversary, and holiday but are also the everyday food. Relations are structured by access to the salmon fishery, where men strive to be boat captains or crew on top boats, women seek out successful fishermen as partners and may fish themselves, and children want to follow in their parents' footsteps. Top fishermen direct most political decisions in the communities. Salmon provides them with greater economic stability than many of their contemporaries but also brings a measure of vulnerability as access to the fish and their marketability fluctuate. The salmon industry has changed to meet a globalized market where the fish circulate in wide networks: salmon from Aleut harvests could land at the house next door or as far away as Japan.

False Pass and Nelson Lagoon are both small villages dependent on salmon fisheries and facing looming desertion.[5] Both formed along with the developing salmon fishery infrastructure. Nelson Lagoon was chosen as a territorial school site in 1960 and is located next to a major salmon-producing system with cannery operations across the lagoon. False Pass has a longer history, having formed in 1917 with the opening of a P. E. Harris cannery. This cannery went through multiple owners, the last being Peter Pan Seafoods. The facility burned in 1981 and thereafter remained only a supply base and fueling station, indicating a locally understood "disregard" for False Pass and a corporate desire to concentrate operations in King Cove.

The salmon industry is largely controlled by transnational corporations. The canneries did not directly invest in the welfare of the villages in which they were situated. Instead, canneries kept communities, laborers, and fishermen in debt systems and controlled local access to products and services from the moment they were installed. This continues today, as cash advances on fishing efforts are often issued at the start of the season and paid off during the summer. In Nelson Lagoon, this cash advance coincides with a spring barge.

The limited entry permit regime, though initially a scramble to qualify during which some fishermen unjustly lost out (to a "cartel" between permit distributors and qualifiers, as elder Alex Samuelson put it [interview with author, January 13, 2000]), is now scarcely controversial in the villages (as opposed to conditions in the Kodiak archipelago, see Carothers, chapter 7, this volume) because currently active fishermen or their fathers fared well in the initial permit distribution. Those who initially lost out are a minority in the villages; others have left the communities, their complaints silenced. Decades later, salmon access is being redistributed once again, with limited entry shaping the results and the compositions of the villages. A fixed number of permits are traded on the open market, making them increasingly likely to be purchased by those living outside the villages. Since there can be no local or Native entitlement to the commercial resource, rights to harvest salmon are purchased and maintained. Similar to other coastal community trends (Donkersloot 2005), the loss of permits from Aleut and local hands has been dramatic since 1975 (see also Reedy-Maschner 2007, 2008). Permits are typically sold due to the cost burdens of fishing or lost as a result of poor financial decisions by the fishermen. Aleut fishermen see these losses both as having structural roots and as individual failures.

These villages and the Aleutians East Borough in which they reside depend almost exclusively on a raw fish tax. Pounds harvested within the borough are taxed for its benefit and the benefit of the various villages, so the size and performance of the fleet, not its composition, is what matters. The borough treats a transient "outside" fleet as equal to residents in this regard. The fleets have expanded both in size and harvest capacity, some even skirting the vessel length limit laws by widening and deepening their boats.

Villages and the borough seek funds for docks and harbors, airport improvements, and other infrastructure. Capital improvement projects amount to millions of dollars invested in the region, and one might expect the state to be committed to maintaining communities and protecting their investments. But the state is not seen as directly supporting the fisheries' economic base in the villages, and some local people have interpreted the funds as "hush money," as if their eroding fisheries access might hurt less with shiny new infrastructure. The concern today is that the infrastructure can no longer be supported, and human mobility is no longer an option.

Nelson Lagoon

The region in which the present-day village of Nelson Lagoon is located was used traditionally by Aleuts for fish camps and hunting grounds. A few families lived on the Nelson Lagoon spit prior to its founding, but the majority lived in Herendeen Bay. Arthur Johnson, ancestor to many modern families, ran a saltery in the late 1800s in Nelson Lagoon. A Pacific American Fisheries cannery/saltery was built on Egg Island, a tiny island in the lagoon, and operated between 1906 and 1923. Five commercial fish traps were built in the lagoon (later outlawed by the Statehood Act of 1959) and one in a channel that forms at low tide, a tender moved the fish to the cannery, and a potable water barge brought freshwater from upriver. This facility was then moved to Port Moller in 1923 under Pacific American Fisheries, which later became Peter Pan Seafoods, Inc., and residents and fishermen remained scattered around the lagoon, coming together only during commercial fishing seasons. In the 1950s four families lived in Herendeen Bay and operated two small fish canneries. At the end of the decade, they and others in the lagoon region began to coalesce around the modern town site of Nelson Lagoon. Beginning in 1960, families from the nearby Port Moller, Bear River, Herendeen Bay, and Ilnik regions moved to Nelson Lagoon where a town grew up around a school.

Commercial fishing was the primary occupation of the families, and salmon-fishing boats operated between Nelson Lagoon and Bear River, earning a solid income from the sockeye salmon fishery. Boats were typically 32 ft long and privately owned, which was an improvement from the decades before in which small wooden boats were leased from Pacific American Fisheries. The fish-processing vessel *Akutan* came into the lagoon to buy, fillet, and freeze fish.

Nelson Lagoon is thus a new village site but is led by families who have been in Herendeen Bay or Port Moller for generations. Today the population totals fifty-two (82 percent Native Aleuts; United States Census Bureau 2010). In 2009 twenty-three residents held twenty-six commercial salmon fishing permits, the majority of which were set gill net.[6] Nelson Lagoon retains its village status. Aleut villages that incorporated as cities wanted the ability to tax a cannery, but here there was nothing to tax, and residents hoped village status would help them maintain their lifestyle.

One cannot acquire basic necessities in the villages without experiencing some level of sticker shock. In the early 1980s, Nelson Lagoon still had no store or post office. Residents waited in the spring for the *North Star III*, the supply ship that brought fishing equipment, housewares, lumber, vehicles, fuel, and food. No store exists today, and the village still receives one barge per year at enormous freight costs. Port Moller is the landing site of a barge from Seattle that brings food and supplies for the facility and for Nelson Lagoon in the summer months. Most food is air freighted from Cold Bay on a constant basis, and residents have experienced numerous fuel shortages because they must plan for the whole year.

Although it is a salmon-fishing community, the primary subsistence food for Nelson Lagoon used to be caribou. The second-ranked food for the community was goose. Today, hunting both species is prohibited by regulation due to population concerns.[7] People subsist on fish and buy crab and cod from King Cove, but most meat is ordered "from outside" now, although moose are occasionally hunted in the area. Families generally put up fish by freezing, smoking, and salting and share the labor since not everyone owns a smokehouse.

Nelson Lagoon does not have access to a greater variety of sea life due partly to its location. People do not harvest many sea mammals there in part because the Scandinavians who intermarried with the Indigenous population were not interested in them, and their descendants did not develop the taste. Sea otters instead are competition for clams and sea urchins. However, residents maintain hunting cabins around the lagoon and along the Bering Sea coast. Bird hunters go after ducks, brants, emperor and Canada geese, and ptarmigan. Berries are harvested by the gallon, especially salmonberries, mossberries, and wild strawberries.

Poor commercial salmon seasons affect subsistence in a negative way. Rather than retain more subsistence fish, people in Nelson Lagoon instead tend to "deliver every one you got for every penny," said Ray Johnson (interview with author, August 20, 2009). To put it in more concrete terms, "One fish equals one gallon of gas; three fish used to buy a whole drum" (August 20, 2009). The price of fuel ($5.71 per gallon of gasoline in 2009) negatively affects harvesting range. Sharing remains a key feature of relationships in Nelson Lagoon and incorporates everything from fish to labor to fuel and groceries.

Nelson Lagoon Fisheries

The composition of the salmon fleet is a critical variable for the success of Nelson Lagoon fishermen. The Port Moller North Peninsula fishery is dominated by a group called Concerned Area M Fishermen (CAMF). A few locals from the region are part of CAMF, but it is largely an "outsider" fleet whose members reside in other parts of Alaska and Washington State. Only a few CAMF fishermen ever come in to Nelson Lagoon. They are locally called the "Northern Fleet" or the "Moller Fleet" and pejoratively the "Unconcerned Area M Fishermen." Today the fleet has 147 boats; in 1974 it had 47. "You can't put any more permits in here," observed Ray Johnson of Nelson Lagoon (interview with author, August 20, 2009). The Northern Fleet fishes hard, around the clock during openings, with multiple crewmen on board. People in Nelson Lagoon harbor strong resentment toward this fleet: "They come in for three weeks, make sixty or seventy grand, and take off. We make thirty grand, but both spouses need to work here" (Leslie Nelson, interview with author, August 18, 2009). Fish migrate into the Bering Sea and go north toward Bristol Bay before coming toward the shore and turning south. Thus, the Northern Fleet impacts the southbound run into Nelson Lagoon. The Northern Fleet is stretched out 100 mi long, and Ray Johnson noted, "They can intercept our fishery in a great way" (interview with author, August 20, 2009). Nelson Lagoon fishermen estimate they have lost 60 percent of the harvestable surplus in the lagoon in recent years because of outside interception.[8]

Transient fishermen on the North Peninsula need not pass through a village on their way to and from the cannery or the fishing grounds and may barge their boats to and from Alaska, never storing them there. Since the members of CAMF can operate entirely without setting foot in an Aleut community, they generally do not have a sense of their own impact, nor any doubts about the appropriateness of their roles. CAMF is also self-traditionalizing, having fished the region for multiple generations now, and makes its own historical claims to the fishery.

Because Nelson Lagoon is a terminal fishery, the fishery "on the outside"—that is, CAMF—can have a dramatic impact on the fishery inside the lagoon. The outside fishery now opens in June instead of July, and its range up the peninsula between Nelson Lagoon and Meshik Bay has expanded. "Fifteen years ago, we took one million fish in Nelson Lagoon. We live here! They can go back and get other jobs. We have no options," said Justine Gundersen of Nelson Lagoon (interview with author, August 19, 2009). "Fishing is going to the dogs," stated Leslie Nelson (interview with author, August 18, 2009). When locals buy groceries and fuel on credit from Peter Pan Seafoods and then fish all summer to try to pay it off, their situation becomes even more difficult. People have built up debt even before the season starts.

In 2009 coho (silver salmon) fetched $0.25 per pound, and fishermen received $0.85 per pound for sockeye. Peter Pan Seafoods in Port Moller is the only local buyer for these fishermen, so market competition does not work in their favor. No local people work in the processing plant, nor do they want to; instead, Peter Pan Seafoods supports about three hundred migrant employees working three shifts.

Nelson Lagoon participates in the federal community development quota (CDQ) program APICDA (Aleutian Pribilof Islands Community Development Quota), which guarantees fisheries allocations and royalties from Bering Sea and Aleutian Islands fisheries to participating communities.[9] This village receives benefits primarily through profit sharing and the development of a storage company for boats and gear. Economic diversification is virtually non-existent. Two small companies of people in Nelson Lagoon sell smoked salmon out of their houses, which they make using alder and cottonwood driftwood (a scarce resource), but business is difficult for these types of enterprises because they have to market outside the village.

False Pass

False Pass is an Aleut village located on the eastern end of Unimak Island facing Isanotski Strait. Isanax, "The Pass" in Aleut, was renamed False Pass because of the difficulty of navigating the channel. Established in 1917 around a P. E. Harris cannery with residents from the dwindling nearby villages of Morzhovoi and Ikatan and from Sanak Island, the community has been a small commercial fishing port for the past century. Today, the community struggles to stay viable; False Pass has an official population of thirty-five (63 percent Aleut; United States Census Bureau 2010), but several families return for fishing in the summer. Only six local fishermen held seven commercial salmon fishing permits in 2009, with a few additional permit holdings in halibut, cod, and herring fisheries.

The salmon cannery was the focal point of False Pass, and the cannery company owned fish traps nearby. It processed salmon, crab, and other Bering Sea and Pacific Ocean fish but was always a smaller operation than the facility in King Cove. Food and supply orders came to the cannery store on the *M/V Dolphin* from Seattle, a small monthly barge. The P. E. Harris facility was sold to Pacific American Fisheries and later to Peter Pan Seafoods. When Peter Pan burned in 1981, the False Pass economy struggled. Commercial fishing remained the local focus, but fishermen deliver to tenders for the King Cove plant, and some people moved to King Cove and Sand Point permanently. The old Peter Pan Seafoods facility and dock (figure 6.3) is now a fueling station with one operator.

The village itself is in danger of becoming a ghost town. A school was built in False Pass in 1929 but did not operate every year as the number of children in the community fluctuated; the school in Ikatan operated until 1956, and many families moved between communities. The current school has struggled to stay open with only a few children (three for the 2009–2010 academic year). Recent out-migration has been caused by partners leaving failed relationships (with their children), youth choosing to attend school in Anchorage, and others leaving for work. Several recent "younger deaths" that were alcohol related also contribute to the decline. Despite this drop in population, the city has still secured improvement monies for a planned airport expansion, a new landfill, a new liquor store, a new harbor, and new crab pot storage space from the harbor dredge.[10] Revenue is generated from a fish tax and mooring fees related to the harbor facility. Four boats hold slips year-round.

Figure 6.3

Old Peter Pan Seafoods, Inc. sign lying in the tundra, False Pass, Alaska, August 2009. Source: Katherine Reedy-Maschner.

No one is purely subsistence oriented given greater access to and desire for Western foods. Salmon is the main subsistence food, followed by halibut and an abundance of berries that are picked right in town. People go *bidarki* (chiton) picking all year, gather sea (urchin) eggs, catch octopus, and collect *pushki* (cow parsnip) and *petrushki* (wild parsley). Other prize foods are seal oil and *ulla* (whale meat that is scavenged from beached whales, not hunted), which is usually traded in from other communities such as King Cove. Like on the Alaska Peninsula, caribou hunting is closed on Unimak Island; families used to take two to three each year. People also frequently hunt waterfowl on Unimak Island. Sharing is frequent; as Eric Weber of False Pass said, "It is a responsibility of mine. I have the ability and the opportunity" (interview with author, August 14, 2009). For those who do not hunt and fish, access depends upon their relationships with the harvesters.

Some families order groceries from Seattle once or twice a year, but freight prices make this practice very expensive. Some also shop for groceries at the costly local store. No credit is extended at the store unless one is working on a boat. Fuel costs concern everyone. A 50 gal drum of oil costs

$500 and lasts only a month. The village is now so spread out along the shore that a vehicle is necessary, as is gasoline. Fear of bears and wolves also necessitates the use of cars.

False Pass Fisheries. Fishing occurs on the Pacific side or in the pass during short openings from June to August. Peter Pan Seafoods in King Cove sends tenders, vessels that move fish from boats to canneries, over to the False Pass area to collect fish off the boats. A tender operated by the seafood processor SnoPac also motors down from Bristol Bay.

False Pass also participates in APICDA. In 2000 APICDA-funded Bering Pacific Seafoods opened as a local cooperative cannery, but it closed after two years. It reopened for the 2008, 2009, and 2010 salmon seasons. BP, as it is called, is primarily a salmon "slime line," which is a fish-gutting and fish-cleaning assembly line to ready fish for market, and it has a mixed reputation with the region's fishermen for its fish prices and procedures. BP hires workers at $9 per hour and provides housing, food, and transportation. Although it provides some economic relief in the form of profit sharing, local Aleut John Shellikoff, who gave me a tour of town, said, "Outsiders work there," as he drove me past the cannery (interview with author, August 14, 2009).

Commercial fishing issues weigh heavily on False Pass as a community and as a fishery (Reedy-Maschner 2010). In the late 1990s and early 2000s, the False Pass fishery became hotly contested by people of the Arctic-Yukon-Kuskokwim and Bristol Bay regions who accused False Pass of intercepting salmon bound for those streams. "False Pass was a convenient target," Eric Weber said (interview with author, August 14, 2009). The controversy and subsequent fluctuations in fishing regulations for the Area M fishery added stress to an already volatile and fragile community.

Fishermen complain that they used to fish only in the summer to make a living but now must fish all year long. Only a few men in False Pass fish cod commercially even though they are located near prime fishing grounds. Cod fishery traditions were lost to the future generations through the North Pacific Fisheries Management Council (NPFMC) management allocations. "Handliners" were cod fishermen of the late nineteenth and early twentieth centuries who fished commercially from dories using handlines. These men married locally and are ancestors to many in the region. As Eric Weber said, "Our fathers and grandfathers were handliners. It's in my heritage but where's my portion?" (interview with author, August 14, 2009).

Locals describe crab fishing as a "huge tragedy," referring to the 2005 rationalization of the fishery. That year, the crab fisheries were restructured by the NPFMC to give quotas to both vessels and processors based on historical participation, effectively reducing the crab fleet by 75 percent. In 2008, perhaps 85 boats fished in what had previously been a 350-boat fishery. False Pass collected a fishery tax on a Peter Pan Seafoods floating processor that was put across the bay in season, sold fuel and hanging bait to crab fishermen, and offered pot storage. A local man worked by making alterations on the pots for the different fisheries and species. Industries within the industry have dwindled or no longer exist. Before rationalization, five thousand pots were stored in False Pass. Now twenty-two hundred crab pots for forty-six boats are stored there. Two False Pass men participate in crabbing, but most subsistence crab comes to the village by way of charity from the crab fleet, illegal harvests, or *purchases* from Peter Pan Seafoods in King Cove. Because "customary and traditional" use of crab was never documented, few legal provisions exist for local access.

SUSTAINABLE SALMON FISHERIES?

Salmon (and other) fisheries are moving out of local hands as people and the salmon infrastructure relocate to larger villages. Maintaining viable villages seems to be a goal only for the villagers themselves, and they lack compelling arguments and population strength to move the centers of salmon fisheries back to their villages. Gerald Sider (2003) in his study of Newfoundland found that a professionalization of the cod fishery by the Canadian government undermined the inshore fleets and villages, and a comparable local neglect is occurring even without deliberate policy objectives. The borough tax base is unaffected by a dwindling local fleet, and the canneries have a reliable fleet of nonlocal "hard fishermen" supplying them,[11] so no one is motivated to consciously support the local communities.

APICDA was intended to provide fisheries-related economic development and "support sustainable and diversified local economies" (Shellikoff 2009). While the program has "success stories," local situations reveal enormous concerns. The shoreside processing plant constructed in False Pass had a goal of providing needed jobs to local villagers, but no locals are employed there, nor do they want to be. APICDA is now pursuing the direct marketing of frozen fish from Nelson Lagoon in order to fly it out of the village instead of Port Moller, having grown weary of Peter Pan Seafood's apparent disinterest in the success of their community. This new plan would involve putting a processor in the village very similar to the one already found in False Pass. Local people are interested in the plant as competition for Peter Pan and as a guaranteed buyer for their fish, but hard lessons are being learned in False Pass where the plant loses money. And this plant would also be unlikely to employ local people because they have no interest in that type of low-status work.

The pollock fishery is the primary source of revenue for APICDA, but it operates under stricter rules to avoid salmon bycatch, which could potentially lower APICDA revenue. The CDQ program also builds up infrastructure, which then must be maintained. "APICDA's job is to spend money, not make money," said one False Pass fisherman (interview with author, August 16, 2009), which he believed leads to poor business practices. He noted that APICDA investments are losing money "by the hundreds of thousands," yet the organization justifies the loss because the communities' tax bases still benefit. In places like Kamchatka, where these models are being reproduced, we must ask if CDQs will work at all (Sharakhmatova, chapter 5, this volume).

Revisiting the wish list produced from the sustainability project, we see that both communities have access to abundant subsistence resources. Even though they cannot hunt caribou and emperor goose, they harvest multiple other birds and fish. Both communities have wage employment in fishing that is compatible with human–animal–environment relationships, but retaining salmon permits locally is difficult, and crab and halibut are managed by quotas that are largely in the hands of a transient fleet. Employment in processing is available to both communities, but these jobs are low status and undesirable. ANCSA and its emergent political structures provided some measure of local control over lands, resources, and politics, but this control is limited to corporation lands, subsistence resources, and internal politics. The CDQ program offers scholarships for the training and education of youth in areas that can support their communities, but an out-migration of those with skills and education is the unfortunate result. The CDQ, borough, and municipal governments pursue a great deal of funding to improve infrastructure to the villages at a constant rate, but this infrastructure must be maintained by the community. For a village of sixty-four people to gain monies for a new harbor, shore plant, landfill, and an expanded airport in recent years only to lose even more of its population in the meantime (thirty-five residents in the 2010 census) shows socioeconomic failure.

The Aleuts are not unique in this situation. The trends of decreasing local ability to benefit from healthy stocks identified for Bristol Bay (Robards and Greenburg 2007) are evident here, but with added layers of localized constraints. Thus, development projects that threaten the very resources the Aleuts have relied on are now becoming attractive enterprises.

PETROLEUM AS THE AREA'S "OTHER NATURAL RESOURCES"

In 2007 an 8,700 sq mi parcel of outer continental shelf adjacent to Nelson Lagoon was opened for petroleum leasing. If developed, several offshore platforms in the Bering Sea may connect to a pipeline across the peninsula and then to a liquid natural gas terminal on the Pacific side. Aleut interest in offshore development is the result of people out-migrating for work, difficulties in keeping schools open, a depressed salmon fleet, fear of turning into a "welfare state," and villages becoming ghost towns. Salmon fishing can no longer be someone's sole income, and other fisheries are experiencing restructuring that decreases local opportunities to "move laterally." Thus, many locals are interested in developing their "other natural resources" in order to "help maintain our traditional fishing way of life" (Aleutians East Borough 2008).

In March 2010, however, the federal government again placed a moratorium on the North Aleutian Basin and canceled any planned lease sales. The three years of planning nonetheless show both the anxiety of the communities and their commitment to the fisheries. Local leaders imposed a series of mitigation measures aimed at protecting fish resources. They hoped that development would provide extra funding, not replace commercial fishing, to offset declines in fisheries revenue. Leaders spearheading the negotiation were also fishermen and never intended to leave the business for platform work. Nelson Lagoon leader Justine Gundersen instead expected positive outcomes in revenue sharing that would "create entrepreneurship," job development, and infrastructure to "let us survive" (interview with author, August 19, 2009). False Pass leaders were optimistic about the village serving as staging grounds for oil and gas development and spill response. By considering petroleum "other natural resources," they seemed to be diffusing the risks for themselves.

Others were fearful of the prospects. If managed properly, salmon is considered a renewable resource that will last forever, but oil is finite. "Oil and gas has come a long way in safety, but not far enough," said one False Pass man (interview with author, August 16, 2009). Attitudes were shifting in Nelson Lagoon where 40 percent of the population was estimated to be against the development in 2010. Fishermen spoke of the difficulties in getting salmon escapement in the Nelson Lagoon system and their fears that fishing "will dry up" (interview with author, August 20, 2009). Ray Johnson said, "You add oil and gas leases on top of that and now you got something to worry about" (interview with author, August 20, 2009).

Residents of Bristol Bay and Nelson Lagoon visited offshore platforms and fishing communities in Sakhalin in 2009 as part of a global reconnaissance of petroleum and fishing activities. They returned not wholly convinced of compatibility between industries and concerned about the paradox of the oil and gas industry both threatening and investing in salmon conservation (Wilson, chapter 2, this volume). As Justine Gundersen stated, "It is more controversial now than it was" in Nelson Lagoon (interview with author, August 19, 2009).

During development negotiations, local leaders implicitly equated oil and gas with salmon and other foods even though these "other natural resources" pose credible threats to the more traditional ones. This revaluing of salmon, however temporary, reflects an attitude that was markedly different from attitudes in the transient fleet: they come to the region only for the salmon and are strongly opposed to development that threatens the fish.

DISCUSSION AND CONCLUSIONS

"Sustainable" salmon fisheries of Alaska represent the rationalized management of human behavior and imply healthy fleets and communities that are implementing better fishing practices. However, community benefits are merely implied with sustainability certification, not necessarily realized. As Governor Tony Knowles (2000) stated, "In Alaska, fishing is an inseparable part of our history and culture.... When consumers buy MSC labeled salmon, they are supporting a sustainable future for fishing in Alaska." More abstractly, criteria for sustainability identified in other arctic locations show that the models and aspirations for maintaining these northern communities will still likely fall short. The wish list is already being implemented in Aleut communities, but each condition also includes a layer of difficulty that will prevent long-term maintenance of the villages.

Perhaps entry into the market economy steered coastal villages down this uncertain path. A life based upon subsistence harvesting may have offered more local control. The view of some (mostly non-Native) people in the Aleutian region is that the export economy is too volatile, and "traditional subsistence economies can last forever" (interview with author, February 26, 2010). But subsistence-dominant communities depend heavily, and in some cases exclusively, on government transfer payments. Subsistence harvesting costs money, and the villages have expensive infrastructure—this is not an economic base and cannot be sustained in the long run. The point is moot, however, in Aleut villages where people have embraced the market economy, and their participation in it has become a cultural foundation even as they attempt to mitigate its unpredictability. Any romanticism about Indigenous peoples in harmony with natural ecosystems, operating outside market systems and the nation-state, and defending their culture against global powers will find no footing in the Aleutians (Kearney 1996:107).

The model for ecological and sustainable management of salmon is relatively sound, but it does not emphasize supporting people economically, socially, or politically, which may have more to do with sustaining the development process itself (Sachs 1992). Salmon-dependent communities are entering into new agreements with developers while the nonlocal portions of the fishing fleets voice opposition, yet the nonlocal presence in the fishery is what makes these alternative options attractive. The ability to enter the salmon fishery is open to a fixed number of participants, and a growing nonlocal fleet means that the local fleet must shrink. When permits become available, nonlocal fishermen are typically in a better position to acquire them. The communities are having increasing difficulty retaining young skilled people, and the villages are not reproducing themselves. Svein Jentoft (2000) has shown that when communities disintegrate, the resource can be vulnerable as well, yet the "fishing community" in this case includes transients.

Maintaining village sources of revenue appears not to be a priority of fisheries management as control of and participation in fisheries increasingly shifts away from local communities. Both villages face rural school closures, which would drive young families out. Villages and processing plants are both distant from markets and have high costs associated with them. Processors became economically more efficient by consolidating operations (in this case away from False Pass to King Cove) and by investing in a more efficient, reliable fleet (away from Nelson Lagoon to Port Moller). Processors must *choose* to support the communities as part of their bottom line; they may hire seasonally engaged people from around the globe, and these workers support local businesses, but this level of support is insufficient. Local government structures must keep permits in local hands, rather than blindly supporting the entire fleet. The region needs policy intervention that keeps both permits and revenue local.

These issues are seen as constraints, not barriers, by the Aleuts. The Aleuts do not passively accept their precarious positions but instead encounter, resist, transform, and incorporate political and economic influences all the time. The villages exist because of deliberate commitments from the people. They fish commercially because they have made deliberate choices around lifestyles and economics. Where possible, they have made deliberate choices to diversify into other fisheries. The irregular abundance of salmon allows for other efforts at other times, and this time is not wasted.

Community members are trying to maintain themselves as salmon fishermen by turning toward revenue-sharing opportunities and investing in nonrenewable resources. These strategies may ultimately undermine salmon-based fishing communities, but the volatility of salmon fishing offers petroleum companies space for negotiation. Aleut participation in development of this kind is read locally as both participating in self-determination *and* capitulating under duress, while they succumb to pressures all around them.

Local people are constantly exploring economic opportunities by allowing or pursuing development, which now includes tidal and geothermal energy in nearby communities. New development ventures must be explored at a constant rate, and the villages currently have the leadership to realize their goals. Would job creation make a difference? The global labor pool for processing closes off job prospects for locals. But locals do not want this meaningless work with low pay and low status, so another facility in Nelson Lagoon seems inappropriate even though its purpose is to compete with Peter Pan Seafoods and possibly compel Peter Pan Seafoods to pay closer attention to the resident fleet.

Sustainability is only tenable when consciously rooted in cultural identities, economies, and local environments (Escobar 2008), all of which must be understood as part of global processes (Kearney 1996). The two Aleut villages of Nelson Lagoon and False Pass are struggling politically, socially, and economically despite, and because of, the healthy, "sustainably" managed local salmon resources. Managing salmon to be compatible with markets frequently creates inequality for local, less efficient fleets. By studying the realities of villages on the cusp of collapse, and their efforts to stay on life support, we can consider their future. The salmon fisheries of these two eastern Aleutian communities are social failures amid ecological success. They are in an unsustainable socioeconomic trap with sustainable resources all around them. As Martin Robards and Joshua Greenburg assert (2007), village sustainability has more to do with flexibility and the ability to reinvent oneself again and again as the market, the resource, the villages, and salmon management evolve. Historically, the Aleuts met ecological or economic change with trade, a shift in resource emphasis, or mobility. Today, this resilience is still a necessary ingredient for village viability.

Notes

1. The Sustainability of Arctic Communities project is a National Science Foundation–funded interdisciplinary, multiyear study of how climate change, oil development, tourism, and reduced government funding affect four arctic communities (Kofinas and Braund 1996).

2. This paper dwells on recent salmon industry development and the role of Indigenous people, which should not be seen as separate from a millennia-long history showing the stability of salmon consumption in the Aleutian region (Maschner 1998). Its abundance throughout Aleutian history could explain its unremarkable status in Aleutian lore (see also Koester, chapter 3, this volume).

3. Cold Bay is also a modern community, founded during World War II, and is primarily the headquarters of the US Fish & Wildlife Service and the National Weather Service. Aleuts represent a small fraction of the town.

4. A "tribe" in Alaska is a village designation from a moment in the recent past, not an ethnic distinction. Tribal councils of many of these now abandoned villages remain intact in nearby communities; for example, the Pauloff Harbor Tribe from Sanak Island is located in Sand Point, 170 km to the northeast of Sanak Island.

5. Population maintenance is also threatened by high mortality rates. For example, Nelson Lagoon lost two adult men in the summer of 2010, or 9 percent of its salmon permit holders.

6. Set gill nets are fishing nets set out in a stationary site in the path of moving fish. Seine nets are laid out around milling fish from a boat using a skiff, then closed at the bottom and lifted onto the boat.

7. An overpopulation of wolves is frequently blamed for the decline in caribou herds. Human overharvesting is also mentioned.

8. The harvest for the last several seasons is approximately 210,000 sockeye after escapement needs are met. The Port Moller fleet harvests two million sockeye.

9. The program is meant to stabilize local economies by providing employment opportunities, raw product for business development, tax revenue to local governments, training and education, and economic growth.

10. False Pass boats used to be anchored in the pass with huge 750 lb anchors during the fishing season and pulled up onto the beach in the off-season. This was very hard on all the vessels due to the harsh weather.

11. This term refers to fishermen who are the first to set their nets and the last to pull them, fishing every possible moment that they can.

7

Enduring Ties

Salmon and the Alutiiq/Sugpiaq Peoples of the Kodiak Archipelago, Alaska

Courtney Carothers

INTRODUCTION

> Our lives revolve around fish. It's something that's been in our life forever. It's the mainstay of the people. [Old Harbor fisherman, interview with author, March 7, 2010]

In a recent set of interviews about the changing nature of fishing in small coastal villages of the Kodiak Archipelago in the south-central Gulf of Alaska, I asked people to talk about the historic and current importance of salmon to their communities. Many said plainly, "Without salmon, the Kodiak villages wouldn't exist." For over a hundred years salmon in particular have formed the backbone of life in the Kodiak region. The singularity and importance of such a resource was, of course, difficult for people to articulate. Salmon are so commonplace, so unquestionably part of daily life, and so vital that they easily become submerged in thought and expressive culture, as David Koester (chapter 3) discusses in this volume.

While making explicit the importance of salmon is difficult in directed conversation, the tangible marks of such significance are easy to observe. On a recent visit to the village of Old Harbor (plate 2) on the southeastern coast of Kodiak Island (figure 7.1), I detected the physical and symbolic presence of salmon all around me. As I visited with an elder on a blustery winter day and talked about fishing in the old days, her nephew walked in

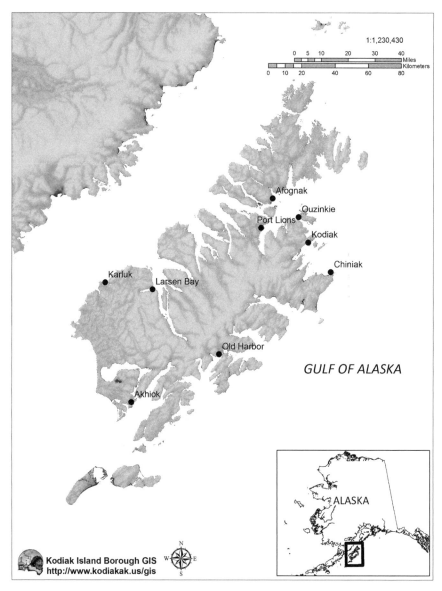

FIGURE 7.1

Map of the Kodiak Archipelago.

the door and dropped off a frozen red salmon (*Oncorhynchus nerka*) into her sink. "For you, Auntie," he said and was out the door. The headed and gutted red salmon was a welcome treat, but like many of the elders in the village, my companion especially craves the humps of the spawning male pink salmon (*O. gorbuscha*) and salmon heads. On the table that afternoon sat a bowl of silver salmon (*O. kisutch*) spread, along with dried salmon, *tamuuq*, with seal oil for dipping. On the walls of the house, like nearly all of the houses in the village, hung photographs and paintings of salmon-fishing boats and fathers, brothers, daughters, and nephews working on the water or processing fish. Had I been visiting in the fall, young and old would have been casting for silvers in the creeks or setting a net to catch a winter pack of fish. The entire village would have been alight with many working smokehouses and fragrant with the smells of salmon slowly smoking. Conversation would inevitably circle back to the perpetual tending of the fires and the patrolling for bears. Had I arrived in summer, I would have witnessed the commercial salmon purse-seine season luring recent village out-migrants back to their boats and communities for a few months. The six to eight active salmon fishermen of Old Harbor and their crews would be out in the nearby bays setting their seine nets and pulling in load after load of first red, then pink salmon. Salmon "jumpers" would be sailing out of the water along the coast of the village as they migrated back to their natal streams, creating peaceful sounds in the surrounding silence.

While the singular importance of the marine environment has always been a core feature of human life in the Kodiak Archipelago, the nature of the dependence on salmon has shifted over time. The first peoples of Kodiak utilized fish to supplement their marine mammal diet. Later cultures took advantage of shifting climates to locate their villages along rich salmon streams and lakes. Dried salmon played a role as a vital local food source and trade good during the Russian invasion and subsequent sea otter fur trade. The capital expansion of the salmon-salting and salmon-canning complexes of the American colonial period near the turn of the nineteenth century set in motion the development of the contemporary dependence of Kodiak economies on salmon fishing. The salmon canneries and developing ties to commercial fishing have had perhaps the most lasting effect on the current context of Sugpiaq communities and their relationships to salmon. In addition to being unable to imagine the existence of their communities without salmon, many informants stress the importance of cannery relationships in developing contemporary fishing economies and village communities.

The story of salmon and Sugpiaq peoples is a complex one with many contradictions and ironies. Drawing on insights from political ecology and postcolonial studies, this chapter explores the changing and enduring ties of salmon and Kodiak Sugpiaq peoples. The colonization of the Kodiak Archipelago by Russia and the United States has had a lasting effect on the social ecologies of place in the contemporary period. Throughout these histories, resistance, domination, and adaptation have shaped unique social, economic, and cultural hybridities of contemporary village lifeways (Crowell, Steffian, and Pullar 2001). Embracing difference as an analytical concept opens up possibilities for exploring the current challenges to fisheries engagement in the Sugpiaq region. On the concept of difference, Arturo Escobar (2008:6) notes, "People engage in the defense of place from the perspective of the economic, ecological, and cultural difference that their landscapes, cultures, and economies embody in relation to those of more dominant sectors of society." Through an investigation of major waves of social change in Sugpiaq communities and the hybridizations that have resulted, I will be able to trace the economic, ecological, and cultural differences that have come to characterize contemporary Sugpiaq villages. These differences have not meshed well with the recent enclosure and commodification of fishing access rights, which has constricted the nature of human–environment relationships in Kodiak villages (Carothers 2010). While Sugpiaq economies are becoming less connected to commercial fishing, subsistence practices, individual and community identities, and place attachments still embody the close connections to salmon and marine resources. However, the recent economic severing of Kodiak villages from the resources of the sea will have profound impacts on the future of these practices and identities.

In this chapter I provide a brief historical review of the waves of influence that have shaped contemporary Sugpiaq communities and salmon fisheries. These historical details are central to understanding contemporary human–salmon relationships. After introducing Kodiak prehistory, I summarize the Russian colonization that dramatically impacted Indigenous ways of life in the Kodiak Archipelago and created lasting hybridities in local cultures and identities. Next, I review the subsequent period of Americanization that created new extractive industries and political relationships, further altering the social and economic relationships within Kodiak communities and between communities and the state. Drawing on archival and ethnographic research, I trace the transitions experienced in Sugpiaq communities in the first half of the twentieth century to illustrate the development of seasonal, flexible, place-based fishing lifestyles in the period of cannery development in the Alaskan territory. I conclude by exploring the nature of the economies, cultures, and identities of difference that developed in the cannery period in light of neoliberal policies that increasingly bring about an alienation of local resource rights because they demand utterly different social and economic arrangements.

KODIAK PREHISTORY

The human history of the Kodiak Archipelago spans over seven thousand years (Clark 1998). The cultural traditions evident in the archaeological record are shared across the neighboring Alaska Peninsula, Chirikof Island, Prince William Sound, and Kachemak Bay regions. Since the earliest cultural period identified by archaeologists, Ocean Bay I, inhabitants of this region seasonally located their settlements at the mouths of salmon-rich streams. In this early phase, hunting of marine mammals including seals, sea lions, whales, otter, and porpoises was the dominant livelihood. By about 2000 BC, the Kachemak cultural tradition developed in this region of the Pacific. Throughout this period, people were increasingly pursuing fishing, as evidenced by the prevalence of notched pebbles and grooved-stone fishing weights in the archaeological record (Clark 1984). The late Kachemak period in the Kodiak region was one of central winter village settlements of semisubterranean houses at the mouths of bays and seasonal occupation along salmon streams (Fitzhugh 2003; Steffian and Saltonstall 2004; Steffian, Saltonstall, and Kopperl 2006; Yesner 1989). The maritime hunting and fishing cultures and economies of the archipelago supported over ten thousand people organized into a complex coastal village–based social system that involved social stratification, territoriality, and trade (Clark 1979, 1998; Fitzhugh 2003). While a detailed, traditional account was never fully documented, the cultural history of the ancestors of Indigenous peoples of Kodiak Archipelago has been pieced together from oral history; explorers', colonizers', and missionaries' accounts; and archaeological study (Clark 1984). Donald W. Clark (1984:148) remarks on the cultural mixing that has characterized Kodiak peoples in prehistory as well as the current era: "The Koniag phase, and in general the Pacific Eskimo, is neither an in situ development nor a direct result of a population and cultural replacement; rather it is an amalgamation of old and new elements and replacement or loss of numerous former traits during the course of several centuries, accompanied by population mobility."

Anthropologists and others have used various names to classify the Indigenous peoples of the Kodiak Archipelago, including Koniag, Russian Aleut, Pacific Eskimo, and Suk Eskimo (Clark 1998). Many Indigenous people from the Kodiak region today refer to themselves as Aleut or increasingly as Alutiiq (the self-referent for "Aleut" in the Indigenous Sugt'stun language). This name dates back to the eighteenth-century fur trade period when Russians referred to Indigenous peoples of the Aleutian Islands, the Unangan (see Reedy-Maschner, chapter 6, this volume), and the Kodiak Archipelago and other coastal areas as Aleuts. The term *Sugpiaq* (from *suk* meaning "person" and *piaq* meaning "real" or "genuine") in Sugt'stun is used by Native speakers, anthropologists, and others to refer to the Indigenous peoples of the central Gulf of Alaska, including the Kodiak Archipelago, along with the Alaska Peninsula, Kenai Peninsula, and Prince William Sound. In a recent volume Sven Haakanson Jr. and Amy Steffian (2009:205) note the preferred usage of *Sugpiaq* (plural: Sugpiat) to refer to the Indigenous peoples of these regions and *Alutiiq* to refer to their language. I follow that convention in this chapter.

RUSSIAN PERIOD

According to written records, Indigenous Kodiak Islanders successfully repelled several Russian ships that made contact between 1760 and 1780 (Black 1992; Pierce 1981). In August 1784, Grigorii I. Shelikov, along with 130 Russians, ten Aleut "volunteers" from the Fox Islands, and two interpreters, established the first Russian settlement on Kodiak Island (Black 1992). The Russians were received with violence by the Sugpiaq peoples on the east side of the island; Shelikov (1981[1786]:40) describes being "warned about the aggressiveness of the Koniag people." According to his accounts, the local people repeatedly attacked the Russian *baidaras* (large skin boats) with their weapons of arrows and spears, expressing "their desire that we leave their shores or be killed" (Shelikov 1981[1786]:39). The guns and cannons of the Russian fleet eventually brutally overpowered Sugpiaq resistance. The massacre of Refuge Rock (Awa'uq) occurred shortly after their arrival when an estimated three hundred to four hundred Sugpiaq men, women, and children were killed (Crowell, Steffian, and Pullar 2001:54; Lisiansky 1968[1814]:180); none of the Russians were reported to have been killed during this slaughter, although five or six were wounded (Pierce 1981; Shelikov (1981[1786]). Shelikov (1981[1786]:40) documents taking one thousand hostages (retaining four hundred as captives), including children abducted from their families "as a pledge of their good faith." Some of the adult male captives were reported to have been executed (Pierce 1981:12). After these violent attacks and other displays of the dominance of their gunpowder and weapons, the Russians were able to erect a settlement at Three Saints Bay (Staraia Gavan) in the southeast of Kodiak Island and another eight years later at Saint Paul's Harbor (Pavlovskaia; present-day Kodiak City) (Black 2004).[1]

By 1805 the population of Sugpiat in the Kodiak Archipelago was estimated to number only four thousand (Lisiansky 1968[1814]). This number would drop even lower in the next several decades as continued violence, forced labor, and disease further decimated the Indigenous population

(Clark 1984). A respiratory disease was documented in 1804, influenza-like attacks in 1819–1820 and 1827–1828, and a smallpox epidemic reached Kodiak in 1837–1838. The smallpox epidemic was particularly devastating and had lasting effects on village life in Kodiak. Prior to the smallpox epidemic sixty-five to seventy-five villages existed in the Kodiak Archipelago. These villages were fused into only seven to enable medical care to be administered more efficiently (Pullar 2009).

By the turn of the eighteenth century, the Russian American Company (formerly the Shelikov-Golikov Company) and its base in Kodiak had gained monopolistic control over the lucrative Asian fur trade in the North Pacific (Black 2004; Lightfoot 2003). Local men were conscripted into sea otter hunting to supply pelts to the company and to a lesser extent whale hunting to supply meat and oil to the company settlements at Kodiak and Afognak. Hiermonk Gideon comments that while the language and reports of the Russian American Company express "kindly and friendly treatment" toward the Indigenous peoples of the islands, this was not what he observed. He reported, "On the west end of Kad'iak, the Russian *promyshlennye*,[2] coming ashore, formed a line with firearms loaded, and announced: 'Now, tell us if you are not joining the (hunting) party, [just] say so!' [The guns were cocked.]—'We'll shoot.' Under such threats who would dare to express dissatisfaction?" (1989[1805]:69).

The hunting parties were often absent from their homes from March to September (Gideon 1989[1805]), or even longer. Urey Lisiansky (1968 [1814]:177), a captain of the Russian Navy, notes encountering a village settlement in the winter of 1805 made up entirely of "emaciated beings," "literally half-starved" women and children who in the year-long absence of the male hunters servicing the Russian company were without provisions. Indeed, throughout his travels, Lisiansky remarks on the lack of resources in the Sugpiaq settlements he visits. While the Russian Navy captain is quick to blame "sloth and idleness" for such poverty, he is surprised to learn from village leaders (*toyons*) that instead the forced labor and "high price fixed by the Russian company on every necessary article" prevented most village settlements from procuring enough necessary subsistence foods and purchasable items from the Russians during these times (1968[1814]:179).

Perhaps reflecting previous social hierarchies, men who owned their kayaks (*qayaqs* in Alutiiq and *baidarkas* in Russian) were under different obligations to the company than boatless men. In the early 1800s, Gavril Davydov (1977[1809]:168) observed that "he who has a baidarka is rich. Such a person is even now regarded with respect by the Russian; for a Koniaga who has a baidarka always has a source of food. He can hunt animals for which he will get, not very much, but at least something from the company, while his comrade who travels with him and does the same amount of work, must consider himself lucky if he is well-fed and clothed somehow or other."

Elder men and boys were drafted to hunt puffins and other birds for parkas; unfulfilled bird quotas were required to be supplemented with fox and land otter pelts. Sugpiaq women were also forced into laboring for the company for most of the year. Women were responsible for making grass baskets, collecting berries, and constructing bird-skin parkas, *kamleikas* (waterproof layers worn while kayaking), sinew thread, and cordage for seal nets (Gideon 1989[1805]). In compensation for this obligatory labor, the company made small payments of tobacco, beads, and parkas, which Sugpiaq peoples themselves had been forced to procure materials for and produce (Luehrmann 2005).

Sonja Luehrmann (2005, 2008) draws upon Andrei Grinev (1999) to describe the particular colonial arrangements used by the Russians in Alaska in contrast to their colonization of Siberia. In Alaska, the Russian American Company was more deeply involved in Indigenous communities because they forcibly controlled production, labor (very few Russians ever became skilled marine hunters [Gideon 1989(1805)]), and, importantly, the redistribution of goods. By contrast, the Siberian colonies were required to pay tributes to the company in cash or pelts, but they retained local control of hunting practices. As Gideon (1989[1805]) notes, this level of control deprived the Sugpiat of their former economy. Over time the majority of the Sugpiat had been dispossessed of their means of production in the form of baidaras and baidarkas and wealth in the form of fur and feather parkas.

Far from a monolithic entity, the Russian state at the time was made up of a complex set of actors diverse in their visions for the new territory. While the Russian American Company and Russian Navy dominated the economic and militaristic affairs in the Russian colony, processes of social assimilation shifted into the domain of Russian Orthodox missionaries. Shelikov and his partner, Ivan Golikov, financed the first Russian Orthodox church built on Kodiak and lobbied for missionary support in Alaska. Catherine II responded by sending an ecclesiastic mission of ten men in 1794. By the next year, several thousand Sugpiat had been baptized and many formal marriages performed. From early on, the missionaries played a key role in educational assimilation. In the beginning of this process of conversion, Alaska Native boys were kidnapped and forced to attend school. In time, parents would come to willingly send their children to mission schools (Black 2004). Similar to their intrusion into the economic sphere, the penetration of Russian spiritual and cultural practices into Sugpiaq communities was extensive, and as a result, Russian and Sugpiaq practices and beliefs became joined.

Lydia Black (2004) contends that Orthodox missionaries made great efforts to learn local languages and incorporate local beliefs into their teachings. She also provides detailed accounts of how Russian clergy members actively fought the Russian American Company on behalf of Indigenous peoples (2004:237–238, for example). In advance of formal approval from the Russian state, monks began administering an oath of allegiance to the state that would grant Indigenous people citizenship rights. The clergy's support of the local people against the company provides an important historical context that helps explain why many Sugpiaq people today are still firm in their Russian Orthodox beliefs and continue to associate Russian Orthodox faith with their Indigenous identity.

The intermarriage of Russian men and Sugpiaq women created lasting hybridities: cultures and economies of difference that have persisted through current times. Over twenty Russian family names are still common in Sugpiaq communities today (Madsen 2001). Black (2004) discusses the formation of a new social class in Kodiak and throughout Russian America. Black traces the earliest usages of the term *Creole* to church records in 1816. The term is defined in the Second Charter of the Russian American Company (enacted in 1821 and at that time thought to apply to 180 men and 120 women) and used to designate "extraterritorial birth rather than racial descent" (Luehrmann 2008:117). Black states that the term *Creole* comes from *criollo*, used by the Spanish in the late 1500s to refer to individuals of European descent born in the West Indies. As defined by the Russian state, Sugpiaq peoples could claim Creole status without having a Russian parent (Pullar 2010). Residing in a Russian American settlement town or pledging allegiance to the Russian czar granted Sugpiaq individuals entry into the Creole class (Oleksa 1990, cited in Pullar 2010). Mixed marriages were also recognized as legal unions by the Russian state. The children of mixed marriages were considered citizens of the state, entitled to the estate and property of the Russian father. Creoles made up about 90 percent of the Kodiak population when the United States purchased the territory from Russia in 1867 (Oleksa 1992, cited in Pullar 2009).

When the United States took control of the territory, the status of the Creoles changed dramatically; as Black (2004:287) notes, "The proud creoles would become contemptible half-breeds." Descent was racialized in the American period with a loss of status for Native and Creole peoples as a result. We see in this period the introduction of the Euro-American notion of purity that was largely absent in the Russian period. This framing has continued to be a dominant lens through which ethnicity and race are approached in the United States. During this challenging period of transition, many people in the Kodiak region began to identify themselves as Russian (Pullar 2009, 2010) and continued to do so until processes of "political awakening" and revitalization of the Sugpiaq culture gained force in the 1960s (Eaton 2009; Pullar 1992). The civilizing governmentality of the colonial US state was apparent in early "divide and conquer" policies of Indigenous language and cultural suppression, resettlement, and forcible removal of children for placement in boarding schools and continues through recent assimilative policies, such as the corporation model established by the land claims processes in the 1970s. The complex history of changing sociopolitical relationships in the American period deserves more attention than is given here (see, for example, Berger 1985; Davis 1976; Langdon 1986). The following section focuses specifically on the shifts brought about by the capitalization of the salmon industry during this period.

AMERICANIZATION: THE DEVELOPMENT OF FISHING LIVELIHOODS OF DIFFERENCE

Gordon Pullar (2009) has recently synthesized a historical ethnography of Kodiak village communities around 1867, when the United States purchased the Alaska territory from Russia. Contributing to a volume exhibiting Sugpiaq masks collected from Kodiak area villages by Alphonse Pinart in 1871, Pullar ties together various accounts to describe transitioning economic and social communities and imagine what Kodiak villages might have been like in this transitional period. While sea otter populations had declined dramatically by the 1890s, hunting continued until at least 1900 (Pullar 2009). Fish- and whale-processing plants were developed in the Kodiak region during the late 1880s through the middle of the twentieth century. The relationship between Sugpiaq communities and these resource-extractive industries was a complex one of resistance and intimate participation, giving way to cultural and economic hybridization. The social, economic, and cultural shifts brought on by the widespread development of salmon canning in the Kodiak Archipelago, particularly against the backdrop of other widespread changes in the sociopolitical relationships between Indigenous peoples and the state during Americanization, have had perhaps the most lasting impacts on contemporary Sugpiaq villages.

The highly productive Karluk River system on the west side of Kodiak

Island was one of the first locations where US companies established commercial salmon extraction and processing facilities (figure 7.1). A salt house and packing facility in the village of Karluk (Kal'uq) produced salt fish and dried fish for use throughout the Russian colonies in Alaska (Elliot 1886 in Pullar 2009); however, no major commercial trade of fish developed until the American period. Commercial salting and drying of fish was soon to be overshadowed by the burgeoning canning industry. The first cannery in the Kodiak region was built in Karluk in 1882; less than a decade later, five canneries were operating on the congested spit. At the turn of the century, over four million fish were extracted from the Karluk River, canned, and supplied to international markets (Roppel 1994). As salmon populations began to decrease in the Karluk, canneries were built throughout the Kodiak Archipelago, including the sites of Larsen Bay, Afognak Island, Alitak Bay, Olga Bay, Moser Bay, and Uganik Bay. The intense corporate competition of the early cannery period exerted pressure on fish stocks and oversupplied a developing market. Companies began to consolidate and utilize more efficient harvesting technology (particularly fish traps) to cut production and labor costs. The Alaska Packers Association, headquartered in San Francisco, and the Northwestern Fisheries Company began to dominate as the centralized heads of most of the companies operating in the region (Roppel 1994). Throughout south-central and southeast Alaska, the salmon-canning industry reached its peak of production (pre-1978) in 1936 when 25,221 workers caught and canned 129 million salmon, over 600 million lbs (B. King, personal communication 2004).

Rather than being caught in a one-way relationship of structural dominance and passive reception, local peoples were actively involved in these processes of change. Whether engaged in aggressive resistance to loss of resource access rights or adaptive adoption of those elements of the cannery system that fit with their ways of life, Sugpiaq villagers were agents of change during these times; however, as Luehrmann (2008:109) notes, the stakes with cannery development were high: "Canneries not only made the Alutiiq a minority in their homeland but also challenged Native rights to resources they had always used—and salmon were more crucial to survival than were the sea otter pelts the Russians had prohibited the Alutiiq from using."

Acts of Resistance

Several early acts of resistance occurred in the villages of Afognak (Ag'uaneq) and Karluk. In 1889 the chiefs of the village of Afognak sent a letter to the governor of Alaska: "We, the natives and all of Russian population of Afognak, appeal to your excellency to help us retain possession of the fish streams where we are dependent on getting our winter's supply of food for ourselves and families. We can not get any chance of fishing in the streams, as the cannery fishermen of all the companies operating here have taken possession of the mouths of the rivers" (Arnold 1978:77). Salmon depletion by the expanding canning industry prompted a Presidential Proclamation in 1892 prohibiting all commercial and subsistence harvests within a 3 mi limit surrounding Afognak Island. Thus, the Indigenous peoples who built their livelihoods around salmon were now banned from fishing. A hatchery constructed within this newly declared Afognak Forest and Fish Culture Reserve was intended to halt the demise of the salmon fishery. Along with the Afognak peoples, fishery agents fought for the removal of this ban for over fifteen years. Not until 1909 did the Afognak Sugpiat gain back the legal right to harvest fish for their own consumption and small-scale trade, and not until 1912 could they harvest a commercial catch. The right to fish commercially in the reserve was given only to residents of Afognak, where officials had some difficulty making permanent residency decisions. In 1913 commercial fishing rights were extended to residents of several nearby islands and to white men married to Native women. After some debate with the canneries, licenses to fish were issued to Native fishermen. In that year, seventy-two fishermen received licenses and fished in twelve crews of four to six people. The first six days of fish caught were taken for home consumption. Over the next few years, Kadiak Fisheries, based in Seattle but with plants locally, became the major buyer of salmon from Afognak fishermen. The company also loaned fishing gear and supplied transportation to several fishing spots (Roppel 1994).

Afognak Sugpiat also fought to restrict commercial fishing in areas around Afognak to Afognak fishermen only (specifically excluding fishermen from the nearby village of Ouzinkie [Uusenkaaq] on Spruce Island who traditionally were not allowed access to Afognak waters for fishing; see figure 7.1). In 1915 the commissioner of fisheries declared that Ouzinkie fishermen could only access the waters to the east of Afognak Island. As a result, the western waters of Afognak Island were exclusively for Afognak villagers. With the implementation of the White Act in 1924, which imposed conservation measures and legislated against exclusive access rights, these fishing rights for the Afognak residents were repealed (Roppel 1994).

In later decades, Sugpiaq fishermen in Karluk, unsuccessful in earlier battles with canneries and the federal government, continued to fight for a reservation that would preserve their access rights to the fish of their home shores (see Grantham 2011). In 1943 after a decade of petitioning, the Karluk Indian Reservation (Public Land Order No. 128, May 22, 1943) was created to protect Indigenous fishing and trapping rights, in particular from being appropriated by nonlocals. The reserve set aside 35,000 acres of coastline on Shelikof Strait, including the mouth of the Karluk River, for beach seining and offshore purse seining for Sugpiaq fishermen. The Native Village of Karluk set aside a small portion of the Karluk Reservation for their exclusive use, an area that extended 1,000 yds northeast and 500 yds southwest from the mouth of the river and 500 yds from shore at mean low tide (Native Village of Karluk n.d.). The Native Village of Karluk enabled other fishermen to apply for permits to access the other areas of the reservation for fishing. In 1945 at least thirty such permits were issued: twenty-nine to "resident" fishermen (including five fishermen from Karluk, five from Afognak, three from Uganik, two from Old Harbor, two from Ouzinkie, twelve from Kodiak) and one to a "non-resident" (a fisherman from Seattle). Reflecting the close relationship between fishermen and canneries at the time, only three of those thirty fishermen were described as "independent" on their permits; the others listed relationships with nine canneries throughout the Kodiak region (Native Village of Karluk n.d.). As Anjuli Grantham (2011) notes, the Alaska Packers Association (APA) ordered local agents to ignore the designation of the reservation. APA's A. K. Tichenor wrote to the local cannery superintendent (Gordon Jones) on June 8, 1944: "Nothing must be done…which may constitute any recognition on our part that the Karluk Indian Reservation is valid or legal or anyone has any rights in connection with our property. It is important therefore that we continue our fishing operations as we did last year, hiring the Indians as our employees, furnishing them with our gear, and letting them use our beaches to catch our fish for us" (Grantham 2011:2). APA joined six other cannery companies to file a suit against the reservation.[3] Just three years after its creation, the Karluk Indian Reservation was determined by US District Court judge Pratt to violate the White Act's nonexclusion clause based on its inclusion of ocean waters. This legal challenge of reservation domain was the first to include marine space and resources (Roppel 1994).

Cannery Engagements and Changing Communities

Over time, as the remote Kodiak communities began to develop in tandem with salmon canneries, resistance gave way to close participation. Sugpiaq communities and canneries codeveloped, and canneries were the primary vehicle for integrating coastal villages into commercial fish harvesting and wage employment (Davis 1976; Mishler 2003). Remote canneries located near Sugpiaq villages came to offer village services, such as company stores, electricity, communications, and health care. Sugpiaq labor in the canneries varied by community and over time (Luehrmann 2008; Partnow 2001; Roppel 1994). Generally, men harvested fish by beach seine, set gill net, and later by purse-seine vessel. Women worked manually preparing fish and later on the mechanical "slime lines" (Befu 1970; Davis 1971; Dombrowski 2001; Roppel 1994; Taylor 1966). In the early years, fishermen were paid in trade goods or credit at the company stores (Moser 1902), a practice that continued through the second half of the century. Elder fishermen remember fondly these days of "pay after fishing" or "slap it down" (Opheim 1994).[4] Edward Opheim Sr. (1994:93) in a memoir about dory fishing for cod around Kodiak in the 1920s recalled: "After ten years of cod fishing, I did not have a dime to call my own, but at least I had a credit standing at any story or cannery on the islands." Patricia Roppel (1994:249) describes how in the mid-1900s, the sign over a cannery store in Alitak at the south end of Kodiak Island read "'Lum and Abner's Jot Um Down Store' because all bills were settled after the season closed."

The growing commercial fishing industries, particularly salmon, cod, herring, and halibut, began to connect the Kodiak region to large fishing hubs like San Francisco and Seattle. Foreign fishermen, from Norway, Italy, and elsewhere, who had been fishing out of these US ports made their way north to Kodiak. Canneries also brought seasonal workers into the Kodiak region, and Chinese, Filipino, Mexican, and Japanese laborers began working in Alaskan canneries (Roppel 1994). Luehrmann (2008:65) describes how cannery development in Alaska was distinctive from the Russian fur trade: "The Alutiiiq lost the importance of indispensable specialists because the cannery operators brought Asian contract workers up from California and Seattle." The flow of outside labor contributed to a growing ethnic variation and segregation in many Alaska Native villages and seasonal cannery communities. Asian laborers were physically separated in large bunkhouses from Indigenous workers who lived in groups of smaller, more traditional dwellings. Social stratification at the canneries was evident in housing accommodations and differential wage scales and task assignments (Mishler 2003; Roppel 1994).

Beginning in the 1870s and continuing through the mid-twentieth century, foreign fishermen, and Scandinavians in particular, settled permanently in Kodiak Sugpiaq communities, some marrying local women. Roy Madsen (2001) notes the influx of Scandinavians into the region during the early twentieth century and lists over twenty-five family names that were common in Sugpiaq communities and that date back to this period of immigration and intermarriage. In the 1920s, about fifteen Scandinavian men were counted in Kodiak and surrounding villages (Mishler and Mason 1996). Roppel (1994) writes that "the fishermen were from San Franscisco, mostly immigrants—Scandinavians, Danes, Germans, and Italians.… Many of these men returned year after year and began to feel a sense of ownership for 'their' fishing grounds." The integration of foreign fishermen into Sugpiaq communities prompted changes in the sociocultural values of work and wealth accumulation, as well as increased stratification within and between villages (Mishler and Mason 1996). As in the Russian colonial period, cannery development and the social shifts brought about by the inclusion of foreign fishermen into the cultural fabric of Sugpiaq villages helped to form and solidify new identities and assemblages of nation, commerce, and religion. Lucille Antowak Davis, a Sugpiaq elder born in 1926, recalled this scene from her early years growing up in the village of Karluk:

> Fishing season is what I liked most of all because it was from inside. It touched you. We'd be sitting in the grass and mama would have blankets on us and we'd watch. The first thing they would do is blow the cannery whistle, three times. Even if we were sitting there we'd have to stand up. It was just like saluting the flag, okay? The American flag would come up and the guns were shooting. The church bell would ring on the side to wish the men a good season. The men were getting ready to go down with their boats, their fishing boats. With their oars, they pushed out and that's when they would shoot three times. Boom! Boom! Boom! And then they made their haul. That was really special. The flag would come up, the American flag would come up, the church bells were ringing, everybody was happy. They didn't take that day for granted, no way. [Crowell, Steffian, and Pullar 2001:230]

Like Ms. Davis, most current village residents have favorable memories of their involvement with local canneries. Nancy Yaw Davis (1971) described this positive relationship in her ethnographic research in Kodiak communities in the 1960s. Canneries were viewed as "benevolent agent[s]" (Mason 2006). Elder fishermen throughout the archipelago expressed in interviews that they could not imagine their daily lives growing up or their village communities developing without the local cannery. One fisherman remarked, "The cannery used to bring all our fuel and groceries in the fall, fill up our houses with groceries for the winter. They were good people" (interview with author, March 6, 2010). Another added: "I don't know what

FIGURE 7.2

Beach seine crews in Karluk bringing in eighty thousand salmon in one haul, 1901. Source: Alaska State Library, Wickersham State Historical Sites Photography Collection, P277-008-065.

we would have been doing if we didn't have Shearwater [cannery]" (interview with author, March 6, 2010).

Beach seining and fish traps were a primary method of harvesting salmon before purse seining began to dominate after World War II (figure 7.2). During this time, canneries maintained "company boats" that fishermen could lease out for the season for a percentage of their catch. Village men were often skippers or crewmen on these boats. Provided that a fisherman continued to successfully catch fish for the cannery year after year, the cannery would continue to loan or lease the boats. Over time, some families, often with financing from canneries, purchased or built their own vessels. Rates of individual boat ownership varied by village. In Karluk, village fishermen in the 1940s expressed interest in owning their own boats and sought assistance from the federal government for purchasing them (Bingham 1946); however, by the 1960s only one Karluk fisherman owned a purse-seine vessel (Taylor 1966). In Ouzinkie some fishermen were able to build their own dory-style boats to facilitate independence from the canneries. In Old Harbor several fishermen were acquiring their own small wooden boats during this period.

The credit systems established by canneries did contribute to a paternalistic system of dependency and debt (e.g., see Befu 1970; Dombrowski 2001; Sider 2003). An Alaska Native Service schoolteacher based in the village of Karluk provided evidence of this system in a letter to the general superintendent discussing a cannery labor dispute and strike vote: "Folks are afraid to do anything that might annoy the Alaska Packers for fear they will pull out and leave them to starve. They have been so dependent upon the Alaska Packers for their livelihood and for caring [for] them through the winter months on credit that they have lost any initiative they might have ever had" (Bingham 1946). The extension of credit in winter months that fostered these dependency relationships, however, is remembered fondly by informants today. Credit from the canneries has been described repeatedly in interviews as a safety net that often helped village families weather seasonal fluctuations and variations in fish stocks and prices. Many village residents describe their relationships with canneries as mutually dependent and as largely compatible with the flexible nature of the "maintenance economy" that characterized Sugpiaq fishing villages prior to the 1970s (Carothers 2008a, 2008b, 2010; see also Davis 1996 for a discussion of "livelihood" versus "accumulation" focused fishing lifestyles). For many fishermen, working on a beach seine gang, running a cannery boat, or working for wages in plants was to earn enough money to provide for their needs through the winter season. One fisherman recalled, "You could actually fish the summer and live most of the winter off what you made. The canneries back then they'd give you loans or whatever you needed to make it through the winter. They'd carry you, which they don't do nowadays" (interview with author, March 7, 2010). The earnings of village fishermen in the cannery period were modest. The president and secretary of the Native Village of Karluk estimated an average season's earnings for beach seining to be $400–$500 per person in 1948 (Masure and Ellanak 1948). According to four affidavits submitted in support of the Karluk fishing reservation between the years of 1938 and 1945, an average annual income in Karluk ranged from $700 to $1700; between 84 percent and 96 percent of income came directly from fishing (Native Village of Karluk n.d.).

The desire to accumulate and store wealth did not appear to motivate more fishing and cannery work by village households than was needed for winter sufficiency, and the fact that they fished or worked seasonally, or only when income was needed, made the Indigenous workforce "unreliable" in company discourse. Chinese, Japanese, and Italian workers were often described in early literature as preferred employees (Jacka 1990). Several early commentators on the nature of Sugpiaq involvement in fishing and cannery labor stress the mismatch between Sugpiaq ways of life and the desires of cannery employers. John Cobb (1921:98) notes: "In Alaska and at a few places in the States Indians are employed in the canneries. In Alaska more would be employed if they could be secured. They make fair work people, but are rather unreliable about remaining through the season."

Engagements in commercial fishing and ideas about work were changing during the period. As I have mentioned, Craig Mishler and Rachel Mason (1996) discuss how intermarriage patterns between Scandinavian men and Sugpiaq women generated important sociocultural and economic hybridities in contemporary Kodiak villages that began to change the nature of Sugpiaq relationships with commercial fishing. Mishler and Mason discuss how fishermen brought with them a "Scandinavian work ethic" that they passed on to their large families. As the men who settled into the communities came without family, matrilineal kin were particularly important in structuring the community relationships of this generation. For the next generations, these family ties provided collective resources that allowed them to gain entry into commercial fisheries. Older brothers and maternal uncles taught youngsters the trade of fishing and later helped them to acquire boats. A former fishermen in his early forties remarked in an interview that he was part of the last generation that followed the Sugpiaq pattern of children living with and learning from their maternal uncles. He said, "The uncles will watch out for you, they'll still be pretty hard on you. And teach you to work. And give you the lessons in life. Most fathers are very lax on their own kids. I was part of the last of that generation they did that with. That whole system changed starting in the '60s, late '70s" (interview with author, April 6, 2010).

In these times, boys (and often girls) typically began fishing when they were quite young—often at age five or six. By the teenage years, boys were capable of running or captaining a salmon purse-seining operation. Several young adults in Old Harbor were able to purchase their own small 32 ft wooden starter boats, called "grandies" (after the Grandy Boat Company in Seattle that built them), with financial help from canneries, brothers, or uncles. These boats could hold about 70,000 lbs of fish. Memories of the grandies provoke much laughter and stories about how "stink" they smelled from gurry. Village fishermen often gained entry to commercial salmon fishing by leasing grandies from the cannery for a percentage of their season's earnings. After several seasons, some fishermen were able to purchase their own boats. One Old Harbor fisherman described how he got started running his own boat with the help of his older brother: "My older brother had little boats; then he had a bigger boat and he gave us the little boats to run and I started first and my other brother ran the little boat. Then from there we all got bigger boats. The canneries gave us loans to buy bigger boats to fish" (interview with author, March 7, 2010).

Grandies were traded in for larger wooden boats and then fiberglass boats, often referred to collectively as the "tupperware fleet." These vessels tended to range in size from about 40 to 55 ft. As for all Sugpiaq villages, salmon became a mainstay fishery for Old Harbor fishermen. Over time various other species, including cod, herring, halibut, and crab, have fluctuated in importance. A handful of Kodiak Sugpiaq fishermen were able to become highliners in multiple commercial fisheries. The Old Harbor purse-seine fleet in particular became known for aggressive and territorial fishing practices (Mason 1993; Robinson 1996).

The subjectivities of economic and cultural difference in the village communities are evident in written accounts and people's memories of these days. The canneries engendered a seasonal maintenance economy that complemented subsistence lifestyles based in place. Many fishermen note that this economic arrangement was fundamentally different than the one that developed as fishing rights were individualized and commodified beginning in the 1970s. The material and symbolic domination of capitalocentric logics (Gibson-Graham 2006) based on expert knowledge, alienable resource rights, and mobility of labor and capital appears to have made the maintenance and self-sufficiency economies of remote coastal Sugpiaq communities untenable (Carothers 2010). Scholars like Katherine Gibson and Julie Graham have written about deliberately cultivating alternative economic arrangements in looking forward to postcapitalist futures; however, in this case it is important to look back. We have briefly explored how the maintenance economies of the Sugpiaq villages functioned, but what went wrong? Why are these alterative economies disappearing?

ALIENABLE RIGHTS: CHALLENGES TO VILLAGE LIVELIHOODS

> Well that's one thing that was unique back then compared to today where it's difficult to get started. You have to buy everything. Back then, we got a boat that belonged to the cannery. We leased it, of course. And, then, the seine skiff, we purchased that through the cannery. So we didn't have to go to the bank without any kind of loan history or, you know, credit. Young guys just don't have that now. It was a lot easier back then. Once you convinced the cannery that you were capable of doing it, they'd let you have a boat. [Ouzinkie fisherman, interview with author, March 14, 2010]

A series of changes in the 1970s set in motion a displacement of resource wealth from the Sugpiaq communities in the Gulf of Alaska. The salmon Limited Entry Act of 1974, the fall of the price of wild salmon, the catastrophic *Exxon Valdez* oil spill of 1989, the increasing capital requirements of maintaining a legal vessel, and, as one informant described, "free money from the government and Native corporations" have dramatically altered the nature of village economies. Prior to these changes, in the 1960s, nearly every household in each village on Kodiak fished commercially; now, fewer than 30 percent do (Carothers 2008b). The reasons for this dramatic decrease in commercial fishing engagements are multiple. One of the root causes is limitation and commodification of fishing rights, such that they can be bought and sold, detached from place. David Koester (chapter 3, this volume) provides a theoretical discussion of the alienation of resource rights that processes of capitalization and commodification can generate, which is helpful to consider in this case as well.

The centrality of fishing, both as an economic activity and a valued lifeway, has very much changed in Sugpiaq villages within the past generation. This interview excerpt from a former fisherman in his mid-forties draws attention to the importance of fishing and, at the same time, to the displacements of place and resources occurring in contemporary Sugpiaq villages:

> SH: According to my dad and my mom, when I was born [in Kodiak, where women go to give birth] there were no phones or radio and so they [in the village of Old Harbor] didn't know what sex I was. And up until then I had three sisters. My uncle had gone home before my mom and told my dad, "Ah, you had another daughter." And he didn't say anything after that. And so, when I got off the plane, my dad said, "Ma, what'd you name her?" And she—my mom—looked at him and said, "What are you talking about 'name her'? Her name's Sven Jr." He said, "Ah, there's my fisherman." And it stuck. I didn't even know I had another name until I was seven. In first grade, the teacher told me, "You better go home and ask your parents what your real name is." I said, "My real name is 'Fish.'" Even going to church, they asked me (my real name, and I said) "My church name's Fish."

> CC: Did you feel that you had big expectations, then, to be your dad's successful fisherman?

SH: No, not really. But I expected to go fishing after—I had planned on, in college, becoming a teacher so I could fish in the summertime. But my dad had lost his permit when I was eighteen because he couldn't make the boat payments to the State of Alaska. He was one of the old-time fishermen where fishing "was to make enough money to make it through the winter." Not "you have to make enough money to make a boat payment and pay all these other bills." And so he lost his permit and that pretty much left me deciding to either go a couple hundred thousand dollars in debt and fish, struggling to make ends meet, or go off to college and figure out something else. And I think my dad losing his permit and it not being handed to me was a pretty strong impetus for me to go to school.

CC: You've mentioned the permits a couple of times. Could you tell me more about that from your perspective?

SH: Well, the limited entry permits, which I think was—personally, it was a death knell for a lot of the villages, the start of it, for the fishing industry because it's controlled by that. Nobody can just start up and go fishing like they used to. You limit people and, then, you put a monetary value on who can fish and who can't. And you, basically, force people out of an industry. What happened in Old Harbor—I don't know how many permits are left but probably of the twenty or more that was there originally, how many do you have left? Eight that are active? People can't make payments and it becomes, "Hey, I'll sell you my permit if you give me money." So what happens? Just like land. You give people land, and if they don't have any money, land is money. They sell it. It's the same thing. And that's what happened to a lot of the villages or is happening, even. Look at Akhiok, Larsen Bay, Port Lions, Old Harbor, Ouzinkie. I mean, Old Harbor, Port Lions, and Ouzinkie are some of the stronger ones, but if you look at what's happened to Karluk and Ahkiok…you have how many permits fishing in Ahkiok, one? I think one left. Out of everybody that used to have permits. [interview with author, April 6, 2010]

Elsewhere I (2008a, 2008b, 2010) have explored in greater depth the mismatch between the limited entry permit system and Kodiak Sugpiaq fishing economies. In general the individualization and commodification of fishing rights marked a fundamental shift in the economic arrangements that village fishermen secured during the cannery period. One fisherman remarked that individual ownership "was a whole new concept and foreign to having a fleet [of boats] stay at home as opposed to having to go back to the canneries" (interview with author, April 6, 2010). Limited entry in the 1970s ushered in the haves and the have-nots. As one informant described: "Captains became richer, had more things, were able to do more, had more money. And then the folks whose families didn't have permits, that changed" (interview with author, April 6, 2010). In the 1980s, with less support from the canneries, "fishermen [became] more independent after limited entry" (interview with author, March 7, 2010). However, with this independence came a growing dependence on the formal economy—banks, loans, insurance. The more informal engagements that some fishermen had with commercial fishing—crewing for a short season, working in the cannery for a limited time, fishing only the summer salmon season for a cannery—were largely cut out with the change in how fisheries were managed. These alternative economic arrangements of Kodiak villages that seamlessly mixed subsistence and commercial production have been constrained by the recent shifts to capitalocentric fisheries management. Seasonal employment was a valued lifeway. One fisherman described this moral framework underlying the right way to work and structure one's life: "It's not wrong to not be employed in the winter if you've made enough in the summer...you can go hunting, you can build a net, visit with grandkids, you can go traveling...visiting time is gone. You fish so hard. Community exchange is gone—dancing, starring, we don't have time...it's not *immoral* not to be working...the social dynamic is forever changed when you schedule your life like that" (interview with author, February 2, 2011).

Informants are clearly nostalgic about past arrangements when subsistence and commercial fishing lifestyles merged more easily. However, the cannery period that informants remember so fondly was also based on a history of exploitation, exploitation that earlier generations of Sugpiaq peoples forcefully resisted. By attending to informants' harsh criticisms of fisheries enclosure and commodification and their nostalgic longings for previous times, we come to see a strong critique of the crisis of the current era—the economies of difference that have adapted and persisted despite waves of intense change are now largely untenable.[5] Without investment from federal, state, and tribal sources and transfer payments, rural fishing villages in this region would not be able to sustain themselves. This fact marks a truly new period for Sugpiaq communities. Surviving the brutality of the Russian invasion and fur trade, the forced cultural assimilation brought about by US tribal policies, and the economic development of large-scale fisheries extraction is the amalgamated Sugpiaq culture and economy, which has until now been based in place and on the resources of the sea.

ENDURING TIES: ALTERNATIVE ECONOMIES AND IDENTITIES

> Even the critiques of enclosure aid in the erasure of alternative economies by leaving them undocumented and devoid of possibility. [St. Martin 2007:528]

> Rather than vestiges to be swept away by enclosure and a capitalist becoming, the unique characteristics of fisheries economies, which are found throughout the world and represent the conditions under which millions of people labor, might become the conditions of existence of alternative economic futures. [St. Martin 2007:533]

This chapter has spanned a diverse and dramatic history of change in Sugpiaq communities and documented shifts in the nature of place, resource attachments, and the politics of difference occurring over a relatively short period of time. The eldest Sugpiat remember their parents and grandparents hunting sea otters from baidarkas for the Russians. They lived through health epidemics that decimated their villages. They witnessed the development of heavily capitalized salmon fishing—fish harvesting from small beach seines to fish traps to 56 ft fiberglass purse seiners and processing on drying racks on the beach to mechanized "slime lines" in the cannery factories. Many who have since passed never witnessed current trends severing the Sugpiaq people from the sea. The "violence waged against alterity" (Moore, Kosek, and Pandian 2003:6) in this history has taken many forms, from the physical overpowering of Indigenous hunters and communities during the Russian conquest to the symbolic dominations of the cultural logics underpinning widespread resource enclosure in recent decades.

Beginning with Clark's (1984) first assessment of the assemblages of disparate material cultures evident in the archaeological record, this review has covered various kinds of linked social, economic, and cultural hybridities forged by Sugpiaq peoples through time. As the recent volume

Looking Both Ways: Heritage and Identity of the Alutiiq People (Crowell, Steffian, and Pullar 2001; Crowell 2004) demonstrates so richly, the Sugpiat have always challenged notions of purity and boundedness, from early Russian intermarriage and cultural mergings to contemporary alternative fishing economies. The nature of their relationship to salmon has also shifted through time. A mainstay resource throughout their history, salmon became a major vehicle for linking Sugpiaq villages with capital and nonlocal people who were also seeking out new relationships with salmon. The early commodification of salmon led to enduring engagements with capitalist economies, and the relatively recent alienability of these relationship rights marks a new turn for Sugpiaq relationships with salmon. A handful of Sugpiaq commercial fishermen remain, largely those with access to capital that can be fully engaged in commercial enterprises. But many households, though displaced from commercial fishing, do continue to access salmon for subsistence. Salmon remains a keystone species. The enduring ties are active ones—by continuing to harvest, process, share, and consume salmon and other resources of the sea, Sugpiaq peoples continue to form strong attachments to the resources that surround their villages. Setting a subsistence net for salmon to dry, smoke, and freeze for the winter is a common and highly valued practice for many local people. The tie that has been severed is the one to an economic model that works in rural coastal communities in Kodiak—subsistence-based economies supported by rich local resources, the use of those resources as needed, and flexible engagements with commercial enterprises.

Katherine Reedy-Maschner (2009) writes that the notion of "entangled livelihoods," rather than mixed economies, better captures the contemporary coastal village economy in southwestern Alaska. She states that commercial fishing and subsistence fishing in Aleut communities "are mixed seamlessly and with banality; it is simply what you do...the people, gear, fish, and other subsistence foods are so intertwined that disentangling the commercial and subsistence as two separate systems is difficult (and unnecessary)" (2009:141). The economic displacements caused by restricting and commodifying the commercial sector of these entangled livelihoods have been more pronounced in Kodiak communities compared to the Aleutian communities that Reedy-Maschner (chapter 6) explores in this volume. For many in the Kodiak Archipelago, fishing no longer generates any income. Just as Gavriil Davydov (1977[1809]) observed in the early nineteenth century, those who own their means of production, a baidarka in the Russian days or a fishing boat and fishing rights in today's time, are rich, while others must leave rural villages for work or become dependent on support services and transfer payments.

Akhil Gupta (1998) in his exploration of postcolonial realities in farming communities in north India uses the concept of hybridity to describe the impurity, incommensurability, and blending of differing cultural practices, discourses, and structural forces. Gupta (1998:6) is clear that as an analytical concept hybridity must retain the "messiness" of these meldings. Arturo Escobar (2008:13) also notes the importance of not letting the concepts of hybridity overlook the "potential of difference for worlds and knowledges otherwise." The erasure of difference is seen in recent discourses and policies that attempt to imagine human beings as isolated profit-maximizers, mobile in place and livelihood (Davis 1996). But the centrality of hybridity and difference in these theorists' approaches complicates universalizing discourses of market-based resource governance. As Courtland Smith (chapter 1) reviews in this volume, dominant logics from agricultural production systems have dramatically shaped fisheries management to center on increasing production and profit. The economic imaginaries underpinning recent market-based governance propose the sameness of individuals via an ability to pay. The hegemony of economic efficiency as the goal of resource management, and the market as the distributor of resource rights, has dramatically limited the scope of the possibilities of difference, of alternative modernities, persisting in the Sugpiaq region and emerging in others. And yet, even in the past arrangements that informants often recollect as the good life—the cannery period of mutual dependence and a seasonal economy of hard work in the summer that produced time for subsistence and other life pursuits in the winter—certain dependencies were created that have become largely unsustainable. As Reedy-Maschner (chapter 6) argues in this volume, despite the relative abundance of resources and access rights that remain in the eastern Aleut region, many deprivations exist, and she directs us to question the sustainability of places in the global system more generally.

When discussing the disconnections experienced in Sugpiaq communities since the watershed moment of the 1970s when fishing rights became alienable, I am often presented with the question "So what?" Challengers often note that these shifts are part of an inevitable process of change produced by global capitalism in agriculture and other natural resource industries. Katherine Gibson and Julie Graham (Gibson-Graham 1996, 2006) explore deliberate, forward-looking constructions of alternative economies that challenge the perceived inevitability of capitalist globalization.

In this chapter, rather than looking forward, we have looked back and attempted to understand how alternative economies functioned in the past and how different economic-cultural linkages shaped both people and environments. The discourses, motivations, and practices linking people and salmon embody one set of alterative social-political-cultural-economic relationships that scholars like Gibson and Graham propose for future paths. One of the goals of this contribution is to document possible imaginaries of the past that are often overlooked, as Kevin St. Martin (2007) does in his critique of enclosure processes. The "so what" question can be explored as a question of "So what is lost?" The transitions being experienced in Sugpiaq villages are characterized by many locals as a "death knell," a severing of place relationships. As more families leave their home communities in search of work, the links between place and people become more symbolic than experienced. Sugpiaq fishermen from across the region are consistent in their stories and their certainty that without salmon and salmon fishing, their communities would not exist. Reedy-Maschner (2010) describes how Aleut peoples also base their identity on these relationships. As the various authors in this volume attest, the resources of the sea have brought about large-scale interconnections across the North Pacific region, some ephemeral, some enduring. As processes of delinking resources from place are under way, how are local and regional sustainability redefined?

The permanence of people in the Kodiak Archipelago has always depended upon securing the bounty of the sea—not in a timeless history of social-ecological harmony as Marianne Lien (chapter 11, this volume) is careful to note, but through the development of economies and cultures of difference in the face of hegemonic restructuring. These processes of hybridization have also been an enduring feature of Sugpiaq adaptation. What is new about the current changes, and what are the implications? While thinking about economy and culture as bounded spheres is limited, we should note that in the Sugpiaq case, economic dispossessions (e.g., the ability to make income from salmon) outpace cultural change (e.g., the dominant imaginaries that Sugpiaq villages are still fishing villages). Sugpiaq economies have shifted from salmon dependence, but Sugpiaq ecologies, cultures, and identities still very much embody the close connections to salmon and marine resources. The recent economic disconnections of Sugpiaq communities and the resources of the sea have profound implications for the future of these ecologies, cultures, and identities.

My recent winter visit to the village of Old Harbor concluded with a short, bumpy ride on a small five-seater plane. As we headed northeast from Old Harbor toward the central hub of Kodiak town, we passed over

Kiliuda Bay. My elder companion pointed down: "I was born there" (personal communication 2010). It took me a minute to make out the barely visible structure beneath us. Here was the site of the Shearwater Cannery, the cannery that entire families from Old Harbor would relocate to for the summer fishing season. My companion's mother, whom she calls "a full-blooded Aleut," gave birth to her at that site over seventy years ago. Her mother's husband was a Norwegian who settled in the community of Old Harbor in 1931. Together they had nineteen children, fourteen of whom survived into adulthood. Individual and collective Sugpiaq histories are full of stories, experiences, and memories of the mixing of people, places, and economies. These histories of hybridities provide a lens through which we can better understand how nature–culture and human–salmon relationships have shifted over time. We take note of the ephemeral nature of some ties, like the defunct canneries dotting the landscapes near Kodiak villages, and the enduring nature of others that are shaped by these histories but emerge anew as people continue to forge relationships with salmon and other keystone resources and symbols in their defense of place, livelihood, and identity.[6]

Notes

1. Lydia Black (2004:141n2) notes that an earthquake in 1788 left the Three Saints Bay harbor inaccessible to large vessels. According to oral history accounts, Baranov's vessels were said to have found suitable anchorage in a neighboring bay (the current site of the village of Old Harbor). Expanding the headquarters in the southern part of the island was difficult without timber resources. Baranov relocated the settlement to Chiniak Bay.

2. Also *promyshlennik*, a Russian rank-and-file employee of the Russian American Company.

3. The companies included Alaska Packers Association, Grimes Packing Company, Libby, McNeill & Libby, San Juan Fishing and Packing Company, Kadiak Fisheries Company, Frank C. McConaghy Company, and Parks Canning Company. While these companies did not have plants in Karluk at the time of the litigation, they had all processed fish from Karluk previously (Roppel 1994).

4. The acronym PAF for "pay after fishing" was a play on the acronym for Pacific American Fisheries, which operated canneries at Alitak, Zakhar Bay, and elsewhere in Alaska. PAF went out of business in 1966, but the expression meaning "pay after fishing" is still used here today and elsewhere in Alaska (specifically Bristol Bay) (B. King, personal communication 2004).

5. I thank an anonymous reviewer for commenting on the importance of not

valorizing a period of exploitation. The reviewer noted a missing dialogue on the role of nostalgia in people's recollection of past fisheries arrangements. I regret that my short discussion of this topic does not fully respond to this critique.

6. This research was originally supported by the Wenner-Gren Foundation for Anthropological Research (Individual Research Grant 7239), the National Science Foundation (Dissertation Improvement Grant 0514565), and the Washington Sea Grant college program. Additional research and writing funding was provided by the Morris K. Udall Scholarship and Excellence in National Environmental Policy Foundation and the University of Alaska–Fairbanks School of Fisheries and Ocean Sciences. I thank the tribal councils of the Native Village of Larsen Bay, Village of Old Harbor, and the Native Village of Ouzinkie for granting me permission to conduct research in their communities. I appreciate the Kodiak Archipelago map (see figure 7.1) produced by Maya Daurio, Kodiak Island Borough. I extend my sincere gratitude to Benedict Colombi, James F. Brooks, Marianne Lien, Courtland Smith, Katherine L. Reedy-Maschner, and all of the SAR seminarians for providing a fertile context in which to share ideas and push my thinking further. I thank Gordon L. Pullar, Sven Haakanson Jr., and two anonymous reviewers for their comments, which greatly improved this chapter. Any errors or misrepresentations are entirely my own.

8

The Disturbed Environment

The Indigenous Cultivation of Salmon

Charles R. Menzies

INTRODUCTION

I must have been twelve or thirteen the first time I saw an old stone fish trap. It was late July, warm, the sky was crisp and blue. I was playing around on the water at the head of a small cove, marking the time until the commercial seine fishery would begin. Drifting along with the tide, I was watching coho salmon swimming below me, illuminated by the bright sun. Then I saw the walls of stone laid out below on the ocean floor. I was captivated by the intricacies of the stonework, a fascination that has stayed with me for more than three decades. Back on my father's fish boat, I asked him about the stone walls in the water. "That," he said, "that's an old fish trap. They used to drag seine here."

There exists a common misperception that prior to the arrival of the K'msiwah—Europeans—the natural world was pristine and untouched. Indigenous peoples on the Northwest Coast were thought to have lived opportunistically on the bounty of nature. While we do know that they were abundant, these resources were not guaranteed (Suttles 1987); the idea that our Indigenous ancestors had no significant impact on the environment (unless of course they were massacring Pleistocene megafauna—for an informed discussion of this issue, see Kelly and Prasciunas 2007) is a persistent Euro-American myth. In this chapter I challenge the myth of the pristine and untouched natural world. My challenge may not prove the case, but through my reflections, considerations, and speculations I wish to provoke my readers to consider that the world the K'msiwah entered in the late 1700s was no "natural" world, it was the outcome of deliberate and direct human–environment interaction over millennia.

I use the phrase "disturbed environment" in the title deliberately. In contemporary ecology a disturbance is understood as a temporary change in environmental conditions of either natural or anthropogenic cause that has a pronounced effect in a particular ecosystem. The need to explain episodic disruptions or cataclysmic interventions in an ecosystem arises from a theoretical framework that considers a steady state to be normative. Some perspectives and theories, of course, attempt to describe ecosystems differently. However, those charged with governing resources like salmon remain steadfast in their conviction that prior to their own system of industrial resource extraction, salmon, and the world, existed in a natural balance. In this outlook Indigenous peoples become naturalized and located within a prior, prehistorical time in which our effects are generally limited to occasional cataclysmic disruptions. I am not concerned here with the effectiveness of ecological theory in explaining ecosystem change and function. Rather, my concern is with the ways such theories have displaced and ignored Indigenous practices in shaping—and in effect making—the environment that latter-day ecologists now study as natural systems.

This chapter is a collection of reflections woven together. In it I draw from my ongoing research into fishing practices within Gitxaała. This research involves oral history, contemporary ethnography, and archival and archaeological investigations. In what follows I present a context for understanding who Gitxaała are and where they live. I have selected three case studies of traditional fishing sites in order to provide a way to think about how Gitxaała intervention in and interaction with the environment has contributed to an increase and stabilization of salmon biomass through the millennia prior to K'msiwah arrival.

CONTEXT FOR UNDERSTANDING

British Columbia's northern coastline is riddled with fjords, coves, bays, and channels that wrap around and through hundreds of islands from the very tiny—barely a rock—to the grand, comprising hundreds of square miles of land. Our Indigenous ancestors have lived here certainly since the end of the last ice age and possibly even before that time. I grew up working on a salmon seiner skippered by my father. I spent my summers with him on the boat and much of my time in the winter after school working alongside him in gear lockers and engine rooms doing the tasks needed to keep a large wooden boat afloat and ready to fish. In the summer we traveled and fished throughout the north coast. The area of my childhood travels mirrors to a large extent, if imperfectly, the traditional territory of my Gitxaała ancestors. I felt connected to this place and people through the stories my father told me and the places where we fished.

Gitxaała territory stretches from just north of the mouth of the Skeena River south to Aristable Island, including Porcher, Banks, Pitt, and parts of Campania islands (figure 8.1). The territory stretches eastward into the mainland along Grenville Channel and west into Hecate Straights. Beyond this core territory special paces, like Ts'bassa's *oolichan* fishing camp on the shores of the Nass River, figure importantly in Gitxaała's traditions and oral history.

Gitxaała people have made their lives here, fishing, hunting, inventing, telling, singing—in sum, this land is Gitxaała much as Gitxaała are this land. This story of salmon and fish traps is about one small part of Gitxaała's world. The key idea is that our Indigenous practices have contributed to the ecological well-being of salmon and have potentially enhanced them to the level found by K'msiwah at the start of industrial commercial fishing in the 1800s.

My first experience of "seeing" a stone trap has stayed with me. It was a captivating sight for a young boy. But even for an adult the often intensely complex construction is impressive. One cannot leave a stone-trap site without considering the implications of human labor in the environment. I grew up with stories of my great-grandfather's fishing camp in K'moda. Yet seeing the curved walls of stone in the water made me think quite differently about what might actually have been involved in building these structures. As is noted in the three case studies that follow, some significant quantity of labor is required to construct, maintain, and then operate fisheries using stone-trap gear.

In the 1970s and early 1980s I was very much involved in salmon enhancement projects and discussions. Later, as a professional researcher in the 1990s, I was involved in watershed restoration projects that included conducting oral history research into traditional management practices that could be deployed in the present. Throughout these experiences I started to notice a similarity between the ancient practices described to me and inscribed within the creeks and shorelines of Gitxaała territory and the contemporary scientific models of enhancement and restoration.

In interviews, community harvesters frame their explanations for what is done, in terms of creek-scaping and harvesting techniques, in terms of relations with nonhuman social beings and humans. That is, one's behavior

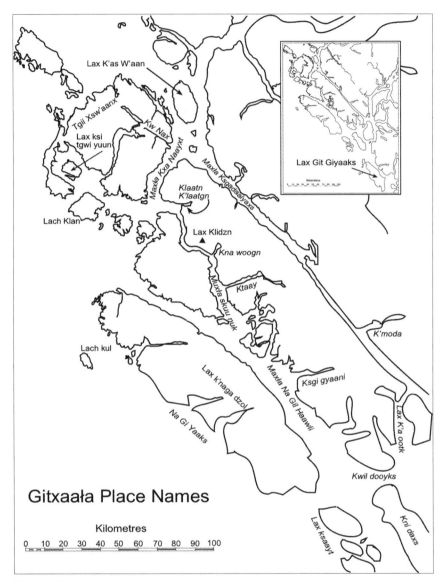

FIGURE 8.1

Map of Laxyuup Gitxaała. Source: Charles Menzies.

is regulated through social relations that are understood as kinlike (see, for example, Langdon 2006). This regulation implies and requires a structure of obligation and reciprocity that one learns about firsthand through experience on the water and land. But these lessons are also heard in and reinforced by the oral histories of Gitxaała people, some of which have been recorded over the course of the last century and a half.

John Tait (Gispaxloats, Tsimshian) recounted a sequence of stories about Txemsum (Raven) to William Beynon in 1954. In his narrative, Tait talks about the time when Txemsum married the princess of the Salmon People. Txemsum "had plenty of food. Whenever they were hungry they would roast a salmon and the woman [Txemsum's wife] would carefully gather all the bones and the remnants and burn these and as she done this they heard a happy cry in the waters of the stream. This was the salmon they had just ate now restored again" (Beynon 1954). As long as Txemsum respected his wife and her relatives he had plenty of food.

Unfortunately for Txemsum he grew jealous of his wife and lost his trust in her. His wife "became very angry. 'I'll go away back to my own people as I am afraid you will do me injury.' So she went out of the house and called out as she went out 'Come my children, come with me.' She went down into the stream, into the water and disappeared and all of the dried salmon now became alive and all jumped into the water and became live salmon and swam away after the woman, who was the Princess of the Salmon. Txemsum's supply of salmon was all gone.… He was now very hungry with nothing to eat" (Beynon 1954).

Jay Miller (1997) describes the results of people not respecting the gifts of their nonhuman relations. In his account of Temlaxham, an ancient Tsimshian community of origin, we learn of how the people are punished for forgetting themselves, for disrespecting our own animal relatives:

> Everyone did as he or she pleased. Great chiefs would give feasts and kill many slaves. They wasted food. The people had become wicked. One day some children went across the Skeena to play by themselves. One of them went for a drink at a small stream. There he saw many trout. He called to the others, and they began to fish for trout even though they already had plenty of food. They abused the trout. When they caught a fish, they would put urine in its mouth and return it to the water to watch it writhe and die. They laughed and mocked the fish in its agony. The trout had come to spawn that fine spring day, but they died instead. Soon a black fog began and a strong wind blew. Then it began to rain torrents. The trout stream began to rise. The children drowned. [Miller 1997:63–64]

Marc Spencer (Ganhada, Gitxaała), in an interview with William Beynon in 1953, related a similar Gitxaała account of a flood brought about by children disrespecting salmon at a village on Banks Island known as K'na'woow (Place of the Snares):

> The salmon were very plentiful in all these creeks and the people had plenty. It was then that some of the young people, now having all of the salmon they required, began to abuse the salmon by catching them in looped snares which they made from fine roots. When the salmon's head swan into the loop they would pull it tight and then leave the salmon hanging by the neck half out of water, then the eagles and other preying animals would come and devour the salmon. The older people begged the young people to stop their abuses to the salmon but these would not heed the warnings of the older people and soon other children in the nearby villages began doing the same. Their elders kept warning them "you will cause the anger of the chief of the Skies, because you are abusing the valuable salmon," but they would pay no attention to their warnings. Soon the weather began to change and the rain began to come down heavy and soon the rivers began to rise and gradually the waters rose and soon the villages at the creeks became submerged and still the waters rose and soon the small islands became submerged and then the people who up till then had kept moving up into the hills now got everything into their large canoes and the high hills and mountains were now all submerged only here and there were small portions of the hills to which the people were gathering to anchor their canoes and soon these disappeared and the people that were saved began to drift apart. The people knew that this was the revenge of the salmon that caused the flood retaliating after the many abuses. [Beynon 1954]

Thus we see that if the salmon or the trout are treated inappropriately they will leave or extract retribution. If respected they will reward the harvester. History has taught us that catching too many salmon at a particular location will result in either a marked decline or total extirpation of the stock. The same history has also shown that not taking enough seems to have a similar effect. Thus, the oral histories provide guidelines for behavior that are reinforced through our direct observations of the behavior of the fish.

The stone fish traps and associated Indigenous practices that I discuss in this chapter exemplify some actual creek-scaping and fishing techniques, and these practices can teach us about purposeful conservation and management practices. The extension of Canadian law into aboriginal fisheries and land management has been an explicit attempt to disrupt and displace aboriginal practices (Harris 2008). Thus, since the 1880s Gitxaała fisheries practices were essentially criminalized and the fisheries transformed into a so-called food fishery for Indians (in which First Nations are allowed to harvest for social and ceremonial purposes) and a commercial fishery for "everyone" (in which the sale of fish for economic benefit is permitted).

When one compares the catch data over the last 150 or so years with the estimates of pre-K'msiwah harvest levels we can see that the pre-K'msiwah harvests were equivalent to the industrial harvests of the twentieth century (Glavin 1996). As Michael Kew (1989:180) notes: "The Indian salmon fishery stands as a prime example of high utilization and dependence by humans over a long period of time with no depletion of the resource." Put another way, the commercial and aboriginal fisheries caught about the same amount of fish, but in the 150 years of the commercial fishery salmon stocks have been pushed to a dangerously low level. What happened? Very likely the criminalization of aboriginal creek-scaping and fisheries practices played a significant role in undermining the health of salmon stocks in British Columbia (Harris 2008; Menzies and Butler 2007).

Prior to the application of the Canadian Fisheries Act to British Columbia in the 1880s, Gitxaała people actively managed and shaped creeks and associated spawning channels to effectively increase spawning areas through modification of the watercourse. In addition, harvesting was managed to control for the numbers of salmon entering into the spawning channels. All of these actions had the effect of stabilizing the amount of salmon available for Gitxaała harvesting.

Essentially, Gitxaała management practices acted as a form of "Keynesian" management. That is, their interactions with the environment cut off the high peaks and low valleys of fish runs to generate a stable and reliable supply of fish. Gitxaała interventions worked in two ways: (1) by expanding and modifying spawning and rearing habitats and (2) by regulating quantities of salmon entering the spawning habitats. Because of their reproductive strategy (r-selection: that is, high number of offspring, low parental investment), salmon can react quickly to changes in their environment. This capacity also allows for the augmentation of particular runs beyond the potential capacity of spawning grounds and as a side consequence provides "surplus" fish that can be harvested without affecting the long-term sustainability of the fish stock. This classic tenet of contemporary salmon management practices appears to have been a successful aspect of Indigenous salmon management prior to the criminalization of Indigenous practices in the late 1800s.

INDIGENOUS SALMON FISHERIES AND STONE TRAPS

The customary fishing methods of Northwest Coast First Nations comprise a highly varied and refined assemblage of technologies, reflecting millennia of development and innovations. These fishing technologies and gear were designed with micro-ecological factors such as tides, eddies and other water features, seasons, and the behavior of target species in mind. The method and gear used at a particular site was selected according to multiple factors in order to improve efficiency without destroying fish stocks for future use. These highly specialized technologies allowed for sustained yields of salmon, providing adequate food supplies for many nations for thousands of years (Berringer 1982; Newell 1993; Stewart 1977).

Traditional fishing gear included gaffs, clubs, traps, weirs, trolling hooks, drag seines, gill nets, tidal traps, spears, dip nets, hooks on lines, and fish rakes (McDonald 1991). Each of these tools was associated with particular fishing sites, species, and seasons. The following case studies explore the interconnections between locally appropriate gear types, Indigenous history, and knowledge systems related to each fishing site and the implications of these connections for the cultivation of salmon.

Each case study offers a unique vantage point from which to consider the specific question at hand: K'moda is a location that figures prominently within my own family's history. It is also the site of one of the first canneries on the north coast and a site of ancient conflict between the northern invaders and Gitxaała and their Gitga'ata cousins. Kxooyax is a place that also figures in the history of early encounters with K'msiwah; here, Captain James Colnett's crew decided to tear apart a portion of a stone fish trap. But this place is also where Gitxaała people learned an early lesson about treating salmon with respect and the cost of not doing so. It is a place where K'msiwah laws came into conflict with Gitxaała laws over the allocation of fishing rights. Kxenk'aa'wen stands out as the location of an amazing complex of stone traps. In fact, the place-name is a direct referent to the special nature of the local stone fish traps. K'msiwah also encountered Gitxaała people here early in their commercial trading ventures along this coast. More importantly, Kxenk'aa'wen is a place where people live and have lived for millennia, harvesting a multitude of resources (not least of which are salmon) in the unique traps the place is named after.

FISHING AT K'MODA: CASE STUDY

K'moda is a river and lake system at the head of Lowe Inlet within Gitxaała territory.[1] This is the traditional territory of Sm'ooygit He:l. Over the course of the past century and a half, this place has been at the center of significant social transformations. K'moda is also the place at the heart of many of the stories that my father would tell me about my great-grandfather Edward Gamble and my uncle Russell Gamble. I have been fortunate to have had the opportunity to visit this place many times over the course of my life. One notable trip stands out.

In March 2000 Marvin (Teddy) Gamble took us to Lowe Inlet on his gillnetter, the *Gamble Lake*. We were joined on this trip by Sm'ooygit He:l (Russell Gamble), my father, my sons, and my colleague Caroline Butler. Being able to listen to my father and uncle speak about this place and their recollections of fishing and the people who once lived there shaped my understanding in ways that my written words may not be able to convey. When I return to this place I still see them there on the beach, talking. My memory of this trip has transformed the abstract landscape into a social space through which my family has passed and with which we retain an important connection (plate 8). Thus, while I write here about the fish trap (plate 9) and the history of salmon fisheries and management, I do so aware of the larger social world within which this place is more than just a place to catch fish.

In the late 1880s one of the earliest salmon canneries in British Columbia was established here. Drawing upon local Gitga'ata and Gitxaała community members, the cannery operated for several decades spanning the late 1800s and early 1900s. Coastal steamers made regular stops here along the inside passage route from Vancouver to Alaska. Members of the Harriman Expedition, notable for the number of Indigenous objects they removed without permission and donated to US museums, passed through here on their way north to Alaska in 1899. Photographer Edward Curtis took a few pictures of the area while other scientists onboard collected plant samples. The 1881 census taker had previously passed through this site. In his personal journal he recorded his trials and tribulations in attempting to take census data during his visit to the Gitxaała houses at the mouth of the K'moda.

Records of customary use and commercial trade by a Gitxaała *sm'ooygit* are inscribed in the Canadian sessional papers.[2] One early reference, dated 1890, notes that "the chief at Lowe's Inlet, assisted by his sons, caught and sold to two canneries on the Skeena River forty thousand fish, at an average of seven and eight cents each" (Sessional Papers no. 12, vol. 10, Ottawa). Oral accounts describe the close interconnection between the customary use of the area and the development of a local—Gitxaała and Gitga'ata—labor force that caught and processed salmon in the Lowe Inlet cannery.

Some find the combination of "traditional" and "commercial" fisheries practices to be either a contradiction or evidence of acculturation. However, this is far from the case in Indigenous fisheries along the west coast of Canada. Those who believe that aboriginal fisheries were always and only used for subsistence are mistaken. This colonial misconception underlies a great deal of historical and contemporary rumination about aboriginal fisheries. In point of fact, Gitxaała harvesters have always harvested for domestic consumption, gift exchange, and exchange for benefit. The development of the K'msiwah commercial salmon fishery, especially in its early decades, fit well within the entrepreneurial culture of Gitxaała and neighboring Indigenous communities.

For generations K'moda has been the home territory of the leading sm'ooygit from Gitxaała, Sm'ooygit He:l. The late Sm'ooygit He:l (Russell Gamble) explained that during the mid-twentieth century K'moda was occupied by the chief and house group from late spring through early fall. The resources they gathered included, but were not limited to, mountain goats, deer, a range of different berries, bark, clams and cockles, seals, and, of course, salmon and other fish. Elders who were young children during the early twentieth century recall the life of the campsite during the leadership of Sm'ooygit Seax/He:l (Edward Gamble), nephew and heir of Tsibassa. Edward Gamble was the named hereditary chief and held this site in the decades before it was held by his heir, Russell Gamble.

Over the course of the twentieth century the fishing patterns at K'moda changed from customary harvesting for consumption and exchange for benefit (up to about 1880) to a pattern of intense industrial harvesting co-existing with customary harvesting (1880–1930) to locally controlled drag seining (1930–1967) and, finally, to less intensive, occasional customary harvesting using gill nets (1967 to present). In what follows I will describe the key aspects of the customary techniques of fish harvesting. The data I draw upon comes from site visits to K'moda with Sm'ooygit He:l and interviews with Gitxaała elders and community members who actively use or used this place for the harvest of fish and other resources.

Three key fishing technologies have been customarily deployed at K'moda: gaffs, stone tidal traps, and drag seines (Menzies and Butler 2007). Up until the late 1800s, most salmon was harvested using gaffs and stone traps. Coincident with the development of the industrial salmon canning fishery, Gitxaała fishers switched to drag seining. This innovation accommodated the reduction in labor force caused by the waves of disease and dislocation brought by invasive non-Indigenous humans. In what follows, only stone-trap fishing is discussed.

Stone traps can be found throughout the Northwest Coast region (see, for example, Langdon 2006; Stewart 1977) and were typically located near streams and rivers in which migrating salmon traveled as they returned to spawn in the fall. Traps consisted of a series of stones arranged in a semicircular design. Boulders and stones were stacked upon each other. No mortar was used to hold the stones together; instead, careful selection and placement of the stones was required. In this way the wall of stones would remain upright in rough weather and throughout vigorous tidal action. Stone traps were used by house groups that relied on collaborative labor under the guidance of the house leader.

Stone fishing traps use the principle of "tidal drift" to catch fish. Salmon gather near the mouth of their birth river or stream in preparation to spawn, and when the water is deep enough, the salmon enter the river system and swim upstream. As the tide comes in the salmon are pushed toward the shore and the waiting trap. When the tide recedes the salmon move downstream, away from the shore, and as the fish swim away from the shore with the current they become trapped by the wall of stones. Fishers would position themselves along the wall as the tide dropped and splash the water to keep the fish from swimming out before the water was lower than the wall.

The K'moda stone trap is located in a small cove near to, but not in or across, the opening of the creek. Its design, like all stone fishing traps, uses tidal drift to capture fish. Elders report that the numbers of salmon returning to spawn in creeks and streams were so vast that a trap located at the beach anywhere close to a stream would provide a rich harvest.

Trap placement, however, typically takes advantage of the micromovements of local currents—this technology is not simply placed near or in a creek mouth. At K'moda, the trap is located to the north of the creek's actual mouth. During our observations of tidal patterns, we noted that at about three-quarters ebb a back eddy formed, which, if fish were around, would have acted as a great broom sweeping the fish into the belly of the trap. Then, as the tide receded, the current would drop the fish behind the trap's wall, allowing the fishers to select those fish that were required for processing that day.

STREAM-SCAPING AT KXOOYAX: CASE STUDY

Kxooyax is a stream and lake system located on the southeastern shore of Banks Island. This ancient fishing site is the territory of Gilasgamgan, Lasgeek. It has been the site of significant Gitxaała fisheries prior to, at, and well past the point of initial encounter with Europeans.

James Colnett, captain of the vessel *Prince of Wales* in October 1787, made the first known European record of this trap. Colnett's crew fished here without permission from the local titleholder. Additionally, his crew dismantled a portion of the trap: "The Wire that was fixed in the Run was to prevent the fish from getting too hastily up as well as down, & some of our people out of pity for the sickly fish above broke part of the wire down by which means the fish had a free passage up & when the run increased nothing to stop them" (Galois 2004:157). Colnett's inability to recognize the existing Indigenous regulations and customs related to use of local resources ultimately resulted in conflict between his crew and Gitxaała people. After Colnett's early account of Kxooyax, this place re-enters the official Euro-Canadian historic record via the assignment of a reserve for Gitxaała and the licensing of fishing rights by the Canadian government.

Following a meeting with Gitxaała hereditary leaders at K'moda in July 1891, Indian Reserve commissioner Peter O'Reilly agreed to establish Indian Reserve 12, Ks-or-yet (a variant of Kxooyax), for Gitxaała. He described the reserve as comprising 28 acres and "situated on the eastern shore of Banks Island, about four miles north of Gale Point" (O'Reilly 1889–1892). F. A. Devereaux (1891–1892) surveyed the reserve in May 1892 and noted the presence of an "Indian house" within the boundary of the surveyed reserve.

In 1911 the Canadian government assigned the commercial drag-seine fishing rights to BC Packers (License No. 18—Bare Bay).[3] The majority of these drag-seine licenses were normally operated by the Indigenous titleholder: those hereditary leaders who would customarily be considered the individual with rights to use and governance over such places. However, the assignment of fishing rights by the nonaboriginal fishing companies was not without problems. In 1890, for example, Sm'ooygit Seax advised a cannery manager operating near his territory to stop fishing. Seax's enactment of his authority and jurisdiction is recorded in a letter from M. K. Morrison, fishery guardian, to Thomas Mowat, inspector of fisheries:

> I was down to Low's Inlet and around Banks Island where I found considerable trouble between the Low's Inlet Canning people and the Indians, the cause I will try and make clear to

you. Part of Low's Inlet is an Indian Reserve (Kitk-a-thla Tribe), the Cannery is not on the Reserve where the fish is caught inside the Reserve line salt water, but close to the falls the same has to be hauled on Indian reserve below high water mark—Chef Shukes [Sm'ooygit Seax] forbid the Cannery people to fish, if they did he and his young men would cut their nets.… I went to Shukes and he told me as follows: Judge O'Reilly gave this land and water to my people, I do not want any Whitemen to fish here please tell your chief I have fished at Low's Inlet for 8 years, it is the principal support of myself and people.… The Indians on Banks Island told the Captain of the "Murrial" if he put out a seine to fish in their water he would be shot, he did not do it had not men enough. [Morrison 1890]

The cannery licensing system also interfered with Gitxaała customary practices by preferentially allocating licenses to community members in ways that were not necessarily in accord with traditional practices. Thus, on September 30, 1915, a petition of complaint was submitted to the Royal Commission on Indian Affairs regarding the process of assigning fishing rights at Kxooyax:

There is a salmon creek running on Eastside of Banks Island below Bare Hill called in our language K'Oyaht [a variant of Kxooyax] and from immemorial our forefathers in our family own it and claim it as their own, and it is from where they generally obtain their living…but, some years ago another man of different family butt in and troubling us by taking advantage of us in taking away that salmon creek from us, and we've been pressed out by him. He has been running that creek since for Lowe Inlet Cannery…and now we want to take it back from him through you by recognizing it to us. It was reserved to our family by or through the late Indian Agent.… This man's name who took that place away from us is Alfred Robinson also of Kitkatla, B.C. He has no right to claim that place and salmon creek other than us. We'll mention the names of only four of our forefathers herewith who own that place mentioned above from immemorial…Milsh, Haqulockgamlahap, Dwilthlagianat and Lthgooshamun.… We are their descendants and therefore we have right to run that salmon creek ourselves for that

> cannery.... We want to be allowed to get our own drag seine
> license for that salmon creek for next season. [Royal Commission
> on Indian Affairs 1912]

Echoes of these disagreements reverberate through to the present.

My own first visit to this place, nearly two centuries later, was in the 1970s while fishing with my father. This is the same area, in fact, where I first saw a stone trap (as I have described). Since the late 1990s I have revisited this place several times in order to record and observe the stone-trap complex in greater detail. The stone-trap complex at Kxooyax differs significantly from the one at K'moda (plate 11). Whereas the K'moda trap adjoins the stream mouth, at Kxooyax the trap complex is located in the creek mouth and entrance channel.

At least eight individual rock alignment features and three retaining pool features are identifiable along both sides of the creek. These extend over an area of approximately 430 m in length and range in elevation from a low of 2.45 m below the current barnacle line to 0.50 m above the barnacle line. The longest border alignment is 81 m in length and is located in the center of the stream in a V-shaped formation that substantially alters the stream flow. Four shorter linear features are present along the lower reaches of the southern stream bank running nearly perpendicular to the stream. These features run parallel to each other but do not match up with similar features on the northern stream bank. A distinct 50 m long arc-shaped boulder alignment follows the stream flow in contrast to the four linear features on the southern shoreline. The alignment located closest to the stream outlet extends all the way across the stream channel. This particular feature is only visible at the lowest point of low tide. The lower reaches of Kxooyax Stream have been extensively modified and engineered to facilitate access to the salmon fishery. The complexity and extent of the features represent a significant intergenerational commitment to securing access to and managing the use of salmon at this place. A canoe run along the north side of the stream mouth (near the "Indian" house documented by Devereaux) further demonstrates the extent of human use of this area.

In no way can Kxooyax be thought of as a "natural" space; it is totally creek-scaped. The path of the stream—from the high tide mark to the lowest low tide mark—shows clear evidence of human modification. Deep V-shaped stone structures provide access points for gaffing and dip netting salmon. Holding pools along the sides of the stream in the upper reaches of the tidal area allow for live storage and selective removal of fish according to processing and consumption needs. This is a human-designed space dedicated to the harvesting of salmon.

KXENK'AA'WEN: CASE STUDY

Kxenk'aa'wen, also known as Bonilla Arm, is an inlet on the west coast of Banks Island noted for, among other things, its seaweed, seals, fish, and range of productive salmon streams. This is an ancient place within the Gitxaała world, and stories link contemporary titleholders to their ancestors back beyond the ken of history. The very name, Kxenk'aa'wen, can be translated as Place of Special Trap. And, indeed, this place contains an amazing example of stone fish traps. Along one side of the inlet, stretching for a full kilometer, is a complex of stone traps the like of which is seldom observed along British Columbia's coast.

Kxenk'aa'wen is also one of the places where the Gitxaała people first met the K'msiwah. Gitxaała people engaged in fishing halibut off of Lax t'xal (Bonilla Island) sighted a strange being floating offshore.

> The greatest number [of Gitxaała people] would gather off the west coast of Banks Island, and Bonilla Island (lax t'xal). Here over a large area they would fish for halibut. One day these people set out as usual for their fishing each choosing a locality and all being very close to one another, in case of sudden danger. Then the chief Sabaan and his slave went the furthest out to sea to get more halibut then the rest. All were busy engaged in fishing and suddenly as if coming from nowhere, there appeared a huge being with many wings and no noise, it came so suddenly among the people that they were barely able to pull up their anchors and escape. [Beynon 1955–1956]

Upon investigation, Sabaan realized the strange being was a vessel with people on board—not a supernatural being.

The academic literature concerning these first encounters distils the various Gitxaała narratives into a singular event in which James Colnett met with Gitxaała at K'swan (Calamity Bay) (discussed previously in relation to Kxooyax; see, for example, Galois 2004). However, an alternative understanding (one that is more in keeping with internal Gitxaała perspectives) is that these historical narratives relate a series of encounters between Gitxaała and K'msiwah peoples. Colnett was not alone in traveling through these waters, and at least half a dozen ships are known to have been here around the time of Colnett's voyage. Thus, the K'msiwah academics writing about this issue have overlooked the possibility that variations in this story may, in fact, be evidence of different "first encounters" rather than errors of memory and discursive flourishes on the part of latter-day storytellers.

The contemporary titleholders, Inta 'we walp and Kaymt Kwa', exercise rights and responsibilities for this unique place that rest upon an ancient history extending back long before the K'msiwah drifted toward these coasts. Both men live on to this day through the products of their labor in Kxenk'aa'wen. In this unique place we find a long history of interconnected resource use within which salmon is a critical, but not exclusive, object of harvest.

Given the nature of the fish traps—how they are laid out along the shoreline, their shape, and their placement in relation to local streams—the target species were likely pink and dog salmon. Unlike sockeye, these two salmon species travel close to shore in dense schools (sockeye tend to run farther off the beach). Pink and dog salmon are thus particularly amenable to harvest using large half-moon-shaped stone barricades. Sockeye, another prime target species, was more likely harvested on its way up the stream mouth, given its different traveling behavior. Thus at Kxooyax, which is a sockeye stream, the stone traps are located within the creek. In Kxenk'aa'wen, where pink and dog salmon predominate (though there are significant sockeye runs here as well) the stone traps are located along the shoreline where they would more effectively intercept pink and dog salmon (plate 10).

With the development of the industrial commercial salmon fishery in the late 1800s came changes in the fishing techniques and gear types used even as the cultural values of Gitxaała remained consistent (Menzies and Butler 2008). In Kxenk'aa'wen a shift occurred away from the use of stone and wooden traps to cotton drag seines and then, in the mid-twentieth century, to seines and gill nets operated from motorized vessels. The operators of the new gear types remained the traditional titleholders and members of their house groups.

The exact date of the transition from stone traps to drag seines is not clear from either oral histories or the documentary record. The transition might have predated K'msiwah arrival, occurred at the moment K'msiwah first arrived (early maritime traders used drag seines in Gitxaała territory to harvest fish for food), or occurred later in the nineteenth century with the emergence of the industrial commercial fishery. Gitxaała people had the knowledge and the capacity to produce nettle-twine nets that could have been used as drag seines prior to the arrival of marine traders using seines. Coast Salish fishers in the Fraser River estuary and surrounding areas used large stationary nets to trap salmon (see, for example, Kew 1989; Suttles 1987). Thus, the leap from drag seines is not a conceptually significant one for experienced coastal fishermen like the Gitxaała. However, given that the catching capacity of the traps appeared to be more than sufficient given the supply of labor available prior to contact, it is also possible that there was no reason to shift technology until the new diseases brought by K'msiwah (smallpox, measles, flu) devastated coastal communities with one wave of death after another (Boyd 1999a; Campbell 2005). What is clear is that the customary laws of access and proprietorship governing these fishing sites date well before K'msiwah arrival and have continued into the present.

Changes in technique and gear type have implications for labor deployment. Fishing stone traps would require a community effort in which intergenerational labor would be deployed. Harvesting and processing would be coordinated. Shifting to drag seining for the commercial fishery would sever the coordination between harvesting and processing. Aside from that processing related to household consumption and trade, the majority of processing would be shifted out of community control into industrial fish-processing plants. Furthermore, the labor requirement would be reduced as the operation of a drag seine requires at most a dozen men. The harvested fish would be immediately loaded onto a tender boat and then transported to the fish-processing plant. Household fish processing would likely drop to about five hundred to one thousand fish per household given that most production of fish for economic benefit had been redirected to the industrial fish-processing plants rather than kept within community processing facilities (i.e., local smokehouses).

Sigyidm hana'a (matriarchs) Agnes Shaw and Charlotte Brown grew up in Kxenk'aa'wen. In a series of interviews and conversations they described the early twentieth-century experience of growing up and living within their father's clan territory. Their father, William Lewis, and his brother James were members of the Gispuwada (Blackfish) house group. As Agnes comments: "When my dad [William Lewis] get some seal, and then he'd call my grandfather [Samuel Wise Lewis] up, his father. And that was Albert Argyle's house, where my Dad stayed, in Kxenk'aa'wen, and then when he [Albert] died, then my dad moved in into his house" (interview, July 4, 2005).[4] Agnes and Charlotte describe an annual cycle that began in May with seaweed and halibut and finished in the late fall when the last salmon was put up in the big smokehouse located near their homes at Kxenk'aa'wen. A short list of resources harvested includes abalone, seal, sea lion, halibut, deer, and several species of berries. The people also maintained a garden out on Lax t'xal that was noted for its large white potatoes.

Agnes Shaw and Charlotte Brown explained that they would stay out at Banks after finishing up the commercial drag-seine fishery to put up their own fish. "There's a big smokehouse in Bonilla Arm. Four women in that big smokehouse. They divided it into four sections for those four ladies. One [section] for each lady" (Agnes Shaw, interview, March 10, 2005). Charlotte Brown estimated that the women put up about "seven hundred fish each for their households" (interview, December 14, 2001). Her sister Agnes comments, "We would dry the fish, my mom and me. Hundreds of fish in the big smokehouse. When they were dry, we put them higher up, to make them really dry. In the winter to eat them, we soak it overnight to get the salt out and then boil it. We did that for halibut too. Seal we would dry it really dry, sea lion too" (interview, February 11, 2002).

Charlotte Brown recalled drag seining in the early part of the twentieth century: "We were drag seining when Albert Argyle was alive. He was the owner of the river before, Killer Whale Clan. Last time we drag seined when I was small. They went into the salt lake and were fishing inside it. They got the boat in on a strong tide" (interview, December 14, 2001). Agnes also recalled:

> I can just remember. It was so good what those guys used to do. And then, when the boat ran along the shore to Gushi'algun, and we'd ride along, we were on there with all the kids. After a while near the rapids [*sxr'adzlaasen*, salt water rapids created by the tide] these guys would get out and pull their canoes along the shoreline [i.e., on foot], and then we'd pull the boat along to fish in the inlet by drag seine. And up by the tree line, that's where we'd sit, me and the rest of the ladies. And these ladies would get ready with their containers, empty cans, and then they'd spear crabs. I really wonder what that area is like today, whether there's lots of crabs there now. They'd build a big fire there. At twelve o'clock [the men] they'd come back and we'd all eat down the beach, they [the ladies] would build a fire and boil crabs. It was so good, what those people used to do." [Agnes Shaw, interview, July 4, 2005]

The contemporary titleholders continue to live on resources harvested in their Kxenk'aa'wen territories. While they still spend time living in their territories, they are less likely to spend as long there as families did during

Agnes and Charlotte's youth in the early years of the twentieth century. Salmon are now fished with gill nets that can be fixed in place or drifting. Whereas the stone traps required several households working together and the drag seines at least a dozen people to operate, gill nets can be fished with one or two people from a small skiff (12–18 ft in length) or a commercial gillnetter (35–40 ft in length). With the use of a small vessel and outboard motor, harvesters can selectively access their traditional territory and return home later the same day without having to camp overnight. Nonetheless, harvesters do remain on-site for periods of time depending upon the particular resources they are harvesting. Despite changes in time spent in the territory and techniques used for harvesting, the customary protocols governing ownership and access still pertain.

LAXYUUP GITXAAŁA AND THE CULTIVATION OF SALMON

These examples of customary fishing sites, and their human-modified environments, provide a backdrop to my contention that Gitxaała people purposefully managed salmon stocks. At each of these places fishing techniques relied upon similar principles that regulated who could fish, when they could fish, and how much fish would be taken. While drag seining was more recently introduced to Gitxaała territory than stone-trap or gaff fishing, it does have historical antecedents within north coast Indigenous fishing techniques. Nets of various sorts, including encircling seine-type nets, have been used for millennia by Indigenous fishers. The key point is that gear selection has always been based upon the particular ecological conditions at a site and the social dynamics of the community actively engaged in fishing the site. I would like to point out that a variety of gear is employed not only across different sites but even at the same site. Thus, fishers vary their harvesting techniques according to time of year, local conditions in weather and fish availability, and targeted species.

K'moda is an intensively productive salmon watershed that, since the regulatory removal of Gitxaała engagement, has seen a marked decline in fish stocks, surely the result of many factors. Nonetheless, the role of Gitxaała titleholders in the health and well-being of salmon resources should not be overlooked. Stories about Edward Gamble relate how he would survey the stream above the tidal falls and direct young members of his household and crew as they cleared and structured the watercourse in that area. The fish trap near the mouth of the creek was designed to take advantage of local tidal currents. The fishery at the falls allowed for selective removal of fish (Menzies and Butler 2007).

At Kooryet, the intensive modification of the creek above and below the high tide line reflected an intensive investment of human labor power, and Kooryet remains a customary harvesting site (in fact, several times while we were there our crew set a net to harvest salmon for our own consumption). Side pools and V-shaped structures point to techniques of fish harvesting that allowed the effective removal of fish from the stream. Again and again in interviews with hereditary leaders and active resource harvesters, we hear accounts of active management of the fish.

Kxenk'aa'wen is notable for the large and expansive set of traps that covers nearly a kilometer of the intertidal zone and is a salmon system of multiple pink, chum, and sockeye runs. Each species requires a somewhat different harvesting approach, and the material remains document a diversity of harvesting techniques. This area remains a key traditional territory from which the local titleholders harvest a range of marine resources.

A critical aspect of these Gitxaała fishing techniques is the ability to avoid, or to release unharmed, nontarget species. One of the problems in the contemporary industrial fishery is the mixed-stock nature of the coastal salmon fisheries. The fleet encounters a mass of fish that can include several species, spawners from a variety of creeks within the same species, and juveniles. Traditionally, the industrial gears have found it difficult to release nontarget species without stress or damage. After it was discovered in 1997 that coho stocks in the Fraser and Skeena River systems had drastically declined, the salmon fleet was required to release coho live at specific times and in particular areas (see Copes 1998). The stress on the fish during harvest required that they be resuscitated in "revival boxes" of fresh flowing seawater before release. Selectivity, both for species and for particular spawning runs, continues to be an issue for commercial salmon harvesters. The priority of weak stock management to preserve biodiversity obligates the Department of Fisheries and Oceans to manage a system according to the needs of the weakest run of spawners. If harvesters cannot identify and avoid salmon from a particular creek that has been identified as weak, then an entire fishery can be reduced or closed. When harvesting occurs at the mouth of a particular creek, the harvester must know exactly which spawning population is being targeted. Harvesting fish individually at close range ensures that the fisher can target a particular species (spring salmon rather than coho, for example) or size of fish.

Similarly, stone traps are located at or near to the mouths of creeks. As I have documented, harvesting was regulated based on the house leaders' observations of spawner abundance, and a specific ratio of harvest was maintained to prevent overly pressuring one run of fish. The traps corral the fish into a small pond of water, and they are then removed by harvesters. The fishers can select by species and age at this point and leave the nontarget or juvenile fish to escape the trap as the tide increases. The drag seine, being very close in function to the stone trap, is selective on the same bases.

Gitxaała technologies are also supported in their conservation potential by the social relations that guide and control their use. Whereas the K'msiwah fishery was driven by capitalist market forces and catching efficiency, Gitxaała fishing techniques and approaches have been regulated by community-based harvesting and use principles within a cultural framework that treats salmon as a relative and a social being deserving of respect.

CONCLUSION

This chapter begins with the assumption that purposeful human–environment interactions are not the sole prerogative of late capitalist society. Of course, this assertion is not new or startling. Empirical evidence exists for many disastrous human–environment interactions and many unintended consequences. The discussions of beneficial and positive outcomes, however, seem to me to be few and far between.

My experience growing up on the north coast of British Columbia, my time working with my father on his fishing boat, and my trips to Gitxaała and through Gitxaała territory lead me to question the idea that there was no intent or design behind all of the human labor that my ancestors gave to our traditional territory. I have more to do, more to say, more to consider as this argument is advanced. Nonetheless, from all that I have seen I believe that the environment that forms Gitxaała territory was a disturbed environment, an environment shaped through millennia of human practices and behaviors. It neither is nor was a pristine wilderness space in which nature wrote her own story. Laxyuup Gitxaała is the outcome of millennia of interactions, purposeful interventions, and human disturbances: this fact is what makes it the place it is today.

Acknowledgments

The ideas that undergird this chapter have grown out of the time spent with my father in conversation and in silence. To him I owe my lifelong fascination with the marine world. My focus on fish and fisheries may not make sense to my undergraduate students, but for those of us who are from this world, the most important things, after family, are unquestionably fish and how to catch and prepare them. The opportunity to bring this conversation into a setting that included others who share my love of fish and fisheries was a real pleasure. My thanks to Ben Colombi and James Brooks for the chance to participate in the School for Advanced Research seminar in Santa Fe that gave birth to the book of which my chapter is part. As part of my scholarly journey, I would like to thank my various research crews and colleagues who have taken the risk of joining me in my own backyard along British Columbia's northern coast. In particular, Caroline Butler, former student and now colleague, has had much to say and to contribute to this study. More recently, and as part of my foray into archaeological research, Iain McKechnie has generously shared his knowledge and—when his own work and family permitted—joined us on the north coast. Thanks also to the various field crew members who have worked with me, but most particularly to Brendan Gray, Kenzie Jessome, and Ken Innes. Thanks also to Naomi Smethurst, crew member and archaeologist, whose own archaeological research is focusing in detail upon aspects of fish traps that I only touch upon here. Ultimately this chapter emerges out of lifelong conversations within and about my family. To Teddy, Russ, Phil, and my dad, I say thanks for making our trips to the sea fun. There is always time for one more!

Notes

1. The section on K'moda is an abridged excerpt from Menzies and Butler 2007.

2. Sessional Papers are reports and papers that have been tabled in the House of Commons (and sometimes the Senate) and deposited with the clerk. These papers include annual reports of government departments and boards, the Estimates, the Public Accounts, and the reports of the Royal Commissions.

3. Bare Bay is the name commonly used to refer to the bay into which Kxooyax Creek empties.

4. Interviews were conducted as part of a research project led by the author.

9

"Salmon and His People"

Encounters with Global Capitalism

Benedict J. Colombi

INTRODUCTION

This chapter is an examination of Nimiipuu culture as it is situated in relation to salmon, a very specific place in northwest North America, and the global economy.[1] It is provocative because it places the analysis of Nimiipuu society in a larger context by exploring this society's reactive, yet unexpected, interactions with a growing capitalist economy. It is practical because it describes Nimiipuu strategies of Indigenous self-governance and self-determination as they invest in a whole range of land and resource uses, including the stewardship of salmon and confronting larger ecosystem processes such as global climate change.

More specifically, this chapter first emphasizes the importance of water, then salmon, and then relates the historical roots of industrial agriculture and dam-building in the Nimiipuu watersheds of the Snake and Columbia rivers. Thus, in order to understand the ways in which the market economy has influenced the lives of Nimiipuu peoples, we must examine the interplay between culture, politics, a new capitalist culture, and its transformative impacts on Nimiipuu people, who are tied to salmon. Applying an analysis of capitalist global economies to the Nimiipuus, however, requires some clarification.

Capitalism in this context refers to the mode of production or "dynamic interplay" of capital accumulation, power, and labor. Global capitalism takes on many forms, first with undercurrents of power and capital accumulation in industrial agriculture, and second with dam-building. In *Europe and the People without History,* Eric Wolf (1982:xiii) argues that "capitalism expands its reach and occupies new niches, it sets up new and diversified entrepreneurial scenarios. These scenarios attract new laborers, as well as new middle classes and entrepreneurial strata. All face the problem of how to fit their varied cultural understandings to the requirements of an ever-changing political economy. How these adaptations unfold is not predictable a priori."

An examination of the Nimiipuus as they engage with a capitalist culture of industrial agriculture and dams and exercise sovereignty in a modern context, I argue, elucidates the contradictions within the flows of money that eddy around salmon. For example, industrial agriculture and dam-building had enormous benefits for individual actors yet had transformative negative impacts on Nimiipuu life in regards to salmon. Industrial agriculture and salmon are connected in extraordinary ways through demands for water—particularly with regard to water for agriculture versus water for migrating salmon. Even more surprising is that the dams have allowed the Nimiipuus to gain capital for themselves, to focus on being practical in the context of the capital economy in which they are lodged, by working toward the restoration of salmon. Ironically, perhaps, the Bonneville Power Administration, the federal agency responsible for marketing hydropower to regional consumers, funds most Nimiipuu restoration work as well as the hatcheries. The precise nature of Nimiipuu salmon, watershed, and forest stewardship is not, however, a simple, happy story of the Nimiipuus ascribing cultural values to a species that many outsiders see in only economic terms. Rather, the Nimiipuus intend that their husbandry efforts and sovereignty work will yield real economic benefits to both tribal programs and individuals.

My emphasis first on water and then on salmon extends beyond riverbanks to the land and forest, to wild game and flora nutrient uptake, and draws from my more than a decade of collaborative research as an anthropologist working with Nimiipuu people and tribal programs, and before that a lifetime of dedicating myself to the understanding of rivers, including serving as a professional fishing guide in the Nimiipuu watersheds of the Snake and Columbia rivers.[2] My examination of Nimiipuu culture, in the context of salmon, also draws from the ethnographic literature, including Nimiipuu accounts of "Salmon and his people," a phrase describing how the fate of fish and the fate of Nimiipuu people are linked in fundamental and inseparable ways (Landeen and Pinkham 1999). According to

Leroy Seth, a Nimiipuu elder, "We learn a lot of lessons from watching the animals. The salmon are one of our best teachers. We learn from them that we have to do certain things by the season. We watch the salmon as smolts going to the ocean and observe them returning home. We see the many obstacles that they have to overcome. We see them fulfill the circle of life, just as we must do. If the salmon aren't here, the circle becomes broken and we all suffer" (Landeen and Pinkham 1999:3).

SALMON AND WATER AS IDEATIONAL AND MATERIAL FOUNDATIONS

The Nimiipuus possess a set of narratives built around their harvesting of several different runs of chinook, coho, chum, and sockeye salmon; cutthroat, lake, Dolly Varden, and steelhead trout; and different varieties of whitefish, sturgeon, suckers, lampreys, and pikeminnows. Before 1850 Nimiipuus are estimated to have consumed an average of 300 to 500 lbs of fish per adult per year (Anastasio 1972; Hewes 1947, 1973, 1998; Hunn 1982; Marshall 2006; Schalk 1986; Walker 1967). Recent archaeological analysis of fish bones recovered from the Northwest Coast and Columbia Plateau suggest seven thousand to eight thousand years of stability in salmon use (Campbell and Butler 2010). Moreover, anthropologists and archaeologists have shown that people in the Pacific Northwest developed remarkable subsistence and social patterns based on the annual return of migrating salmon (Ames and Maschner 1999; Campbell and Butler 2004; Hayden and Schulting 1997; Matson 1992; Schalk 1977; Suttles 1990; Walker 1998a).

Beyond salmon, Nimiipuus' use of plants, for medicinal and industrial purposes, ranks nearly as high as the Nimiipuu preference for fish, deer, elk, moose, and bison. Nimiipuu food-collecting strategies require the active management of seasonal foods in preparation for winter. The Nimiipuus resisted all forms of species-specific agriculture, practicing instead a "mode of agriculture" in their manipulation of wild plant foods (Marshall 1999:173). Nimiipuu men typically hunted game and harvested fish, and women were responsible for harvesting an abundance of plant foods as well as preparing and storing fish and game resources for trade and consumption. Nimiipuu women retained "equal access to power, authority, and autonomy" in all spheres of Nimiipuu life (Ackerman 2003). Equitable Nimiipuu gender roles exist today with women serving on the tribal council and a woman as chair of the tribal executive committee. Women also control the trade and regulation of traditional tribal foods, such as roots, berries, and salmon.

Salmon and water serve as the ideational and material foundations of

Nimiipuu knowledge and survival (Marshall 2006). Horace Axtel (personal communication 2008), a Nez Perce elder, commented on the importance of water and salmon: "According to our spiritual way of life, everything is based on nature. Anything that grows or lives is part of our spiritual life. The most important element we have in way of life is water. The next most important element is the fish because the fish comes from water."

Salmon and water are present in Nez Perce daily life and ceremony and are necessary for the fulfillment of individual and community life (see figure 9.1). In 2006 Alan G. Marshall, an anthropologist with long-standing relationships to the Nimiipuus, published the article "Fish, Water, and Nez Perce Life." In his analysis, which drew from more than four decades of ethnographic fieldwork, Marshall (2006:774) provided vivid descriptions of salmon, both culturally and ecologically, and observed that "some active fishermen take up to 200 or more salmon per year. Men who are able to do this receive high praise and prestige because they provide the necessary raw resources to women for the production of Indian food for their families and communities. Families with enough fish to eat as a normal part of their diets are regarded as traditional. Such families are considered strong spiritually and as authorities on Nez Perce Indian life and history." Marshall also went on to describe deliberate and direct involvement of Nimiipuu culture with the salmon at the start of each year's season:

> The early season fishing sites were not haphazardly located on the great rivers, the Snake, main Clearwater, and Salmon. Nez Perce men knew from long personal and family experience where the fish would stop and rest in their upstream migration. Men also knew the underwater trails that they followed. So the men built structures which made their efforts and tools much more efficient. All day and all night, just as at Celilo Falls in living memory, men dip netted or speared fish with leisters or harpoons from wooden platforms built on steep banks over deep holding water. Fish walls (or rock piers), were built out into the salmon's underwater trails to divert and hold fish that would otherwise simply swim by so that those fish, too, could be taken. Canoes were used, often in flotillas, as platforms for dip netting and spearing fish. As this wealth poured in, women gutted, filleted, smoked, dried, pulverized, and packed fish in large open structures erected for this purpose. Most of these sites were at or near winter villages. There was little resting: everyone knew that

this was the main chance for a winter without hunger. [Marshall 2006:781]

Clearly, Nimiipuu peoples took active roles in shaping outcomes with their purposeful management of watersheds and salmon-based resources (see Menzies, chapter 8, and Kasten, chapter 4, this volume). If Nimiipuus proved selective in their taking of salmon, as were the Gitxaała and Koryaks, their management may also have contributed to the noteworthy abundance of Columbia Basin salmon at the time of Euro-American settlement in the 1850s.

On this abundance, fisheries biologist James Lichatowich (1999:180) noted that "historically, the Columbia produced more chinook and coho salmon and steelhead trout than any other river in the world. Prior to the arrival of Euro-Americans, 10 to 16 million adult salmon of all species entered the river each year. Though all five species of salmon spawned in the Columbia River, the royal chinook was by far the most abundant. About 8 to 10 million Chinook entered the river each year. Many of them, especially the 'June hogs' of the summer run, weighed in at fifty to sixty pounds each."

Nimiipuu peoples continue to use salmon in everyday ceremonial events including births and funerals; testimonial "giveaways" for the first anniversary marking an individual's death; weddings; "name-giving" ceremonies; "first salmon," "first kill," and "first roots" ceremonies marking adulthood; and "pow-wows" and other celebrations, including "dinners" conducted to share and give thanks for the joy of life (Marshall 2006). The dinners, which are both ritual feasts and nonritual meals, include items unavailable for purchase in supermarkets, including "water" (kúus), chinook salmon (nac'óox), meat (elk, deer, moose, and bison; núukt), roots (qáaws), and huckleberries (cemíitx).[3] The capture of Nimiipuu foods is thought of as a gift (pínitiní) from the creator (haniyaw'áat) because these living beings gave up their lives so that people can continue to prosper. The creator made both the world and humanity, and Nimiipuu engagements are a matrix of labor, ceremony, and place, told through water (kúus) and salmon (léwliks).

The Nimiipuus develop family, band, and tribe identities based on their relations to land, water, and salmon. Social cohesion and basic values are enhanced and governed by these relations. "We need the salmon for our future and for our children," proclaimed Nez Perce elder Julia Davis-Wheeler (Landeen and Pinkham 1999:111). "We need the salmon because it is part of our lives and part of our history. The salmon is a part of us, and we are a part of it. Our children need to be able to feel what it is like to catch and eat salmon. They need to be able to experience that sense of respect that many of us have felt in past years" (1999:111).

Former Nez Perce Tribal Executive Committee (NPTEC) member Arthur Taylor, testifying in 1997 on the centrality of water and salmon in Nimiipuu life before a US House of Representatives Subcommittee on Water and Power, stated:

> It is with the utmost respect and honor that I am allowed to submit written testimony on behalf of my people. From time immemorial, the Nez Perce People have utilized the fish, water, animals, and medicinal plants which have been produced by the Columbia River. All living creatures which have been created by the Creator are considered sacred to the Nez Perce People. It is simply for this reason during the springtime, we honor these gifts which have been bestowed upon the Nez Perce. We honor the return of the first salmon back to the river, as well as, honoring the first roots and berries in special ceremonies. The Nez Perce People are proud of their heritage in the Pacific Northwest and in particular our heritage along the Columbia River. [U.S. House of Representatives 1997:1]

In their cultural rankings of fish, Nimiipuu people prefer salmon, first chinook, then sockeye, and lastly coho; then eels (*hésu*); sturgeon (*qíilex*); steelhead (*Oncorhynchus mykiss*; *héyey*), cutthroat (*Oncorhynchus clarki*; *waw'álam*), and bull (*ís'lam*) trout; northern pikeminnows; suckers; and chiselmouths. Introduced fish species, like carp, walleye, and bass, are rarely if ever used and regarded as either culturally insignificant or economically unimportant. Salmon from hatcheries is acceptable but not preferred, and fish other than salmon is generally disliked. One could argue that the preference for endemic species is more healthy and in keeping with the local environment and culture.

Water (kúus), like fish, has an ideational and material importance to Nimiipuu cosmology and everyday survival. Water is home to powerful spirits, and materially, water is used for medicine and healing purposes. According to Nimiipuu cosmology, eddies and confluences of free-flowing rivers and waterfalls are thought to be the homes of spirits (Marshall 2006). Similar to how Nimiipuus regard fish, not all water sources are considered equal in either importance or preference. Springs possess the purest, strongest, and most spiritually powerful water and are used in the ritual sweathouse where the water is poured on hot rocks. Cold flowing water from high mountain snowmelt is less preferred than spring water but is considered "better" than water that runs at lower elevations, with less velocity, and at higher temperatures. Nimiipuu rankings of water types reflect their cultural knowledge because springwater is less likely to contain pollutants than water at lower velocity and higher temperature, which provides a better habitat for pathogens.

Water (kúus) and salmon (léwliks) are found in streams and rivers of great cultural importance. Basic values and beliefs are evident as moral instruction in Nimiipuu stories, such as "Coyote Breaks the Fish Dam at Celilo," "The Maiden and the Salmon," "How Salmon Got Over the Falls," and "Coyote and Salmon" (Phinney 1934; Spinden 1908; Walker 1998b). The creation story as told by tribal elder Allen Pinkham, in his account of "A Meeting between Creator and the Animals," speaks of a time before humans when the creator asked that all the animals, including salmon, come forward to help the new human beings:

> Salmon and Steelhead came forward and said, "We can help the human beings with our flesh." Salmon said, "When we come up the river we will die, so the human beings will have to catch us before that happens. I'll come up only on certain times of the year, and that's when they'll have to catch me." Then Steelhead said, "I want to come in the wintertime, but I'll give them something special. That will be the glue from my skin. This glue can be used to make bows and spears. I'll be in the water all winter long." So Creator let Steelhead become qualified. Sockeye Salmon came forward and he said, "I don't want to be big like Chinook Salmon and Steelhead, and my flesh will be red because I will eat different foods." Then Trout came forward and he said, "I am going to look like Steelhead, but I am not going to go down to the ocean. I'll just stay here in the waters even in the winter, and if these human beings can find me they can have me for food. But in the wintertime I will be down in the gravel and if they can find me that's where I will be." Then Eel came out and said, "I don't want to look like the Steelhead or Salmon or Trout. I want to be long, and when I rest I want to put my mouth on the rocks. But I'll come up the river every year, and they can use my flesh for food." So this is how the fish became qualified. [Axtell et al. 2003:114]

These kinds of stories illuminate the creation of the world and the

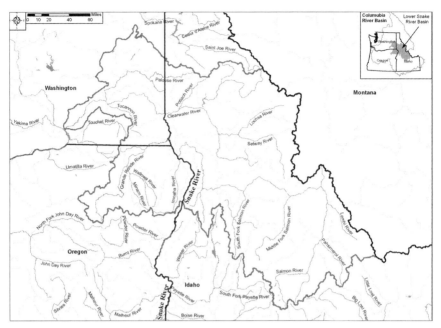

FIGURE 9.1

Nimiipuu salmon drainages of the territorial homeland, lower Snake River. Source: Jeff Cronce, GIS Coordinator, Nez Perce Tribe, 2011.

beings that inhabit it and include moral teachings tied to Nimiipuu drainages, from Celilo Falls on the mid-Columbia to the tributaries of the Snake River, including the Palouse, Tucannon, Clearwater, Grande Ronde, Salmon, Weiser, and Payette rivers (figure 9.1). Except for above the lower falls on the Palouse River, all of these rivers and streams supported annual returns of salmon, and all of the sub-basins, including the Palouse River, flourished with abundant springs, cold running water, waterfalls, deep water holes, and eddies.

ENCOUNTERS WITH EARLY GLOBAL CAPITALISM

The Lewis and Clark Expedition met the Nimiipuus in the upper reaches of the Clearwater River drainage in 1805. This encounter signaled the intrusion of a capitalist global economy into Nimiipuu territory. The relationship between Nimiipuu peoples and global capitalism deepened with the fur trade during which time, as historian Richard White (1983:xv) states in his book *The Roots of Dependency*, "Understanding change involves, not finding the invisible hand of economic interests, but rather finding the reciprocal influences of culture, politics, economics, and the environment. For the Indians, the result of these changes was dependency."

By 1813 some Nimiipuus were actively trading furs with the North West Company. This trade signaled the beginning of Nimiipuu engagements with a monied economy. Fur-trading companies encouraged Nimiipuu men to marry more wives and become "chiefs," which created more fur processors. Institutional shifts increased the pace at which pelts could be trapped, processed, bought from producers, and sold for greater profit, thereby giving way to an imbalance in economic and political relations.

The fur trade brought new forms of prosperity yet caused many Nimiipuu people to abandon traditional subsistence activities. In turn, the Nimiipuus, like other Indigenous peoples, "became specialized laborers in a putting-out system, in which the entrepreneurs advanced both production goods and consumption goods against commodities to be delivered in the future. Such specialization tied the native Americans more firmly into continent-wide and international networks of exchange, as subordinate producers rather than as partners" (Wolf 1982:194). The fur trade also proved indirectly responsible for spreading European pathogens. Epidemics brought to Nimiipuu lands by non-Native trappers ravaged villages, and by 1841 Nimiipuu populations dwindled to two thousand individuals compared to the 1805 estimate of more than six thousand (Walker 1998a).

Increasing demands for land prompted the US government to respond to the Nimiipuus with policies of removal and treaty agreements in the 1850s. The treaties of 1855, 1863, and 1868 established legal ties between the United States and the Nimiipuus, with the young and ambitious governor of Washington territory, Isaac Stevens, granting the Nimiipuus ownership of a large and contiguous reservation and off-reservation rights to fish, hunt, and gather at "all usual and accustomed places" (Axtell et al. 2003:117; also see Diver, chapter 10, in this collection for a discussion of Columbia Basin treaties and rights to salmon). Nimiipuu leaders, in return, ceded large portions of their territorial homeland in order to retain the rights described in the 1855 treaty: "The right of taking fish in all the streams where running through or bordering said reservation is further secured to said Indians; as also the right of taking fish at all usual and accustomed places in common with citizens of the Territory; and of erecting temporary buildings for curing, together with the privilege of hunting, gathering roots and berries, and pasturing their horses and cattle upon open and unclaimed land" (Axtell et al. 2003:117). Idaho became a territory in 1863, and US officials and Nimiipuu representatives renegotiated the 1855 treaty (Phinney 2002). A second treaty emerged in 1863, which reduced Nimiipuu land holdings by 90 percent (i.e., 8 million acres of reservation land retained by the Treaty of 1855 were reduced to a total of 800,000 acres in the Treaty of 1863).

Nimiipuus held reservation land in common and prohibited non-Native trespass. Even so, early settlers wanted access to arable land and other prized natural resources within reservation boundaries. Thus, in 1887 President Grover Cleveland placed the Nimiipuus "on the first list of tribes to be allotted under the newly passed Dawes Act" (Greenwald 2002:59). The Dawes Act allotted each Nimiipuu head of household 160 acres, individuals over eighteen years of age 80 acres, and those under eighteen, who were mostly orphans, 40 acres in fee-simple, and thus alienable, title. More important, the Dawes (or General Allotment) Act was a carefully crafted policy aimed at dividing and destroying communally owned property. It also encouraged capital accumulation through individual labor and private property and set a precedent for the development of industrial agriculture and dam-building on Nimiipuu lands.

Christian converts were the first Nimiipuus to engage in an agricultural economy. Moreover, Nimiipuu farming during this period was small in scale and farmland was located largely along the Clearwater, Salmon, and Snake rivers, taking advantage of the fertile soils created by annual and periodic flooding. Surplus produce was sold to non-Native settlers, mostly miners, who began trespassing in large numbers after the 1855 treaty. Nimiipuu people engaged with this new capitalist economy by bartering and selling agrarian products and became astute at acquiring specific articles of the introduced "monied" economy—for example, alcohol, guns, and tobacco. Besides farming, the Nimiipuus managed household gardens, domesticated animal pastures, and feedlots. The Nimiipuus exacted tolls along all major migratory routes leading to gold mines and off-reservation settlements. They also controlled toll bridges, utilizing natural crossings of fallen logs (Wells 1958).

Some Nimiipuus retained ownership of allotted lands near important fishing areas and along steep canyons and plateaus adjacent to rivers. The Nimiipuus who converted to Christianity usually occupied flat and rolling prairie lands more suitable for large-scale agriculture. Archie Phinney (2002:22), a Nimiipuu anthropologist writing in the 1930s, stated that "this region, once abundant with wild game, fish, berries and roots, had been transformed into a settled territory, dotted with white town sites and farmsteads." By the early twentieth century most farmers cultivated fixed grains, such as wheat, without irrigation. Moreover, Nimiipuu farmers, although few in number, began emulating capital-intensive techniques employed by early industrial farming.

With the passing of the Burke Act in 1906, the Nimiipuus could sell or lease allotted lands, mostly to non-Indians, and the leasing and sale of lands provided many Nimiipuus with needed capital. Subsequent economic downturns devalued the land, and the Nimiipuus were not able to collect as much rent. Allotted lands were divided into smaller fractions, through a process known as "fractionated heirship," wherein smaller and smaller pieces of land get passed to the heirs of the original allottees. Emily Greenwald (2002:86–87) noted that "not many Nez Perces farmed allotments themselves: Superintendent Oscar Lipps reported about 300 Nez Perces cultivating about 5,000 acres in 1908. Lipps also observed that most Nez Perces had homes in the valleys along the streams [near the salmon], although their farms were up on the prairies. Their residence patterns continued to reflect traditional settlement, even though their economy had changed."

Settlement of Nimiipuu lands by outsiders intensified in the twentieth century. Still, considerable numbers of Nimiipuu people resisted ideologies of individualism and self-sale of labor in a capitalist system and continued to practice seasonal movements around fishing for salmon, collecting berries and roots, and hunting wild game. Many Nimiipuus remained committed to group participation and traditional community life, often seeing little value in farming.

The Bureau of Indian Affairs handled all individual and tribally owned trust lands, leasing Nimiipuu properties to white farmers. Renting allotted land provided some Nimiipuus with short-lived economic gains. The money also allowed Nimiipuu people to engage in a growing capitalist economy by purchasing imported foods and manufactured goods or moving to cities and regions outside the territorial homeland for employment purposes.

The Dawes Act, a critical US policy in the history of assimilation and economic development, proved a failure on three levels. First, the federal government had difficulty transcending Nimiipuu values of collective community. Most Nimiipuus failed to be enticed by outside efforts to make land more productive and profitable through capital-intensive agriculture. Second, the leasing and sale of individual trust lands enabled the Nimiipuus to sell reservation land to non-Indians, thus making the Nimiipuus a new class of land-poor Indians. Third, agricultural development on Nimiipuu lands caused great harm to the environment, including watersheds. Phinney reflects on the relationship of degradation and the General Allotment Act:

White Men exploited the territory with a vengeance. Pasturelands were overgrazed, forests were clear-cut by lumber companies with no thought of reforestation, agricultural lands were wastefully farmed out, particularly Indian lands, for the leaseholder had no interest in maintaining the fertility of, or building up, the soil of lands that were his only temporarily. Lack of fertilization and proper summer fallowing soon decreased the productivity of farmlands and resulted in the decrease rental value of Indian lands. On the other hand, the cycles of depression of a capitalistic economy brought hard times for the white farmers. This meant that in some years the Indians received irregular and diminished payments of lease money or they could not rent their lands at all. [Phinney 2002:26]

ENCOUNTERS WITH DAM-BUILDING AND INDUSTRIAL AGRICULTURE

Dam-building and industrial agriculture were driven by pro-growth policies produced during the post–World War II globalization period. Dam-building also gained public support from the national ethos of "public works projects for the public good" that were to bring energy to households and businesses and deliver water to arid regions of the inland Northwest. Dam-building enabled private and public defense industries (i.e., Boeing and Hanford) to harness more energy, produce aluminum for airplanes, and process plutonium for nuclear weapons. It also created year-round river barge transportation, mostly of agricultural commodities, and delivered water to farmers with irrigation. In short, industrial agriculture and dam-building had measurable benefits for individual actors within a growing capitalist economy but had devastating impacts on Nimiipuu salmon watersheds.

The transformation of early farming to large-scale agribusiness was the result of a concentrated effort predicated on economic growth and national defense. Key changes after 1940 replaced self-sufficient farm inputs of human labor and horses with fossil fuel–driven machinery and agricultural chemicals. Industrial farming produced higher yields and tremendous surpluses. For example, per-acre yields on Nimiipuu lands increased threefold from 1910 to 1987 (Bodley 2003). However, industrial agriculture requires the use of fossil fuels, mechanized equipment, and chemical-based fertilizers. Thus, many Nimiipuus were unable to participate in industrial farming because of these capital requirements. Chemical fertilizers and fossil fuels were nonexistent on Nimiipuu lands in 1910; however, by 1940 they comprised 31 percent of total farm inputs (Bodley 2005).

Furthermore, World War II generated new demands for national defense and hydroelectricity. Prior to the war, a rail system provided farmers with the primary mode of transporting grain to consumers. After the Second World War, the push to transport grain by river barge prompted the US Army Corps of Engineers to build four new dams along the lower Snake River. These dams on the lower Snake would link inland economies with those on the middle and lower reaches of the Columbia River. The historian Richard White (1995:108) in his book *The Organic Machine* speaks of a changing river, stating that "the Columbia has become an organic machine which human beings manage without fully understanding what they have created. The organic machine has, in turn, spawned a virtual river whose life influences the actual Columbia."

Nimiipuu leaders and support groups opposed dam-building from its inception. Nevertheless, between 1955 and 1975 the US Army Corps of Engineers built all four dams on the lower Snake River. The greater social power of federal agencies and individual elites facilitated growth in two economic sectors: industrial agriculture and commercial shipping. Individual actors expanded profits by transporting commodities by river barge, which is a heavily subsidized industry, versus shipping grain by either railcar or highway transport.

Proponents of dams argued that dam-building would stimulate economic growth and facilitate national defense—that the dams would supply Hanford and aluminum smelters with electricity from hydropower and facilitate the movement of agricultural commodities by river barge to global markets. The US Army Corps of Engineers built Lower Granite Dam during a time of heightened Indigenous sovereignty actions and environmental consciousness. In 1975 Nimiipuu leaders pointed to the harmful effects of dams on migrating salmon and their habitat. Nimiipuu leaders and other leaders from Columbia Basin tribes began campaigning publicly for dam removal, noting that dams violate the 1855 treaty agreements, thus negating salmon as a reserved property right, which are "those rights that a tribe never expressly surrendered or gave up" (Wilkins and Lomawaima 2001:120).

In the context of treaty rights, salmon are utilized as follows: as food, as an item of trade, and as a necessary component of religious expression. In the 1855 treaty, Nimiipuu people retained the "right of taking fish...at all usual and accustomed fishing sites" (Axtell et al. 2003:117). A century later, the US Supreme Court (*Washington v. Washington State Commercial Passenger*

Fishing Vessel Ass'n., 443 U.S. 658 [1979]) ruled that the original treaties entitled treaty tribes to one-half the total harvest of salmon and approved the use of modern fishing equipment: "Without this technology, the rulings recognizing treaty fishing rights would have been hollow victories: in these times of intensified fishing pressure and dwindling runs of fish due to dams and other developments in the watersheds, modern gear is a necessity if the tribes are to obtain the amount of fish to which they are entitled under court-ordered apportionment" (Wilkinson 1987:73).

As recently as February 2011, the Nez Perce Tribe, the State of Oregon, and a coalition of conservation and fishing groups contended that the federal strategy to mitigate the effects of dams and protect salmon was both inadequate and illegal. A year earlier, in legal briefs filed on October 29, 2010, the Nez Perce and Spokane tribes asked "U.S. District Court Judge James A. Redden to declare the 2008 Biological Opinion and the 2010 supplemental Biological Opinion illegal and required federal agencies to go back to the drawing board" (*Columbia Basin Fish and Wildlife News Bulletin* 2010). However, the courts require an expert biological opinion when a federal action, such as modifying dams on the Snake and Columbia rivers, "is not likely to jeopardize the continued existence of any threatened or endangered species or result in the destruction or adverse modification of designated critical habitat" (NOAA Fisheries 2011).

On one side of the debate are the Nimiipuus allied with environmentalists, the State of Oregon, and non-Native fishing communities. On the other side are dam-building interests, including aluminum producers, industrial agriculturalists, and river barge operations with support from political allies in Idaho, Oregon, Montana, and Washington. Thus, "it would be a mistake to view this as a routine battle between old adversaries. The sides in this struggle represent profoundly divergent views that reflect deep philosophical divisions in our society and in the human community at large" (VanDevelder 2011).

The Nimiipuus have refused on religious grounds to estimate an appropriate monetary amount for repatriation; however, dollar values may be between six and twelve billion. A report by the Institute of Fisheries Resources, titled "The Cost of Doing Nothing," used widely accepted economic methods to calculate a net value of $13 billion for Columbia Basin salmon (Radtke and Davis 1996). As a result of cultural loss, several proposals to repatriate off-reservation Nimiipuu lands, like those located in Oregon's Wallowa Valley (home to Chief Joseph's band), are being considered. In 2009 Vera Sonneck, who directs the Cultural Resource Program for the Nimiipuus, called the Wallowa Valley "almost heaven, the place where [our] Nez Perce ancestors came to hunt, fish and seek visions" (Cockle 2009).

Snake River salmon account for half of all salmon migrating to the Columbia Basin, thus a net value for salmon has been calculated at $6.5 billion. The Nimiipuus participate in some of these market values, too. For example, in the Columbia River Anadromous Fish Restoration Plan of the Nez Perce (Nimiipuu), Umatilla, Warm Springs, and Yakama Tribes, called *Wy-Kan-Ush-Mi Wa-Kish-Wit*, or "Spirit of the Salmon," a restored fishery would amount to an estimated $98 million in annual personal income for Columbia Basin tribal communities (Columbia River Inter-Tribal Fish Commission 2011). The commercialization of salmon requires significant hatchery inputs by all four Columbia Basin treaty tribes. For example, the majority of hatcheries are tribally operated—the Nimiipuus operate fifteen hatchery facilities—and many are co-managed with state and federal facilities. In sum, more than 90 percent of the salmon caught in the Columbia and Snake rivers originate from hatcheries, with tribal hatchery inputs making possible the over $1 billion spent each year by anglers in the regional sport-fishing economy (Washington Department of Fish and Wildlife 2011).

Tribal claims could also include lost land value. By the late 1800s, tribes in the Columbia Basin ceded over 6 million acres of communally managed land to the United States. The Institute for Fisheries Resources attached a value of $2,000 per acre to this land, with the value of tribal land cessations an additional $12 billion (Radtke and Davis 1996). In short, if harvestable fish stocks are not restored, the federal government and taxpayers could be responsible for compensating treaty tribes for roughly $23 billion.

Nimiipuu leadership expends considerable resources in fighting for watershed habitat to support salmon reproduction as well as migration, and not just for cultural purposes. Commercial and sport fisheries yield income for individual members and tribal programs. The Nimiipuus protect tribal fishing activities and economic opportunities through legal actions in which, according to Daniel McCool (2002:79) in his book *Native Waters: Contemporary Indian Water Settlements and the Second Treaty Era*, the Nimiipuus and federal agencies have "spent $10 million preparing their water case for trial and will spend an additional $2 million per year in the years ahead."

The Nimiipuus advocate for salmon in two ways: first by securing adequate flows in the watersheds of the Snake and Columbia rivers and second by maintaining salmon as a reserved right. Nimiipuu elder Levi Holt commented on the importance of water: "The tribes have always treated water as a medicine because it nourishes the life of the earth, flushing poisons out of humans, other creatures, and the land. We know that to be productive, water must be kept clean. When water is kept cold and clean, it takes care of the salmon" (Taylor 2010).

In 1993 remaining salmon counts were at an all-time historical low with roughly 450,000 fish returning to the Columbia Basin, nearly half of which were harvested. Nimiipuu tribal programs, federal agencies, and state fish and game programs, therefore, invested large sums of money in restoring salmon and related habitats. On the Columbia River this type of policy has resulted in skyrocketing costs. In 2003 a retired biologist with the US Army Corps of Engineers stated that roughly $8 to $10 billion had been spent to improve fish passage on the lower Snake River (personal communication 2003). A fish screen, for example, was implemented to allow migrating smolts (i.e., juvenile salmon) to bypass intake valves at McNary Dam. This improvement cost the federal government and US taxpayers roughly $18 million.

More recently, surface bypass structures installed by the US Army Corps of Engineers on most Snake and Columbia River dams cost nearly $10 to $15 million per structure. The bypass structures, however, have led to additional costs well over what the US Army Corps of Engineers initially proposed. Supplementary costs have resulted from complications associated with construction, contract changes, as well as litigation. For example, a former staff attorney working for the US Army Corps of Engineers described a case where the agency had to settle a $6 million lawsuit with a surface bypass fabrication contractor that arose predominantly out of the difficulty of having to work around fish-viewing windows (personal communication 2011). Most important, bypass structures, screens, fish ladders, and the transportation of migrating smolts around dams by river barge and highway are striking examples of how taxpayer monies are expended by federal agencies in the context of dam-building, salmon migrations, legal battles, and environmental impacts.

Columbia Basin dams allow the river barge industry to ship agricultural commodities (i.e., wheat, barley, and lentils) in larger quantities and at lower rates than would be possible by highway or rail transportation. In 2006, according to an agricultural economist at Washington State University, 92 percent of grain production on Nimiipuu lands was exported globally and consumed largely in China (personal communication 2006). Moreover, according to the *Seattle Post-Intelligencer*, "Already this year, China has accepted 1.8 million metric tons of U.S. wheat—nearly 17 times as much as all of last year. And about 60 percent of it was funneled through Columbia and lower Snake river ports. For the first time in 30 years, China has entered the Pacific Northwest wheat market on a dramatic scale" (Wong 2004). With the removal of dams, the cost of shipping grain by railroad and highway increases the price per bushel of wheat by 8 to 10 percent. The irony in wheat production is that none of the wheat producers on Nimiipuu lands, including the reservation, are tribal members. Deep inequalities of this magnitude are social creations with a history (Colombi 2005).

In 2008 officials with the Bush administration and Bonneville Power Administration reached an "agreement" with Columbia Basin tribes.[4] Those signing the agreement, known as the Columbia Basin Fish Accords, included the Colville Confederated Tribes, Confederated Tribes of the Umatilla Reservation, Confederated Tribes of the Warm Springs Reservation, Shoshone-Bannock Tribes, and Yakama Nation.

The Columbia Basin Fish Accords commits Bonneville Power Administration to giving the tribes more than $900 million in ratepayer monies. In turn, the tribes signing the agreement will largely use the money to aid in habitat restoration and hatchery improvements for salmon. Money is also allocated to federal agencies to fund additional spillway weirs and screens in an effort to protect fish on some dams located in the Columbia Basin (Banse 2008). Ironically, however, the agreement also commits participating tribes to refrain from publicly opposing the government's operation of dams or advocating for their removal for a ten-year period from 2008 to 2018. Fearing the loss of self-determination, the Nimiipuus declined to sign the agreement, with leaders stating that "they want[ed] to keep their options open to press for breaching the four lower Snake River dams" (McCall 2008). In the most recent hearing before Judge Redden in 2011, those tribes in support of the Columbia Basin Fish Accords, named previously, filed amicus briefs on behalf of the federal government.

NIMIIPUU ALTERNATIVE FUTURES

Salmon and water give the Nimiipuus power. In the 1855 treaty, the Nimiipuus reserved the right to fish for salmon and the right to water. The treaty established both land and use rights that were critical for Nimiipuu survival: land rights allowed the Nimiipuus to retain a base of power, and use rights allowed them to use salmon. The treaties recognize the Nimiipuus as a sovereign nation, with distinct rights to both salmon and water.

The nineteenth and twentieth centuries marked a period of great change and reorganization, and the 1855 treaty contained Nimiipuu strategies for resolving conflicts and strengthening their sovereignty. During the drafting of the 1855 treaty, the Nimiipuus attempted to influence outcomes, even under difficult circumstances, by arriving late to the treaty negotiations. In doing this, the Nimiipuus served notice with their behavior that they wanted to be treated as equals in the treaty negotiations.

Wild salmon, not hatchery, returns have averaged one-tenth of historic levels, with as few as 200,000 fish returning to the Columbia River each year (Augerot 2005). The current decline in returning salmon can be attributed to the impact of hydroelectric dams, irrigation projects, overharvest, release of too many production-hatchery fish, and overall habitat loss (Blumm 2002; Lichatowich 1999).

Dams also make inland rivers important transportation corridors to world markets. Wheat growers ship commodities downstream on the Snake and Columbia rivers via barges, while agricultural inputs such as petroleum fuel and chemical fertilizers move upstream to production centers (Rother 2001). China consumes over 90 percent of the wheat produced within the boundaries of the Nimiipuu reservation. None of the wheat producers are Nimiipuus, and Nimiipuu lands in non-Indian ownership support this agricultural production (Colombi 2012).

Nimiipuu leaders never expressly surrendered the right to fish at all usual and accustomed places, which was retained by the Nimiipuus in signing the 1855 treaty with the United States, and measurable declines in salmon and water are immediate dangers to Nimiipuu rights and their way of life. However, in response to the impacts of contact, colonization, and the acceleration of global capitalism in the twentieth century, the Nimiipuus are developing alternative futures that reach beyond external policies of assimilation and economics. Nimiipuu salmon management utilizes Indigenous knowledge to fashion current and informed policies and to implement those decisions in their homeland. Beyond salmon's cultural value, the Nimiipuus manage the economic value of salmon, which is critically important for tribal revenue and individual member income, as described by Sibyl Diver's chapter on comanagement (chapter 10, this volume).

Nimiipuu alternatives to the current salmon crisis may also have the capacity to countervail the negative effects of dam-building and industrial agriculture on salmon-related resources. Drawing on the Doctrine of Reserved Rights (Wilkins and Lomawaima 2001) and the Treaty of 1855, the Nimiipuus operate natural resource programs, including a well-established fisheries program. In this context, Nimiipuu efforts to exercise sovereignty allow them to shape an alternative future after having survived for four hundred–plus generations in the face of globalization, non-Native habitat modification, and now climate change.

The primary goal of Nimiipuu fisheries is to recover and restore salmon and related habitat in the Nimiipuu watersheds of the Snake and Columbia rivers, for both cultural and economic reasons. Nimiipuu Fisheries, in partnership with the Columbia River Inter-Tribal Fish Commission (CRITFC), provides scientific, technical, and policy inputs to protect the tribe's reserved rights in salmon and water. The Nimiipuus operate fifteen fish hatcheries, located on and off the reservation lands, and some of their fish culture interests and practices derive from their horse-breeding activities and deliberate management of resources, such as forests, prairies, and watersheds, prior to Euro-American settlement of Nimiipuu territory. The breeding techniques appear to have grown out of their land management and are now used in programs to restore salmon.

The tribe also monitors harvest by Nimiipuu fisherman. The Nimiipuus, along with additional tribes in the Columbia Basin, provide recommendations for the protection and restoration of salmon habitat and populations listed under the federal Endangered Species Act. Consultation between treaty tribes and federal agencies results in the issuance of biological opinions on the survival and recovery of listed salmon species that have been impacted by a federal action that has directly or indirectly altered critical habitat.

At the local level, each CRITFC tribe operates their own fishery program and regional fish supplementation hatcheries (see chapters by Diver, 10, and Smith, 1, in this collection for detailed descriptions of CRITFC and co-management outcomes of fisheries in the Columbia Basin). This means that Columbia Basin tribes extend their jurisdictional boundaries far beyond the reservations to include hatchery programs and restoration projects at "usual and accustomed places." CRITFC tribes monitor the harvest of 50 percent of the available adult salmon migrating in the Columbia River each year for commercial sale and cultural use. Individual tribes place tribally specific restrictions on tribal fishers.

The artificial propagation of salmon (i.e., from hatcheries) takes two forms. One is production hatcheries supported by many nontribal fishing interests and the logic of industrial agriculture. The other is supplementation hatcheries, mostly run by tribes, that involve "thinking like a salmon" and that are designed to restore stocks and salmon diversity. These differing hatchery approaches have differing effects on the natural diversity of salmon stocks in the Columbia Basin.

The Nimiipuus operate hatcheries located on the Clearwater, Salmon, Snake, Imnaha, Grande Ronde, and Wallowa rivers, in the heart of Nimiipuu territory, and co-manage several salmon projects with the State of Idaho and the US Fish and Wildlife Service on Nimiipuu watersheds, located off reservation in traditional use areas. Differences of Nimiipuu hatchery design include the development of a "natural" rearing pond informed by Nimiipuu cultural understandings of the "needs of the salmon," says Ed Larson of Nimiipuu Fisheries (FiveCrows 2011). Conventional hatchery pens are rectangular concrete structures, whereas some Nimiipuu supplemental fish hatcheries are designed to mimic healthy riparian areas, thus implementing lessons learned from Nimiipuu engagements with salmon over the millennia by encouraging salmon fitness and reproductive success. As Dave Johnson, Nimiipuu Fisheries program manager, stated, "We will treat these fish with the respect they deserve.... They are not ours to do with what we will. Rather, they are a part of us; they share our world" (FiveCrows 2011).

In addition to restoring salmon through hatcheries, the Nimiipuus also realize the centrality of water in contemporary Nimiipuu policy. For example, in 2005 the Nimiipuus participated in an agreement between non-Native water users, the Idaho state senate, and the US Congress in the Snake River Basin Adjudication (SRBA)—a water rights case introduced in 1986 to settle more than 150,000 outstanding claims to water in the Snake River drainage. The Nimiipuus drew from their cultural connections to salmon and water and formed an agreement in which the Bureau of Reclamation may lease up to 427,000 acre-feet of water from the State of Idaho to increase flow augmentation in the Snake River drainage and help endangered salmon. Additional water in the Snake River aids in salmon migration and improves Nimiipuu fish and habitat projects. Nimiipuus thus use reserved rights, self-determination, and autonomous self-governance in strengthening their Indigenous culture and homeland against the internal and external conflicts of more than 150 years of outside commercial development.

The newest challenge—confronting global climate change and its associated consequences—has resulted in *novel and innovative Nimiipuu policies* (Hanna 2007). Nimiipuu attempts to mitigate climate change include on- and off-reservation carbon sequestration. The Nimiipuus have committed twenty-nine forest-restoration projects and about 5,000 acres to carbon sequestration. Their plantings of Douglas fir and ponderosa pine saplings are projected to absorb a year's worth of carbon dioxide from nearly 500,000 cars, trucks, and SUVs (Zaffos 2006), which also improves upland habitat for salmon and watersheds. Moreover, the Nimiipuus aim to have corporations offset their greenhouse gas emissions by paying to keep trees growing and forests intact. Few American companies are presently mandated to curb greenhouse emissions with carbon sequestrations, but these Indigenous efforts are models that provide examples for others: the real value in forests lies in allowing them to flourish.

Other mainstream tribal strategies include adjudicating water rights for salmon as a powerful tool in an environment of increasing demands and declining supplies. In addition, the federal Endangered Species Act is a valuable legal strategy for the Nimiipuus as they aim to protect salmon populations from extinction, and additional legal structures, such as contract law, may provide other means by which the Nimiipuus could attempt to secure in-stream flows to protect migrating salmon. Finally, for the protection of salmon Nimiipuu policies aim to designate off-reservation land-holdings by converting land to tribal trust status and in the co-management of federal public lands, including national parks and monuments and in wild and scenic rivers.

Intergovernmental and intertribal cooperation has resulted in the CRITFC and other collaborations with various federal agencies such as the National Oceanographic and Atmospheric Administration, Bonneville Power Administration, and the National Fish and Wildlife Service. These partnerships are effective in co-managing hatchery programs and in developing long-range management strategies for salmon restoration. The Nimiipuus have developed and implemented strong policies related to the future of dams and irrigation projects, and in partnering with other Columbia Basin tribes, they seek to force dam operators to release more water when needed to improve fish passage and when necessary litigate for the decommissioning of dams (see Diver, chapter 10, this volume, for a detailed discussion of co-management of tribal fisheries in the Columbia Basin).

CONCLUSION

In 1980 Idaho's Department of Fish and Game closed fishing on Rapid River, a smaller tributary of the Salmon River in north-central Idaho, due to declining returns of Chinook salmon. The Nimiipuus and other tribal fishermen viewed the closure as a violation of 1855 treaty rights, which prompted those who regularly fished at Rapid River to form an ad hoc committee of tribal fishermen and their families. The closure at Rapid River also impacted Nimiipuu sovereignty work after the creation of the dams, and it jump-started husbandry efforts to produce salmon through supplementation hatcheries and improving off-reservation habitat.

The ad-hoc group, known as the "fishermen's committee," began by meeting regularly and making a collective decision to ignore the ban by continuing to fish for returning salmon at Rapid River (Landeen and Pinkham 1999). Local, non-Native outsiders formed vigilante groups and regularly threatened Nimiipuu fishermen and family members while they

FIGURE 9.2

Nimiipuu child with ceremonially important First Salmon and Idaho law enforcement officials,
Rapid River standoff. Source: Katherine Jones, Idaho Statesman, *1979. Courtesy of The Special*
Collections Department of Albertsons Library, Boise State University, Idaho Statesman Photo col-
lection, MSS 111, 800622b.

fished on Rapid River during the closure. Furthermore, state and county
law enforcement officers arrested over eighty Nimiipuu fishermen, claim-
ing that Nimiipuu fishermen were not only fishing illegally but also pos-
sessed salmon in violation of the state's closure. One of those arrested was
a seven-year-old Nimiipuu child who had caught a ceremonially important
First Salmon (figure 9.2).

Doug Nash, a well-regarded tribal member, law professor, and former
staff attorney for Nimiipuu legal counsel commented on the significance of
Rapid River by stating, "The Fishermen involved directly in the Rapid River
controversy have probably never been given the credit they deserve. Those
people had to face many obstacles including displays of arms and force.
The fact that whole families were involved made an important statement
to the state about how the Nez Perce people felt about their treaty rights"
(Landeen and Pinkham 1999:119).

Also, in an effort to honor salmon, protect treaty rights, and limit economic gain, the Nimiipuu fishermen's committee members limited fishing

to weekends, reducing the number of fish taken. However, the state contended that the decline of salmon was ultimately a result of Nimiipuu overharvest. "We knew we weren't the reason the fish were being wiped out," stated Virgil Holt, a Nimiipuu elder. "It was the dams and the management that were hurting the fish runs. We weren't responsible for either" (Woodward 2005:2). Nimiipuu elder Elmer Crow reflected on Rapid River during the twenty-fifth anniversary of the standoff by proclaiming, "What happened here 25 years ago didn't just change Nez Perce country…it changed the whole country. It was the beginning of co-management of fisheries. Our Nez Perce fisheries department is a good example. It started with three people. Now we have 260" (Woodward 2005:1). After a year of heated conflict, Rapid River came to a close in 1980, with Idaho County magistrate judge George Reinhard throwing out the state's claims on grounds that "the state did not have a right to unilaterally close the fishery" (Woodward 2005:1).

In turn, Nimiipuu actions at Rapid River led to a greater recognition by state and federal authorities of Nimiipuu treaty-based rights to manage fish resources at all the "usual and accustomed places," even those located off reservation. Their actions also showed how Nimiipuu peoples are involved in the stewardship of salmon in unexpected ways, through treaty-based litigation and innovative environmental solutions, such as those imposed from the bottom up at Rapid River.

The Rapid River case also illuminates how the Nimiipuus have combined over four hundred generations of knowledge, their leadership and governance structure, and their powers as a sovereign Indigenous nation to conserve and restore ecosystems that have sustained their culture, while yielding real economic benefits. Moreover, their knowledge, leadership and governance, and sovereignty challenge the future value of industrialized agriculture and dam-building, whose proponents tend to view salmon species in largely economic terms. Thus, Nimiipuu encounters with global capitalism work two ways—the Nimiipuus restore, supplement, and protect salmon with their sovereignty while maintaining a salmon-centric culture and economy amid the dramatic remapping of their homeland.

In conclusion, the divestment of ancestral lands and the introduction of industrial agriculture expanded global capitalism and stimulated dam-building in Nimiipuu watersheds. Yet, Nimiipuu reactions to external influences—the ways they reorganized themselves to cope with the changes—show the ability of the Nimiipuu people to balance both cultural and economic values. They are also creating an alternative future by using their sovereignty, drawing from their experiences, and applying their values and knowledge to make salmon restoration a reality. "The dams may last centuries, true, but to the Columbia's tribes that is a blink of time. Sooner or later dams will fail, or become silted up, or their power will prove unnecessary. When that happens the old river will come back, and the River People will still be there to welcome the return of the Salmon People" (Dietrich 1995:399).

Notes

1. *Nimiipuu* is the name the Nez Perce call themselves, which means "we the people" or "real people." According to tribal elder Cecil Carter, the name also refers to the Nimiipuus before they had horses, meaning "we walked out of the woods" or "we walked out of the mountains." The name Nez Perce was used by Lewis and Clark in 1805 and in French means "pierced nose." However, nose piercing was not a cultural practice of the Nimiipuus (Cultural Resources Program, Nez Perce Tribe). The chapter title "Salmon and His People" is a phrase based on Nimiipuu tribal-traditional teachings and borrowed from the title of Landeen and Pinkham's (1999) book *Salmon and His People: Fish and Fishing in Nez Perce Culture*. The phrase "a very specific place in northwest North America" is adapted from Wright's (2004) book *The World and a Very Small Place in Africa: A History of Globalization in Niumi, The Gambia*.

2. My ongoing collaborations with Nimiipuu tribal programs and people began in 1998. In 2004 the Nez Perce Tribe Executive Committee (NPTEC) and Natural Resource Subcommittee approved a Tribal Research Permit for my research project titled "A Power and Scale Perspective on the Management of the Lower Snake River Watershed." In doing so, Nimiipuu tribal leaders have encouraged my examination of their salmon fisheries, power relationships, industrial agriculture, and encounters with global capitalism.

3. All Nez Perce–language (*nimiipuutimt*) words are in parentheses. The spellings are derived from Aoki 1994.

4. The distinction between *agreement* and *settlement* requires clarification: the term *settlement* connotes litigation, and those tribes that actually signed on to the agreement were never parties to litigation.

10

Columbia River Tribal Fisheries

Life History Stages of a Co-management Institution

Sibyl Diver

INTRODUCTION: COLUMBIA RIVER TRIBAL FISHERIES CO-MANAGEMENT

Co-management refers to "collaborative" or "cooperative" management that has been generally defined as the sharing of management power and responsibility between governments and local people (Berkes and Turner 2006:481; see also Berkes, George, and Preston 1991). Much of the literature suggests that fisheries agency managers should cooperate with local resource users in gathering data and decision-making to achieve more sustainable fisheries (Jentoft, McCay, and Wilson 1998; Loucks, Wilson and Ginter 2003). However, collaboration has various meanings (Berkes 1994, 2007), and equal power-sharing between co-managers is often not achieved (Nadasdy 2003). The Columbia River case discussed here provides an example of tribal fisheries co-management in the Pacific Northwest—generally recognized as one of the longest running examples of successful co-management (Cohen 1989; Dale 1989; Pinkerton 1989).

Historically, Columbia River tribes in Washington, Oregon, and Idaho managed fisheries through their own traditions and institutions. From the 1850s, however, Euro-American settlement displaced many Columbia River tribes from their traditional lands and fisheries, despite their resistance. After years of political organizing, two key court rulings—the 1969 Belloni Decision and the 1974 Boldt Decision—confirmed treaty fishing rights for Columbia River and Puget Sound tribes. These court decisions initiated a significant tenure shift in Columbia River fisheries by defining a new co-management relationship between treaty tribes and state fisheries agencies. Yet despite these rulings, initial fisheries co-management institutions were heavily criticized, and many years of restructuring were required before Columbia River co-management became recognized as an effective governance mechanism. This history raises some questions. Has co-management indeed become a decision-making structure that facilitates more equal power-sharing between tribes and state agencies within Columbia River fisheries management? If so, how did the transformation from an ineffective to a more effective institution occur? And what are the implications for tribal fisheries today? In order to understand the conditions that have led to present-day co-management, this chapter evaluates the effectiveness of Columbia River co-management institutions at specific time periods by deploying Elinor Ostrom's (1990) principles of enduring common property institutions. For this case, I define effective co-management through the attributes of increased power-sharing and adaptive management, where institutions permit structured experimentation and management flexibility, thus allowing managers to incorporate future learning and changing conditions into their decision-making (Armitage, Berkes, and Doubleday 2007).

Through my case analysis, I argue that Columbia River treaty tribes played an integral part in creating co-management institutions through a collective choice process. I also show that co-management is not static, but is rather an evolving and nonlinear process, highly contingent upon shifting sociopolitical and ecological conditions. Finally, I argue that after forty years, Columbia River co-management has become more effective—containing particular institutional and noninstitutional properties—precisely because of tribal participation. One of the properties that I will discuss is internal legitimacy of co-management for tribes, along with the process of integrating Western science and Traditional Ecological Knowledge within intertribal management institutions today.

The scope of this analysis is primarily *U.S. v. Oregon* institutions involving treaty tribes, state and federal agencies, and intertribal co-management structures. The four treaty tribes signed treaties in 1855, reserving their rights to land and fisheries (Cohen 1989:38; CRITFC 1995; Slickpoo and Walker 1973). Together with the US federal government, these tribes filed lawsuits against Oregon over treaty-reserved fishing rights in federal court, which resulted in the decision *U.S. v. Oregon*, Civil No. 68–513 (D. Or. 1969). Emerging from this legal process, the primary Columbia River fisheries co-managers are the Confederated Tribes of the Umatilla Indian Reservation, the Confederated Tribes of the Warm Springs Reservation of Oregon, the Confederated Tribes and Bands of the Yakama Indian Nation, and the Nez Perce Tribe (or Nimiipuus); the states of Oregon, Washington, and Idaho, represented by their respective Departments of Fish and Wildlife; and the US federal government, represented by the Departments of Commerce and the Interior.[1] My analysis focuses on the series of Columbia River Fisheries Management Plans (CRFMPs), adopted at approximately ten-year intervals, following this legal decision. When viewed alongside historical events, the CRFMPs provide useful signposts for understanding how *U.S. v. Oregon* co-management evolved. Personal interviews with Columbia River co-managers also inform the chapter.

LIFE HISTORY STAGES OF MANAGEMENT AND ENDURING INSTITUTIONS

Elinor Ostrom (1990:202) writes, "To understand institutional choice processes, one must view them as historical processes whereby current decisions are built on past decisions." Ostrom (1990:51) has defined institutions as the "sets of working rules" that determine decision-making processes. She has also analyzed institutions that have survived for at least one hundred years to determine a set of underlying design principles shared by long-enduring common property resource institutions. I have adapted these principles here as (1) clear boundaries and use rights, (2) rules that fit local conditions, (3) collective-choice governance, (4) monitoring, (5) graduated sanctions and enforcement, (6) conflict-resolution capacity, (7) recognition of community rights by external authorities, and (8) relationships to nested institutions (Ostrom 1990:90–102).

In addition, I use salmon life history stages, from the egg to adult (Groot and Margolis 1991), to help articulate the different stages of evolving Columbia River tribal co-management institutions and produce a "life history" of co-management for this case (figure 10.1). Following the tenure shift that initiated Columbia River co-management institutions, I break the institutional history into four parts: new institutions, refining rules, reorganization, and recognizing differences. The analogy—comparing development stages of salmon to institutional developments—is intended to help order the complex history of Columbia River management institutions and connect the policy back to a common goal: bringing back the salmon. The salmon life cycle analogy also reminds us that human fisheries management is codependent with the salmon itself. For example, salmon biology and genetics guide the migration behavior that brings salmon to North

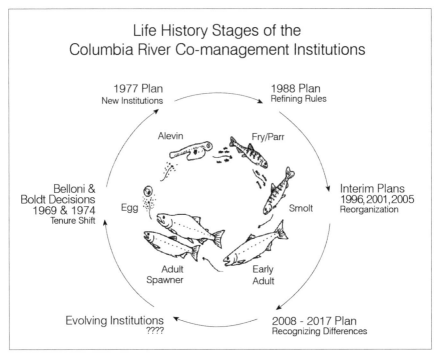

FIGURE 10.1

Analogy comparing salmon life history stages to the institutional history of Columbia River co-management. Source: Life cycle illustration provided by the Vancouver Aquarium. Additional graphic design by Nora Diver.

Pacific coasts and rivers—shaping where humans choose to live and work. At the same time, human management decisions about time, place, and manner of harvest affect salmon biology by determining what runs of fish reach their spawning grounds to reproduce.

(1) Tenure Shift/Egg Stage (Early 1970s)

> Salmon lay their eggs in the upper layers of stream gravels where the pores in the gravel allow oxygen to reach the eggs as they develop.

This section describes the point of origin for Columbia River treaty fisheries co-management in the early 1970s and the initial circumstances that led to new co-management institutions. Prior to Euro-American settlement, Columbia River tribes regulated access to fishing places within and among tribes (Aguilar 2005; Dupris, Hill, and Rodgers 2006; Hunn and Selam 1990; Wilkinson 2007). Starting in the 1850s, however, Euro-American settlers increased competition for fisheries resources, created unregulated open-access fishery conditions, and often displaced tribes from traditional fishing places (Donaldson and Cramer 1971; Montgomery 2003). In addition, tribes fishing in-river were "last in line"—geographically disadvantaged relative to nontribal fishermen harvesting in the ocean or river mouth (Harrison 1986). Canneries introduced new processing technologies and capitalist markets, which made fishing "big business" (Cohen 1986:40). The state legislatures of Oregon and Washington responded by enacting fishing regulations in the 1870s and adopting the 1918 Columbia River Compact to establish uniform harvest codes in state boundary waters (Woods 2008). Still, salmon runs declined due to the combination of unregulated harvest pressure and habitat impacts (Lichatowich 1999; Taylor 1999).

Tribes responded to open-access fishing conditions by filing lawsuits, with direct protest actions, and by creating new institutions. In 1935 a new intertribal management institution was created at Celilo Falls, long an important place for intertribal gatherings (Boyd 2004). The Celilo Fish Committee was formed by representatives of the Mid-Columbia, Umatilla, Warm Springs, and Yakama Indians and was recognized by the commissioner of Indian affairs (Dupris, Hill, and Rodgers 2006). The committee enforced regulations that upheld sharing of traditional fishery resources, limited access to fishing places for outsiders, and also regulated the timing and location of Indian dip-net fishing at Celilo Falls (figure 10.2; Dupris, Hill, and Rodgers 2006:14).

The Celilo Fish Committee was a precursor to present-day intertribal co-management institutions. However, the Celilo Fish Committee's authority was primarily held at the local level. Despite its protests, the organization could not halt the federal government from constructing the Dalles Dam below Celilo Falls. The committee functioned until the dam gates closed in 1957, and the Columbia River rose to submerge the Celilo fishing rocks (Barber 2005).

Since 1887, Columbia River treaty tribes have worked to enforce treaty fishing rights through the courts (Cohen 1986:54). Lawsuits were based on the 1855 treaties, in which all four tribes reserved their exclusive right to fish on reservations and the right of taking fish "at all usual and accustomed places in common with the citizens of the Territory" (Treaty with the Yakima 1855:Article 3). In the early 1960s, treaty fishing rights disputes came to a head when state agencies attempted to regulate Indian fishing for conservation purposes. Game wardens harassed and arrested Indians

FIGURE 10.2

Dip-net fishing by Columbia River tribes at Celilo Falls, ca. 1950s, prior to its inundation by the Dalles Dam. Source: Oregon State Archives, Department of Transportation, highway photographs series, negative #G211.

fishing at off-reservation fishing grounds (AFSC 1970; Cohen 1986). At the same time, American Indian activists engaged in political organizing and direct action to raise public awareness and assert tribal claims to salmon harvests (Burns 1971). Numerous Indian fisheries activists organized "fish-ins" as a civil disobedience tactic (Shreve 2009; Wilkinson 2005).

Yakama Nation members Richard Sohappy and his uncle David staged the fish-in that produced the landmark 1969 court ruling on treaty fishing rights, *Sohappy v. Smith*, Civil No. 68–409 (D. Or. 1969). Later consolidated into *U.S. v. Oregon*, Civil No. 68–513 (D. Or. 1969), this became known as the Belloni Decision (AFSC 1970:201; Cohen 1986:120). *U.S. v. Oregon* initiated a fundamental tenure shift in Columbia River fisheries by upholding tribes' treaty rights to a "fair share" of the fish at usual and accustomed fishing areas, including off-reservation areas. Judge Belloni's ruling stipulated that state regulation of tribal fisheries could still occur in some cases, but only when necessary for conservation. Thus, states needed to take all possible steps to preserve runs, including restricting the non-Indian harvest before restricting Indian fishing (Weaver 1997:680).[2] In the *Sohappy v. Smith* decree, the judge also ordered the states to provide tribes with the opportunity to "participate meaningfully" in rule-making that might restrict off-reservation fisheries.[3] A second landmark case followed. In *U.S. v. Washington*, 384 F. Supp. 312 (W.D. Wash. 1974), Judge Boldt interpreted the "fair share" entitlement to mean 50 percent of the harvestable fish destined for tribes' usual and accustomed fishing places. This established the 50/50 allocation principle: tribes and states could each take 50 percent of the harvestable fish entering the Columbia (Cohen 1986:12).[4] The Belloni court applied the Boldt Decision to *U.S. v. Oregon* the next year. Then in 1979, the US Supreme Court upheld the Boldt Decision principles in *Washington v. Washington State Commercial Passenger Fishing Vessel Ass'n*, 443 U.S. 658 (1979) (Woods 2005).

By the early 1970s, the culmination of tribes' political organizing and court rulings led to the recognition of treaty fishing rights, a major tenure shift. The *U.S. v. Oregon* and *U.S. v. Washington* court decisions established clear use rights for tribal fisheries co-management. Given the historical context, the persistence of tribal leaders and their allies that led to key court decisions was a remarkable endeavor. However, these "paper rights" needed to be implemented. Although court rulings laid the groundwork for co-management, a comprehensive management plan was not developed for several years. Thus, we can view this initial, emergent stage of Columbia River fisheries co-management as the "egg" stage.

(2) New Institutions/Alevin Stage (Late 1970s)

When the eggs hatch, tiny fish called alevin remain attached to their yolk sacs and stay hidden in the gravels.

New fisheries co-management institutions were created in the 1970s; however, initial implementation was highly dependent on court interventions and limited in scope. The *U.S. v. Oregon* decision initiated Columbia River fisheries co-management as a set of legal institutions backed by the courts. The courts recognized treaty tribes and states as co-managers and convened all parties to jointly approve fisheries management regulations. In Washington State, changes were met with strong resistance from non-Indian fishermen and only sporadic state enforcement (Cohen 1986). But in Oregon, Judge Belloni took swift action to enforce his ruling and issued court injunctions to close sections of the Columbia River to non-Indian fishermen. The Department of the Interior also arranged for US marshals to patrol the Columbia (Berg 2008). The states and treaty tribes initially operated under single-year management plans developed under *U.S. v. Oregon* jurisdiction. However, after almost eight years of continuous litigation and strong convincing from Judge Belloni, tribal, state, and federal co-managers jointly developed and signed the first five-year management plan, "A Plan for Managing Fisheries on Stocks Originating from the Columbia River to Its Tributaries above Bonneville Dam." In February 1977, Judge Belloni adopted this plan as a court order, maintaining federal district court jurisdiction over treaty fishing rights (Dale 1989; Weaver 1997).[5] After this plan expired in 1982, the federal judge presiding over *U.S. v. Oregon* ordered the parties to negotiate another plan (Smith 1998; Weaver 1997).

The purpose of the 1977 plan was to create a sharing agreement for the river that addressed harvest allocations and conservation issues. The stated goal was to "maintain, perpetuate, and enhance...fish stocks," as well as to provide treaty tribes and nontreaty users with "a fair share of the harvest" (CRFMP1977:1). The plan determined clear boundaries and use rights. It defined the shared resource as "stocks originating from the Columbia River and its tributaries above Bonneville Dam" (CRFMP 1977:1). It also confirmed the geographic limits for shared resources, previously established through the court as "fish caught in the Columbia River below McNary Dam and any other inland off-reservation catch placed in commercial channels" (CRFMP 1977:5). For the most part, this created a two-part fishery. Non-Indians could fish commercially from the mouth of the Columbia River to the Bonneville Dam (a 140 mi stretch, designated as Zones 1–5). Only treaty Indians could fish commercially above Bonneville to the McNary Dam (a 130 mi stretch, Zone 6, which included the now submerged Celilo Falls) (Cohen 1986).[6] We should note that tribal commercial fishing was included in the initial and subsequent agreements. From other chapters in this volume, we see that Indigenous peoples are often excluded from fisheries because tribal fishermen are banned from making commercial sales or using modern fishing gear—also a topic of dispute on the Columbia (see Sharakhmatova, chapter 5, and Carothers, chapter 7, as well as Colombi's discussion of *Washington v. Washington State Commercial Passenger Fishing Vessel Ass'n*, 443 U.S. 658 [1979], chapter 9, this volume).

The agreement also defined the percentage of catch harvestable by treaty Indian fishermen and non-Indian fishermen for each salmon run. For the fall chinook run, the plan allotted 60 percent of the harvestable fish to treaty fishermen—for ceremonial, subsistence, and commercial harvest—and 40 percent to nontreaty fishermen. For the spring chinook run, the sharing formula was reversed with a 40/60 allocation, although tribes' ceremonial and subsistence harvests received first priority (CRFMP 1977). In summary, Indian fishermen received more fall fish, their principal run, and non-Indian fishermen received a greater share of the spring run of sport fish (Berg 2008).[7]

In addition, the plan established specific rules for harvest and conservation. The plan stipulated escapement goals, or the number of fish that must be allowed to pass through harvest areas unharmed for spawning. Allowable harvest levels were scaled proportionally to the size of fish returns. As an essential institution for collective choice governance, the Technical Advisory Committee (TAC) was created so that tribal, state, and federal representatives could suggest joint recommendations to the state and federal commissions setting fisheries harvest regulations (Cohen 1986).[8]

The Columbia River Inter-Tribal Fish Commission (CRITFC) was established in August 1977, shortly after the first five-year plan was adopted. Organized "in the manner of the Celilo Fish Committee," CRITFC was founded to serve the four Columbia River treaty tribes as a tribal technical and coordinating agency (CRITFC 1977). CRITFC hired its own policy, legal, and fisheries science experts and represented tribes in fisheries management policy arenas. Following the passage of the 1975 Indian Self-Determination and Education Assistance Act, CRITFC was able to receive recognition and funding through an agreement among tribes, the Bonneville Power Administration, and the Bureau of Indian Affairs (CRITFC 2003; Dompier 2005). A CRITFC (1987) report described the organization's purpose and limitations: "The tribes structured CRITFC to insure that policy is set by the four tribes through their fish and wildlife committees...CRITFC can take action only with the approval from each of the four fish and wildlife committees." Also, "CRITFC is accountable only to its member tribes, not to the states, BIA or any other entity." Along with negotiating with state agencies, CRITFC also facilitated allocations and enforcement among the four tribes, an important function not addressed through *U.S. v. Oregon* (Cohen 1986). In addition to CRITFC, individual tribes established their own fisheries programs to reflect their distinct values and management goals (see Colombi, chapter 9, this volume).

Lack of external authority, however, prevented intertribal fisheries institutions from effectively co-managing. For example, states did not fully recognize the legitimacy of tribal fisheries representatives. The 1977 plan set off a period of constant litigation, tying up fisheries management resources (Dale 1989; Harrison 1986). Also, the Technical Advisory Committee did not give tribes a sufficient role in decision-making. For example, state biologists provided their own separate reports to the joint state agency that sets fishery regulations, and recommendations from tribal program biologists were given little consideration. Lack of tribal recognition and representation was also a problem with the Pacific Fisheries Management Council (PFMC), partly because representatives from state fisheries agencies had seats on the PFMC, while tribes did not (Cohen 1986:127).

Another problem was the lack of restrictions on ocean harvests. Although ocean fisheries intercepted salmon destined to spawn in the upper Columbia River, the management plan primarily addressed in-river fisheries (Weaver 1997). At this time, there was limited understanding of mixed-stock ocean fishery effects, and limited technologies were available for tracking fish migration patterns (Rich Lincoln, personal communication 2009). In January 1982, the Columbia River tribes' Council of Councils unanimously declared the five-year plan a failure. The Umatilla and the Yakama tribes formally notified the US District Court of their withdrawal from the plan (Cohen 1986:135). In September 1983, Judge Craig ordered further negotiation to develop a new management plan (CRITFC 1987).

In summary, the first five-year management plan defined fishery use rights and boundaries. In this early stage, we see mixed progress with negotiating in-river harvest allocations; however, rules did not address the broader scope of management issues. CRITFC emerged to represent the interests of tribal fishermen regarding shared intertribal fisheries. But the problem of ocean-based fisheries regulation was not adequately addressed, and conflict resolution mechanisms beyond litigation were lacking. Also, tribal management authority was still not widely recognized. The dependency of co-management institutions on court challenges and the partial function of co-management institutions recall the "alevin" stage of development, when young salmon are still attached to the yolk sac.

(3) Refining Rules/Fry or Parr Stage (1980s to Early 1990s)

> At this juvenile stage, the fry emerge from the gravels into the stream and begin feeding on stream insects. As the fry grow larger, they become parr and develop dark vertical markings that help conceal young fish from predators.

The 1980s and early 1990s were an important growth period for Columbia River co-management, during which co-managers built upon initial institutional structures. States and tribes spent ten years negotiating the 1988 Columbia River Fisheries Management Plan (CRFMP), a ten-year plan, which vastly improved co-management effectiveness. A key factor was increased technical capacity for tribes, as well as for state agencies. A CRITFC Special Report (1987) stated, "Without their own technical experts, the tribes' victory in *U.S. v. Oregon* was almost meaningless." CRITFC provided the policy and science background to support the many successful lawsuits initiated by tribes (Sanders 2008). Norman Dale (1989:66) described how co-management processes also drove improved technical capacity for the state: "The Boldt and Belloni decisions forced the state fisheries agencies to search for state-of-the-art models and even to support development of new more advanced approaches to handling the dilemmas of many mixed stocks. In turn, tribal managers responded by bringing staff into the inter-tribal commissions who could understand and work with these new models." This description suggests a co-production process (Jasanoff 2004) in which co-management institutions and fisheries science essentially co-evolved. Through initial co-management institutions and the courts, tribes were empowered to push for new scientific models and fisheries-monitoring technologies. And when fisheries managers developed and adopted such new methods of doing fisheries science, this shift essentially changed the co-management institution, which could now require more meaningful decision-making and accountability regarding mixed-stock fisheries. As a case in point, tribes filed suit against the secretary of commerce prior to the 1988 plan (Cohen 1986), which helped drive some of the improvements in ocean fishery monitoring and regulation. As a result, the 1988 plan included a 50/50 fall chinook allocation that took into account ocean fisheries (CRFMP 1988:29).

One of the biggest changes in the co-management institution was more detailed rules of use that provided a better fit with local conditions. The scope of rules expanded to address hatchery management issues. Both tribes and state agencies supported hatcheries as a strategy for supporting salmon harvests in the highly developed Columbia Basin; however, the contentious issue of who received hatchery benefits needed to be addressed. First, the plan set out rules for where and how hatchery enhancement should occur. The location of initial hatchery facilities, all built below Zone 6 in locations outside of primary Indian commercial fishing areas, was of particular concern (CRITFC 2003). Second, the plan created a framework that defined sub-basin jurisdiction over harvest and hatchery management decisions by clarifying which individual parties were responsible for developing different sub-basin plans. The plan also adopted more specific rules for harvest allocation and rules to prevent harvest of more depressed stocks (CRFMP 1988). To establish relationships with nested institutions, particularly higher level decision-making institutions, this management plan set a specific meeting schedule for co-managers to discuss yearly ocean and in-river harvest regulations with the PFMC and secretary of commerce (CRFMP 1988; CRITFC 2009).

This plan also introduced new institutional structures for collective decision-making and conflict resolution. A new Production Advisory Committee (PAC) and a Policy Committee were formed. A new conflict resolution procedure directed co-managers to initially address disputes within committees. Co-managers were directed to first review potential fishing regulations within the committee and then bring unresolved issues to the court's technical adviser for facilitated discussion (not arbitration). If the co-managers still did not reach consensus, the issue went to the Policy Committee. If the Policy Committee was unable to reach consensus, co-managers were required to document their position in a written statement to be distributed among parties (CRFMP 1988).

In the time leading up to the 1988 plan, tribal representatives increasingly engaged with higher-level, nested fishery management institutions beyond *U.S. v. Oregon* structures. Through the 1980s, tribes participated in international negotiations over ocean harvests of Columbia River–bound fish through the Pacific Salmon Commission, which was composed of four US and four Canadian commissioners. Holding one commission seat and one vote, tribes had a voice equal to the states (CRITFC 1987). In addition, President Reagan appointed CRITFC director S. Timothy Wapato to serve as chairman of the US section of the commission (CRITFC 1987). At the regional level, the 1980 Northwest Power Act marked congressional recognition of tribal salmon co-management in the Columbia Basin and supported tribal fisheries and restoration programs (Weaver 1997). Having established their own sanctioning and enforcement programs, tribes pledged to increase their police, prosecutorial, and judicial capacities (CRFMP 1988).

Thus, the 1988 ten-year plan built new rules onto existing institutions to address specific harvest and hatchery issues and to create improved conflict resolution structures. Passage of the Northwest Power Act helped co-managers address habitat restoration needs specific to the Columbia River context. In addition, tribes' authority expanded into higher-level nested institutions. Although litigation still occurred, improved conflict resolution meant co-managers could increasingly make time-sensitive decisions benefiting fisheries. These improvements in co-management may be compared to the "fry" and "parr" stages of development, when juvenile salmon become better able to fend for themselves in local streams.

(4) Reorganization/Smolt Stage (Mid-1990s to Early 2000s)

> During the smolt stage, the salmon's internal physiology changes from its freshwater form to its saltwater form, and the fish prepares to out-migrate to the ocean.

In the early 1990s, National Marine Fisheries Service (NMFS)initiated Endangered Species Act (ESA) listings for several Columbia River salmon runs originating in the Snake River, thus beginning a challenging period of renegotiation and reorganization for Columbia River co-management institutions. Instead of building on existing institutional arrangements, some fundamental tenants of initial co-management institutions were questioned during this period. Co-managers responded by adopting several three-year interim management agreements for 1996–1998, 2001–2003, and 2005–2007. The upset in co-management relationships occurred when the ESA triggered regulations legally requiring federal agencies, including Columbia hydropower agencies, to "conserve" threatened or endangered salmon runs (Weaver 1997). By changing jurisdictional authority and the allocation process, the ESA had the potential to substantially erode treaty fishing rights. Legal disputes targeted NMFS regulatory actions, which tribes viewed as a violation of the 50/50 allocation principle, the established CRFMP, and *U.S. v. Oregon* standards for reasonable and necessary conservation measures. Also, despite their initial hopes, tribes were disappointed that ESA listing did not prompt the federal government to consider dam-breaching (Weaver 1997). Interestingly, one state fisheries agency staffer commented that federal ESA listings unexpectedly led to a new "mutual interest" among tribes and the states in maintaining harvests on unlisted salmon runs (interview with author, June 30, 2009).

In a second shift, new ESA requirements forced a new level of vigilance around conservation measures for declining stocks. Fisheries management now had to address fishing from mixed stocks, or listed and unlisted runs that intermingle in the river. Federal regulatory processes limited harvest levels through Biological Opinions and incidental take permits for ESA-listed fish (CRITFC 1995). Incidental take permits complicated the 50/50 established use right. In addition, new hatchery production rules attempted to prevent genetic mixing of fish that originated in the hatchery and wild fish. Third, ESA provisions led to increased institutional complexity. Multiple institutions engaged in fisheries management, including Northwest Power Act committees, the Pacific Fisheries Management Council, the Pacific Salmon Treaty Commission, and the Department of the Interior. New multistakeholder processes, such as the NMFS Regional

Forum, were initiated (Smith 1998). Don Sampson (1996:682) described the effect as "nothing less than slow strangulation by paperwork and process." As co-managers negotiated deeper issues, they adopted interim plans that focused on immediate harvest and production actions and continued to follow the 1988 CRFMP procedures (CRFMP 1996–1998b).

In addition, tribes responded by publishing their own restoration plan, *Wy-Kan-Ush-Mi Wa-Kish-Wit (Spirit of the Salmon): The Columbia River Anadromous Fish Restoration Plan of the Nez Perce, Umatilla, Warm Springs, and Yakama Tribes* (CRITFC 1995), which called for the implementation of fisheries management within existing institutional structures. The plan (1995:Legal Context) aimed to protect tribal sovereignty and tribal conservation interests, and it bluntly stated, "Rights are meaningless if there are no fish to be taken or resources to be managed." The restoration plan set out a salmon recovery agenda, aiming to "put fish back in the rivers and protect the watersheds where fish live" (1995:Executive Summary). Organized in two parts, the plan set out policy action recommendations and also presented sub-basin–by–sub-basin restoration and management goals for twenty major watersheds. The plan (1995:Cultural Context) emphasized the cultural context of salmon recovery: "Salmon are a part of our spiritual and cultural identity.... Without salmon returning to our rivers and streams, we would cease to be Indian people" (also see Colombi, chapter 9, this volume).

During the 1996–2007 period, ESA listing led to the renegotiation of Columbia River co-management. Co-managers adopted interim plans while they negotiated new rules to address ESA requirements. The new role of the federal government led to an alliance between tribes and the states, despite previous animosities. These transformational changes demonstrate that Columbia River co-management did not always evolve through gradual change. Rather, the institutions went through an abrupt reorganization in response to changing sociopolitical events, analogous to the abrupt transformational changes in juvenile salmon physiology that occur during the "smolt" stage.

(5) Recognizing Differences/Early Adult Stage (Early 2000s)

> As an adult in the highly productive ocean system, the salmon now switches to feeding on plankton and matures to its adult size.

By the late 2000s, Columbia River co-management had become a more mature institution, though it was still imperfect. After developing the necessary capacity and legitimacy, these institutions had become a more effective forum where differing views on fisheries management could be heard. After the previous ten years of interim agreements and negotiations, *U.S. v. Oregon* parties arrived at the "2008–2017 *United States v. Oregon* Management Agreement." Although the 2008 agreement's goals were consistent with the 1988 plan, the new plan demonstrated a more sophisticated approach, allowing concurrent management of the treaty Indian fishery alongside the non-Indian fishery and recognizing differences between the two.

To address some of the conflicts that arose with ESA listings, the 2008 plan introduced the "catch balance model" to define harvest allocation in a mixed-stock fishery. This model attempted to balance the tension between the use right (the 50/50 allocation) and rules of use (ESA-driven harvest limits). The model recognized the different fishing methods practiced by Indian and non-Indian fishermen: nontribal fishermen practice "catch-and-release" or "selective" fishing, while tribal fisheries do not. In other words, nontribal fishermen keep marked hatchery fish and throw back wild fish, while tribal fishermen harvest all the fish in their nets. Hatchery fish are typically "marked" by the removal of the adipose fin (Dompier 2005). This difference in fishing practices reflects the belief of many tribal members that catch-and-release methods are disrespectful to salmon (CRITFC policy staffer, interview with author, June 29, 2009). Importantly, the 2008 agreement allowed tribal and nontribal fishermen to use the fishing method of their choice but attempted to incorporate the potential difference in total harvest numbers and wild fish mortality that could result from using selective versus nonselective methods.[9] Tribal and state fisheries managers reported controversy over implementing the catch balance model (CRITFC science staffer, interview with author, June 30, 2009; state fisheries agency staffers, interviews with author, July 1, 2009, April 20, 2010). Although non-Indian fisheries received a lower percentage of ESA incidental take, they were allowed a higher harvest rate on marked hatchery fish since unmarked wild fish would be thrown back (CRFMP 2008–2017:35–36).[10] Yet despite these differences, co-managers were still able to move forward with jointly developing the ten-year plan.

Hatchery reform was another significant issue in the 2008 plan that was negotiated but not resolved. Both the release location of hatchery fish and marking protocols affect tribal access to returning salmon. Some tribal members also view marking with fin clips as harmful to the salmon and therefore a culturally inappropriate practice. The 2008 rule changes included detailed, stock-specific hatchery production guidelines. For example, summer chinook production regulations stipulated release site, rearing facility, origin of the stock, life stage of release, target numbers for release, and whether the hatchery fish would be marked. This agreement highlighted hatchery marking programs as an area of concern for tribes and prescribed a "basin by basin" approach to developing marking protocols (CRFMP 2008–2017).

The 2008 plan also included new approaches to monitoring, enforcement, and conflict resolution. First, co-managers agreed to use performance measures for harvest and production, with 1988–2007 stock performance as a baseline. Declines from the reference period would trigger an "analysis of causes," which might lead parties to adjust the management agreement or engage outside entities in problem-solving. Second, the agreement created a new Regulatory Coordination Committee to monitor regulations for consistency. Third, the parties agreed to monitor the performance of the upriver spring chinook catch balance model. Fourth, to improve graduated sanctions and enforcement, the tribes continued to emphasize the importance of increasing tribal enforcement capacity. Fifth, to promote conflict resolution, strategic work groups were created to assist the Policy Committee by reviewing technical information (CRFMP 2008–2017). Both CRITFC and state fisheries agency staffers have reported they are now relatively successful at conflict resolution within *U.S. v. Oregon* committees (interviews with author, June 30, 2009).

Although tribal authority stems from *U.S. v. Oregon* and associated court decisions, recent events highlight how tribal authorities have accessed nested institutions beyond *U.S. v. Oregon* structures. For example, treaty tribes helped negotiate the recently adopted US-Canada agreement that decreased ocean harvests of upper Columbia River spring and fall chinook (CRITFC 2009). In addition, CRITFC, Umatilla, Warm Springs, Yakama, and Colville tribes signed the 2008 Columbia Basin Fish Accords with the Bonneville Power Administration, US Army Corps of Engineers, and the Bureau of Reclamation. In the accords, Bonneville Power agreed to provide $900 million for salmon restoration actions, with significant funds for tribal watershed restoration projects. In return, the signatory treaty tribes agreed not to litigate on dam removal for a ten-year period. The Nez Perce, or Nimiipuu, chose not to enter the accords (CRITFC 2009), as is further discussed by Benedict Colombi, chapter 9, this volume.

Under the 2008 agreement, more sophisticated rules addressed tribal interests in harvests and hatcheries as well as ESA listings. The plan introduced additional performance monitoring. It also acknowledged differences in harvest methods between tribes and the states. Over time, the decision-making role of the four treaty tribes and CRITFC has increasingly been recognized by external authorities and nested institutions. As with thc adult stage of the salmon life cycle, this stage of Columbia River co-management has reached a certain level of maturity in which differences among co-managers are recognized.

(6) Evolving Institutions

I am tempted to bring the salmon life cycle metaphor to completion here with a narrative of salmon returning home to spawn, which reveals a key limitation of the life cycle metaphor. Although the salmon life cycle provides a useful communication tool that helps us to synthesize the complex history of Columbia River institutional developments, the metaphor is imperfect and certainly not predictive. Importantly, the life cycle metaphor suggests change and rejects a linear trajectory, yet identifying a metaphor that precludes a deterministic pattern of growth and progress is a challenge. Columbia River institutions will continue to evolve into the future, extending beyond a single life cycle, and the next round of changes in a highly context-dependent system is unlikely to replicate the first. Thus, we have reached the point of departure from the metaphor.

Still, the metaphor helps us to construct a mental model for recognizing and recalling patterns in the institutional changes that have occurred over forty years of Columbia River tribal fisheries co-management history. Based on this historical analysis, it seems clear that co-management institutions will continue to change and that the wild salmon, which is identified as a "cultural talisman" for the North Pacific region, as "our fish" (Smith 1979; White 1995:91), will remain important to tribal and nontribal people. Furthermore, tribes have demonstrated a long-term commitment to protecting salmon and the fisheries and will continue to drive the search for creative solutions to challenges facing Columbia River salmon and peoples, who are codependent on one another. Looking at the history of Columbia River co-management through Ostrom's framework of enduring common property institutions also helps us to learn from this case.

APPLYING OSTROM'S PRINCIPLES

In this chapter I ask, how did the ineffective initial stages of Columbia River co-management develop into a set of institutions that support increased power-sharing and adaptive management—the co-management of today? Applying Ostrom's (1990) framework to the Columbia River case further demonstrates that Columbia River co-management institutions are not static. Rather, the co-management institution is made up of a shifting set of rules that are being constantly negotiated and interpreted. Other scholars have also viewed co-management as a long and continuous process (Berkes 2007; Pinkerton 1992). This stage-based approach, however, allows us to consider iterations of institutional design and the precise role of "incremental changes in existing rules" (Ostrom 1990:140). At the same time, Ostrom (1990:140) distinguishes such gradual change from the institution's moment of origin "as a major, one-step transformation."

Applying Ostrom's principles to the Columbia reveals that landmark legal decisions provided the transformational origin for Columbia River co-management institutions (early 1970s, egg stage). Then key changes were introduced, increasing co-management effectiveness in fits and starts, over time. First, management institutions required new conflict resolution mechanisms to define and enforce treaty rights—facilitated by the courts (late 1970s to 1980s, alevin and fry/parr stages). Second, institutions needed rules that fit the specific social and ecological conditions shaping Columbia salmon runs and harvests—equitable, timely, and adaptive structures for decision-making (1980s, fry/parr stage and onward). Finally, co-managers needed to gain access to nested institutions at the regional and international levels in order to impact decisions at the ecological and geopolitical scale of Columbia River salmon runs, which can migrate up to Alaska and the Bering Sea (1980s, fry/parr stage and onward). This history leads to the question of how much access do treaty tribes now have to the broad range of decision-making processes affecting Columbia River fish?

To this end I ask, does today's co-management facilitate equal power-sharing among co-managers? The answer depends on the type of decision-making or rule-making process.[11] At the level of day-to-day operational rules and collective choice rules, tribes appear to have a strong voice alongside state agencies through *U.S. v. Oregon* structures. Ironically, one tribal policy staffer expressed the concern that more limited funding for state fisheries agencies is hampering states' capacity to participate in co-management processes (interview with author, June 29, 2009). However, at the level of constitutional rules, which are important for higher level governance and legal frameworks, tribes are more likely to be in a consultative role, such as tribal delegations lobbying the US Congress. At the same time, Columbia River treaty tribes are participating in certain constitutional-level decisions, such as drafting international treaties.

Despite some backwards steps, the overall trend has been toward more equitable decision-making, especially given the 1970s as a reference point. Unlike the early stages of co-management, present-day structures address all elements of Ostrom's framework for enduring common property resource institutions, at least in part (table 10.1). Once tribes developed

TABLE 10.1

A stage-based comparison of Columbia River co-management evolution

Life cycle stage ▶	A) Egg (early 1970s) Tenure Shift 1969 & 1974 Decisions	B) Alevin (late 1970s) New Institutions 1977 Plan	C) Fry/Parr (1980s to early 1990s) Redefining Rules 1988 Plan	D) Smolt (mid-1990s to mid-2000s) ESA Listings 1996, 2001, & 2005 Plans	E) Early Adult (late 2000s) Recognizing Differences 2008 Plan
Ostrom (1990) Framework ▼					
1) Clear boundaries and use rights	X	XX	XXX	X	XX
2) Rules that fit local conditions[a]		X	XX	X	XX
3) Collective-choice governance[b]		X	XXX	XX	XXX
4) Monitoring[c]		X	XX	XXX	XXX
5) Graduated sanctions and enforcement			X	XX	XX
6) Conflict resolution	X	XX	XXX	XX	XXX
7) Recognition of community rights by external authorities	X	X	XX	X	XX
8) Relationship to nested institutions		X	XX	XX	XXX

Qualitative scores summarize relative changes in fisheries co-management institutions, interpreted through Ostrom's (1990) framework as follows:

X = co-management institutions begin to address a given design principle at a minimal level.

XX = changes in co-management institutions allow additional, yet still partial, fulfillment of the design principle.

XXX = institutional changes now meet the primary tenants of the design principle. (For a supplemental appendix that further explains qualitative score choices, please contact the author.)

Definitions of Ostrom's principles include (a) congruence between local conditions and rules restricting multiple factors, including time, place, manner, or amount of fish harvests; (b) most individuals affected by the rules can participate in changing them; and (c) monitors are accountable to the resource user.
Source: Sibyl Diver.

---

their capacity, they successfully represented their interests within newly created decision-making structures that they themselves took part in creating. Although tribes litigated constantly in the past, disputes today are typically handled out of court. Of particular note, tribes now participate in a range of nested institutions governing Columbia River fisheries at regional and international levels. As a result, treaty tribes have had a strong hand in shaping current fisheries science and policy, including ocean harvest monitoring and hatchery management standards. Davis Washines (interview with author, April 19, 2010), CRITFC's chief of law enforcement and Yakama Nation member, commented on *U.S. v. Oregon*: "It got us to the table as equals. Once it allowed that through the legal channels, then you have this organization called CRITFC. All of a sudden they are trying to play catch up to us in a lot of areas."

Co-management has also increased the capacity for adaptive management in the Columbia River basin. In particular, co-management structures have precipitated an adaptive feedback loop in which learning among co-managers can better inform future fisheries management decisions. I also suggest that Columbia River co-management institutions and fisheries science were essentially co-produced, perhaps themselves a form of adaptive management. In Jasanoff's (2004) co-production framework, the making of an institution does not occur through a linear, unidirectional process. Rather, it results from an interplay between scientific knowledge and governance institutions so that scientific and political practices are simultaneously shaping one another. In the Columbia River case, having tribes involved in both knowledge-making and institution-making through the co-management process has led to some important lessons and improvements in fisheries management, namely improved ocean fisheries monitoring, hatchery reform, and successful watershed restorations.

For example, tribal involvement in fisheries management triggered a set of policies in the 1970s and 1980s including the Northwest Power Act, which, according to Kai Lee (1993:42), led to an increase in tribal shares of the harvest, even while total catch of Columbia River stocks decreased relative to previous years. Having treaty tribes at the table has increased the political will and funding to support fish passage and habitat conservation. And tribal restoration projects have brought salmon back to places like the Umatilla River (CTUIR n.d.). In addition, tribes have also encouraged hatchery development and reform. Although hatcheries can be a contentious topic, the Columbia Basin currently depends on a combination of production and conservation hatcheries to meet people's cultural and economic needs for salmon and to mitigate the negative impacts of dams. The question of whether we can bring back historic runs of Columbia River salmon depends on how we define our goals, political will, and many additional factors. In the 1995 restoration plan *Wy-Kan-Ush-Mi Wa-Kish-Wit*, tribes set the following goal: "Within 25 years, increase the total adult salmon returns of stocks originating above Bonneville Dam to 4 million annually and in a manner that sustains natural production to support tribal commercial as well as ceremonial and subsistence harvests" (CRITFC 1995:Executive Summary). An analysis of the tribes' plan for achieving this vision includes co-management but goes beyond the scope of the current chapter.

INSTITUTIONAL FACTORS ENCOURAGING EFFECTIVE CO-MANAGEMENT

This brings us to the final question: what were the factors or conditions that allowed this shift from initial institutional processes to more effective co-management to occur? Given the time-sensitive nature of the harvest and lengthy nature of legal disputes, parties required *additional conflict resolution mechanisms* beyond the courts. Although the external authority of federal district courts was necessary, litigation was insufficient for establishing effective co-management. One lawyer working for the tribes explained, "So one of the reasons why it works, is, I'll be frank, is because there's a federal judge sitting over there. That if there's a problem with how people are getting on, he's the backstop." But she continued, "And every season, the tribes would go back to court. They would go back to court, and the court would say,...'States, you screwed up.' But by that time...you know, the fish come in, they're there, and they go to spawn" (CRITFC policy staffer, interview with author, June 29, 2009). Additional conflict resolution capacity provided by the *U.S. vs. Oregon* committees has been essential.

For effective co-management, institutions also needed to *address the tension between treaty rights and conservation rules*. Historically, conservation rules have been used as a pretext for preventing Columbia River tribes from catching their fair share of the fish. Because Indian fishermen were located upstream from most non-Indian commercial fishermen—"last in line" and "in plain sight"—late season fishery closures occurred only after non-Indians had caught their share. Thus, tribes often bore the burden of conservation regulations. Given the greater visibility of in-river Indian fishers compared to non-Indians fishing offshore, as well as issues of racial discrimination, tribes often became scapegoats for declining runs, despite the reality of tribes catching smaller amounts relative to non-Indian fishermen (Cohen 1986; Montgomery 2003). Yet there have been times when declining stocks have warranted fisheries closures. This tension was recognized in the initial Belloni Decision and its appeals, which placed limits on the rights of states to regulate tribes for conservation purposes (Gartland 1977), and it continues to be present in the Columbia River today with ocean harvest limits, hatchery placement, ESA listings, and catch balance models. A similar tension exists for other Indigenous communities, such as the Afognak Sugpiat example discussed by Courtney Carothers, chapter 7, this volume.

Another condition for effective co-management was *increased organizational capacity for tribes*, which helped establish the legitimacy of tribes as co-managers. Not for many years after the Belloni and Boldt decisions were treaty tribes broadly recognized as fisheries management authorities. Treaty tribes gained this recognition by building institutional capacity and leadership through CRITFC and individual tribal fisheries departments. They waged a series of court battles to uphold treaty fishing rights. Tribes also asserted their authority through the day-to-day practice of negotiating with state managers through *U.S. v. Oregon* structures. Building legitimacy for tribal co-managers has required extensive funding from multiple sources, including federal and state governments, hydroelectric companies, and private grants (CRITFC policy staffer, interview with author, June 29, 2009). Funding from the Bonneville Power Administration, supported by hydropower ratepayers, has been critical for the development of co-management capacity. CRITFC (1995) suggests that this cost is bearable and worthwhile if it is shared among the wide range of citizens in the basin who benefit from the resource. Yet funding salmon recovery through hydropower-producing dams that often block the passage of fish highlights the tricky business of working with established industry, an issue that has also arisen on Sakhalin with oil companies (Wilson, chapter 2, this volume).

FACTORS BEYOND THE INSTITUTIONAL LENS: TRADITIONAL ECOLOGICAL KNOWLEDGE, SCIENCE, AND SOCIAL NORMS

Going beyond institutional frameworks reveals additional factors essential for effective co-management. Researchers have found that effective co-management is highly dependent on local community attributes, particularly leadership and social capital (Gutiérrez, Hilborn, and Defeo 2011; Pinkerton and John 2008). In this same vein, I found that an additional condition for effective Columbia River co-management was *building internal legitimacy in practice*. A common critique of co-management with tribes is that institutions are typically based on dominant society's structures and values (Deloria and Lytle 1984; Weir 2009). Thus, some co-management may increase the marginalization of Indigenous peoples (Nadasdy 2003). This fact raises an important question for Columbia River co-management: to what extent have the treaty tribes been able to shape governance structures and practice tribal fisheries management based on current community values? In other words, does the practice of co-management have internal legitimacy for Columbia River treaty tribes? The answer may differ among and within tribes. But to address one aspect of the question at the intertribal level, we may ask how does Traditional Ecological Knowledge (TEK) interact with Western scientific knowledge at CRITFC?[12] In the literature, TEK has been defined as "a cumulative body of knowledge and beliefs handed down through generations by cultural transmission, about the relationship of living beings (including humans) with one another and with their environment" (Berkes, Colding, and Folke 2000:1252).

At first glance, TEK appears to be absent from Columbia River co-management. For example, the fisheries management plans (CRFMPs) contain no language addressing traditional or Indigenous knowledge, and the CRFMPs only mention *Wy-Kan-Ush-Mi Wa-Kish-Wit* once in passing (CRFMP 1996–1998b:12). Granted, *U.S. v. Oregon* structures for collective governance were initially established through the courts and primarily based on scientific management principles. In order to engage on equal footing with states, CRITFC and individual tribes have prioritized building strong fisheries science programs. CRITFC, however, sees itself as an organization that integrates conventional Western science and TEK. In interviews, CRITFC staffers reported that TEK shapes the organization's policy. One policy staffer described efforts to integrate TEK and science: "Here at our commission…we don't have a tribal longhouse department.… We are very much science, law, and co-management program functions." Yet, TEK still guides decision-making, he explained. "Our tribal commissioners, those identified by the tribal governments as their representatives, guiding our commission, are expected to have an awareness and ability to fuse the tribal reconciliation of culture and governance into an intertribal program" (interview with author, June 29, 2009). Because of the people who come together through CRITFC—scientists, tribal leaders, and combinations of the two—both science and TEK inform CRITFC decisions and co-management policy.

Despite its relative absence from the management plans, there are numerous examples of TEK shaping current intertribal fisheries co-management at CRITFC.[13] One example is management practices that ensure fishing can occur at family-owned fishing places. A scientist working for CRITFC explained that this sometimes means putting social criteria ahead of economics. "If you want to maximize the efficiency of your fishery, you basically want to get as many fish out of the water as soon as you can, as far downstream as you can," he said. Yet, the tribes do not manage this way. "We have to figure out how to do fisheries so that we've got a reasonable balance of opportunity to catch some fish in different areas" in order to serve tribal members, he explained (interview with author, June 30, 2009).

A second example involves incorporating tribal worldviews into fisheries management policy, particularly tribes' cultural and spiritual relationships to salmon. One tribal policy manager explained, "If you are catching a fish…it is due to the Creator's benevolence. It is not the man's, human's role or authority to say, 'Oh no, Mr. Fish, you fought to the near death. Now you are to be placed back in the water.'" Respect for the fish is important, and recreational fishing is typically looked down upon as "playing with the fish" (interview with author, June 29, 2009). This relationship leads tribal fishermen to harvest all the salmon from their nets, including wild and hatchery-origin fish, a practice that is accounted for with catch balance rules, as I have discussed.

A third example of how TEK guides current fisheries management is related to subsistence and ceremonial fishing, which has a specific allocation and is managed separately from the commercial fishery. The importance of providing salmon for spring ceremonies is held above other fishing priorities, and co-managers have written explicit contingencies into CRFMPs for providing ceremonial fish to tribes, even when spring salmon runs are low.

A fourth example is selected tribal hatcheries, which incorporate both the latest hatchery technologies and "thinking like a salmon" into their designs (see Colombi, chapter 9, this volume.) The Nez Perce or Nimiipuu have built a tribal hatchery near Cherry Lane, Idaho, whose ponds are free from hard, straight lines; incorporate high-velocity flow, sunken logs, and other structures that mimic natural habitat; and include subsurface feeding systems that encourage fish to learn predator avoidance, along with other innovations not used in conventional hatcheries (FiveCrows 2003; Bonneville Power Administration et al. 1997).

Finally, tribes are often using conventional Western science in the service of a deeply important cultural practice—caring for the salmon—thus complicating the division between Western science and TEK.

While acknowledging that today's co-management structures are undeniably shaped by state institutions and Western science, we can see many instances where TEK interacts with scientific management. I would suggest this is an example of tribes producing a new Indigenous knowledge system. This knowledge system includes a strong science program, incorporates TEK through tribal representatives, and requires consensus-based decision-making, among other attributes. Viewing CRITFC's ongoing process of integrating TEK with science as a new and evolving knowledge system highlights how tribal cultures are both flexible and dynamic. This approach brings together old and new ways, reflects tribes' particular ways of knowing salmon, and recalls the principles of adaptive management and learning.

Another condition that goes beyond Ostrom's (1990) framework is *shifting social norms.* Ostrom (1990:35) discusses shared norms as incentives for upholding agreements even when breaking the rules results in no immediate consequences. Yet, shared norms are insufficient for creating an enduring resource management institution; otherwise, institutionalized rule systems would not be needed (Ostrom 1990:93–94). This limited treatment unfortunately does not reflect the importance of shifting social norms that drive the evolution of effective co-management. Despite having combative co-management interactions in the past, some co-managers report that shared norms among co-managers have changed, making negotiations easier: "There's been occasion when it's felt a little bit like the old Warner Brothers cartoons. This was in the Bugs Bunny series, where you've got the sheep dog and the coyote and they go to work every day. And so at the beginning of the cartoon, they're going to work with their lunchboxes, and they check in a little time clock at the tree or something. And then they do battle with each other. And then at the end of the cartoon, the day is done, and they clock out, and they're talking to each other on the way home" (CRITFC science staffer, interview with author, June 30, 2009).

This statement is not intended to suggest that disputes no longer occur, but it suggests how social norms guiding interactions among co-managers have shifted. Some authors have ascribed this change to "social learning" (Dale 1989; Lee 1993), and multiple staffers at CRITFC and state fisheries agencies referred to building "trust" among co-managers (interviews with author, June 29, 2009, June 30, 2009; Rich Lincoln, personal communication 2009). However, these interpretations focus on individual co-managers and personal intent. In reality, this change in attitude has been shaped within a broader social context. As an area of future study, this pattern of shifting norms could perhaps be better explained through Michel Foucault's (1990:92) analytic of power as a "multiplicity of force relations." This approach could help identify key areas of shifting power relations for Columbia River fisheries, shaped by salmon declines, hydropower development, and changing perceptions about American Indians.

CONCLUSION: GETTING TO CO-MANAGEMENT

In conclusion, I suggest that Columbia River fisheries co-management has produced a set of institutional structures that harness the tension among co-management partners and drive improved decision-making and innovation. However, getting to co-management first required that institutions were established and legitimized. Columbia River treaty tribes then worked within the conditions of the time to help produce the necessary political space and mechanisms for tribes and state agencies to interact on a more equal playing field. As fisheries science and co-management institutions co-evolved, more effective fisheries management rules could then emerge. Thus, I suggest that important changes in fisheries management occurred not in spite of but rather because of the differences in perspective among co-managers, which became visible through co-management processes. One fisheries scientist at CRITFC put it this way: "And whereas, if without the co-management tension there, there would be a lot more pressure to deal with short-term economic issues that would make it seem like salmon recovery is just a little too expensive, and these fish really aren't worth it. So I think by having a lot of people working, representing different constituencies, haranguing each other, saying, 'No, no this stuff is important. We gotta keep working on this,' I think, actually, it works well" (interview with author, June 30, 2009).

At one level, this idea supports Kai Lee's view that the "gyroscope" of democratic political processes has helped to improve Columbia River salmon management. However, in recalling co-management history, we see that treaty tribes were included in fisheries management only after a key legal decision clearly recognized and defined treaty fishing rights—a decision opposed by many dominant political interests at the time. Representative democracy was insufficient to address treaty fishing rights, but when the judiciary intervened through *U.S. v. Oregon*, thus producing a new institutional framework based on collective choice decision-making, the work of building an effective institution could begin. Over forty years, co-managers negotiated to establish a co-management institution that, at some level, supports more equal power-sharing and facilitates adaptive management.

In considering what this case means for other Indigenous communities struggling to have a voice in salmon fisheries management (see Kasten, chapter 4, and Sharakhmatova, chapter 5, this volume), we must acknowledge that Columbia River co-management has been a struggle. One CRITFC policy staffer commented, "There is an enormous weight of maintenance around co-management that many people have shouldered for an awful lot of days" (interview with author, June 30, 2009). In this struggle, we should not underestimate the importance of the transformational origin of Columbia River management with the Boldt and Belloni decisions, tribal leadership and commitment to building legitimacy for Columbia River co-management, and key conditions that allowed the institutions to become more effective over time.

Although each place has its unique sociopolitical and ecological context, and its own history of institutional changes, we see the beginning of similar struggles for Russian Indigenous peoples. In Victoria Sharakhmatova's chapter (this volume), she critiques the Russian legal system for failing to enforce even the subsistence fishing rights that are guaranteed Russian Indigenous peoples by law. In response, we see Russian Indigenous leaders taking steps to build capacity and engage with the Russian legal system on fisheries management policy. For example, national organizations like the Association of Indigenous Peoples of the North, Siberia, and Far East of the Russian Federation (RAIPON) are building external legitimacy for their cause through the United Nations and through Russian national bodies such as the Public Forum. Russian Indigenous community-based organizations have filed lawsuits and engaged with regional governments to allege violations of Indigenous fishing rights and discuss policy solutions. Allocating fishery resources to Indigenous people becomes extremely difficult, however, when those resources are highly valued on the global market. New legal mechanisms may play a role in addressing this challenge. But where is the opportunity to transform institutions and encourage the enforcement of Indigenous fishing rights in a place like Kamchatka, given the Russian context? Ostrom's theory and the Columbia River experience have demonstrated that fisheries management can be more effective when tribal representatives with a strong interest in maintaining fisheries for the long term participate meaningfully in forming governance institutions. So even as offshore oil development is being considered by keystone salmon nations of Sakhalin, Kamchatka, and the Aleutians, how do we ensure that our governments on both sides of the Pacific make room for Indigenous voices that are advocating both for a fair share and for the protection of vital salmon resources?

Acknowledgments

My deepest thanks to the individuals at CRITFC and the Washington and Oregon Departments of Fish and Wildlife who shared their co-management experiences with me and to Stephanie Carlson, Benedict Colombi, Louise Fortmann, Charles Hudson, Courtland Smith, Kim TallBear, Sara Thompson, and the SAR advanced seminar group for their useful comments. I also wish to thank Hekia Bodwitch, Esther Conrad, Margot Higgins, Guillermo James, Dan Sarna, Miriam Tsalyuk, Seth White, and Mary Woolsey for their help in reviewing the manuscript. Nora Diver provided essential graphic design assistance. This work was supported by the National Science Foundation, the Berkeley Fellowship, and the School for Advanced Research.

Notes

1. Columbia River tribal fisheries co-management involves additional groups, including the Shoshone-Bannock Tribe of Idaho and nontreaty tribes, which participate in specific co-management processes. Although nontreaty tribes along the Columbia

River generally have less influence than treaty tribes in fisheries management decisions, their role in Columbia River fisheries is a research topic in its own right. Beyond the intertribal institutions discussed in this chapter, we should also note that individual tribes have separate relationships with relevant states, and tribes have additional management rights and responsibilities over usual and accustomed fishing areas within their individually ceded territories and Columbia River sub-basins.

2. In the context of Columbia River fisheries policy, the terms *Indian harvest* versus *non-Indian harvest,* or *tribal fisheries* versus *nontribal fisheries*, are often used to distinguish the 50/50 harvest allocation between the two groups.

3. Noted in *Sohappy v. Oregon*, 302 F. Supp. 899, 912 (D. Ore. 1969).

4. The category "harvestable fish" excluded fish caught by Indians on reservations, fish caught by Indians for ceremonial or subsistence purposes, and the "escapement" set by fisheries managers, meaning the number of fish that must be allowed to pass through fishing areas and return to their home rivers to spawn (Cohen 1986:12).

5. The co-management plans for Columbia River tribal fisheries are court filings, developed by co-managers and issued as judicial orders under *U.S. v. Oregon*, Civil No. 68–513 (D. Or. 1969). Recent agreements can be accessed online or through www.pacer. gov/. Older plans or agreements may be accessed through the District Court or attorneys working with *U.S. v. Oregon*. This chapter uses the abbreviation CRFMP (Columbia River Fisheries Management Plan) to refer to the various plans. The full names of the plans are (1) A Plan for Managing Fisheries on Stocks Originating from the Columbia River and its Tributaries above Bonneville Dam, February 28, 1977; (2) 1988 Columbia River Fish Management Plan; (3) 1996–1998 Management Agreement for Upper Columbia River Spring Chinook, Summer Chinook and Sockeye; (4) 1996–1998 Management Agreement for Upper Columbia River Fall Chinook; (5) 2001–2003 Interim Management Agreement for Upriver Spring Chinook, Summer Chinook, and Sockeye; (6) 2005–2007 Interim Management Agreement for Upriver Chinook, Sockeye, Steelhead, Coho and White Sturgeon; (7) 2008–2017 United States v. Oregon Management Agreement, May 2008, and they are available at www.critfc.org/text/press/20080813.html.

6. Importantly, Zone 6 does not cover all "usual and accustomed fishing areas" for treaty tribes. Individual tribes have additional fishing rights within their ceded territories and reservations. Intertribal fishing areas also include in-lieu fishing sites that extend beyond Zone 6. In 1939 Columbia River treaty tribes and the United States reached a settlement agreement in which the United States promised to acquire alternative fisheries sites for tribes in lieu of those inundated by construction of Bonneville Dam. Only five "in-lieu" sites were initially acquired. In the 1980s, tribes pushed for additional sites, which were established by law in November 1988 (www.critfc.org; Ulrich 2007).

7. There are different types of nontribal fishermen, including sport fishers, gill-netters (commercial fishermen), and ocean trollers (commercial fishermen and also charter services for sport fishers). All these groups have different fishing practices and interests and are primarily regulated by state agencies. However, sport fishers currently have the greatest political influence on state regulatory bodies (White 1995:98).

8. Although co-managers provide data and recommendations, the Columbia River Compact and Pacific Fisheries Management Council are the legally designated bodies that set fisheries harvest regulations (Cohen 1986).

9. "Selective fishing methods" refers to non-Indian release of wild fish and retention of hatchery fish, while "nonselective fishing" refers to Indian retention of both wild and hatchery fish (state fisheries agency staffer, interview with author, July 1, 2009).

10. One state fisheries manager reported that a higher harvest rate on mixed stocks is possible because wild fish that are released from nets do not fully count toward the total harvest number. Rather, harvest estimates incorporate the expected mortality of released fish. A state agency staffer explained, "We say that the number of hatchery fish we keep and the number of wild fish that die after they are caught and released, i.e., the incidental catch, are equal to the total harvest" (interview with author, July 1, 2009).

11. Ostrom (1990) distinguishes three hierarchical levels of rule-making processes. *Operational rules* affect day-to-day decisions, such as appropriation, provisioning, monitoring, and enforcement. *Collective choice rules* are used in policy-making by appropriators, their officials, or external authorities. *Constitutional rules* affect who is eligible to craft the rules governing both operational and collective choice rule-making, and they impact higher-level rule formulation, governance, adjudication, and modification in constitutional-level decisions.

12. Additional research is needed to assess the internal legitimacy of co-management among and within the four treaty tribes as distinct nations.

13. Understandings of TEK can vary widely among different tribes and individuals. Although the intertribal forum at CRITFC does allow TEK to guide policy, additional research is needed to reflect on how TEK is understood and practiced by each individual treaty tribe.

11

Conclusion:
Salmon Trajectories along the North Pacific Rim

Diversity, Exchange, and
Human–Animal Relations

Marianne Elisabeth Lien

INTRODUCTION

Salmon realities are fraught with paradox: Never before has salmon been so readily available for so many people. From being the "king of fish," a precious luxury item and the backbone of subsistence economies in the North, salmon has become what some would call "the chicken of the sea," an affordable source of protein sold in large quantities in supermarkets and restaurants across the world. But the story can also be told as one of loss and decline: Previously found in rivers across most of the northern hemisphere, Pacific salmon is now under threat in areas where it was previously abundant. Its decline is most pronounced around the eastern Pacific Rim, in British Columbia and the United States south of the Canadian border, while it is more abundant further north and west, with Kamchatka, Sakhalin, and Alaska being the richest salmon regions in the world. In a similar retreat toward the remote North, its Atlantic cousin vanished more than a hundred years ago from the industrialized regions of continental Europe and is now mainly found in the rivers of Scotland and Norway.

These contradictory realities of abundance and decline are not entirely unrelated. As Courtland Smith shows in the first chapter of this volume, models and metaphors of agriculture have redefined human–salmon relations and introduced ideals of cultivation, exploitation, and control. These practices have, in turn, altered circuits of reciprocity that previously favored the return of salmon year after year. The emergence of salmon aquaculture on a massive scale is the most direct example of the way terrestrial agricultural practices have informed our relations with, and been tried out in relation to, marine species (Lien 2007a). Salmon aquaculture thus explains Atlantic salmon's affordability and worldwide abundance today[1] but is simultaneously a threat: aquaculture may affect wild salmon fisheries both directly, through the exchange of pathogens, parasites, and genes (Naylor et al. 2005), and indirectly, through the pricing of salmon in a global market of consumers who do not always differentiate "*Salmo domesticus*" from its more self-sustaining river cousins.[2]

But the relation is also more complex. The current threat of salmon aquaculture to self-reproducing salmon rivers is only the most recent in a series of dramatic and devastating changes to human–salmon environments. These include alterations of river systems by dams for hydroelectric power, river transport, dumping of industrial waste, pollution, overfishing, and other intended and unintended consequences of industrial growth, urbanization, and increased population densities. As demonstrated in the case of the Columbia River basin, as well as in France and England, such alterations severely undermined or destroyed the viability of what were previously abundant salmon rivers, long before the advent of modern salmon aquaculture (see Colombi, chapter 9). To some extent, salmon appear to do well as long as humans are relatively few and far between, such as in remote parts of Alaska and eastern Russia.[3] Paul Greenberg (2010:35) in his book *Four Fish* argues that while Alaskan salmon outnumber Alaskan humans by a ratio of fifteen hundred to one, the corresponding ratio for the world of humans and salmon globally is one in which humans outnumber salmon somewhere around seven to one.

But the simple conclusion that humans represent a threat to salmon overlooks the ways in which humans have sustained salmon and contributed to the proliferation and well-being of both. As this book demonstrates, humans have intervened in the lives of salmon in a variety of ways, from the stocking of rivers with fry (see Colombi, chapter 9, and Reedy-Maschner, chapter 6) to the rearrangement of rocks to create resting ponds for salmon swimming upstream (see Menzies, chapter 8, on Gitxaała management practices). This was the case in the Pacific Northwest, where salmon sustained large Indigenous populations.

This chapter draws together and elaborates some of the insights that have emerged from the preceding chapters. Presented with such a broad range of case studies of salmon and indigeneity along the north Pacific Rim, my response could be to draw some generalized conclusions, or grand narratives, that could summarize our present knowledge of human–salmon relations and serve as a guide to better governance. I have chosen a different approach. Acknowledging that the ethnographies presented here are both extremely rich and at the same time only partial accounts of the realities they seek to reveal, I ask instead how they may challenge our assumptions about both salmon and indigeneity, and I look for differences rather than for generalizing traits. In this way I hope to avoid erasing those very differences that may serve as templates for alternative futures.

One insight that emerges from the previous chapters is that Pacific salmon both grow out of and shape relations between humans and non-humans in ways that defy a sharp distinction between nature and culture. This insight implies that the distinction between the domesticated and the wild, which tends to structure environmental policies, cannot be taken for granted. Rather, as I shall argue, salmon and humans have taken part in each other's lives through forms of co-evolution that have important implications for the ways we may conceptualize sustainable human–animal relationships in the future. Furthermore, we see from the studies presented here that such sustained relations can take many different forms, which may or may not involve forms of domestication, monetary exchange, symbolic elaboration, exclusive fishing rights, and permanent settlements.

Another insight that emerges from these case studies relates to the different ways in which salmon are known and their elusiveness in the human–salmon encounter. As we attempt to trace salmon lives through various spatio-temporal trajectories, the salmon itself emerges as largely unknown and mostly out of sight. Its migratory routes from rivers to the sea and back again, and the simple fact that it lives under water, make it hard to grasp (Lien 2007a, 2007b; Lien and Law in press). But although salmon migratory routes have been a puzzle for salmon biologists, the fact that salmon must pass through coastal waters and river mouths to get into the rivers to spawn brings them into closer proximity with humans than many other migratory fish. Because coasts are where most people tend to gather, salmon–human contact is almost inevitable.[4] Furthermore, as we shall see, salmon not only defy sharp distinctions between nature and culture but also challenge the assumption that nature can be known as something completely separate from the human realm. As we shall see, salmon may be known in a number of different ways, and human ways of knowing salmon fundamentally depend upon the techniques of knowing that are available to us. Unpredictability thus remains a feature of human–salmon relations (see, for example, Kasten, chapter 4), yet the entangled livelihoods that salmon enable also involve particular ways of knowing that are, in turn, as diverse as the sociomaterial relations that sustain them. Hence, as we shall see, the scientific mode of knowing salmon emerges as only one mode of knowing among many. In the following sections I will elaborate these ideas, in conjunction with findings from the previous chapters.

"NOT WILD, YET NOT NOT-WILD"

In the opening paragraphs of his book *Soul Hunters,* anthropologist Rane Willerslev (2007) tells the story of a Yukaghir hunter in northern Siberia who dressed up as the elk he is about to shoot. Willerslev portrays the hunter as he hid behind a tree, covered in elk skin and under the weight of elk antlers, as someone who was "not an elk, and yet he was also not *not* an elk" (Willerslev 2007:1, emphasis in original). Rather than presenting the hunter as occupying a position of liminality, which is a conventional approach in anthropology, he uses this story to challenge conventional categorical distinctions of animals versus humans, subjects versus objects, and nature versus culture. Willerslev thus explores the human–animal relation as a terrain of ambiguity, one in which what appear to be differences are systematically transcended by notions of similarity and identification. Thus, he positions himself within the broad body of literature that challenges dualist conceptions of nature (Cronon 1995a; Haraway 2008; Ingold 2000; Latour 2004; Pálsson 2009).

In a similar vein, we may infer from the cases presented in this volume that Pacific salmon can hardly be classified as simply "wild," yet at the same time, its association with particular landscapes and seascapes implies that it cannot be said to be "*not* wild." The trouble with "salmon as wild" rests not so much with the salmon as with the term *wild* and the corresponding notion of wilderness in Euro-American thought. William Cronon (1995a:69–70) has famously and somewhat ironically depicted the notion of wilderness as representing "an island in the polluted sea of urban-industrial modernity," the last place where civilization "has not fully infected the earth." According to Cronon (1995b), who is an environmental historian, the trouble with wilderness is not its nonhuman nature or the tracts of land and sea that it refers to, but rather that the concept "embodies a dualistic vision in which the human is entirely outside the natural." Thus, it embodies a fantasy of people who never themselves had to work the land or sea to make a living. Cronon continues:

> If we allow ourselves to believe that nature, to be true, must also be wild, then our very presence in nature represents its fall. The place where we are is the place where nature is not. If this is so—

if by definition wilderness leaves no place for human beings, save perhaps as contemplative sojourners enjoying their leisurely reverie in God's natural cathedral—then also by definition it can offer no solution to the environmental and other problems that confront us. To the extent that we celebrate wilderness as the measure with which we judge civilization, we reproduce the dualism that sets humanity and nature at opposite poles. We thereby leave ourselves little hope of discovering what an ethical, sustainable, honorable human place in nature might actually look like. [Cronon 1995b]

"Wild salmon" is a relatively recent concept. It has emerged as a way of differentiating farmed salmon raised in pens from the migratory salmon whose life cycle is less marked by human intervention (Lien and Law 2011). Thus, in an era when farmed Atlantic salmon flood the supermarkets and *Salmo domesticus* has greatly outnumbered its river-bound relatives, the notion of "wild salmon" is intuitively grasped as the salmon that is not farmed. The distinction helps differentiate phenomena that are in many ways dissimilar. The problem with the term *wild salmon*, however, is that it carries with it the dualism of humanity and nature as opposite poles, a dualism that has been challenged both ethnographically and philosophically (e.g., Ebert 2010; Latour 1993). The adjective *wild* thus portrays salmon as a species that has evolved completely independently of humans and will survive only as long as they are protected from human interference.[5] The problem with such assumptions is not only that they are wrong (Losey 2010; Menzies, chapter 8; Swanson 2009)[6] but, more importantly, that they leave us with few options to discover what sustainable human–salmon entanglements might look like.

One of the merits of the case studies presented in this collection is that they do exactly the opposite. More precisely, they demonstrate that even in areas where salmon would generally be classified by outsiders as wild (certainly not farmed), their movements and innate properties are still shaped and modified. Landscapes we tend to think of as "wilderness," do indeed leave a place for humans whose lives and movements are similarly shaped and modified by the presence of salmon.

A striking example of such co-existence, if not co-evolution, is provided in Charles Menzies's (chapter 8) account of Gitxaała fishing practices on the Pacific coast of northern British Columbia. Menzies challenges the notion of terra nullius in arguing that the coastline that the Europeans encountered in the late 1700s was the "outcome of deliberate and direct human–environment interaction over millennia," but his argument goes further. Drawing on a wide range of ethnographic sources, he suggests that the Gitxaała, who still inhabit the region, had in fact purposefully managed salmon stocks in ways that are likely to have contributed to their increase or stabilization prior to European arrival. Traditionally, Gitxaała caught salmon with gaffs and stone traps and later by drag seining. In fact, specific boulder alignments currently being recorded in rivers document the ancient use of fish traps. According to Menzies, these gaffs and stone traps allow for the selective removal of fish, in relation to both specific creeks (runs) and individual salmon. Thus, the Gitxaała may have been able to target specific salmon as they returned and ensured that a sufficient number of healthy individuals had the chance to reproduce. The fishing gear employed was more labor intensive (gaff fishing involves selectively removing one fish at a time with a hook) but also more sophisticated than contemporary technologies that generally do not differentiate between juvenile and adult stock or between salmon from creeks that need protection and those that are less vulnerable. In other words, Gitxaała harvesting methods appear to have taken advantage of a nuanced understanding of salmon behavior and the ecology of various stocks. Menzies shows how fishing practices were embedded in a relational approach to nonhuman social beings in which an understanding of obligation and reciprocity was central. Human–salmon relations were kinlike, and ill treatment of salmon would cause them to leave (Losey 2010).

After about 150 years of European presence, this is exactly what happened. With the introduction of new production technologies such as canning and fishing gear that was both economically "efficient" and less sophisticated in the sense that it did not differentiate between types of salmon caught, the salmon stocks declined dramatically.[7] At the same time, with the introduction of processing technology and expanded possibilities for trade, (canned) salmon found its way to distant cities, which involved a dramatic and uneven upscaling of the human–salmon assemblage that could hardly be sustainable. Ironically, and following the decline in salmon stocks, Gitxaała fishing practices were essentially criminalized by Canadian authorities beginning in the 1880s.[8] Unraveling the complex entanglement of people and fish through such restrictions has, according to Menzies, contributed to the decline of both.[9] The Gitxaała account indicates how selective and careful harvesting represents a form of contact, a way of knowing, that in turn allows for the sustainable management of fish stocks.

A similar entanglement is found among the treaty tribes of the Columbia River basin, where there has been a dramatic decline of salmon due to the introduction of hydropower dams and the greater harvesting pressures resulting from commercial opportunities that arose with the opening of the river to non-Indian settlers. Since the 1980s, numerous programs intended to protect Indigenous fishing rights have therefore simultaneously involved measures to enhance the salmon in the rivers through hatchery techniques (see Diver, chapter 10). An example is the Nez Perce, for whom the salmon are key to subsistence, kinship , trade, and commerce. In his chapter, Ben Colombi (chapter 9) describes how their efforts to recover and restore salmon involve the operation of several fish hatcheries, partly through partnerships with governmental institutions. In this case then, human involvement in salmon lives is taken a step further, in that it involves some control of the reproductive process, without which there would be very few salmon left. Salmon are thus involved in a process of sovereignty that in turn represents culturally specific solutions to broader environmental problems.

Inspired by the success of hatcheries in the Columbia River, Hokkaido (then a recently annexed part of Japan) opened its first full-fledged salmon hatchery in 1877 (Swanson 2009:80). But hatcheries were not unique to the Pacific Northwest. According to Greenberg (2010), records of human-controlled reproduction of Atlantic salmon from France are about six hundred years old. In Norway, publicly funded hatcheries were established in the mid-1800s as a response to a decline in Atlantic salmon stocks. By 1900, more than two million fry were produced by local Norwegian hatcheries, and a number of fish ladders were built to facilitate salmon runs (Treimo 2007). These interventions represent systematic efforts at cultivating salmon and suggest that domestication is indeed a gradual and ongoing process. Most importantly, we are reminded that humans and salmons intervened in each other's lives long before the most recent turn to intensive aquaculture on a massive scale.

Hatcheries sustain Alaska's salmon populations as well. The Alaska Department of Fish and Game stocks many millions of hatchery-raised fish to supplement the rivers in the southern part of the state. According to Greenberg (2010:59), nearly one in three so-called wild Alaskan salmon begins its life in a hatchery. And yet in spite of, or perhaps because of, such human interventions, Alaskan salmon is doing well compared, for example, with its cousins in the lower forty-eight. A hatchery could be considered a necessary "life support" or an "unnatural" intervention. However, the fact that a caught salmon may have been spawned in a hatchery does not prevent it from being classified as wild on the North American market. Furthermore, a distinction is often made between "conservation hatcheries" and "production hatcheries," which further emphasizes their distinct aims of supplying either the rivers or the aquaculture companies with salmon parr. The boundaries of "wildness" are, in other words, highly arbitrary, as well as culturally and historically specific, and the striking mobility and adaptability of salmon challenge whatever attempts we humans make to hold them in place.

In Norway, where hatcheries are primarily associated with aquaculture production and conservation hatcheries have a much less important role in the stocking of rivers than in the United States, the categories operate slightly differently. Where "life-supporting" hatchery practices *do* take place, such as in the once famous salmon river Vossovassdraget, a fin-clipped, hatchery-produced parr that is released in the river with the aim of re-establishing salmon is referred to as *forsøkslaks* (experimental salmon), not *villaks* (wild salmon) (Barlaup 2008). The term *villaks* refers only to those salmon originating from eggs fertilized "naturally" in the river, but again, boundaries are difficult to establish. When I asked whether the large salmon he had caught was wild or escaped farmed salmon, a young salmon fisherman who had grown up near the Hardangerfjord replied, "It depends on what you mean. I could spot a mark that indicates that it was vaccinated, and I could tell by the shape of its back that it was probably raised as a smolt at a production hatchery. But then it must have escaped early on, because the fins were perfectly alright, and not worn as they tend to be with farmed salmon. So it has spent most of its adult life out in the ocean with what you would call wild salmon" (interview with author, June 14, 2010).[10]

Escaped farmed salmon are seen as a serious threat to the self-sustaining salmon populations in Norwegian rivers, and the recent discovery that a third of all salmon caught in the Alta River were escapees (i.e., net-pen salmon raised for commercial purposes) from farms caused considerable worry. As a result of such concern in Norway in recent years, escaped farmed salmon have, somewhat controversially, been reclassified as alien species (Lien and Law 2011).[11] This example is yet another indication that the differentiations between "wild" and "not-wild," "native" and "not-native" are done differently in different situations and socioenvironmental contexts.

As this book shows, salmon come in different forms in different places. Some were born in hatcheries, some were not. Rather than nurturing an image of salmon as wild, we should draw attention to the wide scope of possibilities available to humans and salmon and their entangled practices. Furthermore, we need to focus not only on the way hatcheries sustain salmon populations, but also on the ways in which the presence of salmon sustains human populations and human networks on a broader scale. Let us turn to salmon as food.

SALMON TRAJECTORIES: SALMON AS FOOD, GIFT, AND COMMODITY

"About the only sociable thing to do with food is to give it away" (Sahlins 1974:217). This statement is taken from Marshall Sahlins's classic book *Stone Age Economics*, and the same could be said for salmon. As many of the preceding chapters demonstrate, salmon moves along networks of reciprocity that often defy Euro-American notions of individual property rights.

Saying that salmon are crucial to the Indigenous people on the western Pacific Rim is an understatement. Among the Itelmens in northern Kamchatka (maritime Koryaks), salmon constitutes life in so many ways that any simple analysis of household economics, nutrition, trade, or cultural identity would miss the complexity that characterizes human–salmon relations in this region. On the shores of Sakhalin, salmon fishing is crucial to Nivkh identity and subsistence practices (see Wilson, chapter 2). Dried salmon has traditionally been the main staple of people whose subsistence practices are now under pressure, even though the salmon of Kamchatka and Sakhalin is currently abundant. Eric Kasten (chapter 4) describes how dried salmon nurtures people as well as dogs in northern Kamchatka and thus allows movement in a region where the ground is covered by snow a great part of the year. Salmon feed people sharing households, as well as extended families. But salmon feed larger social networks, too. Maritime Koryaks supplied salmon and seal to the reindeer Koryaks, who supplied them with reindeer meat in return, in long-lasting barter relations (Kasten, chapter 4). Such relations resemble the reciprocal exchange between coastal and reindeer-herding Sámis in Norway, an institution also known as *verrde* (Kramvig 2006).

During the Soviet period, subsistence fishing continued in Kamchatka, but the socioeconomic unit was expanded to include the entire village *kolkhoz*. David Koester (chapter 3) sees this shift as a step toward alienation, bureaucratization, and rationalization. In order to meet the Soviet state requirements for accounting, salmon quantities were expressed as written numbers, which in turn reflected the kolkhoz's relative success in producing "surpluses that could be directed into the stream of national Soviet production" (Koester, chapter 3; see also Sharakmatova, chapter 5). Koester notes how this introduction of numbers as a way of representing salmon foreshadowed a shift from description (of catch from particular villages) to prescription (of quotas for particular rivers), a shift that also relates to ways of knowing salmon. Accompanying the shift to numbers was a shift toward commoditization: instead of being a subsistence food and gift, distributed within known social networks, salmon soon became a product (smoked, dried, or salted) that could be sold and consumed in towns as far away as Moscow.

Across the Bering Strait, on the islands of southern Alaska, a similar shift toward commoditization took place with the establishment of cannery operations in the early twentieth century. Village settlements grew as the local demand for salmon rocketed, and the new industry linked the local population to a fluctuating global commodity market. But the dependence on global markets also caused vulnerability in a region where people's lives revolve around fish. Contrary to many accounts that portray Indigenous villagers merely as victims of globalizing forces, Katherine Reedy-Maschner (chapter 6) notes how the market economy has been embraced in the villages of the eastern Aleutian Islands. Rather than passively accepting the current conditions of vulnerability, the Aleuts "resist, transform, and incorporate political and economic influences all the time" (Reedy-Maschner, chapter 6). Salmon is central to these entangled livelihoods (Reedy-Maschner 2009:135)[12] as it is caught, eaten, sold, given away, or even transferred in the form of fishing permits when the need for cash is acute (see also Carothers, chapter 7).[13] Again, we see how salmon enters ever widening circuits of exchange, only some of which sustain the lives of Indigenous people.

Reedy-Maschner takes us through two fishing villages that may or may not remain viable settlements in the years to come. As in many other chapters of this volume, we hear of people who move, of old settlements that dwindle, and of new ones that emerge. These are villages that depend on the sea, rather than on the land, and on what is caught, rather than on what is grown. Embedded in nation-states that are founded on the idea of the successful cultivation of land, such nonagricultural settlements challenge our notion of what a settlement is and ought to be. How, for instance, should we think of resilience? Are opportunistic resettlements to follow salmon and the socioeconomic relations that this resettling enables (jobs in processing and export, for example) a sign of resilience or of vulnerability? Are villages with a stable population an indication of a prosperous and viable region? Or does stability signal a lack of flexibility? Emma Wilson (chapter 2) describes how the Nivkh people of Sakhalin were forced to move to new kolkhoz settlements when Soviet officials deemed their salmon livelihoods "nonprofitable." While the Nivkh people today recall these demographic upheavals as rather dramatic, Wilson argues that they have adapted to such changes while retaining their close engagement with salmon. As Heather Swanson (2009) points out, the viable diversity that salmon have spawned around the Pacific Rim comes from dynamic connections and migration, not from isolation. Trained in anthropology and Indigenous studies, we tend to think of culture lost every time a village is deserted (see also Creed 2006). Trained in biological sciences and conservation biology, we tend to think of species lost every time a salmon run becomes extinct. But salmon, like people, are remarkably mobile.[14] Are we programmed to read catastrophic change into shifts that are perhaps better seen as flexible and resilient?

Raising these questions is not a way of arguing for a neoliberal ideal in which change is embraced as opportunity and therefore is essentially good. Clearly, as some of these chapters demonstrate, some changes do indeed have negative impacts, and the current state of both Indigenous people and salmon along the Pacific Rim is in many cases deeply problematic. The question then becomes, how do we identify the problems in a way that also acknowledges the diverse forms of co-evolution and entanglement that sustain both humans and salmon in their wider networks of reciprocity? How do we problematize the current situation without reproducing nostalgic images of timeless Indigenous settlements embedded in relations of profound ecological balance? How can we draw on the rich variety of human–salmon relations to imagine alternative futures?

Courtney Carothers (chapter 7), in her chapter about the Sugpiaq people of southern Alaska, reminds us that while the marine environment has always remained a core feature of people's lives on Kodiak Island, "the nature of the dependence on salmon has shifted over time." Over the last seven thousand years, they have used salmon to supplement a marine mammal diet, forge settlements along streams and lakes, and trade during the Russian conquest. Yet, salmon canneries constitute the historical core of communities in the eyes of villagers today. In other words, global trade and capitalization are part and parcel of how the Sugpiaq villagers see themselves and their salmon.

On Kodiak Island, as in other parts of Alaska, salmon not only constitutes a movement of food *out* of the region, it also attracts flows of people *into* the region. Waves of Scandinavian migration contributed to modernization of the fishing fleet in the twentieth century; waves of Asian, North African, and Mexican migrants fill the industrial factories today.[15] This influx of people to the canneries made the Sugpiat a minority in their homeland and undermined the sovereignty that had traditionally ensured local people access to salmon. Not only did fish become a scarce resource,

Indigenous fishing practices were temporarily banned around the turn of the twentieth century (as was also the case in Canada and in northern Norway). During the twentieth century, commercial and subsistence economies were increasingly entangled, and like the Aleuts farther east, the Kodiak islanders embraced the opportunities that the cannery industry brought about.

Carothers points to the individualization of fishing rights of the 1970s and the notion of limited entry as representing a fundamental shift of the local economy. The problem, she argues, is not change as such, but the ways in which hegemonies of science and of the market dramatically limit the scope for difference and thus for carving out alternative approaches to the socionatural environment. The recent economic disconnection of Sugpiaq communities from resources of the sea significantly limits their possibilities for participating in an economy that, she argues, is based on an image of humans as "isolated profit-maximizers" of what their surroundings may offer. The limited relevance of this model is vividly illustrated by the preceding chapters, too, which together provide a variety of accounts of people whose relations to salmon are far more complex than one of mere resource exploitation. The case of the Kodiak islanders indicates that the problem is not capital as such (canneries encouraged flexible fishing lifestyles, for example), but rather the ways in which it is accompanied by forms of governance that give rise to particular subjectivities, practices, and ontologies, while restricting others. It also reminds us that struggles over sea and land are embedded in historical contexts of colonial inequities and that struggles over salmon are no exception.

Colonial inequities are also played out in the shadows of an emerging market economy, as exemplified in Russia, where an urban demand for caviar among affluent Muscovites forges unsustainable salmon relations in Kamchatka and Sakhalin. Erich Kasten (chapter 4) describes how the high price of caviar underpins a lucrative trade that involves poachers who catch heaps of salmon just to extract the roe and then dump the remains along the riverbanks to rot. While decomposing salmon may facilitate marine nutrient redistribution (Helfield and Naiman 2001), the removal of roe disrupts the salmon reproduction cycle. Most importantly, such fishing practices dramatically disrupt the traditional Koryak notions of reciprocity in relation to salmon. Rather than being merely a resource to be exploited, the Koryak River is also a sacred place that should be treated with respect, which entails a respectful relation to salmon. As one woman put it: "You must never fish more fish than you are later able to prepare. You must think about how these fish are given to us" (Kasten, chapter 4; see also Sharakmatova, chapter 5; Koester, chapter 3).

What went wrong is not so much that salmon (or roe) found its way to people elsewhere, but rather that the terms of exchange involved in these journeys disembedded salmon from the relations of reciprocity (between the river and people) that constitute human–salmon assemblages in the local region. That Muscovite, rather than Koryak, notions of what a salmon is emerge as dominant even in Kamchatka relates, in turn, to issues of power and involve not only who gets access to certain resources (Indigenous people are poachers, too) but who gets to define what a salmon—and a river—is and how it should be treated. In other words, it relates to diverging salmon ontologies as well as diverging interests.[16]

How do we accommodate such ontological difference? How can we account for different ways of knowing salmon, different biosocial realities, without erasing that very difference (in practices and relations) through which such realities are enacted? These questions are crucial in a situation in which struggles need to be settled and policies will be made. Let us turn to questions of what salmon might be and the different practices through which it may be known and differentiated.

KNOWING SALMON

How do we, as humans, *know* salmon? And how do we, as anthropologists, come to terms with the different ways that salmon are known? To what extent are the salmon of the Koryak, for example, so different from the salmon described by natural science that we may in fact think of them as different entities? Is our analysis of cultural difference premised on the notion "mononaturalism," as Bruno Latour (2004:33) argues? Or do we allow a more radical epistemology in which other people's ways of knowing nature are as valid as those of natural science, and if so, how do we do that?

While Traditional Ecological Knowledge is often viewed as insight that may supplement, confirm, or enhance scientific knowledge, but not challenge its very foundation, Helen Verran takes a different view. In her study of different fire practices (ways of making the bush burn) in Australian Arnhem land, she describes a workshop where aboriginal landowners and environmental scientists came together to learn from each other (Verran 2002). Acknowledging that both Yolngu Aborigines and scientific knowledge rely on specific performances or ways of mobilizing collective memory (science as written texts, tables, and graphs; Yolngu as song, dance, and design), she then proposes an analysis that respects these epistemic differences. Her analysis respects different knowledges as "real" rather than trying to reduce them to a universalizing Western metaphysics.

Verran notes, for example, how Yolngu firing practices mobilize *wänga*, which she loosely translates to "people-places." This term is an attempt to hold on to the Yolngu reality that people and place are in fact one entity, to express an imminent relationality that cannot be reduced to the entities of "people" or "places" as autonomous. Could a similar term be applied to describe the human–salmon nexus? Perhaps it would need to include rivers, too, such as a human–salmon–river assemblage that might even include manmade rock formations on the riverbed (Menzies, chapter 8) or particular forms of fishing gear? In the Koryak case, nonhuman spirits should probably be included, while on Kodiak Island, it might be difficult to conceive of human–salmon relations without including the presence of the cannery. The specific ways in which these entities hold together would obviously differ, and the extent of these assemblages would vary and be to some extent negotiable. What is at stake, I suggest, is not so much what to include but that we think of knowledge as an aspect of relations that are already established and premised on the techniques through which salmon become apparent and relevant to us. Hence, we cannot know the salmon of the Koryaks without taking notice of the relations of reciprocity through which their world is perceived (differentiating gift relations from other nonreciprocal relations, for example), just as we cannot know the salmon of a fish biologist without taking into the account the way science differentiates species, for example, as separable entities of the natural world.

Different epistemic worlds do not evolve in isolation. Koester's (chapter 3) account of the written enumeration of salmon in the Soviet period may be seen as an example of the mechanisms through which one ontology gradually comes to replace, or encompass, another. Numbers, according to Verran (2012), are deeply embedded in and constitutive of the real. Hence, the calculation of numbers is also an act of politics, and the question becomes not only whether to do salmon as numbers (see also Lien 2007b; Lien and Law 2011), but also whose numbers to use, what to count, and what to leave out of the equation.

These dilemmas are dealt with in several of the chapters, and their relevance for policy and governance are illustrated in particular by Victoria Sharakhmatova (chapter 5). In her chapter on community development on the west coast of Kamchatka, she points out huge gaps in knowledge, not only in what is seen as a necessary basis for effective and sustainable nature management, but also between the different groups of people involved, from Indigenous peoples to global nongovernmental organizations. The dilemmas she reveals are instances of ontologies that rub up against one another, and in which no easy consensus can be achieved in relation to what counts as relevant "data" or "truth" (Law 2008). Such dilemmas are also exemplified by Sibyl Diver (chapter 10) as she writes about the historical development of co-management in the Columbia River basin, where court decisions and printed records constitute paper trails of shifting policies and different ways of knowing salmon.

Diver's description of conflicts over access to resources allow us, as readers, to notice how these different ways of knowing play out within the regulatory context, as in the dispute between tribal members and nontribal environmental agencies in relation, for example, to catch-and-release fishing. While catch-and-release fishing is commonly practiced and also promoted in North American rivers, tribal members around the Columbia River see fish as food and have little patience with recreational fishing and catch-and-release, which they look down on as "playing with the fish" (Diver, chapter 10). A similar view is held by Sámi fishermen in Tana (Ween n.d.), and also by many non-Sámi people in Norway, where both inland and coastal fishing have traditionally been crucial forms of food procurement. More recently, however, nature management institutions in Norway promote catch-and-release for conservation purposes, triggering disputes similar to those described by Diver. Such disputes suggest that what is important is not whether or not to look after the salmon, as Diver clearly shows, but rather what belongs, and what does not belong in the category of "salmon." If salmon is known as food and gift and the act of catching it is a reflection of "the creator's benevolence" (Diver, chapter 10), then catching salmon simply to let it go again disrupts the relations that constitute salmon. If, on the other hand, salmon is known as a distinct species, separate from humans, and each individual returning to the river is a reflection—or a prediction—of the viability of the local salmon stock of that particular river, then removing the salmon from its route to spawn simply to eat it disrupts the cycle that constitutes a healthy salmon river.

SALMON TEMPORALITIES: CONCLUDING REMARKS

Humans and salmon are both migratory species with an amazing capacity to adapt, and to evolve, in their explorations of new habitats. In some instances, this capacity has brought us into close engagement with one another, and the preceding chapters elaborate some examples. Sometimes the relation is fragile and temporary, as in the case of some fishing practices. Sometimes it is cyclical and more enduring, as when rock structures, salmon ladders, waders, and simple hatchery tools such as buckets facilitate human–salmon encounters. These, in turn, have allowed the creation of long-term mutual relations of dependence but also of exploitation, loss, and decline. However, the encounter has always remained somewhat unpredictable: while humans tend to attach themselves to a particular settlement infrastructure on shore, salmon travel lightly and do not always return to their spawning grounds, or even to the same river, when they are expected to. Thus, not until the invention of the marine net-pen technology of modern aquaculture did the relation tighten in the sense that the salmon, quite literally, stayed in place. This development facilitated another chapter in the biography of human–salmon encounters and, through the control of both reproduction and feed, another instance in human history of animal domestication.

The lessons to be learned from this collection are many. We have seen that humans and salmon together create particular biosocial configurations that contribute to shaping our collective future. We have seen that these may sustain particular ways of life and thus be beneficial to all, but also that they can get out of hand and become detrimental both to salmon and to people. We have also seen that while they share similarities, each biosocial configuration is also unique, and lessons from one part of the world do not necessarily travel easily to another. Finally, we have seen that with each way of "doing salmon," with each set of relations and the practices and technologies that underpin them, comes another way of knowing salmon. While salmon remains in some sense elusive, and our (human) knowledge is always somewhat incomplete, knowledge also rests in particular places, with particular people, and with the particular strains of migrating salmon that *they* know.

Presented with such diversity, we should treat with caution any claim about how to best deal with the challenges that the salmon–human nexus poses. Sustainable biosocial configurations of salmons and humans may—or may not—involve hatcheries, money, trade, canneries, cosmologies, science, net pens, or a notion of the wild. This is not to say that anything goes, but that the future of human–salmon relations is open-ended. Chapters of our story together are being written every day and perhaps with an even greater intensity and diversity than ever before. What we can do now is share some of these stories and use them as templates for imagining a rich variety of alternative futures, uniquely adapted to the particular ways in which our human–salmon habitats evolve.

Acknowledgments

All scientific work is collaborative, but some papers rely more on collaboration than others. As a native of the Atlantic Rim studying Atlantic salmon, I am deeply grateful for the invitation to take part in discussions about Pacific salmon, species that I initially knew very little about. The School for Advanced Research in Santa Fe provided a perfect location for our exchanges, and I wish to acknowledge the contribution of all fellow seminarians in making this a very stimulating event. I also want to thank the editors, Ben Colombi and James Brooks, and especially Sibyl Diver and Kathy Reedy-Maschner for reading an earlier draft and for providing very constructive comments. Closer to home, I wish to acknowledge the continuous support and inspiration of John Law, Gro Ween, Kristin Asdal, and Line Dalheim and express my gratitude to them for making our ongoing project "Newcomers to the Farm: Atlantic Salmon between the Wild and the Industrial" (funded by the Norwegian Research Council) such an interesting and stimulating journey. A special thanks to John for his patience and inspiration on and off salmon farms and for always pushing me to think again.

Notes

1. The total global production of farmed Atlantic salmon in 2010 was 1.46 million tons. Sixty-five percent of the total production takes place in Norway where the production has more than doubled since 2001 (laksefakta.no/nokkelinfo.html, accessed April 2, 2011).

2. The term "*Salmo domesticus*" is derived from Gross 1998.

3. Most salmon counts rely on salmon returning to rivers to spawn. The number of salmon out at sea is, of course, far more difficult to pin down, and thus the "scientific salmon" is in large part a fish in the river.

4. I wish to thank Sibyl Diver for pointing this out.

5. I do not claim that salmon caught in a river and salmon raised in a net pen are identical or that the way they are often distinguished makes no sense. I wish to emphasize, however, that the boundary thus established rests upon fundamental divisions, both in popular discourse (wild versus not wild) and in anthropology (the human versus the nonhuman realm), that are neither self-evident nor particularly helpful.

6. Heather Swanson points out how the remarkable adaptability of salmon has made them specialists in the art of adapting to particularities, thus indicating a co-evolution with humans.

7. "Efficient" in terms of economic calculations of labor investment versus catch output, measured in the short term. This is a way of modeling that, in itself, represented a "new technology" in the human–salmon assemblage of the Pacific Northwest.

8. Weir-based fisheries were used by non-Indians as well and had the capacity to be incredibly efficient. Unless they were managed carefully (as they were in precolonial times, when some salmon were allowed to move up the river), one could catch the entire run at a single weir. Thus, they were potentially highly efficient, even before the arrival of Europeans.

9. A similar criminalization of Indigenous fishing practices took place in Norway in the Tana River where Sámi fishing practices were made illegal (see Ween 2012).

10. This interview, and the analysis of the case of "Vossolaks" is part of the ethnographic material in the project "Newcomers to the Farm: Atlantic Salmon between the Wild and the Industrial," funded by the Norwegian Research Council. I am indebted to Line Dalheim for pointing out the difference between "wild" and "experimental" salmon.

11. They have been reclassified in spite of the fact that they are offspring of Atlantic salmon stock that was taken from Norwegian rivers some seven to eight generations ago. In the meantime, selective breeding has changed certain characteristics, particularly related to appetite and growth rate. Genetic modification is not practiced in Norwegian aquaculture.

12. "Entangled livelihoods" was coined by Reedy-Maschner to describe the particular coastal village economy characteristic of the southern Alaskan region (see also Carothers, chapter 7).

13. Salmon fishing permits may be transferred temporarily or permanently between friends or kin (with the assumption that the transfer will be compensated by a hired position or other community favors) or sold for cash. People without permits can still fish for subsistence, but this is more difficult without commercial equipment. I wish to thank Kathy Reedy-Maschner for pointing this out.

14. Heather Swanson further suggests that North Americans' impression that salmon is "gone" is a reflection not so much of the salmon's disappearance as of its redistribution throughout the North Pacific. She describes how in the mid-1990s, for example, the US government declared the fisheries of the Columbia River region an "ecological disaster," and salmon populations were seen as endangered (see also Smith and Gilden 2000:6), while Japanese fishermen in Hokkaido hauled in fifty-seven million chum salmon, an all-time record (Swanson 2009:79).

15. The overwhelming majority of cannery workers are immigrants from the Philippines, Mexico, and North Africa. The first major group was made up of Filipinos recruited after American military occupation in the 1930s. Subsequently, when migrant labor laws were relaxed, recruitment moved to Mexico and elsewhere. I wish to thank Kathy Reedy-Maschner for elaborating this point.

16. By "diverging salmon ontologies," I refer to the way in which order is generated through practices that involve both humans and nonhumans. It is a way of stating that the world is not a single order in which difference is merely a question of interpretations and diverging interests. This approach, which sees reality as a relational effect, involves a turn from questions of epistemology to questions of ontology (Abram and Lien 2011:8; Lien and Law in press; see also Mol 2002).

References

Abram, Simone, and Marianne E. Lien

2011   Performing Nature at the World's Ends. Ethnos 76(1):3–19.

Ackerman, Lillian A.

2003   A Necessary Balance: Gender and Power among Indians of the Columbia Plateau. Norman: University of Oklahoma Press.

AEA Technology

2007   Independent Environmental Consultant Final Report—Agency Lenders Sakhalin II Phase 2 Project Health, Safety, Environmental and Social Review. London: AEA Technology plc.

2009   Lenders' Independent Environmental Consultant Site Visit Report: September 2009, Sakhalin II (Phase 2) Project. London: AEA Technology plc.

2010   IEC Lenders Independent Environmental Consultant: Monitoring Report April 2010, Sakhalin-2 Phase 2 Project. London: AEA Technology plc.

AEK (Archive of Erich Kasten)

2003   Digital video recordings of Even texts. 03–05 Natalya Ionovna Grigor'eva, October 4, 2003. Kulturstiftung Sibirien, Fuerstenberg.

AFSC (American Friends Service Committee)

1970   Uncommon Controversy; Fishing Rights of the Muckleshoot, Puyallup, and Nisqually Indians. A Report Prepared for the American Friends Service Committee. Seattle: University of Washington Press.

Aguilar, George

2005   When the River Ran Wild! Indian Traditions on the Mid-Columbia and the Warm Springs Reservation. Portland/Seattle: Oregon Historical Society Press, in association with University of Washington Press.

References

AKD (Archive of Erich Kasten and Elena Dul'chenko)
1998   Digital video recordings on Even/Koryak TEK, Bystrinski rayon. 98–06 Nadezhda Grigor'evna Barkavtova, August 18, 1998. Kulturstiftung Sibirien, Fuerstenberg.

Aleutians East Borough
2008   New Opportunities on the Alaska Peninsula. www.aleutianseast.org/index. asp?Type=B_BASIC&SEC={9CB60AA3–359D-409B-A80C-5187DFB4C1F9}, accessed November 10, 2009.

Ames, Kenneth M., and Herbert G. Maschner
1999   Peoples of the Northwest Coast: Their Archaeology and Prehistory. London: Thames and Hudson.

Anastasio, Angelo
1972   The Southern Plateau: An Ecological Analysis of Intergroup Relations. Northwest Anthropological Research Notes 6(2):109–229.

Anderson, David G.
2000   Identity and Ecology in Arctic Siberia: The Number One Reindeer Brigade. New York: Oxford University Press.

Andersson, Lars
1997   Alienation: En genomgående linje i Karl Marx' tänkande. Nora: Bokförlaget Nya Doxa.

Aoki, Haruo
1994   Nez Perce Dictionary. Berkeley: University of California Press.

Appert, Nicholas
1814   Le livre de tous les ménages, ou l'art de conserver, pendant plusieurs années, toutes les substances animales et végétales. Paris: Patris et Cie.

Appolon, Aleksei Pavlovich
2010   Natsional'nye osobennosti izgotovleniya orudii lova, predmetov byta korennogo naseleniya Koryakii. In Fol'klor i khudozhestvennoe tvorchestvo narodov Severa Kamchatki: Traditsii, sovremennost' i budushzhee. Erich Kasten, ed. Pp. 79–86. Fürstenberg/H.: Kulturstiftung Sibirien; Norderstedt: BoD.

Armitage, Derek, Fikret Berkes, and Nancy Doubleday
2007   Introduction: Moving beyond Co-Management. In Adaptive Co-management: Collaboration, Learning, and Multi-level Governance. Fikret Berkes, Derek R. Armitage, and Nancy Doubleday, eds. Pp. 1–15. Vancouver: University of British Columbia Press.

Arnold, David
2008   The Fishermen's Frontier: People and Salmon in Southeast Alaska. Seattle: University of Washington Press.

Arnold, Robert D.
1978   Alaska Native Land Claims. Anchorage: The Alaska Native Foundation.

Augerot, Xanthippe

2000   An Environmental History of the Salmon Management Philosophies of the North Pacific: Japan, Russia, Canada, Alaska and the Pacific Northwest United States. PhD dissertation, Department of Geography, Oregon State University. ir.library.oregonstate.edu/jspui/handle/1957/9015, accessed February 29, 2012.

2005   Atlas of Pacific Salmon: The First Map-Based Status Assessment of Salmon in the North Pacific. Berkeley: University of California Press.

Augerot, Xanthippe, and Courtland L. Smith

2011   Comparative Resilience in Five North Pacific Regional Salmon Fisheries. *In* Pathways to Resilience: Sustaining Salmon Ecosystems in a Changing World. Daniel L. Bottom, Kim K. Jones, Charles A. Simenstad, and Courtland L. Smith, eds. Pp. 229–264. Corvallis: Oregon Sea Grant ORESU-B-11-001.

Axtell, Horace, Kristie Baptiste, Dave Cummings, Rick Eichstaedt, Carla HighEagle, Dave Johnson, Julie Kane, Diane Mallickan, Allen Pinkham, Julie Simpson, Antonio Smith, Patrick Sobotta, Angela Sondenaa, William Swagerty, Rev. Henry Sugden, and Rebecca Miles Williams

2003   Treaties: Nez Perce Perspectives. Lewiston, ID: Confluence Press.

Banse, Tom

2008   Shoshone-Bannock Tribes Sign Fish Pact with BPA. OPB News, September 19. news.opb.org/article/3103-shoshone-bannock-tribes-sign-fish-pact-bpa/, accessed November 12, 2010.

Barber, Katrine

2005   Death of Celilo Falls. Seattle: University of Washington Press.

Barber, W. E.

1988   Circuli Spacing and Annulus Formation: Is There More Than Meets the Eye? The Case for Sockeye Salmon, *Oncorhynchus nerka*. Journal of Fish Biology 32(2):237–245.

Barlaup, Bjørn T., ed.

2008   Nå eller aldri for Vossolaksen—Anbefalte tiltak med bakgrunn i bestandsutvikling og trusselfaktorer [Now or Never for the Vosso Salmon—Recommendations Based on Population Development and Threats]. DN Report 2008-9. Trondheim: Direktoratet for Naturforvaltning (The Norwegian Directorate for Nature Management).

Bazarkin, Valeri Nikolaevich

1996   Otchet po proektu, Prirodnye resursy zapadnogo poberezhiya Kamchatki. Razdel: 2.6.4 Ikhtiofauna presnykh vod; 3.4.3 rybnye resursy rek. European-Russian Project INTAS 94–0981. Unpublished project report, Freie Universität Berlin and Kamchatski Institute of Ecology and of Natural Resource Use, Russian Academy of Sciences.

Befu, Harumi

1970   An Ethnographic Sketch of Old Harbor, Kodiak: An Eskimo Village. Arctic Anthropology 6:29–42.

REFERENCES

Berg, Laura
2008   Interview with George Dysart. *U.S. v. Oregon:* The Columbia River Salmon Fishing Case. CRITFC Seminar Materials. Late 1989–early 1990.

Berger, Thomas R.
1985   Village Journey: The Report of the Alaska Native Review Commission. New York: Hill and Wang.

Bergman, Sten
1923   Kamtchatka, skildringar från en treårig forskningsfärd. Stockholm: Albert Bonniers Förlag.

Berkes, Fikret
1994   Co-management: Bridging the Two Solitudes. Northern Perspectives 22:18–20.

2007   Adaptive Co-management and Complexity: Exploring the Many Faces of Co-management. *In* Adaptive Co-management: Collaboration, Learning, and Multi-level Governance. Fikret Berkes, Derek R. Armitage, and Nancy Doubleday, eds. Pp. 19–37. Vancouver: University of British Columbia Press.

Berkes, Fikret, Johan Colding, and Carl Folke
2000   Rediscovering of Traditional Ecological Knowledge as Adaptive Management. Ecological Applications 10:1251–1262.

Berkes, Fikret, Peter George, and Richard J. Preston
1991   Co-management—The Evolution in Theory and Practice of the Joint Administration of Living Resources. Alternatives-Perspectives on Society, Technology and Environment 18:12–18.

Berkes, Fikret, and Nancy J. Turner
2006   Knowledge, Learning and the Evolution of Conservation Practice for Social-Ecological System Resilience. Human Ecology 34:479–94.

Berringer, Patricia
1982   Northwest Coast Traditional Salmon Fisheries Systems of Resource Utilization. MA thesis, Department of Anthropology and Sociology, University of British Columbia, Vancouver.

Beverton, R. J. H., and S. J. Holt
1957   On the Dynamics of Exploited Fish Populations. London: H. M. Stationery Office.

Beynon, William
1954   Beynon Notebooks. Canadian Museum of Civilization, Library, Archives and Documentation, Ottawa.

1955–1956 Beynon Notebooks. Canadian Museum of Civilization, Library, Archives and Documentation, Ottawa.

Bingham, Isabelle
1946   Letter to General Superintendent, May 1, 1946. Charles Lucier Collection, Box 1. Archives, Alaska and Polar Regions Collections, Rasmuson Library, University of Alaska–Fairbanks, Fairbanks, AK.

Black, Lydia T.

1992   The Russian Conquest of Kodiak. Anthropological Papers of the University of Alaska 24(1–2):165–182.

2004   Russians in Alaska, 1732–1867. Fairbanks: University of Alaska Press.

Blumm, Michael

2002   Sacrificing the Salmon: A Legal and Policy History of the Decline of Columbia Basin Salmon. Den Bosch, Netherlands: BookWorld.

Bodley, John H.

2003   The Power of Scale: A Global History Approach. Armonk, NY: M. E. Sharpe.

2005   Cultural Anthropology: Tribes, States, and the Global System. Boston: McGraw Hill.

Boettke, Peter J.

1990   The Political Economy of Soviet Socialism: The Formative Years, 1918–1928. Boston: Kluwer Academic.

Bonneville Power Administration, US Department of Energy, Bureau of Indian Affairs, US Department of the Interior, Nez Perce Tribe

1997   Final Environmental Impact Statement. Nez Perce Tribal Hatchery Program.

Botkin, Daniel B.

1990   Discordant Harmonies: A New Ecology for the Twenty-first Century. New York: Oxford University Press.

Botkin, Daniel, Kenneth Cummins, Thomas Dunne, Henry Regier, Matthew Sobel, Lee Talbot, and Lloyd Simpson

1995   Status and Future of Salmon of Western Oregon and Northern California: Findings and Options. Santa Barbara, CA: Center for the Study of the Environment.

Bottom, Daniel

1997   To Till the Water—A History of Ideas in Fisheries Conservation. *In* Pacific Salmon and Their Ecosystems: Status and Future Options. Deanna J. Stouder, Peter A. Bisson, and Robert J. Naiman, eds. Pp. 569–597. New York: Chapman & Hall.

Bottom, Daniel, Kim Jones, Charles Simenstad, and Courtland Smith

2009   Reconnecting Social and Ecological Resilience in Salmon Ecosystems. Ecology and Society 14(1):5. www.ecologyandsociety.org/v0114/iss1/art5/, accessed February 28, 2012.

Bourdieu, Pierre

1977   Outline of a Theory of Practice. Cambridge: Cambridge University Press.

1991   Language and Symbolic Power. John B. Thompson, ed. Cambridge, MA: Harvard University Press.

Boyd, Robert

1999a   The Coming of the Spirit of Pestilence: Introduced Infectious Diseases and Population Decline among Northwest Coast Indians, 1774–1874. Vancouver: University of British Columbia Press.

1999b   Indians, Fire and the Land in the Pacific Northwest. Corvallis: Oregon State University Press.

2004   People of the Dalles: The Indians of Wascopam Mission; A Historical Ethnography Based on the Papers of the Methodist Missionaries. Studies in the Anthropology of North American Indians. Lincoln/Bloomington: University of Nebraska Press, in cooperation with the American Indian Studies Research Institute, Indiana University.

Bugaev, Viktor Fedorovich

2007   Ryby basseina reki Kamchatki. Petropavlovsk-Kamchatski: Kamchatpress.

Bugaev, Viktor Fedorovich, and Viktor Evgeneevich Kirichenko

2008   Nagul'no-nerestovye ozero aziatskoi nerki. Petropavlovsk-Kamchatski: Kamchatpress.

Burns, Carol

1971   As Long as the Rivers Run. Video recording. Olympia, Washington: Survival of American Indians Association.

Butler, Virginia L., and Sarah K. Campbell

2004   Resource Intensification and Resource Depression in the Pacific Northwest of North America: A Zooarchaeological Review. Journal of World Prehistory 18(4):327–405.

Campbell, Kenneth

2005   Persistence and Continuity: A History of the Tsimshian Nation. Prince Rupert, British Columbia: Prince Rupert School District, #52.

Campbell, Sarah K., and Virginia L. Butler

2004   Resource Intensification and Resource Depression in the Pacific Northwest of North America: A Zooarchaeological Review. Journal of World Prehistory 18(4):327–405.

2010   Archaeological Evidence for Resilience of Pacific Northwest Salmon Populations and the Socioecological System over the Last ~7,500 Years. Ecology and Society 15(1):17.

Carothers, Courtney

2008a   Privatizing the Right to Fish: Challenges to Livelihood and Community in Kodiak, Alaska. PhD dissertation, Department of Anthropology, University of Washington, Seattle.

2008b   "Rationalized Out": Discourses and Realities of Fisheries Privatization in Kodiak, Alaska. In Enclosing the Fisheries: People, Places, and Power. M. Lowe and C. Carothers, eds. Pp. 55–74. Symposium 68. Bethesda: American Fisheries Society.

2010   Tragedies of Commodification: Transitions in Alutiiq Fishing Communities in the Gulf of Alaska. MAST 9(2):95–120.

Caulfield, Richard

1997   Greenlanders, Whales, and Whaling: Sustainability and Self-determination in the Arctic. Hanover: University Press of New England.

Cederholm, C. Jeff, David H. Johnson, Robert E. Bilby, Lawrence G. Dominguez, Ann M. Garrett, William H. Graeber, Eva L. Greda, Matt D. Kunze, Bruce G. Marcot, John F. Palmisano, Rob W. Plotnikoff, William G. Pearcy, Charles A. Simenstad, and Patrick C. Trotter

2001   Pacific Salmon and Wildlife-Ecological Contexts, Relationships, and
        Implications for Management. *In* Wildlife-Habitat Relationships in Oregon
        and Washington. David H. Johnson and Thomas A. O'Neil, eds. Pp. 628–
        684. Corvallis: Oregon State University.

Chapman, Donald W.

1986   Salmon and Steelhead Abundance in the Columbia River in the Nineteenth
        Century. Transactions of the American Fisheries Society 117:1–21.

Childe, V. Gordon

1936   Man Makes Himself. London: Watts.

Clark, Donald W.

1979   Ocean Bay: An Early North Pacific Maritime Culture. National Museum of
        Man Mercury Series, Archaeological Survey of Canada, 86. Ottawa: National
        Museums of Canada.

1984   Pacific Eskimo: Historical Ethnography. *In* Handbook of North American
        Indians, vol. 5. D. Damas, ed. Pp. 185–197. Washington, DC: Smithsonian
        Institution Press.

1998   Kodiak Island: The Later Cultures. Arctic Anthropology 35:172–186.

Clifford, James

1986   Writing Culture: The Poetics and Politics of Ethnography. Berkeley:
        University of California Press.

Cobb, John N.

1921   Pacific Salmon Fisheries. Bureau of Fisheries Document, 902. Washington,
        DC: Government Printing Office.

Cockle, Richard

2009   Nez Perce Own 15,000 Acres in Wallowa County. The Oregonian,
        February 22. www.oregonlive.com/news/oregonian/index.ssf?/base/
        news/1235190309180160.xml&coll=72009, accessed August 31, 2010.

Cohen, Fay G.

1986   Treaties on Trial: The Continuing Controversy over Northwest Indian
        Fishing Rights. Seattle: University of Washington Press.

1989   Treaty Indian Tribes and Washington State: The Evolution of Tribal
        Involvement in Fisheries Management in the U.S. Pacific Northwest. *In*
        Co-operative Management of Local Fisheries: New Directions for Improved
        Management and Community Development. Evelyn Pinkerton, ed. Pp.
        37–48. Vancouver: University of British Columbia Press.

Cohen, Felix S.

1953   The Erosion of Indian Rights, 1950–1953: A Case Study in Bureaucracy. Yale
        Law Journal 62(3):348–390.

REFERENCES

Cohen, Norman A.

2005   Community Development in Kamchatka. Unpublished paper on file at the Russian Association of Indigenous Peoples of the North (Kamchatsky), United Nations Development Programme.

Colombi, Benedict J.

2005   Dammed in Region Six: The Nez Perce Tribe, Agricultural Development, and the Inequality of Scale. American Indian Quarterly 29(3/4):560–589.

2012   Declining Salmon, Large Dams, and the Capitalist World-Economy: A Case Study of Biocultural Diversity in the Nez Perce Homeland. *In* Water, Cultural Diversity & Global Environmental Change: Emerging Trends, Sustainable Futures? Barbara R. Johnston, Lisa Hiwasaki, Irene J. Klaver, Ameyali Ramos Castillo, and Veronica Strang, eds. Pp. 388-391. Jakarta: UNESCO; Dordrecht, Netherlands: Springer.

Columbia Basin Fish and Wildlife News Bulletin

2010   BiOp Challengers: 2010 Supplemental Salmon BiOp "Adds Nothing of Legal Significance." www.cbbulletin.com/401381.aspx, accessed November 11, 2010.

Columbia River Inter-Tribal Fish Commission

2011   Wy-Kan-Ush-Mi Wa-Kish-Wit: The Columbia River Anadromous Fish Restoration Plan of the Nez Perce, Umatilla, Warm Springs and Yakama Tribes. www.critfc.org/text/cost.html, accessed October 17, 2011.

Cone, Joseph

1995   A Common Fate: Endangered Salmon and the People of the Pacific Northwest. New York: H. Holt.

Cooke, Bill, and Uma Kothari, eds.

2001   Participation: The New Tyranny? London, New York: Zed Books.

Copes, Parcival

1998   Coping with the Coho Crisis: A Conservation-Minded, Stakeholder-Sensitive, and Community-Oriented Strategy. Victoria: British Columbia Ministry of Fisheries.

Crate, Susan

2006   Investigating Local Definitions of Sustainability in the Arctic: Insights from Post-Soviet Sakha Villages. Arctic 59(3):294–310.

Creed, Gerald W.

2006   The Seductions of Community. Santa Fe, NM: SAR Press.

CRFMP (Columbia River Fisheries Management Plan)

1977   A Plan for Managing Fisheries on Stocks Originating from the Columbia River and its Tributaries above Bonneville Dam. February 28.

1988   Columbia River Fish Management Plan.

1996–1998a   Management Agreement for Upper Columbia River Spring Chinook, Summer Chinook and Sockeye.

1996–1998b Management Agreement for Upper Columbia River Fall Chinook.

2001–2003 Interim Management Agreement for Upriver Spring Chinook, Summer Chinook, and Sockeye.

2005–2007 Interim Management Agreement for Upriver Chinook, Sockeye, Steelhead, Coho and White Sturgeon.

2008–2017 United States v. Oregon Management Agreement. May 2008.

CRITFC (Columbia River Inter-Tribal Fish Commission)

1977 Constitution and Bylaws of the Columbia River Inter-Tribal Fish Commission.

1987 Special Report to Tribal Members. Newspaper.

1994 Chinook Trilogy. Portland, OR: Wild Hare Media. www.critfc.org/text/trilogy.html, accessed February 29, 2012.

1995 Wy-Kan-Ush-Mi Wa-Kish-Wit (Spirit of the Salmon): The Columbia River Anadromous Fish Restoration Plan of the Nez Perce, Umatilla, Warm Springs, and Yakama Tribes, vol. 1. www.critfc.org/oldsite/text/contents.htm, accessed March 20, 2012.

1996 Wy-kan-ush-mi Wa-kish-wit. Old file. www.critfc.org/oldsite/text/contents.htm, accessed February 29, 2012.

2003 Silver Anniversary. Wana Chinook Tymoo Winter:8.

2009 Salmon Win a Triple Crown. Wana Chinook Tymoo Winter:6.

2011 Wy-kan-ush-mi Wa-kish-wit. www.critfc.org/text/trp.html, accessed February 29, 2012.

Cronon, William

1995a The Trouble with Wilderness; Or, Getting Back to the Wrong Nature. *In* Uncommon Ground: Rethinking the Human Place in Nature. William Cronon, ed. Pp.69–90. New York: W. W. Norton.

1995b The Trouble with Wilderness; or, Getting Back to the Wrong Nature. http://www.williamcronon.net/writing/Trouble_with_Wilderness_Main.html, accessed April 2, 2011.

Crowell, Aron L.

2004 Terms of Engagement: The Collaborative Representation of Alutiiq Identity. Études/Inuit/Studies 28(1):9–35.

Crowell, Aron L., Amy F. Steffian, Gordon L. Pullar, eds.

2001 Looking Both Ways: Heritage and Identity of the Alutiiq People. Fairbanks: University of Alaska Press.

Cruikshank, Julie

1998 The Social Life of Stories: Narrative and Knowledge in the Yukon Territory. Lincoln and London: University of Nebraska Press.

CTUIR (Confederated Tribes of the Umatilla Indian Reservation)

N.d. Salmon Success in the Umatilla River! www.umatilla.nsn.us/umariver.html, accessed October 4, 2011.

REFERENCES

Dale, Norman

1989   Getting to Co-Management: Social Learning in the Redesign of Fisheries Management. *In* Co-operative Management of Local Fisheries: New Directions for Improved Management and Community Development. Evelyn Pinkerton, ed. Pp. 49–72. Vancouver: University of British Columbia Press.

Davis, Anthony

1996   Barbed Wire and Bandwagons: A Comment on ITQ Fisheries Management. Reviews in Fish Biology and Fisheries 6:97–107.

Davis, Nancy Yaw

1971   The Effects of the 1964 Earthquake, Tsunami, and Resettlement on Two Koniag Eskimo Villages. PhD dissertation, Department of Anthropology, University of Washington, Seattle.

1976   Steps toward Understanding Rapid Cultural Change in Native Rural Alaska. Report submitted to Federal–State Land Use Planning Commission for Alaska, Anchorage.

Davydov, Gavriil I.

1977[1809] Two Voyages to Russian America, 1802–1807. Colin Bearne, trans. Richard A. Pierce, ed. Kingston, Ontario: Limestone Press.

Deloria, Vine, and Clifford M. Lytle

1984   The Nations Within: The Past and Future of American Indian Sovereignty. New York: Pantheon Books.

Devereaux, F. A.

1891–1892 Field Books. British Columbia Archives, Victoria, BC, CLRS—FBBC 448, 449, 450, 451.

Dietrich, William

1995   Northwest Passage: The Great Columbia River. New York: Simon & Schuster.

Dietz, Thomas, Amy Fitzgerald, and Rachael Shwom

2005   Environmental Values. Annual Reviews in Environmental Resources 30:335–372.

Dodds, Gordon

1959   The Salmon King of Oregon: R. D. Hume and the Pacific Fisheries. Chapel Hill: University of North Carolina Press.

Dombrowski, Kirk

2001   Against Culture: Development, Politics, and Religion in Indian Alaska. Lincoln: University of Nebraska Press.

Dompier, Douglas W.

2005   The Fight of the Salmon People: Blending Tribal Tradition with Modern Science to Save Sacred Fish. Philadelphia, PA: Xlibris.

Donaldson, Ivan J., and Frederick K. Cramer

1971   Fishwheels of the Columbia. Portland, OR: Binfords & Mort.

Donkersloot, Rachel

2005   Ecological Crisis, Social Change and the Life Paths of Young Alaskans: An Analysis of the Impacts of Shifting Patterns in Human–Environment Interactions in the Fisheries Dependent Region of Bristol Bay, Alaska. MA thesis, Department of Anthropology, University of Montana.

Dul'chenko, Elena Vladimirovna

2007   Koncentraciia mikroelementov v nekotorykh vidakh ryb, traditsionno izpol'zuemykh korennym naseleniem Central'noi Kamchatki. *In* Sokhranenie biomnogoobraziia Kamchatki i prilegayushzhikh morei. A. M. Tokranov, ed. Pp. 212–215. Petropavlovsk-Kamchatski: Kamchatpress.

Dupris, Joseph C., Kathleen S. Hill, and William H. Rodgers

2006   The Si'lailo Way: Indians, Salmon, and Law on the Columbia River. Durham, NC: Carolina Academic Press.

Durham, William H.

1991   Coevolution: Genes, Culture, and Human Diversity. Stanford, CA: Stanford University Press.

Dürr, Michael, Erich Kasten, and Klavdiya Khaloimova

2001   Itelmen Language and Culture: Text & Songs; Journey to the Reindeer Camp. CD. Münster: Waxmann Verlag. (Revised DVD edition in preparation, see also www.siberian-studies.org/publications/PDF/ILC3texts_songs_E.pdf, accessed March 18, 2012.)

Eaton, Perry

2009   From the Artist's Point of View. *In* Giinaquq Like a Face: Sugpiaq Masks of the Kodiak Archipelago. S. Haakanson Jr. and A. Steffian, eds. Pp. 167–177. Fairbanks: University of Alaska Press.

Ebert, Mark

2010   Human versus Person: An Examination of Nature/Culture on the Northwest Coast. Nature Studies Review 19(1):29–51.

Ehrlich, Paul R.

1968   Coevolution and the Biology of Communities. *In* Biochemical Coevolution. Kenton L. Chambers, ed. Pp. 3–9. Proceedings of the 29th Annual Biology Colloquium. Corvallis: Oregon State University Press.

Ehrlich, Paul R., and Peter H. Raven

1964   Butterflies and Plants: A Study in Coevolution. Evolution 18(4):586–608.

Elliot, Henry W.

1886   Our Arctic Promise, Alaska and Seal Islands. New York: C. Scribner's Sons.

Engels, Friedrich

1902   The Origin of the Family, Private Property and the State. Chicago: C. H. Kerr.

Escobar, Arturo

1995   Encountering Development: The Making and Unmaking of the Third World. Princeton, NJ: Princeton University Press.

REFERENCES

2008 Territories of Difference: Place, Movements, Life, Redes. Durham, NC: Duke University Press.

FAO (Fish and Agriculture Organisation, United Nations), Fisheries and Aquaculture Department
2011 Fishery Statistical Collections Global Production. Rome: FAO. www.fao.org/ fishery/statistics/global-production/en, accessed February 29, 2012.

Feit, Harvey
2004 James Bay Crees' Life Projects and Politics: Histories of Place, Animal Partners and Enduring Relationships. *In* In the Way of Development: Indigenous Peoples, Life Projects and Globalization. M. Blaser, H. Feit, and G. McRae, eds. Pp. 92–110. London and Ottawa: Zed Books and the Canadian International Development Research Center.

Finley, Carmel
2009 The Social Construction of Fishing, 1949. Ecology and Society 14(1):6. www.ecologyandsociety.org/v0114/iss1/art6, accessed February 28, 2012.

Fitzhugh, Ben
2003 The Evolution of Complex Hunter-Gatherers: Archaeological Evidence from the North Pacific. New York: Kluwer-Plenum.

Fitzhugh, William W., and Aron Crowell
1988 Crossroads of Continents: Cultures of Siberia and Alaska. Washington, DC: Smithsonian Institution Press.

FiveCrows, Jeremy
2003 A Lesson from Nature. Wana Chinook Tymoo Winter. www.critfc.org/wana/ hatchery.html, accessed October 4, 2011.

2011 The Nez Perce Tribe Has Combined Traditional Knowledge with State-of-the-Art Science to Create an Innovative Hatchery in the Heart of Their Reservation. CRITFC, A Lesson from Nature. www.critfc.org/wana/ hatchery.html, accessed October 17, 2011.

Foucault, Michel
1990 The History of Sexuality: An Introduction, vol. 1. New York: Vintage Books.

Foucault, Michel, and Colin Gordon
1980 Power/Knowledge: Selected Interviews and Other Writings, 1972–1977. New York: Vintage.

Galois, Robert
2004 A Voyage to the North West Side of America: The Journals of James Colnett, 1786–89. Vancouver: University of British Columbia Press.

Garibaldi, Ann, and Nancy Turner
2004 Cultural Keystone Species: Implications for Ecological Conservation and Restoration. Ecology & Society 9(3):1.

Gartland, John C.
1977 *Sohappy v. Smith*: Eight Years of Litigation over Indian Fishing Rights. Oregon Law Review 56:680–791.

Geertz, Clifford

1963   Agricultural Involution: The Process of Ecological Change in Indonesia. Berkeley: Published for the Association of Asian Studies by University of California Press.

Gibson-Graham, J. K. (Julie Graham and Katherine Gibson)

1996   The End of Capitalism (As We Knew It): A Feminist Critique of Political Economy. Cambridge: Blackwell.

2006   A Postcapitalist Politics. Minneapolis: University of Minnesota Press.

Gideon, Hiermonk

1989[1805]   The Round the World Voyage of Hieromonk Gideon, 1803–1809. Lydia. T. Black, trans. Richard A. Pierce, ed. Fairbanks: Limestone Press.

Glavin, Terry

1996   Dead Reckoning: Confronting the Crisis in Pacific Fisheries. Vancouver: Greystone Books.

Goldenberg, Suzanne

2011   Obama Administration "Bailed Out" GM Salmon Firm. Guardian, October.

Goodwin, Philip

1998   "Hired Hands" or "Local Voice": Understandings and Experience of Local Participation in Conservation. Transactions of the Institute of British Geographers ns 23:481–499.

Gordon, H. Scott

1953   An Economic Approach to the Optimum Utilization of Fishery Resources. Journal of the Fisheries Research Board of Canada 10(7):442–457.

Grant, Bruce

1999   Foreword and Afterword to Lev Shternberg "The Social Organisation of the Gilyak." Anthropological Papers of the American Museum of Natural History, 82. Seattle: University of Washington Press.

Grantham, Anjuli

2011   Fishing at Karluk: Nature, Technology, and the Creation of the Karluk Reservation in Territorial Alaska. MA thesis, Department of Public History, University of South Carolina, Columbia.

Greenberg, Paul

2010   Four Fish: The Future of the Last Wild Food. New York: Penguin Press.

Greenwald, Emily

2002   Reconfiguring the Reservation: The Nez Perces, Jicarilla Apaches, and the Dawes Act. Albuquerque: University of New Mexico Press.

Grinev, Andrei V.

1999   Russkie kolonii na Aliaske na rubezhe XIX. *In* Istoriia Russkoi Ameriki. N. Bolkhovitinov, ed. Pp. 15–52. Moscow: Mezhdunarodnye Otnosheniia.

References

Groot, Cornelis, and Leo Margolis
1991   Pacific Salmon Life Histories. Vancouver: University of British Columbia Press.

Gross, Mart
1998   One Species with Two Biologies: Atlantic Salmon (*Salmo salar*) in the Wild and in Aquaculture. Canadian Journal of Fisheries and Aquatic Sciences 55(S1):131–144.

Guldin, Gregory Eliyu, Oleg Vasilyevich Kapkaun, and Alexander Timofeyevich Konkov
2010   Sakhalin Indigenous Minorities Development Plan: Plan Completion Evaluation Report. Sakhalin, Russia: Sakhalin Energy Investment Company Ltd.

Gülden, Werner Friedrich, ed.
2011   Forschungsreise nach Kamtschatka. Reisen und Erlebnisse des Johann Karl Ehrenfried Kegel von 1841 bis 1847. Bibliotheca Kamtschatica. Fürstenberg/H.: Kulturstiftung Sibirien.

Gunther, Erna
1926   An Analysis of the First Salmon Ceremony. American Anthropologist 28:605–617.

Gupta, Akhil
1998   Postcolonial Developments: Agriculture in the Making of Modern India. Durham, NC: Duke University Press.

Gurvich, I. S
1974   Malye narody Severa. *In* Bol'shaia sovetskaia entsiklopediia, vol. 15. A. M. Prokhorov, ed. Pp. 861–862. Moscow: Sovetskaia Entsiklopediia.

Gustafson R. G., R. S. Waples, J. M. Myers, L. A. Weitkkamp, G. J. Bryant, O. W. Johnson, and J. J. Hard
2007   Pacific Salmon Extinctions: Quantifying Lost and Remaining Diversity. Conservation Biology 21:1009–1020.

Gutiérrez, Nicolás L., Ray Hilborn, and Omar Defeo
2011   Leadership, Social Capital and Incentives Promote Successful Fisheries. Nature 470:386–389.

Haakanson, Sven, Jr., and Amy F. Steffian, eds.
2009   Giinaquq Like a Face: Sugpiaq Masks of the Kodiak Archipelago. Fairbanks: University of Alaska Press.

Hanna, Jonathan M.
2007   Native Communities and Climate Change: Protecting Tribal Resources as Part of National Climate Policy. Boulder: Natural Resources Law Center, Colorado Law School, University of Colorado.

Haraway, Donna
2008   When Species Meet. Minneapolis: University of Minnesota Press.

Hardin, Garett
1968   The Tragedy of the Commons. Science 162:1243–1248.

Harkin, Michael E., and David Rich Lewis

2007   Native Americans and the Environment: Perspectives on the Ecological Indian. Lincoln: University of Nebraska Press.

Harris, Douglas C.

2008   Landing Native Fisheries: Indian Reserves and Fishing Rights in British Columbia. Vancouver: University of British Columbia Press.

Harris, Marvin

1979   Cultural Materialism: The Struggle for a Science of Culture. New York: Random House.

1980   Culture, People, and Nature: An Introduction to General Anthropology. New York: Harper and Row.

Harrison, Penny H.

1986   Symposium on Salmon Law: Restoration and Harvest Allocation; The Evolution of a New Comprehensive Plan for Managing Columbia River Anadromous Fish. Environmental Law 16:705–727.

Hayden, Brian, and Rick Schulting

1997   The Plateau Interaction Sphere and Late Prehistoric Cultural Complexity. American Antiquity 62(1):51–85.

Helfield, James M., and Robert J. Naiman

2001   Effects of Salmon-Derived Nitrogen on Riparian Forest Growth and Implications for Stream Productivity. Ecology 82:2403–2409.

Hewes, Gordon Winant

1947   Aboriginal Use of Fishery Resources in Northwestern North America. PhD dissertation, University of California, Berkeley.

1973   Indian Fisheries Productivity in Pre-contact Times in the Pacific Salmon Area. Northwest Anthropological Research Notes 7:133–155.

1998   Fishing. *In* Handbook of North American Indians, vol. 12: Plateau. Deward E. Walker Jr., ed. Pp. 620–640. Washington, DC: Smithsonian Institution.

Hilborn, Ray

1999   Confessions of a Reformed Hatchery Basher. Fisheries 24:30–31.

2006   Fisheries Success and Failure: The Case of the Bristol Bay Salmon Fishery. Bulletin of Marine Science 78(3):487–498.

Hublou, Wallace F., Joe Wallis, Thomas B. McKee, Duncan K. Law, Russell O. Sinnhuber, and T. C. Yu

1959   Development of the Oregon Pellet Diet. Research Briefs. Pp. 28–46. Portland: Oregon Fish Commission.

Hunn, Eugene S.

1982   Mobility as a Factor Limiting Resource Use in the Columbia Plateau of North America. *In* Resource Managers: North American and Australian Hunter-Gatherers. Nancy M. Williams and Eugene S. Hunn, eds. Pp. 17–43. Boulder, CO: Westview Press.

REFERENCES

Hunn, Eugene S., and James Selam
1990   Nch'i-Wána, "The Big River": Mid-Columbia Indians and Their Land.
        Seattle: University of Washington Press.

Hunn, Eugene S., and Nancy M. Williams
1982   Resource Managers: North American and Australian Hunter-Gatherers.
        Boulder, CO: Westview Press.

Igoe, James
2004   Conservation and Globalization: A Study of the National Parks and
        Indigenous Communities from East Africa to South Dakota. Case Studies
        in Contemporary Social Issues. Belmont, CA: Thomson/Wadsworth.

Ingold, Tim
2000   The Perception of the Environment. London: Routledge.

Jacka, Jerry K.
1990   Fishing. *In* The History and Ethnohistory of the Aleutians East Borough.
        Lydia T. Black, ed. Pp. 213–240. Fairbanks: Limestone Press.

Jasanoff, Sheila, ed.
2004   States of Knowledge: The Co-production of Science and the Social Order.
        London: Routledge.

Jentoft, Svein
2000   The Community: A Missing Link of Fisheries Management. Marine Policy
        24:53–59.

Jentoft, Svein, Bonnie J. McCay, and Douglas C. Wilson
1998   Social Theory and Fisheries Co-management. Marine Policy 22:423–436.

Jochelson, Vladimir Il'ich
1908   The Koryak. American Museum of Natural History Memoirs, 10. The Jesup
        North Pacific Expedition Publications, 6. Leiden: E. J. Brill; New York: G. E.
        Stechert.

Jochelson, Waldemar
N.d.   The Kamchadals. New York Public Library, Manuscripts and Archives
        Division.
1928   Peoples of Asiatic Russia. New York: AMNH.

Kasten, Erich
1990   Maskentänze der Kwakiutl. Berlin: Dietrich Reimer Verlag.
2009   Das O-lo-lo-Fest der Nymylanen Küsten-Korjaken. *In* Schamanen Sibiriens.
        Magier, Mittler, Heiler. Erich Kasten, ed. Pp. 32–35. Berlin: Dietrich Reimer
        Verlag.
2011   Johann Karl Ehrenfried Kegel. Ein deutscher Agronom bezieht Stellung
        zur Land- und Naturnutzung auf Kamtschatka. *In* Forschungsreise nach
        Kamtschatka. Reisen und Erlebnisse des Johann Karl Ehrenfried Kegel von
        1841 bis 1847. W. F. Gülden, ed. Pp. 307–320. Fürstenberg/H.: Kulturstiftung
        Sibirien.

Kasten, Erich, ed.

2011   Koryak Language and Culture: Traditional Ecological Knowledge, Part 2; Fishing. DVD with booklet (KLC2–02). 4 vols. Fürstenberg/H.: Kulturstiftung Sibirien.

Kearney, Michael

1996   Reconceptualizing the Peasantry: Anthropology in Global Perspective. Boulder, CO: Westview Press.

Kelly, R. L., and M. Prasciunas

2007   Did the Ancestors of Native Americans Cause Animal Extinctions in Late Pleistocene North America? *In* Native Americans and the Environment: Perspectives on the Ecological Indian. M. E. Harkin and D. R. Lewis, eds. Pp. 95–122. Lincoln: University of Nebraska Press.

Kew, Michael

1989   Salmon Availability, Technology and Cultural Adaptations on the Fraser River. *In* A Complex Culture of the British Columbia Plateau: Traditional Stl'atl'imx Resource Use. Bryan Hayden, ed. Pp. 177–221. Vancouver: University of British Columbia Press.

Kittlitz, Friedrich Heinrich von

2011[1858] Denkwürdigkeiten einer Reise nach dem russischen Amerika, nach Mikronesien und durch Kamtschatka. *In* Denkwürdigkeiten einer Reise nach dem russischen Amerika, nach Mikronesien und durch Kamtschatka. Auszüge aus den Werken, mit einem Essay von Lisa Strecker. Bibliotheca Kamtschatica. Erich Kasten, ed. Pp. 37–177. Fürstenberg/H.: Kulturstiftung Sibirien.

Knapp, Gunnar, Cathy A. Roheim, and James L. Anderson

2007   The Great Salmon Run: Competition between Wild and Farmed Salmon. TRAFFIC North America, World Wildlife Fund. 12 D:\Data\Documents\swd\ WSCNorth Pacific salmon.doc. www.worldwildlife.org/what/globalmarkets/ wildlifetrade/WWFBinaryitem4985.pdf, accessed February 29, 2012.

Knowles, Governor Tony

2000   Marine Stewardship Council awards Sustainability Label to Alaska Salmon. Press release of the Marine Stewardship Council. www.msc.org/newsroom/ news/marine-stewardship-council-awards-sustainability, accessed February 28, 2012.

Kofinas, Gary, and Stephen Braund

1996   Defining Community Sustainability: A Report from Community Involvement Phase 1 of the NSF Community Sustainability Project. taiga.net/sustain/lib/ reports/sustainability.html, accessed November 10, 2010.

Kramvig, Britt

2006   Finnmarksbilder. Report no 17/2006. Tromsø: NORUT (Northern Research Institute).

References

Krasheninnikov, Stepan Petrovich
1972   Explorations of Kamchatka, North Pacific Scitimar: Report of a journey
        made to explore eastern Siberia in 1735–1751; by order of the Russian
        Imperial Government. Portland: Oregon Historical Society.

Krech, Shepard, III
2005   Reflection on Conservation, Sustainability, and Environmentalism in
        Indigenous North America. American Anthropologist 107(1):78–86.
2007   Afterword. *In* Native Americans and the Environment: Perspectives on
        the Ecological Indian. Michael E. Harkin and David Rich Lewis, eds.
        Pp. 343–353. Lincoln: University of Nebraska Press.

Krupnik, Igor
1993   Arctic Adaptations: Native Whalers and Reindeer Herders of Northern
        Eurasia. Hanover and London: University Press of New England.

**Kruse, Jack A., Robert G. White, Howard E. Epstein, Billy Archie, Matt Berman,
Stephen R. Braund, F. Stuart Chapin III, Johnny Charlie Sr., Colin J. Daniel,
Joan Eamer, Nick Flanders, Brad Griffith, Sharman Haley, Lee Huskey, Bernice Joseph,
David R. Klein, Gary P. Kofinas, Stephanie M. Martin, Stephen M. Murphy,
William Nebesky, Craig Nicolson, Don E. Russell, Joe Tetlichi, Arlon Tussing,
Marilyn D. Walker, and Oran R. Young**
2004   Modeling Sustainability of Arctic Communities: An Interdisciplinary
        Collaboration of Researchers and Local Knowledge Holders. Ecosystems
        7:815–828.

Ksenofontov, M. Y., and I. A. Goldenberg
2008   Economika lososevogo khozaistva [Economy of Salmon Fishery Farming].
        Moscow: Human Rights Press.

Lackey, Robert T., Denise H. Lach, and Sally L. Duncan
2006   Salmon 2100: The Future of Wild Pacific Salmon. Bethesda, MD: American
        Fisheries Society.

Lake, Frank
2007   Traditional Ecological Knowledge to Develop and Maintain Fire Regimes
        in Northwestern California, Klamath-Siskiyou Bioregion: Management
        and Restoration of Culturally Significant Habitats. PhD dissertation,
        Environmental Science, Oregon State University. ir.library.oregonstate.edu/
        dspace/handle/1957/6222, accessed February 29, 2012.

Lakoff, George, and Mark Johnson.
1980   Metaphors We Live By. Chicago: University of Chicago Press.

Landeen, Dan, and Allen Pinkham
1999   Salmon and His People: Fish and Fishing in Nez Perce Culture. Lewiston,
        ID: Confluence Press.

Langdon, Stephen J.
1986   Conditions in Alaskan Native Economy and Society. *In* Contemporary
        Alaskan Native Economies. Stephen J. Langdon, ed. Pp. 29–46. Lanham,
        MD: University Press of America.

2006   Tidal Pulse Fishing: Selective Traditional Tlingit Salmon Fishing Techniques on the West Coast of the Prince of Wales Archipelago. *In* Traditional Ecological Knowledge and Natural Resource Management. Charles R. Menzies, ed. Pp. 177–211. Lincoln: University of Nebraska Press.

2007   Sustaining a Relationship. *In* Native Americans and the Environment: Perspectives on the Ecological Indian. Michael E. Harkin and David Rich Lewis, eds. Pp. 233–273. Lincoln: University of Nebraska Press.

2008   The Community Quota Program in the Gulf of Alaska: A Vehicle for Alaska Native Village Sustainability? *In* Enclosing the Fisheries: People, Places, and Power. Marie E. Lowe and Courtney Carothers, eds. Pp. 155–194. Symposium 68. Bethesda, MD: American Fisheries Society.

Larkin, Peter A.

1979   Maybe You Can't Get There From Here: A Foreshortened History of Research in Relation to Management of Pacific Salmon. Journal of the Fisheries Research Board of Canada 36(1):98–106.

Latour, Bruno

1993   We Have Never Been Modern. Cambridge, MA: Harvard University Press.

2004   Politics of Nature: How to Bring the Sciences into Democracy. Cambridge, MA: Harvard University Press.

Law, John

2008   Actor Network Theory and Material Semiotics. *In* The New Blackwell Companion to Social Theory. Bryan S. Turner, ed. Pp. 141–158. Oxford: Blackwell.

Lee, Kai N.

1993   Compass and Gyroscope: Integrating Science and Politics for the Environment. Washington, DC: Island Press.

Le Gall, Jean

1951   The Present World Problem of Sea Fisheries. United Nations Conference on the Conservation and Utilization of Resources. Wildlife and Fish Resources 7:11–13.

Lichatowich, James A.

1999   Salmon without Rivers: A History of the Pacific Salmon Crisis. Washington, DC: Island Press.

Lien, Marianne E.

2007a   Domestication "Downunder": Tasmanian Atlantic Salmon. *In* Where the Wild Things Are Now: Domestication Reconsidered. Rebecca Cassidy and Molly Mullin, eds. Pp. 205–227. Oxford: Berg.

2007b   Feeding Fish Efficiently; Mobilising Knowledge in Tasmanian Salmon Farming. Social Anthropology 15(2):169–185.

Lien, Marianne E., and John Law

2011   "Emergent Aliens": On Salmon, Nature and Their Enactment. Ethnos 76(1):65–87.

In press Slippery—Field Notes on Empirical Ontology. Social Studies of Science.

REFERENCES

Lightfoot, Kent G.

2003   Russian Colonization: The Implications of Mercantile Colonial Practices in the North Pacific. Historical Archaeology 37:14–28.

Lisiansky, Urey

1968[1814] Voyage Round the World in the Years 1803, 1804, 1805, and 1806. New York: De Capo Press.

Locke, John

1969   Two Treatises of Government. New York and London: Hafner.

Loring, Philip, and Craig Gerlach

2010   Outpost Agriculture: Food System Innovation in Rural Alaskan Communities. Ethnohistory 57(2):183–199.

Losey, Robert

2010   Animism as a Means of Exploring Archaeological Fishing Structures on Willapa Bay, Washington, USA. Cambridge Anthropological Journal 20(1):17–32.

Loucks, Laura, James A. Wilson, and Jay J. C. Ginter

2003   Experiences with Fisheries Co-management in North America. *In* The Fisheries Co-management Experience: Accomplishments, Challenges, and Prospects. Douglas Clyde Wilson, Jesper Raakjaer Nielson, and Poul Degnbol, eds. Pp. 153–170. Boston: Kluwer Academic.

Luehrmann, Sonja

2005   Russian Colonialism and the Asiatic Model of Production: (Post)-Soviet Ethnography Goes to Alaska. Slavic Review 64:851–871.

2008   Alutiiq Villages under Russian and U.S. Rule. Fairbanks: University of Alaska Press.

Lukashkina, Tatiana P.

1944   Unpublished personal document.

1991   Skazki babushki Petrovny. Petropavlovsk-Kamchatskii: Kamshat.

Madsen, Roy

2001   Tides and Ties of Our Culture. *In* Looking Both Ways: Heritage and Identity of the Alutiiq People. A. Crowell, A. Steffian, and G. Pullar, eds. Pp. 75. Fairbanks: University of Alaska Press.

Marshall, Alan G.

1999   Unusual Gardens: The Nez Perce and Wild Horticulture on the Eastern Columbia Plateau. *In* Northwest Lands, Northwest Peoples: Readings in Environmental History. Dale D. Goble and Paul W. Hirt, eds. Pp. 173–187. Seattle: University of Washington Press.

2006   Fish, Water, and Nez Perce Life. Idaho Law Review 42(3):763–793.

Martin, Irene

2008   Resilience in Lower Columbia River Salmon Fishing Communities. Ecology and Society 13:23. www.ecologyandsociety.org/vol13/iss2/art23/, accessed February 29, 2012.

Marx, Karl

1970   Contribution to the Critique of Political Economy. Maurice Dobb, ed. New York: International.

1972   Ethnological Notebooks. Assen: Van Gorcum.

Maschner, Herbert

1998   Salmon Run Volatility, Subsistence, and the Development of North Pacific Societies. *In* Proceedings of the 12th International Abashiri Symposium: Salmon Fishery in the North and Its Change through Time. Hokkaido Museum of Northern Peoples, ed. Pp. 11–28. Abashiri, Hokkaido: Association for the Promotion of Northern Cultures.

Mason, Rachel

1993   Fishing and Drinking in Kodiak, Alaska: The Sporadic Re-Creation of an Endangered Lifestyle. PhD dissertation, Department of Anthropology, University of Virginia, Charlottesville.

2006   Summers in Hollywood: The Shearwater Bay Cannery and the Community of Old Harbor. Paper presented at the Alaska Anthropological Association Annual Meeting, Kodiak, March 2–4.

Masure, Nestor C., and Larry M. Ellanak

1948   Letter to William L. Paul Jr., May 31, 1948. Charles Lucier Collection, Box 2. Archives, Alaska and Polar Regions Collections, Rasmuson Library, University of Alaska–Fairbanks, Fairbanks, AK.

Matson, R. G.

1992   The Evolution of Northwest Coast Subsistence. Research in Economic Anthropology, Supplement:367–428.

McCall, William

2008   BPA, Tribes Reach $900 Million Deal to Help Columbia River Salmon. Seattle Times, April 7. seattletimes.nwsource.com/html/local-news/2004332803_webtribes07m.html, accessed November 12, 2010.

McCool, Daniel

2002   Native Waters: Contemporary Indian Water Settlements and the Second Treaty Era. Tucson: University of Arizona Press.

McDonald, James A.

1991   The Marginalization of the Tsimshian Cultural Ecology: The Seasonal Cycle. *In* Native Peoples, Native Lands: Canadian Indians, Inuit and Metis. Bruce Alden Cox, ed. Pp. 109–216. Ottawa: Carleton University Press.

McEvoy, Arthur F.

1988   Towards an Interactive Theory of Nature and Culture: Ecology, Production, and Cognition in the California Fishing Industry. *In* The Ends of the Earth: Perspectives on Modern Environmental History. D. Worster, ed. Pp. 211–229. Cambridge: Cambridge University Press.

Menovshchikov, G. A.

1974   Skazki i mify narodov Chukotki i Kamchatki. Moscow: Nauka.

REFERENCES

Menzies, Charles R., and Caroline F. Butler

2007   Returning to Selective Fishing through Indigenous Fisheries Knowledge: The Example of K'moda, Gitxaala Territory. American Indian Quarterly 33(3):441–464.

2008   The Indigenous Foundation of the Resource Economy of BC's North Coast. Labour/Le Travail 61:131–149.

Miller, Jay

1997   Tsimshian Culture: A Light through the Ages. Lincoln: Nebraska University Press.

Mishler, Craig

2003   Black Ducks and Salmon Bellies: An Ethnography of Old Harbor and Ouzinkie, Alaska. Virginia Beach: Donning.

Mishler, Craig, and Rachel Mason

1996   Alutiiq Vikings: Kinship and Fishing in Old Harbor, Alaska. Human Organization 55:263–269.

Mol, Annemarie

2002   The Body Multiple. Durham: Duke University Press.

Montgomery, David R.

2003   King of Fish: The Thousand-Year Run of Salmon. Boulder, CO: Westview Press.

Moore, Donald S., Jake Kosek, and Anand Pandian, eds.

2003   Race, Nature, and the Politics of Difference. Durham, NC: Duke University Press.

Morrison, M. K.

1890   Letter to Thomas Mowat. University of British Columbia Library microfilm, Indian Affairs, RG 10, vol. 3828, file 60,926 (reel C 10145).

Moser, Jefferson F.

1902   The Salmon and Salmon Fisheries of Alaska: Reports of the Alaskan Salmon Investigations of the United States Commission Steamer Albatross in 1900 and 1901. Washington, DC: Government Printing Office.

Nadasdy, Paul

1999   The Politics of TEK: Power and the "Integration" of Knowledge. Arctic Anthropology 36(1–2):1–18.

2003   Hunters and Bureaucrats: Power, Knowledge, and Aboriginal-State Relations in the Southwest Yukon. Vancouver: University of British Columbia Press.

2011   We Don't Harvest Animals: We Kill Them. *In* Knowing Nature: Conversations at the Intersection of Political Ecology and Science Studies. Mara J. Goodman, Paul Nadasdy, and Mathew D. Turner, eds. Pp.135–151. Chicago: University of Chicago Press.

Naish, K. A., J. E. Taylor III, P. S. Levin, T. P. Quinn, J. R. Winton, D. Huppert, and R. Hilborn

2007   An Evaluation of the Effects of Conservation and Fishery Enhancement

Hatcheries on Wild Populations of Salmon. Advances in Marine Biology 53:61–194.

Native Village of Karluk

N.d.   Charles Lucier Collection, Boxes 1 and 2. Archives, Alaska and Polar Regions Collections, Rasmuson Library, University of Alaska–Fairbanks, Fairbanks, AK.

Naylor, Rosalind, Kjetil Hindar, Ian A. Fleming, Rebecca Goldberg, Susan Williams, John Volpe, Fred Whoriskey, Josh Eagle, Dennis Kelso, and Marc Mangel

2005   Fugitive Salmon: Assessing the Risks of Escaped Fish from Net-Pen Aquaculture. BioScience 55(5):427–437.

Nehlsen, Willa, Jack E. Williams, and James A. Lichatowich

1991   Pacific Salmon at the Crossroads: Stocks at Risk from California, Oregon, Idaho, and Washington. Fisheries 16:4–21.

Netboy, Anthony

1974   The Salmon: Their Fight for Survival. Boston, MA: Houghton Mifflin.

Newell, Dianne

1993   Tangled Webs of History: Indians and the Law in Canada's Pacific Coast Fisheries. Toronto: University of Toronto Press.

Newell, Josh, and Emma Wilson

1996   The Russian Far East: Forests, Biodiversity Hotspots, and Industrial Developments. Tokyo: Friends of the Earth–Japan.

NOAA (National Oceanic and Atmospheric Administration)

2006   The History of Fisheries Stewardship. celebrating200years.noaa.gov/foundations/fisheries/#commission, accessed February 29, 2012.

NOAA Fisheries

2011   Glossary. Office of Protected Resources. www.nmfs.noaa.gov/pr/glossary.htm, accessed March 7, 2012.

NPCC (Northwest Power and Conservation Council)

2009   Eighth Annual Report to the Northwest Governors on Expenditures of the Bonneville Power Administration, Northwest Power and Conservation Council document 2009–06. Portland, OR: Northwest Power and Conservation Council. www.nwcouncil.org/library/2009/2009-06.htm, accessed February 29, 2012 .

NPPC (Northwest Power and Planning Council)

1986   Compilation of Information on Salmon and Steelhead Losses in the Columbia River Basin. Portland, OR: Northwest Power Planning Council. www.nwcouncil.org/library/1986/Compilation.htm, accessed February 29, 2012.

NRC (National Research Council)

1996   Upstream: Salmon and Society in the Pacific Northwest. Washington, DC: National Academies Press.

REFERENCES

ODFW (Oregon Department of Fish and Wildlife)
2011   Columbia River Fisheries. Portland, OR: Oregon Department of Fish and
        Wildlife, Fish Division. www.dfw.state.or.us/fish/OSCRP/CRM/reports.asp,
        accessed February 29, 2012.

Oleksa, Michael J.
1990   The Creoles and Their Contributions to the Development of Alaska. *In*
        Russian America: The Forgotten Frontier. B. S. Smith and R. J. Barnett, eds.
        Pp. 185–195. Tacoma: Washington State Historical Society.
1992   Orthodox Alaska: A Theology of Mission. Crestwood, NY: St. Vladimir's
        Seminary Press.

Opheim, Edward N., Sr.
1994   The Memoirs and Saga of a Cod Fisherman's Son: Ten Years of Dory-Fishing
        Cod (1923–1933) at Sunny Cove, Spruce Island, Alaska. New York: Vantage
        Press.

O'Reilly, Peter
1889–1892 Correspondence and Sketches, Minutes of Decision, Federal Collection,
        April 1889 to January 1892, file 29858, vol. 6 (Reg. No. B-64647). British
        Columbia Archives, Victoria.

Orlova, Elizaveta P.
1999   Itel'meny—Istoriko-etnograficheskii ocherk. Saint Petersburg: Nauka.

Ortony, Andrew
1993   Metaphor and Thought. New York: Cambridge University Press.

Ostrom, Elinor
1990   Governing the Commons: The Evolution of Institutions for Collective
        Action. Cambridge: Cambridge University Press.

Pálsson, Gísli
2009   The Biosocial Relations of Production. Comparative Studies in Society and
        History 51(2):288–313.

Partnow, Patricia H.
2001   Making History: Alutiiq/Sugpiaq Life on the Alaska Peninsula. Fairbanks:
        University of Alaska Press.

Peña, Devon G.
1998   Chicano Culture, Ecology, Politics: Subversive Kin. Tucson: University of
        Arizona Press.

Perkins, John H.
1997   Geopolitics and the Green Revolution: Wheat, Genes, and the Cold War.
        New York: Oxford University Press.

Petersen, C. G. Johannes
1903   What Is Overfishing? Journal of the Marine Biological Association
        6:587–594.

Phinney, Archie M.
1934   Nez Perce Texts. New York: Columbia University Press.

2002 Numipu among the White Settlers. William Willard, ed. Wicazo Sa Review 17:21–42.

Pierce, Richard A.

1981 Introduction. *In* A Voyage to America, 1783–1786. M. Ramsay, trans. R. A. Pierce, ed. Pp. 1–35. Kingston, Ontario: Limestone Press.

Pilyasov, A. N.

2007 Soobshestva severnoi pereferi na etape postindustrialnoi transformazi [Communities of Northern Periphery on the Stage of the Postindustrial Transformation]. Pp. 32–54. Moscow: The Federation Council.

Pinkerton, Evelyn W.

1992 Translating Legal-Rights into Management Practice—Overcoming Barriers to the Exercise of Co-management. Human Organization 51:330–341.

Pinkerton, Evelyn, ed.

1989 Co-operative Management of Local Fisheries: New Directions for Improved Management and Community Development. Vancouver: University of British Columbia Press.

Pinkerton, Evelyn W., and Leonard John

2008 Creating Local Management Legitimacy: Building a Local System of Clam Management in a Northwest Coast Community. Marine Policy 32:680–691.

Power, Mary E., David Tilman, James A. Esters, Bruce A. Menge, William J. Bond, L. Scott Mills, Gretchen Daily, Juan Carlos Castilla, Jane Lubchenco, and Robert T. Paine

1996 Challenges in the Quest for Keystones. Bioscience 46(8):609–620.

Pullar, Gordon L.

1992 Ethnic Identity, Cultural Pride, and Generations of Baggage: A Personal Experience. Arctic Anthropology 29(2):182–191.

2009 Historical Ethnography of Nineteenth-Century Kodiak Villages. *In* Giinaquq Like a Face: Sugpiaq Masks of the Kodiak Archipelago. S. Haakanson Jr. and A. Steffian, eds. Pp. 41–60. Fairbanks: University of Alaska Press.

2010 The Creoles of Ostrov Leisnoi: A History of Survival, Adaptation, and Success. Paper presented at the International Conference on Russian America, Sitka, August 19–21. www.2010rac.com/papers/Pullar.pdf, accessed October 11, 2011.

Quammen, David

2009 Where the Salmon Rule. National Geographic Magazine, August.

Radchenko, Vladimir I., Olga S. Temnykh, and Viktor V. Lapko

2007 Trends in Abundance and Biological Characteristics of Pink Salmon (*Oncorhynchus gorbuscha*) in the North Pacific Ocean. North Pacific Anadromous Fish Commission Bulletin 4:7–21.

Radtke, Hans D., and Shannon W. Davis

1996 The Cost of Doing Nothing: The Economic Burden of Salmon Declines in the Columbia River Basin. Eugene, OR: Institute for Fisheries Resources.

References

Reedy-Maschner, Katherine

2007   The Best-Laid Plans: Limited Entry Permits and Limited Entry Systems in Eastern Aleut Culture. Human Organization 66(2):210–225.

2008   Eastern Aleut Society under Three Decades of Limited Entry. *In* Community Impacts of Fisheries Privatization. Marie Lowe and Courtney Carothers, eds. Pp. 13–33. Bethesda, MD: American Fisheries Society Press.

2009   Entangled Livelihoods: Economic Integration and Diversity in the Western Arctic. Alaska Journal of Anthropology 7(2):135–146.

2010   Aleut Identities: Tradition and Modernity in an Indigenous Fishery. Montreal: McGill-Queen's University Press.

Ricker, William Edwin

1975   Computation and Interpretation of Biological Statistics of Fish Populations. Ottawa, ON: Fisheries and Marine Service.

Robards, Martin, and Joshua Greenberg

2007   Global Constraints on Rural Fishing Communities: Whose Resilience Is It Anyway? Fish and Fisheries 8(1):14–30.

Roberts, Paul Craig

1971   Alienation and the Soviet Economy: Toward a General Theory of Marxian Alienation, Organizational Principles, and the Soviet Economy. Albuquerque: University of New Mexico Press.

Robinson, Debra

1996   Changing Relationships to Marine Resource: The Commercial Salmon Fishery in Old Harbor, Alaska. MA thesis, Department of Geography, McGill University, Montreal.

Roon, Tatiana

1996   UIl'ta Sakhalina [The Uil'ta of Sakhalin]. Yuzhno-Sakhalinsk, Russia: Sakhalin Regional Publishers, Sakhalin Regional Museum.

1999   Promyshlennoe osvoenie i pravovye problemy korrenykh narodov Sakhalina [Industrial Development and Legal Issues Relating to the Indigenous Peoples of Sakhalin]. *In* Obychnoe pravo i pravovoi pliuralism [Customary Law and Legal Pluralism]. Papers from the International Conference on Customary Law and Legal Pluralism. N. Novikova and V. A. Tishkov, eds. Pp. 131–136. Moscow: Institute of Ethnology and Anthropology, Russian Academy of Sciences.

2006   Globalization of Sakhalin's Oil Industry: Partnership or Conflict? A Reflection on the Etnologicheskaia Ekspertiza. Theme issue on the oil and gas industry, local communities, and the state. Emma Wilson and Florian Stammler, eds. Sibirica 5(2):95–114. Oxford and New York: Berghahn.

Roppel, Patricia

1994   Salmon from Kodiak: An History of the Salmon Fishery of Kodiak Island, Alaska. Anchorage: Alaska Historical Commission.

Rother, Henrik

2001 The Pacific Northwest Salmon Crisis: Snake River Drawdown and the Impact on Multimodal Transportation with an Emphasis on Wheat Movements in Nez Perce County, Idaho. MA thesis, Department of Geography, University of Idaho.

Royal Commission on Indian Affairs for the Province of BC

1912 Transcripts of Evidence; Questions Affecting the Fishing Rights, Interests and Privileges of Indians in British Columbia—Bella Coola Agency. Pp. 1–33. British Columbia Archives, Victoria, BC.

Rue, Frank

2000 Alaska's Salmon Fishery Certified as Sustainable. Press Release, September 5, 2000. www.adfg.state.ak.us/news/99–02/9–5gov.php, accessed October 26, 2010.

Ruggerone, Gregory T., Randall M. Peterman, Brigitte Dorner, Katherine W. Myers, and Nathan J. Mantua

2010 Abundance of Adult Hatchery and Wild Salmon by Region of the North Pacific. Publication No. SAFS-UW-1001. Seattle: School of Aquatic Sciences and Fisheries, University of Washington.

Russell, Edward Stuart

1931 Some Theoretical Consideration on the "Overfishing" Problem. Journal du Conseil International pour l'Exploration de la Mer 6(1):3–20.

1942 The Overfishing Problem: De Lamar Lectures Delivered in the School of Hygiene of the Johns Hopkins University. Cambridge: The University Press.

Sachs, Wolfgang

1992 Environment. *In* The Development Dictionary: A Guide to Knowledge as Power. Wolfgang Sachs, ed. Pp. 26–37. London: Zed Books.

Sahlins, Marshall

1974 Stone Age Economics. London: Tavistock.

Sakhalin Energy

2005 Phase 2 Project Onshore Pipelines River Crossing Strategy. Sakhalin, Russia: Sakhalin Energy Investment Company.

2006 Sakhalin Indigenous Minorities Development Plan, First Five-Year Plan (2006–2010). Sakhalin, Russia: Sakhalin Energy Investment Company Ltd.

2010 Analysis of Traditional Economic Activities of Sakhalin Indigenous People: Discussion Paper for Preparation of Second SIMDP (2011–2015). Sakhalin, Russia: Sakhalin Energy Investment Company Ltd.

Sampson, Don

1996 One Tribe's Perspective on "Who Runs the Reservoirs." Environmental Law 26:681–691.

Sanders, Marren

2008 Ecosystem Co-Management Agreements: A Study of Nation Building or a Lesson on Erosion of Tribal Sovereignty? Buffalo Environmental Law Journal 15:176.

REFERENCES

Schaefer, Milner B.

1957   Some Considerations of Population Dynamics and Economics in Relation to the Management of Commercial Marine Fisheries. Journal of the Fisheries Research Board of Canada 14(5):669–681.

Schalk, Randall F.

1986   Estimating Salmon and Steelhead Usage in the Columbia Basin before 1850: The Anthropological Perspective. Northwest Environmental Journal 2(2):1–29.

1977   The Structure of an Anadromous Fish Resource. *In* For Theory Building in Archaeology: Essays on Faunal Remains, Aquatic Resources, and Systematic Modeling. Lewis R. Binford, ed. Pp. 207–250. New York: Academic Press.

Sharma, R., A. Cooper, and R. Hilborn

2005   A Quantitative Framework for the Analysis of Habitat and Hatchery Practices on Pacific Salmon. Ecological Modelling 183:231–250.

Shelikov, Gregorii I.

1981[1786] A Voyage to America, 1783–1786. M. Ramsay, trans. R. A. Pierce, ed. Kingston, Ontario: Limestone Press.

Shellikoff, Gilda

2009   APICDA Annual Report 2008. www.apicda.com/News_Reports/ APICDA_08AR.pdf, accessed April 12, 2010.

Shreve, Bradley G.

2009   "From Time Immemorial": The Fish-in Movement and the Rise of Intertribal Activism. Pacific Historical Review 78:403–434.

Shternberg, Lev

1999   The Social Organization of the Gilyak. Anthropological Papers of the American Museum of Natural History, 82. Seattle: University of Washington Press.

Sider, Gerald

2003   Between History and Tomorrow: Making and Breaking Everyday Life in Rural Newfoundland. Toronto: University of Toronto Press.

Sinyakov, Sergei

2006   Ribnaya promishlennost' i promysl lososei v sravnenii s drugimi otrasly-ami ekonomiki v regionakh Dal'nego vostoka. Petropavlovsk-Kamchatski: Kamchatpress.

Sirina, Anna Anatol'evna

2011   Problemy tipologii i preemstvennosti etnicheskoi kul'tury evenkov i evenov (konec XIX–nachalo XXI vekov). PhD dissertation, Institute of Ethnology and Anthropology, Russian Academy of Sciences.

Skempton, Simon

2010   Alienation after Derrida. London and New York: Continuum.

Slezkine, Y.

1994   Arctic Mirrors: Russia and the Small Peoples of the North. Ithaca, NY: Cornell University Press.

Slickpoo, Allen P., and Deward E. Walker

1973   Noon nee-me-poo (We, the Nez Perces): Culture and History of the Nez Perces. Lapwai: Nez Perce Tribe of Idaho.

Smith, C., and J. Gilden

2000   Human and Habitat Needs in Disaster Relief for Pacific Northwest Salmon Fisheries. Fisheries 25(1):6–14.

Smith, Courtland L.

1979   Salmon Fishers of the Columbia. Corvallis: Oregon State University Press.

Smith, Susan L.

1998   Collaborative Approaches to Pacific Northwest Fisheries Management: The Salmon Experience. Willamette Journal of International Law and Dispute Resolution 6:29–68.

Spinden, Herbert Joseph

1908   The Nez Percé Indians. Lancaster, PA: New Era Printing.

Starkova, Nadezhda K.

1974   Morskoi zveroboinyi promysel u itel'menov. Kraevedcheskie Zapiski 5:146–148.

1976   Itel'meny: Material'naia kul'tura XVIII v.—60-e gody XX v. Moscow: Nauka.

1978   Rybolovstvo i orudiia promysla u Itel'menov (konets XIX—nachalo XX c.). *In* Kul'tura narodov dal'nego vostoka SSSR XIX–XX vv. L. I. Sem, ed. Pp. 75–80. Vladivostock: Akademiia Nauk.

Steffian, Amy F., and Patrick G. Saltonstall

2004   Settlement of the Ayakulik-Red River Drainage, Kodiak Island, Alaska: Comprehensive Report 2001–2004. Report prepared for the U.S. Fish and Wildlife Service. Kodiak: Alutiiq Museum and Archaeological Repository.

Steffian, Amy F., Patrick G. Saltonstall, and Robert E. Kopperl

2006   Expanding the Kachemak: Surplus Production and the Development of Multi-Season Storage in Alaska's Kodiak Archipelago. Arctic Anthropology 43(2):93–129.

Steller, Georg Wilhelm

2003   Steller's History of Kamchatka: Collected Information Concerning the History of Kamchatka, Its Peoples, Their Manners, Names, Lifestyles, and Various Customary Practices. Fairbanks: University of Alaska Press.

2012[1774] Beschreibung von dem Lande Kamtschatka, dessen Einwohnern, deren Sitten, Nahmen, Lebensart und verschiedenen Gewohnheiten. Erich Kasten and Michael Dürr, eds. Bibliotheca Kamtschatica. Fürstenberg/H.: Kulturstiftung Sibirien.

REFERENCES

Stephan, John J.
1971   Sakhalin: A History. Oxford: Clarendon Press.

Stevens, Stan, ed.
1997   Conservation through Cultural Survival: Indigenous Peoples and Protected Areas. Washington, DC: Island Press.

Stewart, Hillary
1977   Indian Fishing: Early Methods on the Northwest Coast. Seattle: University of Washington Press.

St. Martin, Kevin
2007   The Difference That Class Makes: Neoliberalization and Non-Capitalism in the Fishing Industry of New England. Antipode 39(3):527–549.

Sturgeon, Noël
2009   Environmentalism in Popular Culture: Gender, Race, Sexuality, and the Politics of the Natural. Tucson: University of Arizona Press.

Suttles, Wayne
1987   Coast Salish Essays. Seattle: University of Washington Press.
1990   Environment. *In* Handbook of North American Indians, vol. 7: Northwest Coast. Wayne P. Suttles, ed. Pp. 16–29. Washington, DC: Smithsonian Institution.

Swanson, Heather
2009   Patterns of Naturecultures: The Spatial Redistribution of Pacific Salmon. *In* Changing Nature of Nature: New Perspectives from Transdisciplinary Field Science. Pp. 77–90. Global COE Program, Proceedings of the Third International Conference, December 14–17. Kyoto: Kyoto University.

Swezey, S. L., and R. F. Heizer
1977   Ritual Management of Salmonid Resources in California. Journal of California Anthropology 4:6–29.

Tanner, Adrian
1979   Bringing Home Animals: Religious Ideology and Mode of Production of the Mistassini Cree Hunters. New York: St. Martin Press.

Taylor, Emmit E., Jr.
2010   Impacts of Dams: Nez Perce Tribal Perspective. Department of Fisheries Resource Management—Watershed Division. Paper presented at the University of Idaho.

Taylor, Joseph E., III
1999   Making Salmon: An Environmental History of the Northwest Fisheries Crisis. Seattle: University of Washington Press.

Taylor, Kenneth J.
1966   A Demographic Study of Karluk, Kodiak Island, Alaska, 1962–1964. Arctic Anthropology 3:211–239.

The Research Group

2009   North Pacific Salmon Fisheries Economic Measurement Estimates, Version 1.2. Report prepared for the Wild Salmon Center, Portland, OR. Corvalllis, OR: The Research Group.

Thornton, Thomas F.

2008   Being and Place among the Tlingit. Seattle: University of Washington Press.

Thornton, Thomas F., and Nadia Manasfi

2010   Adaptation—Genuine and Spurious: Demystifying Adaptation Processes in Relation to Climate Change. Environment and Society: Advances in Research 1:132–155.

Treaty with the Yakima

1855   *In* Indian Affairs: Laws and Treaties, vol. 2: Treaties, in part. 1904. Charles J. Kappler, ed. Pp. 698–702. Washington, DC: Government Printing Office. digital.library.okstate.edu/kappler/Vol2/treaties/yak0698.htm, accessed March 20, 2012.

Treimo, Henrik

2007   Laks, kart og mening. PhD dissertation, Centre for Technology, Innovation and Culture, University of Oslo.

Turaev, Vadim Anatol'evich

1990   Narodnoe obrazovanie i podgotovka kadrov. *In* Istoria i kul'tura itel'menov. A. I. Krushanov, ed. Pp. 153–164. Leningrad: Nauka.

Ulrich, Roberta

2007   Empty Nets: Indians, Dams, and the Columbia River. Corvallis: Oregon State University Press.

United States Census Bureau

2010   Census 2010. www.census.gov; live.laborstats.alaska.gov/cen/dp.cfm, accessed April 15, 2011.

Urkachan, Aleksandra Trifonovna

2002   Veemlen—Zemlya moikh predkov. Petropavlovsk-Kamchatski: Izdatel'stvo Kamshat.

US House of Representatives

1997   Testimony of Arthur M. Taylor, Chairman of Fish, Water, and Wildlife Subcommittee, Nez Perce Tribal Executive Committee. Committee on Resources, Subcommittee on Water and Power. Field Hearing, Lewiston, Idaho. May 31.

Valderrama, Diego, and James Anderson

2010   Market Interactions between Aquaculture and Common-Property Fisheries: Recent Evidence from the Bristol Bay Sockeye Salmon Fishery in Alaska. Journal of Environmental Economics & Management 59(2):115–128.

REFERENCES

VanDevelder, Paul

2011   The Reckoning: A Looming Decision on Endangered Salmon Will Set the Stage for Momentous Battles over the Future. The Oregonian, February 12. www.oregonlive.com/opinion/index.ssf/2011/02/the_reckoning_a_looming_decisi.html, accessed April 4, 2011.

Verran, Helen

2002   A Postcolonial Moment in Science Studies: Alternative Firing Regimes of Environmental Scientists and Aboriginal Landowners. Social Studies of Science 32(5/6):729–762.

2012   Number as Generative Device: Ordering and Valuing Our Relations with Nature. *In* Inventive Methods: The Happening of the Social. N. Wakeford and C. Lury, eds. London: Routledge. www.dasts.dk/wp-content/uploads/Verran_Number_as_Generative_Device.pdf, accessed March 21, 2012.

Vitebsky, Piers

2005   The Reindeer People: Living with Animals and Spirits in Siberia. New York: Mariner Books.

Vysokov, Mikhail

1995   Istoriya Sakhalinskoi oblasti [A History of Sakhalin Region]. Yuzhno-Sakhalinsk, Russia: Sakhalin Centre for New Historical Documentation.

Walker, Deward E., Jr.

1967   Mutual Cross-Utilization of Economic Resources in the Plateau: An Example from Aboriginal Nez Perce Fishing Practices. Report of Investigations, 41. Pullman: Washington State University Laboratory of Anthropology.

1998a   Nez Perce. *In* Handbook of North American Indians, vol. 12: Plateau. Deward E. Walker Jr., ed. Pp. 420–438. Washington, DC: Smithsonian Institution.

1998b   Nez Perce Coyote Tales: The Myth Cycle. Norman: University of Oklahoma Press.

Washington Department of Fish and Wildlife

2011   Hatcheries. wdfw.wa.gov/hatcheries/overview.html, accessed October 17, 2011.

Weaver, Timothy

1997   Litigation and Negotiation: The History of Salmon in the Columbia River Basin. Ecology Law Quarterly 24:677–687.

Ween, Gro

2012   Enacting Human and Non-human Indigenous: Salmon, Sami and Norwegian Natural Resource Management. *In* Eco-Global Crimes: Contemporary and Future Challenges. Guri Larsen, Ragnhild Sollund, Rune Ellefsen, and Toivo Jukkola, eds. Burlington, VT: Ashgate.

N.d.   Honouring Life or Playing with Food? Life and Death in Human-Salmon Relations. Paper submitted for publication in special issue on sentient salmon.

Weir, Jessica K.

2009   Murray River Country: An Ecological Dialogue with Traditional Owners. Canberra: Aboriginal Studies Press.

Wells, Donald N.

1958   Farmers Forgotten: Nez Perce Suppliers of the North Idaho Gold Rush Days. Idaho Yesterdays 2(2):28–32.

Wendling, Amy E.

2009   Karl Marx on Technology and Alienation. New York: Palgrave Macmillan.

Western, David, and R. Michael Wright, eds.

1994   Natural Connections: Perspectives on Community-Based Conservation. Washington, DC: Island Press.

White, Leslie A.

1949   The Science of Culture: A Study of Man and Civilization. New York: Farrar, Straus.

1959   The Evolution of Culture: The Development of Civilization to the Fall of Rome. New York: McGraw-Hill.

White, Richard

1983   The Roots of Dependency: Subsistence, Environment, and Social Change among the Choctaws, Pawnees, and Navajos. Lincoln: University of Nebraska Press.

1995   The Organic Machine: The Remaking of the Columbia River. New York: Hill and Wang.

Wild Salmon Center

2007   Annual Report. Portland, OR: Wild Salmon Center.

2008   Annual Report. Portland, OR: Wild Salmon Center.

Wilkins, David E., and K. Tsianina Lomawaima

2001   Uneven Ground: American Indian Sovereignty and Federal Law. Norman: University of Oklahoma Press.

Wilkinson, Charles

2007   Celilo Falls: At the Center of Western History. Oregon Historical Quarterly 108:532–542.

Wilkinson, Charles F.

1987   American Indians, Time, and the Law: Native Societies in a Modern Constitutional Democracy. New Haven, CT: Yale University Press.

2005   Blood Struggle: The Rise of Modern Indian Nations. New York: W. W. Norton.

Willerslev, Rane

2007   Soul Hunters. Berkeley: University of California Press.

Williams, Chuck

1980   Bridge of the Gods, Mountains of Fire. New York: Friends of the Earth.

REFERENCES

Williams, Richard N.

2006   Return to the River: Restoring Salmon to the Columbia River. Boston, MA: Elsevier Academic Press.

Wilson, Emma

2002a   Est' zakon, est' i svoi zakony: Legal and Moral Entitlements to the Fish Resources of Nyski Bay, North-Eastern Sakhalin. *In* People and the Land: Pathways to Reform in Post-Soviet Siberia. Erich Kasten, ed. Pp. 149–168. Berlin: Dietrich Reimer Verlag.

2002b   Making Space for Local Voices: Local Participation in Natural Resource Management on Sakhalin Island, the Russian Far East. PhD dissertation, Scott Polar Research Institute, Department of Geography, University of Cambridge.

Wolf, Eric

1982   Europe and the People without History. Berkeley: University of California Press.

1997   Europe and the People without History. Berkeley: University of California Press.

Wolf, Edward C., and Seth Zuckerman

1999   Salmon Nation: People and Fish at the Edge. Portland, OR: EcoTrust.

Wong, Brad

2004   State Wheat Supply in Demand: China's Appetite for Grain Could Be Northwest's Gain. Seattle Post-Intelligencer Reporter. www.seattlepi.com/business/200765_wheat23.html, accessed July 10, 2005.

Woods, Fronda

2005   Who's in Charge of Fishing? Oregon Historical Quarterly 106(3). www.jstor.org/action/showPublication?journalCode=oregonhistq, accessed March 20, 2012.

2008   The Columbia River Compact. Washington, DC: Washington Attorney General's Office.

Woodward, Tim

2005   Nez Perce Honor "Warriors" Who Fought for Fishing Rights. Idaho Statesmen, July 9.

Worth, Dean Stoddard

1961   Kamchadal Texts Collected by W. Jochelson. The Hague: Mouton.

Wright, Donald R.

2004   The World and a Very Small Place in Africa: A History of Globalization in Niumi, the Gambia. Armonk, NY: M. E. Sharpe.

Yakel, Y.

2002   The Results of Census of Population [Itogi vserossiskoi perepisi naseleniya]. Petropavlovsk-Kamchatsky: Ltd. Kamchatstat.

2009   The Collection of Normative Documents and Relevant Legislation

Regulating Local Communities' Access to the Water Bioresources. Moscow: Ltd. Scientific Press.

2010   Northeastern Territorial Department of Federal Agency for Fisheries. www.terkamfish.ru, accessed March 19, 2012.

Yesner, David R.

1989   Osteological Remains from Larsen Bay, Kodiak Island, Alaska. Arctic Anthropology 26(2):96–106.

Yurchak, Alexei

1997   The Cynical Reason of Late Socialism: Power, Pretense and the *Anekdot*. Public Culture 9(2):161–188.

Zaffos, Joshua

2006   Tribes Look to Cash In with "Tree-Market" Environmentalism. High Country News, June 12. www.hcn.org/issues/324/16356, accessed March 7, 2012.

"Zashchitim glavnoe bogatstvo Kamchatki" [Let's Protect the Chief Wealth of Kamchatka]

2009   Aborigen Kamchatki, September 8.

Zhuravleva, I. V, V. N. Sharakhmatova, and J. Y. Yakel

2009   Konsepziya razvitya soobshest rodovyx obshin korennyx malochislennyx narodov severa, prpzivayushix v otdalennyx pribreznyx raonax zapadnoi Kamchatki [Concept Paper on Development of Indigenous Peoples of the North Living in Remote Coastal Regions of Western Kamchatka]. Moscow: Ltd. Scientific Press.

Index

School for Advanced Research Advanced Seminar Series

PUBLISHED BY SAR PRESS

GRAY AREAS: ETHNOGRAPHIC
ENCOUNTERS WITH NURSING HOME
CULTURE
Philip B. Stafford, ed.

PLURALIZING ETHNOGRAPHY: COMPARISON
AND REPRESENTATION IN MAYA CULTURES,
HISTORIES, AND IDENTITIES
John M. Watanabe & Edward F. Fischer, eds.

AMERICAN ARRIVALS: ANTHROPOLOGY
ENGAGES THE NEW IMMIGRATION
Nancy Foner, ed.

VIOLENCE
Neil L. Whitehead, ed.

LAW & EMPIRE IN THE PACIFIC:
FIJI AND HAWAI'I
Sally Engle Merry & Donald Brenneis, eds.

ANTHROPOLOGY IN THE MARGINS
OF THE STATE
Veena Das & Deborah Poole, eds.

THE ARCHAEOLOGY OF COLONIAL
ENCOUNTERS: COMPARATIVE
PERSPECTIVES
Gil J. Stein, ed.

GLOBALIZATION, WATER, & HEALTH:
RESOURCE MANAGEMENT IN TIMES OF
SCARCITY
Linda Whiteford & Scott Whiteford, eds.

A CATALYST FOR IDEAS: ANTHROPOLOGICAL
ARCHAEOLOGY AND THE LEGACY OF
DOUGLAS W. SCHWARTZ
Vernon L. Scarborough, ed.

THE ARCHAEOLOGY OF CHACO CANYON:
AN ELEVENTH-CENTURY PUEBLO
REGIONAL CENTER
Stephen H. Lekson, ed.

COMMUNITY BUILDING IN THE TWENTY-
FIRST CENTURY
Stanley E. Hyland, ed.

AFRO-ATLANTIC DIALOGUES:
ANTHROPOLOGY IN THE DIASPORA
Kevin A. Yelvington, ed.

COPÁN: THE HISTORY OF AN ANCIENT
MAYA KINGDOM
E. Wyllys Andrews & William L. Fash, eds.

THE EVOLUTION OF HUMAN LIFE HISTORY
Kristen Hawkes & Richard R. Paine, eds.

THE SEDUCTIONS OF COMMUNITY:
EMANCIPATIONS, OPPRESSIONS,
QUANDARIES
Gerald W. Creed, ed.

THE GENDER OF GLOBALIZATION: WOMEN
NAVIGATING CULTURAL AND ECONOMIC
MARGINALITIES
*Nandini Gunewardena &
Ann Kingsolver, eds.*

NEW LANDSCAPES OF INEQUALITY:
NEOLIBERALISM AND THE EROSION OF
DEMOCRACY IN AMERICA
*Jane L. Collins, Micaela di Leonardo,
& Brett Williams, eds.*

IMPERIAL FORMATIONS
*Ann Laura Stoler, Carole McGranahan,
& Peter C. Perdue, eds.*

OPENING ARCHAEOLOGY: REPATRIATION'S
IMPACT ON CONTEMPORARY RESEARCH
AND PRACTICE
Thomas W. Killion, ed.

SMALL WORLDS: METHOD, MEANING,
& NARRATIVE IN MICROHISTORY
*James F. Brooks, Christopher R. N. DeCorse,
& John Walton, eds.*

MEMORY WORK: ARCHAEOLOGIES OF
MATERIAL PRACTICES
Barbara J. Mills & William H. Walker, eds.

FIGURING THE FUTURE: GLOBALIZATION
AND THE TEMPORALITIES OF CHILDREN
AND YOUTH
Jennifer Cole & Deborah Durham, eds.

TIMELY ASSETS: THE POLITICS OF
RESOURCES AND THEIR TEMPORALITIES
*Elizabeth Emma Ferry &
Mandana E. Limbert, eds.*

DEMOCRACY: ANTHROPOLOGICAL
APPROACHES
Julia Paley, ed.

CONFRONTING CANCER: METAPHORS,
INEQUALITY, AND ADVOCACY
Juliet McMullin & Diane Weiner, eds.

Participants in the School for Advanced Research advanced seminar "Indigenous Peoples and Salmon in the Northern Pacific" co-chaired by James F. Brooks and Benedict J. Colombi, May 15–21, 2010. *Standing, from left:* Charles R. Menzies, Sibyl Diver, Courtland L. Smith, Marianne Elisabeth Lien, Erich Kasten, Katherine Reedy-Maschner, Courtney Carothers, David Koester; *seated, from left:* Victoria N. Sharakhmatova, James F. Brooks, Benedict J. Colombi. Photograph by Jason S. Ordaz.